Gnostic Wars

Gnostic Wars

The Cold War in the Context of a History of Western Spirituality

Stefan Rossbach

Edinburgh University Press

Transferred to Digital Print 2012

Edinburgh University Press
22 George Square, Edinburgh

Typeset in New Century Schoolbook
by Norman Tilley Graphics, Northampton
Printed and bound by CPI Group (UK) Ltd, Croydon, CR0 4YY

A CIP record for this book is available
from the British Library

ISBN 0 7486 1024 3 (hardback)

Contents

Acknowledgements	ix
1 Introduction	1
Politics and spirituality	2
Liminality and *communitas*	5
Spirituality and history: The Axial Age	11
A note on method: Exploring lines of meaning	14
The importance of history	19
Overview	21
2 Liminality in Platonic philosophy and early Christian thought	25
Plato's *metaxy*	25
Periagoge and *metanoia*	38
3 Issues in 'Gnostic Studies'	47
Aspects of Hans Jonas's analysis of 'Gnosticism'	49
Cosmology: Anticosmic dualism	49
Humanity's place in the cosmic drama and the problem of evil	50
'This' world	52
The soul	54
The self-objectification of being and the literary form of the 'system'	55
Antinomian tendencies	57
The debate about origins	59
Marcion, Valentinus, Mani	60
'Gnosticism' and classical culture	68
4 Lines of meaning I: From Manichaeism to 'Neo-Manichaeism'	72
Manichaeans, Paulicians, Bogomils and Cathars	73
Monasticism and heresy	84
Neo-Platonism, mysticism and heresy	90
Apocalypticism	94

5 Intersections: Renaissance syncretism 103
Joachim of Fiore 104
Marsilio Ficino's Hermeticism 116
Pico della Mirandola's 'Christian Cabala' 130

6 Lines of meaning II: Boehme, Hegel, Marx 142
Jacob Boehme 142
Hegel 147
Marx 152

7 Lines of meaning III: The Third Rome against the New World 163
Boehme in Russia 163
The Third Rome 167
The New World 170
Prophetic events in American history 176

8 *Parrhesia* against *Gnosis*: George F. Kennan on the spiritual dimension of the Cold War 186
Excursion I: Mani, Augustine and the two cities 187
Excursion II: The myth of the prince 192
George F. Kennan 196
Kennan as a philosopher 199
Philosophy, politics and the limits of power 202
Philosophical leadership and the need for introspection 204
Totalitarianism as the corruption of the soul 206
The decline of the West 215

9 Epilogue 223

Bibliography 232
Index 248

To my parents

Maria Rossbach
Hans-Paul Rossbach

Acknowledgements

The following is the result of an intellectual journey that has carried me from Chaos Theory and the Sciences of Complexity to the historical analysis of order and spirituality. During the eight years it has taken me to organise my thoughts on these matters, I have incurred many debts and owe gratitude to many. Among those I would like to thank here are Katherine E. Absher, Stephen Hicklin, Nicholas Higgins, Agnes Horvath, Alexandra Morgan, Ruth Purchase, Richard Sakwa, Sebastian Rinken, and Hongying Wang.

I was fortunate to have patient and inspiring teachers who accompanied my itinerary with open minds and constructive criticism. I am thus particularly grateful to Bernd Steeger, Friedrich Hirzebruch, Uwe Nerlich, John Lewis Gaddis, Lawrence Freedman, Gunther Teubner, Ole Waever, and Arpad Szakolczai. Arpad's seminars in Florence were an important source of inspiration – not merely for this project. I have hereby, in many ways, striven to live up to standards defined by him; my efforts may fail in this respect, but the attempt has always been worth while.

The assistance I received through grants from the Social Science Research Council, New York; the John D. and Catherine T. MacArthur Foundation, Chicago; the German Academic Exchange Organisation (DAAD), Bonn; and the European University Institute, Florence, is gratefully acknowledged.

As I was preparing this manuscript, Phil Deans, Patricia de Mesquita and Fred Whitemore took time from their busy schedules to provide detailed comments on style and contents. I am responsible, of course, for all remaining deficiencies.

Patricia's presence in my life has greatly helped me to go through the more arduous, concluding stages of this enterprise. I am indebted to her for her understanding and loving support. My sisters and their families have been the most loyal friends throughout; while the immense gratitude I owe to my parents can only be expressed on the dedication page. Sadly, my father did not live long enough to see this work completed.

S. R.
Canterbury, 1999

1
Introduction

In a letter to a friend, Max Weber called the second part of his *The Protestant Ethic and the Spirit of Capitalism* 'a sort of "spiritualist" construction of the modern economy'.[1] Weber realised that an account of modern capitalism required an investigation into its spiritual preconditions. The arrival of the 'spirit of capitalism', which turned labour into an absolute end in itself, signified a change in the subjectivity of the modern individual. The 'modern economy' asked individuals to rearrange their life-conduct and therefore demanded a change in the mode in which human beings experience and reflect upon themselves and their purpose in relation to others, to nature and to the divine.[2]

By opening the present work with a reference to Weber I do not mean to make pretentious claims about its context or relevance. I merely want to acknowledge an affinity at the level of questions. *Gnostic Wars* is an investigation into the spiritual preconditions of the Cold War. I am concerned with a historical analysis of developments in the very self-understanding of human existence through which the continuous threat of nuclear annihilation could become accepted in the context of a defence of ideas on how to live.

The growing literature which interprets the Cold War is commonly published under headlines such as 'international relations' or 'international politics' and accordingly focuses on economic, political, diplomatic and sometimes ideological issues.[3] The very nature of these disciplines ensured that the sense of epoch evoked by the end of the Cold War was not translated into an overcoming of the past but into policy-relevant anticipations of possible futures. Accordingly, the original task of interpreting the Cold War, of assigning meaning to the Cold War experience, remains to be accomplished. The present work *complements* the existing literature in that it argues that there was a 'spiritual' dimension to the conflict, for the willingness to defend one's life-conduct at the expense of the destruction of the one and only natural environment in which civilisation can flourish appears to presuppose a self-understanding of human existence which does not accept limits in the imposition of human designs on the world.

POLITICS AND SPIRITUALITY

In order to characterise the nature of this dimension of the conflict I prefer to use words such as 'spiritual' and 'spirituality' over the more familiar notions 'religious' and 'religion'. The term 'religion' would be entirely appropriate for my purposes if today's usage had preserved the term's original purpose as defined by Cicero, who introduced it in order to protect the symbolism which classical philosophy had used to refer to the experience and meditation of the transcendent source of order in reality. However, as a result of a long historical process, modern usage of the word 'religion' differs greatly from Cicero's.

Today 'religions' are thought to be closed bodies and 'systems' of beliefs, doctrines, and dogmas. Moreover, as the suspicion grew that religious symbols had no immediate basis in empirical reality, the idea seemed compelling that 'religion' had a 'function' – that is, to both rationalise and conceal ulterior motives which were not necessarily conscious but were, in any case, more 'empirical'. As such – as fictions with a purpose, as *meta-récits* – all religions appeared fundamentally similar and rational arguments about and between them were considered impossible. As a consequence of these changes of interpretation, the modern mind cannot but treat composites of religion and politics as instances of 'fundamentalism' or 'ideology'. Accordingly, well-meaning appeals to 'pluralism' or 'secularisation' count as evidence of liberality and broadmindedness.

This approach is untenable for a number of reasons. First of all, being itself the result of a complicated historical process, modern attitudes towards 'religion' should not easily be taken at face value. The experiences which Cicero subsumed under the label of 'religio' – and which I, in the following, will refer to as 'spirituality' — do not always express themselves in terms of systems of 'fixed' doctrines or 'absolutes'. A good example of the political relevance of what I call spirituality is provided by the various Greek practices of 'truth-telling' – *parrhesia* – which we find discussed in Greek literature from about 400 BC, especially in the tragedies of Euripides, up to the patristic texts of the fifth century AD. The etymological roots of *parrhesia* or *parrhesiazesthai* are *pan*, 'everything', and *rhema*, 'that which is said'. *Parrhesia* is a particular mode of speaking. The *parrhesiast*, the person who speaks in the mode of *parrhesia*, says everything he has in mind without hiding anything. Hence, *parrhesia* is opposed to rhetoric in that the person who makes use of rhetoric uses language as an instrument. Rhetoric has ulterior motives; there is something behind the words which the words both conceal and serve. In contrast, the *parrhesiast* speaks 'in full': he gives a truthful account of himself and firmly believes that what he says is in fact the truth. The term *parrhesia* has no literal translation in English. 'Honest self-expression' captures some of its aspects, as does '*franc parler*' in French.

Typically, a *parrhesiastic* act involves risks – the risk, namely, of being punished for having been the one who showed frankness in speaking the truth. *Parrhesia* therefore occurs mostly in situations in which the speaker faces superior forces who can inflict such punishments. A famous, paradigmatic example of *parrhesia* comes from the sixteenth century. Facing the Emperor Charles V during his second hearing at Worms on 18 April 1521, Martin Luther decided to give a truthful account of himself and his teaching. His famous words – 'Here I stand, I cannot do otherwise', by now proverbial in the German language – reduced the audience to tears. In order to appreciate the tension of this moment, it is important to understand that Luther had a choice when he acted as he did. Confronting the authorities after the failed Calabrian Revolt of 1599/1600, Tommaso Campanella, in contrast, preferred feigned madness over *parrhesia*. Over several years he convinced his prison guards and the Inquisitioners that he was not responsible for what he had said and done; that he was a madman rather than a heretic or a rebel.

The juxtaposition of Luther and Campanella clarifies what is at stake in a *parrhesiastic* moment. *Parrhesia* is a mode of speaking in which language and being touch each other. The *parrhesiastic* enunciation involves the speaker in his being as he makes a commitment to a personal truth for which he is prepared to die. According to Luther's own account of the situation, he had the courage to say what he said because he was aware that ultimately he would not be judged by the Emperor but that both he and the Emperor had to give an account of themselves before God, that they were at last both liable to God's judgement. In front of a non-human force that cannot be deceived it is pointless to speak in the mode of rhetoric.

What compels the *parrhesiast* to speak the truth in spite of the risks he faces is his spirituality – in Luther's case the tension of standing and acting, as an individual, in front of God. The courage to speak up does not flow from a certainty which wants to assert itself against the opinions of others. The *parrhesiast*, in this sense, is not a powerful person; his own fate is not in his hands. The purpose of the speaker's firmness is primarily 'defensive': he speaks because he 'cannot do otherwise'. And the firmness is complemented by the humility of a human being who has run out of choices. Although he sincerely believes in what he must say, the *parrhesiast* also knows that he is not infallible. Therefore, he cannot claim more than that his speech reflects a personal truth. The point of the *parrhesiastic* experience is not, then, that the speaker recites a doctrine which is binding for everyone; rather, the point is that the speaker knows that he will be judged as the one who will have said what he is about to say. The moment of *parrhesia* is a moment of truth only for the speaker, for he makes a commitment to the person he wants to be judged as. The *parrhesiast*, in other words, reveals who he truly is: 'I am the one who thinks this or that.'[4]

The political relevance of *parrhesia* stems from the fact that it functioned as a guideline for the Greek *polis* in antiquity. The Athenian democracy was defined as a constitution in which people enjoyed the equal right of speech (*demokratia*, *isegoria*), the equal participation of all citizens in the exercise of power (*isonomia*), and *parrhesia*. *Parrhesia* in particular was singled out, by Herodotus, as the 'pride of Athens'. As a central aspect of democratic life in Athens, *parrhesia* took place between citizens as individuals, and between citizens construed as an assembly. The *agora* was the place where *parrhesia* typically occurred.

The fate of *parrhesia* in the *polis* and the fate of democracy in Athens are inextricably linked, for the right to democratic participation contributes to the well-being of the *polis* at large only as long as the citizens use it for speaking the truth for the benefit of all. As soon as they begin to abuse their right and to deceive and manipulate in order to advance their own individual interests, the *polis* is doomed. The rise of democracy in Greek Antiquity thus corresponds to the respect which *parrhesia* commanded in the *polis*. In turn, the crisis of democracy corresponds to the increasing difficulty in distinguishing between *parrhesia* and rhetoric. According to Plato, the effect of Sophist teaching was precisely to blur this distinction as it emphasised style over substance. In 355 BC, Isocrates complained that the Athenians listened to the most depraved orators and denied the truly good speakers the possibility of being heard. He considered his own society a 'perversion' of the 'old' *polis*; once the citizens lacked 'self-restraint', *parrhesia* became a problem rather than a blessing.

The importance of *parrhesia* for the functioning of democracy in Greek antiquity draws attention to the spiritual preconditions for the rise of democracy and, indeed, politics.[5] Given that international organisations today cultivate 'democracy' as the standard according to which they assess the performance of political regimes all over the world, the historical fact that democracy had theological roots is not of minor significance. In fact, it has been a commonplace throughout the history of political philosophy that 'good laws' are not sufficient for the establishment of a meaningful and lasting political order. Laws, if they are to be observed, are in need of *buoni costumi*, of good morals, as Machiavelli explained.[6] There is no law, no 'human right', which cannot be abused. As the example of the demise of *parrhesia* demonstrates, the existence of such laws and rights must be complemented by the citizens' disposition to use whatever rights or liberties are granted to them for the benefit of the community at large. Societies in crisis are not so much characterised by the absence of laws but by the absence of this disposition to use the laws as a *means* to advance towards a higher good which transcends the selfish interests of the individual citizen. The restoration of a disintegrating society therefore requires more than a new legal framework or a new governmental system.

The spiritual dimension of political order always transcends the legal framework which it in many ways complements, and yet, as the previous discussion made clear, it is one of its essential aspects. As such it should be studied within the confines of political philosophy in relation to the political institutions and ideas which grew on the soil it provided. The argument about the complex link between *parrhesia* and democracy may also serve here as a first hint at the *contemporary* relevance of an inquiry into the spiritual dimension of politics.

LIMINALITY AND *COMMUNITAS*

In theoretical terms, the spiritual dimension of politics can be understood as the interplay between two models of human interrelatedness: community and *communitas*. The term *communitas* was introduced by the anthropologist Victor Turner in order to denote a sense of 'comradeship' which transcends the structured positions human beings occupy in the societies of which they are members. A sense of *communitas* emerges in certain classes of rituals – rites of passage – whereby a society or tribe guides its members through important changes of place, state, social position or age. Turner, following Arnold van Gennep, divides rites of passage into three stages: separation, margin or 'liminality', and aggregation.[7] The first phase comprises symbolic behaviour signifying the detachment of the individual (or group) from an earlier fixed point in the social structure or an earlier social or cultural condition. The third and final phase deals with the reaggregation of the individual into a 'state' or condition recognised within the community. The second, intervening phase is the 'liminal period', the period 'in between'. 'Liminality' and 'liminal' derive from the Latin *limen*, which denotes a threshold between spaces or times.[8]

If society is understood as a 'structure of positions', then liminality can be thought of as an 'interstructural situation', interposed between stretches of 'ordinary' time. During the liminal phase, the subject of the passage ritual assumes a mode of being defined by ambiguity. Turner refers to such persons as 'liminal beings' or 'neophytes'.

Liminal beings are neither what they were nor what they are going to be. They are, in Turner's words, '"betwixt and between" all the recognised fixed points in spacetime of structural classification'.[9] Neophytes are 'invisible' in that they are outside that which is thinkable or doable in the given society.

During the separation rites, the neophytes lose those aspects of their personality and appearance which identified them as the occupants of specific structured positions within society. Accordingly, relationships among the members of this uniform group are characterised by homogeneity, equality, anonymity, absence of property, suspension of kinship rights and obligations, abolition of rank, and humility. Their sameness is the result of a process or journey in which they have left behind the artifices of society. Hence, the liminal group is a community of 'comrades', not a structure of hierarchically arranged positions, and their comradeship transcends distinctions of rank, age, kinship and other components of social status.

If, in this manner, human beings are stripped of the artifices of society, what remains? According to a common viewpoint, the nakedness of liminality reveals that which is genuinely human. Outside their institutionalised and socialised roles, people, it is said, can be 'themselves'. Liminality would then become a moment of truth as the neophytes reveal who they truly are. The process which brings about this truth could then be understood as a process of 'emancipation' in which individuals 'free themselves' from what is added to their personalities, to their being. The bonds which emerge in such moments are generic bonds between human beings, and as such may evoke a sentiment of 'humankind-ness'.[10] Entering the liminal phase thus amounts to a transformative experience which goes to the root of each person's being and, given the surrounding uniformity, finds in that root something profoundly communal and shared.

This new kind of society which emerges in the liminal period is a relatively undifferentiated and unstructured community, a homogeneous totality. Turner uses the Latin term *communitas* instead of 'community' in order to distinguish such uniformity from an understanding of society as a sphere in which human interrelatedness is mediated by structures, differentiations, and conventions.[11] From now on, the term 'community' will be reserved to this latter, traditional conception.

The powers and forces shaping the neophytes in liminality are often felt to be more than human even though they are invoked and channelled by the representatives of the community. Liminality thus brings the neophyte into close connection with the sacred or with superhuman powers of great potency, with what is regarded as the unbounded, the infinite, the limitless. Accordingly, *communitas* is held to be sacred or holy, and its manifestations may be regarded with both awe and suspicion as they transgress or dissolve the norms which govern structured or institutionalised relationships in an area of 'common living'.

Turner suggests that no society can function without a 'dialectic' between community and *communitas*. By itself, the spontaneity and immediacy of *communitas* cannot endure for longer periods of time. After all, the production of life's necessities calls for social organisation in terms of 'ends' and 'means'; it involves the making of decisions, the 'deferment of gratifications' and, therefore, 'the careful ordering of human relationships and of man's knowledge of nature'.[12] Moreover, the uniformity of *communitas* becomes evident and accessible only through juxtaposition with aspects of social structure. It comes into being through a process of negation and in that sense *requires* that which it negates.

In turn, the community is bound to disintegrate unless it succeeds in re-evocating *communitas* with some regularity. Without *communitas* societies will suffer from structural rigidification, which is then likely to cause extreme responses. *Communitas* provides a complementary realm of speculation, of reflection; it forms a background which lets structures regain contour and meaning. Alternatively, societies may be torn apart by factions and divisions of interests growing out of their internal differentiation. *Communitas* reminds society's members of the generic bond which holds them together underneath the structured positions which separate them. Seen in this light, *communitas* is an aspect of all societies.

The tribal societies studied by Turner understand the relationship between community and *communitas* as symbiotic, with the latter solving the problem of change for the former. As long as the communal life is based on the assumption that the cosmic order within which the community exists is not subject to human will, the transgression of boundaries and movements from one status to another are problematic. For if such changes are possible, what is the nature of the rigidity and firmness of the order of being? The solution to the problem is that, during liminal phases in rites of passage, responsibility for the changes is ultimately placed outside the community: the neophytes are brought into contact with the divine, and it is this contact which imprints on them new insights into the order of things. The outcome of the procedure is therefore bound to be in harmony with the comprehensive order. Through the ritual, the community collectively and the neophytes individually submit themselves to a self-evoked openness whereby their future state is made dependent on forces beyond their control. It is a situation in which the community and the neophytes let themselves be ordered by the forces governing the cosmos. In most cases, the ritual will confirm the harmony between communal and comprehensive order but there is also a genuine element of unpredictability which is inherent in liminality.

In these societies, liminality results in a greater involvement in the rich manifold of social relations and role-playing in society. By allowing neophytes to see those ideas, sentiments and facts which they had hitherto accepted unthinkingly deconstructed into their constituents rites of passage leave the 'new' reaggregated beings with more alert faculties and with an enhanced understanding of 'how things work'. For example, a rite of passage initiating a child into adulthood may expose popular myths which the child was not allowed to question as fictions with educational purposes. The not-boy-not-man may then reflect, during the liminal period, on both the myth as fiction *and* the purpose which it served. Thereafter, while he will no longer be able to believe that the contents of the myth *is* the truth, he will nevertheless appreciate its usefulness in *representing* a truth which he, as a child, would have been unable to understand. This is a useful insight for, although he has ceased to believe, he will continue to respect the myth and to use it for raising his own children. The community's practices and traditions are thereby upheld. Moreover, exposing the myth *as myth* does not provoke a sense of disillusionment. On the contrary, the neophyte learns that the symbols and practices of his culture have meaning regardless of their truth status. He will therefore be all the more willing to let himself be guided by them.

However, the form of interplay between community and *communitas* can vary – among societies or among different epochs within the same society – and such variations may become driving forces in political controversy. An awareness of a tension between the two models exists even in societies in which their relationship is considered complementary, for liminality is a stage of reflection, a realm of 'primitive hypothesis' with a certain freedom 'to juggle with the factors of existence'.[13] Of course, this encounter with contingency has the pedagogical purpose of confronting the neophytes with the dangers inherent in ways of acting and thinking alternative to those laid down by the deities or ancestors. But the mere insight that the order of society is not what it appears to be, that there are layers of meaning which can be 'deconstructed' if necessary, may evoke a form of curiosity which, if unchecked, could destroy the various myths which both define and protect essential communal practices.

There is, therefore, always the possibility of envisioning the two models of communal existence as *competing* rather than as *complementary*. Liminal existence may be approached not as a means but as an end in itself, the result of a liberation and emancipation from the artificialities of society. From this angle, liminal existence outside society appears as *true* existence, representing the purity of humanness. By implication, liminality ceases to be transitional and becomes a 'status' in itself.

As a status, rather than as a non-status 'in-between', *communitas* has a certain magic appeal. Subjectively, the experience of liminality may well arouse feelings of unlimited power, liberty and equality as all social constraints are left behind. Given the undoubted attractiveness of these features, the fact that this power cannot readily be applied to the organisational details of social existence can easily turn into an argument *against* organised social existence. Protest movements may now proclaim the actualisation of the *communitas* as the end of their activities within society.

The rise of monasticism in the third and fourth centuries as well as the success of the mendicant orders during the late Middle Ages – both phenomena to which I will return later – are good examples of this phenomenon. But these examples also show the intrinsic problems of such a programme. The experience of *communitas* is bound to lose intensity once the number of neophytes increases. The success of the movement requires impersonal organisation, roles, routines and institutions. The post-apostolic phase of Christianity and the problems of the Franciscan Order after their founder's death illustrate this dilemma. Compared to the vision of the *communitas*, organisation and structure appear like signs of hypocrisy and loss of faith. Hence, movements driven by this vision always tend to generate successor or offshoot movements which, appealing to 'authenticity', surpass them in radicality.

The struggle for *communitas* is potentially unlimited and total because it may entail the emancipation from precisely the kinds of structured constraints which could contain it. In the communities studied by Turner, the equality and liberty among the neophytes was balanced by their complete submission to the commands of their instructors. If the balance is lost, the neophytes may well turn against the instructors on the grounds that the full truth of generic human existence will remain hidden as long as the process of emancipation is not allowed to run its complete course. Furthermore, the cry for *communitas* tends to appeal to a reality which transcends the context from where it originated and to which, at some stage, it might have been addressed. For the radicals, the 'revolution' will not be over unless it has spread. The true *communitas* encompasses the whole of mankind almost by definition. Because it transcends all cultural divisions and indeed everything which is, in the modern sense, 'socially constructed', the strive for *communitas* easily extends its ambition to the limits of humanity. Its actualisation must be envisioned as a climacteric moment in which the full truth of the meaning of humanness is finally revealed; a moment in which faith is at last replaced by knowledge.

However, the road to *communitas* is covered with problems, sacrifices and postponements of vision. Moreover, as I observed before, the nature of the struggle is such that even success is bound to cause frustration, and the one pragmatic response to the problems – compromise – is precisely the one which stands in the way of fulfilment. But continuous frustration and disappointment must eventually affect the vision of *communitas* itself. The struggle must turn away from society against the necessities which cause and determine the oppressiveness of communal life, but these necessities flow from the human dependency on nature, from humble needs such as food, drink and clothing. The vision of permanent liminality may thus demand emancipation not only from society but also from the body. The truth of humanness is within or, in a figurative sense, beneath the body, possibly even beneath the soul depending on the radicalness of the quest for *communitas*. That which is truly human is thus reduced to some spiritual substance shared by all human beings. Their re-union in *communitas* will then result in one uniform realm not unlike an ocean which consists of millions of drops of water. True emancipation, in this vision, is an emancipation from the necessities of cosmic existence and a reversal of the process of individuation. The resulting *communitas* is not a 'brotherhood' of individuals but a realm of perfect uniformity. Hence, the vision of *communitas* and permanent liminality can develop along three dimensions: the dimension of space (and conquest), of time (and endurance), and of abstraction.

Radical visions of liminality gain credibility and imminence especially if reality itself assumes attributes of liminality. The distinction between community and *communitas* is obvious in periods of stability when the structures and hierarchies of society are taken for granted. However, during periods of upheaval and change when hierarchies are reversed and the whole of society turned upside down, the claim that liminal existence is the 'true' existence appears far more plausible. Dissolutions of order and moments of social transition may evoke liminal experiences comparable to those of the neophytes in rites of passage. As societies are passing from one cultural 'state' to another, the *communitas* may appear closer than ever. The centres of hope will usually be among the outsiders, the marginalised and those who perhaps have more reason than others to experience social life as oppression. The contrast between the comradeship among these groups and their submission to the powers governing society corresponds to the opposition between the *communitas* among neophytes and their submission to their instructors. *Communitas* generally tends to break into society through the interstices of structure, at the edges of structure, and from beneath structure. In other words, from positions of liminality, marginality, and inferiority.[14]

Although the question of the 'status' of liminality is at the centre of the spiritual dimension of politics, it is important not to misinterpret the conceptual distinction between community and *communitas* in terms of the modern separation of a realm of secular politics from a sphere of religious belief and practices. The struggle for *communitas* may well turn against a church organisation – to the extent, that is, that a church is seen as part of the structured positions which define society. The cry for *communitas* may then be deliberately phrased in what appear to be *anti-religious* formulae. The programme of 'de-Christianisation' during the French Revolution may serve here as an example.

SPIRITUALITY AND HISTORY: THE AXIAL AGE

The concrete manner in which the interplay of community and *communitas* may become problematic for a society depends on historical factors. Each social order entails a commitment to symbolisms whereby its members delineate and then refer to the various layers of reality they encounter. These symbolisms embody particular conceptions of the relation between cosmic and social order and of the human being's place within both. If the struggle for *communitas* erupts into society as a political movement it will have to develop its own symbols which share in the cultural context of society precisely because they are *negative* symbols, antipodal to what counts as orthodoxy.

Some of the principal parameters for the unfolding of the problem of liminality and *communitas* were set in the period known as the 'Axial Age'. In the time period from approximately 800 BC to 500 BC there emerged and became institutionalised in some of the major civilisations a conception of a basic tension and chasm between the transcendental and the mundane orders. These civilisations included Ancient Israel, and later Christianity; Ancient Greece; China in the early imperial period; Hinduism; and Buddhism.[15] The clear differentiation and separation of the transcendent – the infinite, the unlimited — and the mundane marked a significant departure from a conception of a close parallelism between the two orders and their mutual embeddedness which had prevailed in the societies from which the post-Axial Age civilisations emerged.

In the Greek context we find early indications of these changes already in the Homeric epics. To be sure, for most parts of the *Illiad* and *Odyssey*, the presentation of the temporal and transcendent realms still emphasises mutual embeddedness. The disorder in temporal society reaches into the divine sphere and vice versa. Gods and humans are interacting forces in an order which embraces them both. Within this comprehensive order, the borderline between human and transhuman is often blurred, and the extent to which the actions of human beings are their actions at all is left open. However, an important reflection by Zeus at the beginning of the *Odyssey* introduces a theme which seems to necessitate a clearer differentiation between the mundane and the divine. Zeus reflects on the responsibility for evil, and argues that the mortals are wrong when they say that evil comes from the gods. Zeus's argument does not settle the issue; on the contrary, it merely invites his daughter, Athena, to draw his attention to the fate of Odysseus, who is held captive by the goddess Calypso because she wants him as a lover. Still, Zeus's reflection reveals Homer's concern with a search for truth about the source of evil, about the causes of the disorder of human existence in society. It is this concern which, in the writings of Hesiod, Xenophanes, Heraclitus and Parmenides, led to the perception of a basic discontinuity, *chorismos*, in the relation between human and divine realms.[16]

The clearer the temporal and transcendent realms are differentiated, the more the former comes into focus as the sphere of human action proper, as the arena in which humans act 'before' or 'below' the divine and in which they carry responsibility for their actions. The social order or disorder is no longer a copy of a transhuman realm or the immediate outflow of a divine will but becomes the concrete result of concrete actions performed by individuals or groups. Because the temporal sphere was subordinated to the transcendent realm, the former had to be structured according to the precepts of the latter or, more importantly, according to the prevailing perception of the proper mode of overcoming and resolving the tension between 'lower' and 'higher' order. While this remains the problem – encountered earlier – of harmonising social and cosmic order through insights gained during liminal periods, it has now assumed a more specific shape with at least two important institutional implications.

The first novelty in post-Axial Age civilisations is the accountability of rulers. As Eisenstadt points out, in a pre-Axial Age society such as Egypt the Pharaoh was God-King, embodying and epitomising a comprehensive order which incorporated society. As such he was not accountable to anyone; he was not even responsible for upholding the customs of the community. He could, of course, be killed or deprived of actual power by force and coercion but he could not be deposed through any customary process.[17] In post-Axial Age societies, the tension between the mundane and the transcendent order becomes the decisive, 'independent' criterion for an assessment of the ruler's performance. The balancing or resolving of tension between the two orders now required deliberate, purposeful action within the temporal sphere – action for which the protagonists could be held responsible.

The second important consequence of the Axial Age transition is the emergence of a new social element. A new type of élite concentrated on the contemplation of the tension between the temporal and the transcendent. The Jewish prophets and priests, the Greek philosophers, the Chinese literati, the Hindu brahmins, the Buddhist sangha – these groups not only initially formulated and carried the perception of this tension but were also implicated in the institutionalisation of its derivatives. The ritual, magical and sacral activities of the former priest thereby became aspects of the premeditated and autonomous construction of the cultural and social order. Whenever any given conception of tension was institutionalised, the corresponding élite could become a relatively autonomous partner within the major ruling coalitions or, depending on the ruling groups' orientation, within opposition and protest movements.[18] Such developments in turn reinforced a status consciousness among these élites as autonomous 'intellectuals' who measured rulers and society in terms of criteria derived from 'higher' principles and therefore held to be 'universal'. In Greece, these changes were reflected in the simultaneous rise of democracy and philosophy.

In their self-understanding, human beings increasingly assumed responsibility for the order prevailing in their society. At the same time, their ordering activity was perceived to be liable to a transcendent measure, to a 'higher' order. The result of these developments was a problematisation of political order in terms of universal principles. The institutionalisation of particular visions of the tension between the mundane and divine orders inevitably implied the exclusion of alternative visions. While such alternatives could be pushed away from the political centre into the periphery, they could never be eliminated entirely because the very process of assessing the ruling majority in terms of 'higher' principles evokes the contemplation of alternative courses of action. Thus, as such alternative visions remained intact, they were able to develop into symbolically and organisationally fully-fledged *heterodoxies*.

The subsequent struggle between the orthodox and the heterodox became a major driving force behind the dynamics of Axial Age civilisations. To the extent that certain groups and institutional spheres succeeded in presenting themselves as the carriers of the attributes of overcoming the tension between the mundane and the transcendent they became endowed with a special meaning which transcended the mundane world within which they operated. What had previously been conflicts between 'primordial' groups, cults or tribes mutated into 'ideological' conflicts or missionary crusades for the transformation of entire civilisations and, indeed, mankind. The intensity and orientation of this dynamics differed, of course, among the various civilisations which emerged from these changes. Eisenstadt observes that the 'fullest ideological and institutional articulation of the political process' developed within the three great monotheistic civilisations: Judaism, Christianity, and later, after the Axial Age proper, Islam.[19]

A NOTE ON METHOD: EXPLORING LINES OF MEANING

In tribal societies, liminality enters the community through rites of passage. More complex societies will usually have a more diverse spectrum of organised practices whereby the community opens itself to liminal experiences. In the Greek *polis*, for example, the right of *parrhesia* could fulfil this function. The *parrhesiast* stood naked before superior powers but his non-status gave him the right to criticise all status-bound personae in terms of a comprehensive order which was binding on all.

I referred to *parrhesia* earlier in order to demonstrate that spirituality does not necessarily manifest itself in the form of explicit doctrines or systems of beliefs – a fact which poses significant methodological problems. For if, in fact, such doctrines can only be treated as *secondary* developments, then how can 'spirituality' be identified empirically? It seems that the study of spirituality must attempt to go beneath the symbols, ideas and doctrines which were used to refer to and illuminate their origins in experience. In other words, the investigation must refer to the experiential context which engendered symbols with spiritual meaning; and it must, by implication, allow for the possibility that such symbols and their corresponding experiences have a basis in reality.

The crucial task of the investigation is thus to bridge the step from the original experience to the symbol evoked by the experience. For this purpose, it is important to realise that the symbol itself is already an attempt at the clarification and denotation of the experience. The texts, utterances, statements, doctrines and records of practices which engulf history are sedimentations of a self-interpreting reality. In a sense, the scholarly investigation of these records participates in and contributes to the very same process of illuminating social existence through an appropriate symbolism.

To participate in this process means, in practice, that the analysis has to begin from the self-interpretations of experiences as they can be found within history, and to follow their subsequent explications, for symbols, ideas and doctrines do become the object of controversies which extend over centuries. Of particular significance are those affinities which are established whenever writers, thinkers or activists express their own experiences by deliberately adopting symbols suggested and used by earlier writers, thinkers or activists. For example, a writer may reveal important details of his self-understanding by identifying 'predecessors'; that is, thinkers of the past who, in his view, pursued projects similar or equivalent to his own. If such lineages are continued by future thinkers, history may generate continuities of meaning which extend over long periods of time. In the following I will refer to these affinities as 'lines of meaning'. By definition, lines of meaning form sequences of self-interpretations of reality which refer to each other *as interpretations of the same reality*. Thus, because the various symbols used in such interpretations are explications of the *same* experience, comparing them ought to provide important insights into the latter.

Lines of meaning may, but do not have to, give rise to 'traditions' with a fully developed identity, or even to 'movements' which are politically active within history.[20] Once a line of meaning achieves such a status, its development becomes more systematic as the movement's future becomes an explicit concern of its members. However, in general, the continuation of a line of meaning is not a systematic process. Experiences are reported, interpreted and elaborated in writing, speech and habits all the time. Potentially, such reports and interpretations are all beginnings of lines of meaning but only an infinitesimal minority will extend into the future beyond the immediate context from which they came. The lonely mystic who struggles to condense his experiences into words, the soldier in the trenches who in rare quiet moments compiles a diary of what he has gone through, they may or may not hope that their reports are somehow of value to others, but they can never be sure.

If lines of meaning are understood as 'communication' in a broader sense, a number of tools from linguistics and linguistic philosophy become available for their investigation. Ever since Karl Bühler's theory of language (1934), it has become common practice to distinguish three functions of language: *Darstellung*, *Ausdruck* and *Appell*, which I, following Niklas Luhmann, translate and change slightly into 'information', 'utterance' and 'understanding' (which includes 'misunderstanding') respectively.[21] Thus, a full account of communication through language must include an account of: that which is being communicated, that is, the information contents of the communication; the way in which this contents is being communicated, that is, the form of the utterance which turns the information into a 'message'; and how the utterance was understood *as an utterance*. In both Bühler's and Luhmann's theories this last point is crucial. Bühler, elaborating the 'function' of language, speaks of its 'appeal' function: an utterance through language entails an 'appeal' to an (imagined or real) audience to 'accept' the utterance as an act of communication. Luhmann, whose systems theory wants to explain the 'successful' emergence of communication, makes this 'acceptance' – the 'understanding' of the utterance *as utterance* – an integral part of his definition of 'communication'. He speaks of 'communication' only if this acceptance has occurred. Similarly, a first segment of a line of meaning is established if a text of the past is accepted as an explication of an experience to which a later audience can relate.

Luhmann *defines* communication as the synthesis of three selections. First, something has to be selected as information. Second, a decision has to be made to turn the selected information into the 'occasion' of an utterance and the precise form or style of the utterance has to be selected. Finally, the utterance has to be accepted as utterance and the precise manner of acceptance – of 'understanding' – has to be selected. This emphasis on the threefold *selectivity* which constitutes 'communication' points to the complexity which the historical analysis of 'texts' – I use the term here in its broadest sense – confronts. The historical meaning of each of these selections does not only depend on the selection itself but on the entire range of options – the 'wider linguistic context' as Quentin Skinner explains – from which the selection was made and hence on the social conventions which frame the selection process. In other words, the reconstruction of the historical meaning of a text cannot simply look at what was being said but must also take into account what was *not* being said of all the things that could have been said.[22] For example, as Skinner argues, given that the discussion of political principles in seventeenth-century England 'virtually hinged on the study of rival versions of the English past', Locke's failure to use any historical arguments in the *Second Treatise* must somehow be relevant for its interpretation.[23]

An obvious but important implication of these methodological considerations is the practical impossibility of a full assessment of the historical meaning of a 'text'.[24] The scarcity of sources, the resulting difficulties in reconstructing the 'wider linguistic context', and indeed other contextual factors, the inevitable ambiguity of symbols and signs, the variety of ways in which a 'text' influences its audience are just a few of the technical reasons why the analysis of lines of meaning always amounts to an exercise in interpretation rather than mere reporting. However, this commonplace does not imply that any history is as good or appropriate as any other. For example, a 'history of ideas' is unsuitable for participating in the self-interpretation of reality by following lines of meaning. A 'history of ideas' typically starts with an abstract definition of the idea or concept whose history is to be examined. In that the definition separates the idea from its basis in real experience, the idea assumes an existence outside history. History is then scanned in a search for 'similar' or 'congruent' ideas which, once arranged in chronological order, form the material for the 'history' of the idea in question. 'Similarity' and 'congruence', however, are extremely ambiguous categories. If 'similarity' is all that is required to move from one idea to another, it will not be difficult to establish a connection between the idea under examination and any other idea.[25]

Lines of meaning are not defined through the similarity of symbols or ideas. They emerge from within history when thinkers, activists or movements refer to each other in order to clarify their concerns to themselves and to others. In contrast to the 'similarity' which defines a history of ideas, the affinities which constitute a line of meaning are assumed and proclaimed within history rather than imposed by the investigator. For example, Hegel occurs in this work not only because the architecture of his *Phenomenology* resembles the architecture of the 'Gnostic' systems from late Antiquity but because of the way in which he links his own efforts to the work of the German mystic Jacob Boehme. Boehme, in turn, is included not only because of the design of his system but because of the fact that he – and indeed his contemporaries – related his mystic experiences to Pico della Mirandola's 'Christian Cabala'. And Pico's interest in Jewish mysticism finally introduces the analysis to the whole context of Renaissance syncretism.

The investigation of lines of meaning must therefore avoid, to the extent that this is possible, referring to entities which are assumed to exist outside history. In other words, lines of meaning are to be 'followed' rather than 'constructed'. It lies in the nature of this approach that it cannot distinguish in an *a priori* manner classes of events, facts or phenomena which are relevant to its purpose from those which are not. What is relevant must emerge from the analysis once a starting point has been chosen, but certain kinds of information seem particularly helpful for the exploration of lines of meaning. The reflection of thinkers, writers and political activists upon their own endeavours is often their own way of connecting to and continuing lines of meaning as they perceive them, especially if they define 'predecessors' of their own enterprises. While this information may occasionally be found in written documents such as diary entries, manifestos or prefaces, it can also be hidden in the person's biography, personal affiliations, the geometry of his intellectual trajectory, and is sometimes revealed not by himself but by acquaintances.

In practice, for the reasons noted above, the principle that lines of meaning are to be followed rather than fabricated does not absolve the analyst from the burden of making decisions. When reflecting on their work, writers and activists can acknowledge 'influences' in a variety of ways, some of which may be 'weaker' and others 'stronger'. If, for example, the writer composed academic treatises, how much significance should be assigned to a footnote? And how much to a casual conversation in which, say, a future revolutionary was instructed in the teachings of Joachim of Fiore? Although footnotes may well convey important information about the 'wider linguistic context' within which an author operates, and although conversations – however casual – can change lives, the examples still allude to the speculative dangers which my approach entails.

While these dangers can be controlled to some extent – a diary entry may turn the inconspicious footnote into evidence of a dramatic reading experience – they cannot be avoided entirely. There is no method which would transform the required interpretations into a mere technicality. In fact, it would be quite absurd to expect that such a method should exist. As I explained earlier, by exploring lines of meaning the investigator *participates* in the self-interpretation of reality. There is a sense in which both the writer who, centuries ago, continued a particular line of meaning, and the researcher who today follows this continuation participate in the same process. Hence, they should be expected to face the same problems: they *both* need to decide which path to follow.

In the absence of a general method which decides on mere technical grounds whether a 'link' between two thinkers or movements qualifies as a constitutive element in a line of meaning, decisions have to be made on a case-by-case basis. It is crucial, of course, that such links are based on *experience* rather than 'similarity' or 'congruence'. There must be evidence of a real encounter between the beginning and endpoint of a line segment – preferrably in the form of an explicit acknowledgement of an 'impact' or 'influence' which the beginning had on the ending. Ideally this evidence would come from the self-interpretation of the thinkers or movements involved; yet, depending on the situation and the availability of sources, circumstancial and secondary biographical information may well be equally relevant.

It seems that the notion of 'influence' is in fact difficult to avoid in this context – an insight which may appear disappointingly unoriginal. Political theorists have traditionally appealed to 'influence' whenever they compared thinkers separated by long stretches of time. This practice naturally invited the predictable criticism that the notion is open to abuse because of its opacity. To be sure, in some sense everyone is 'influenced' by Plato. Quentin Skinner agrees that the notion of 'influence' becomes 'extremely elusive' if it is to be distinguished, as it has to be, from a cause. Yet, he also acknowledges that it is 'far from being empty of explanatory force' because it allows for a kind of causality which is neither 'necessary' nor 'sufficient' and hence incorporates contingency.[26] The previous discussion supports this assessment. The concept of 'influence' is appropriate precisely because it is sufficiently ambiguous – even though it must be acknowledged that one can speak of 'influence' in a more or less disciplined manner. If the concept is used, for example, to denote a segment in a line of meaning, it is crucial that 'influence' must be acknowledged in some form by the 'influenced'. Moreover, the origin of 'influence' must be concrete and empirical – another person, movement, or text rather than the obscure *Zeitgeist*, the 'spirit of the times'. However, there can be no question that regardless of how disciplined the investigation attempts to be, its ultimate appeal must be to 'plausibility'.

It is not clear to me why, as is sometimes suggested, this lack of 'objectivity' should imply arbitrariness. The view that it does so seems to gain popularity with each episodic revival of scepticism. The classical tradition in political science, in contrast, established the validity of theories precisely on the assumption that experiences can be *shared*. In this tradition, the political scientist is a person capable of the 'imaginative re-enactment of the experiences of which theory is an explication'. The theories, in turn, are intelligible to others only if they will call forth 'parallel experiences as the empirical basis for testing the truth of theory'.[27] A theory will be 'plausible' if it succeeds in engendering precisely the experience which it explicates.

Similarly, the exploration of lines of meaning is an exploration of concrete people acting within their concrete situations, driven by their hopes to find warmth and friendship, by their search for something to hold on to, by their striving for fulfilment, their fear of loneliness, of death, of personal responsibility and alienation. An account of such acts will be 'plausible' to the extent that the reader can *share* in the experiences which they expressed and to which they responded. In this sense, lines of meaning come into being through the sharing of experiences. Therefore, the criterion of *shared experience* also enters this work at three different levels. First, it composes the lines of meaning to be investigated in that it lets writers, thinkers and activists acknowledge an affinity at the level of experience. Second, it lets the investigator participate in the self-interpretation of a reality as it is actualised in the line of meaning. And finally, it stands between my work and its readers. The validity or 'truth' of my work does not reside at any of these levels but will, or will not, *emerge* only in their coincidence.

THE IMPORTANCE OF HISTORY

I originally introduced 'lines of meaning' as *means* for participating in the self-interpretation of experiences, for bridging the step between an experience and its symbolic expression. Thus, as the previous discussion on method dealt almost exclusively with the methodological and technical problems involved in following lines of meaning within history, it might now be appropriate to remember that the presentation of such lines of meaning is not the primary objective of the investigation.

As I explained above, lines of meaning consist of self-interpretations of reality which refer to each other as interpretations of the *same* reality. The comparative analysis of these interpretations will therefore assist the *contemplation* of their underlying reality. In other words, once the line of meaning has been laid open, a further interpretive effort is required to go beneath the variety of symbols, ideas, and actions 'down' to the experienced reality which they express. At this point, the analysis of history moves into the background. Lines of meaning will be considered as 'horizontal' rather than 'vertical'; the emphasis will be on the sameness and equivalence of experiences rather than on the diversity of symbols and historical circumstances. As lines of meaning turn into foci of contemplation, the analysis becomes *philosophical* in the proper sense. Leo Strauss's observation that, ultimately, political philosophy cannot be considered a historical discipline corresponds here to this conceptual distinction between *following* and *contemplating* lines of meaning.[28]

The equivalence of experiences underlying a line of meaning is a locus of contemplation rather than an 'object' of knowledge because the drama of history is not completed. The emergent meanings of the experiences remain open towards the future of the process, and as such they can never be more than provisional. Thus, reality must be approached as 'a mystery in process of revelation'.[29] While the analyst participates in the process of revelation, he is not in a position to dissolve the mystery. The contemplation thus does not turn the analyst into an observer but rather confirms his status as a participant in the continuing drama.

My views on the equivalence of experiences and the analysis of lines of meaning have been influenced by Eric Voegelin.[30] If, as I believe, Voegelin's work shares some of the methodological principles of this introduction, then it is not surprising that Voegelin's late, meditative essays both analyse and exemplify precisely the kind of contemplation which in many ways consummates his lifelong occupation with the historical analysis of experiences. For Voegelin, this contemplation corresponds to the experience of a tension 'between the poles of time and eternity'; this tension of the 'in-between' is the characteristic philosophical experience – Plato's *metaxy* – in which temporal being becomes aware of the 'flowing presence' of eternal Being.[31]

If the insights or tension evoked by this contemplation are expressed in symbols, the contemplation itself can re-enter the temporal flow and becomes a constituent of history – as it did, according to Voegelin, with the rise of philosophy in Greece. At this point, of course, the argument has run full circle because the historical sediments of such contemplation now become available for precisely the kind of analysis which they emerged from. In a sense, this circle simply restates that, because of the incompleteness of history, a full investigation of lines of meaning must end in a practice of contemplation and meditation rather than with a concluding act.

The contemplation of history is not the only route leading to the meditative insights of the 'in-between'. But it frames the contemplation in important ways which greatly assist my inquiry. First, history breaks the meditative circle and thus prevents it from becoming a tautology. As the investigator follows lines of meaning and then contemplates the equivalence of experiences beneath the variety of symbols, he becomes conscious of the fact that he is *adding* new symbols to the already existing ones. However, this addition will have relevance to him only in relation to the meaning and concrete historical implications of earlier symbolisms. In other words, the awareness of 'participation' ought to impose on the investigator the responsibility of measuring his own contribution in relationship to past achievements. Ideally, his contemplation re-enters the temporal flow through new myths and symbols with the awareness of a real advance. This advancement does not amount to an accumulation of knowledge but instead offers a *refinement of the symbols* available for the self-interpretation of reality.

A second important benefit of a historical analysis of experience is that it provides a *relativisation of the present*. Contemporary interest in a line of meaning turns the present into a line segment. The subsequent contemplation of the underlying experiences emphasises their sameness and equivalence so that the symbolisms of the present are bound to lose their absoluteness. The 'climax of modernity', the 'postmodern' sense of epoch, the 'finality' of 'liberal democracy': these and other popular myths now appear in a horizontal line together with earlier symbols expressing equivalent experiences. This procedure acknowledges that human nature is articulated *in the whole of history* and not simply in selected periods. Only the contemplation of history can prevent one from mistaking the specific features of one's own time for the nature of things and human existence in general.[32]

OVERVIEW

The present work analyses the spiritual dimension of the Cold War by connecting, through a line of meaning, the self-understanding of the conflict's protagonists with the heterodox beliefs of Manichaeism and

Marcionism. In the terminology developed earlier, Chapters 4 to 7 'follow' or 'lay open' this line of meaning, while Chapters 8 and 9 'contemplate' the experience or problem underlying such continuity. Chapter 8 uses the life work of the American diplomat, historian and writer George F. Kennan as a magnifying lens through which to investigate the line's twentieth century segment. Two brief 'excursions' at the beginning of the same chapter suggest that studies of Augustine and Machiavelli could serve analogous purposes for late Antiquity and the Renaissance respectively. The Epilogue in Chapter 9 adds my own conclusions to Kennan's reflections.

Because Manichaeism plays such an important role in this investigation, I need to devote some attention to 'Gnosticism' and 'Gnostic Studies' in Chapter 3. While I found much of interest in this field, I do not accept its fundamental assumption: that 'Gnosticism' or a 'Gnostic religion' can be defined, in an ahistorical manner, as a category or an 'ideal type'. This supposition is problematic not only because the phenomena commonly labelled as 'Gnostic' are too diverse to warrant such classification. The deeper question raised by the controversy surrounding 'Gnosticism' is whether a religion can indeed be fully characterised through its symbolism. I have alluded to these problems earlier in this chapter, and concluded that the pursuit of 'lines of meaning' is a more suitable approach to the study of spirituality than the categorisation of symbols.

Accordingly, my methodology prevents me from debating whether someone or something actually *is* 'Gnostic' – unless, of course, the label is used in the self-interpretation of the phenomenon in question. Such self-imposed constraint also places the long-standing dispute on the alleged 'Gnostic' features of modernity beyond this project's reach. The historical narrative focuses on the self-understanding of concrete people acting in concrete historical situations. I consequently leave the division of history into epochs to the central characters of the story. The expression 'Gnostic war' is introduced in the Epilogue only in order to give a name to a certain kind of antagonism, of which the Cold War, I suggest, represents an example. The label does not, however, entail a statement about religious movements in late Antiquity.

The discussion of Plato and early Christianity in Chapter 2 stands somewhat outside the historical flow of subsequent chapters. Yet, given that so many thinkers in the history of philosophy revealed vital information about their self-understanding through their references to Plato and Christianity, it seemed logical to make my own interpretation of their spirituality known before I proceed to use such sources in later parts of this book.

NOTES

1. Quoted in Philip J. Lee, *Against the Protestant Gnostics* (New York: Oxford University Press, 1987), p. 125.
2. For the sake of conciseness I have opted to use the pronoun 'he' when speaking of humanity in general.
3. A non-representative selection: Pierre Allan and Kjell Goldmann (eds), *The End of the Cold War: Evaluating Theories of International Relations* (Dordrecht: Nijhoff, 1992); John Lewis Gaddis, *We Now Know: Rethinking Cold War History* (Oxford: Clarendon Press, 1998); Chester Hartman and Pedro Vilanova (eds), *Paradigms Lost: The Post Cold War Era* (London: Pluto Press, 1992); Michael J. Hogan, *The End of the Cold War: Its Meaning and Implications* (Cambridge: Cambridge University Press, 1992); Richard Ned Lebow and Janice Gross Stein, *We All Lost the Cold War* (Princeton: Princeton University Press, 1994); Geir Lundestad and Odd Arne Westad (eds), *Beyond the Cold War: New Dimensions in International Relations* (Oslo: Scandinavian University Press, 1993). Outside the discipline of 'international relations' some work has been done on the impact of the Cold War on culture and society. See, for example, Fred Inglis, *The Cruel Peace: Everyday Life and the Cold War* (New York: Basic Books, 1991); Alan Nadel, *Containment Culture: American Narratives, Postmodernism, and the Atomic Age* (Durham: Duke University Press, 1995); Stephen J. Whitfield, *The Culture of the Cold War* (Baltimore: The Johns Hopkins University Press, 1991).
4. This discussion draws on Michel Foucault, *Discourse and Truth: The Problematization of Parrhesia*, Notes to the Seminar given by Foucault at Berkeley in autumn 1983, manuscript edited by Joseph Pearson. Foucault also lectured on *parrhesia* at the Collège de France. A German translation of two of these lectures of 1983/4 was edited by Ulrike Reuter, Lothar Wolfstetter, Hermann Kocyba and Bernd Heiter as *Michel Foucault: Das Wahrsprechen des Anderen* (Frankfurt a.M.: Materialis Verlag, 1988), pp. 15–42. See also Heinrich Schlier, 'parrhesia', in Gerhard Kittel (ed., trans. Geoffrey W. Bromiley), *The Theological Dictionary of the New Testament*, Volume 5 (Grand Rapids: Eerdmans, 1967), pp. 871–86. On Luther's hearing at Worms see Roland Bainton, *Here I stand* (Icknield Way: Lion Publishing, 1983), pp. 167–90.
5. See Christian Meier, *Die Entstehung des Politischen bei den Griechen* (Frankfurt a.M.: Suhrkamp, 1980).
6. Niccolò Machiavelli, *Discorsi*, Book 1, Chapter 18 in *Il Principe e altre opere politiche* (Milan: Garzanti, 1993).
7. Arnold van Gennep, *The Rites of Passage* (London: Routledge & Kegan Paul, 1960).
8. Victor W. Turner, 'Betwixt and Between: The Liminal Period in *Rites de Passage*', in Turner, *The Forest of Symbols: Aspects of Ndembu Ritual* (Ithaca: Cornell University Press, 1967), pp. 93–111.
9. Turner, 'Betwixt and Between', p. 97.
10. Victor W. Turner, 'Liminality and Communitas', in Turner, *The Ritual Process: Structure and Anti-Structure* (Chicago: Aldine, 1969), pp. 94–130 (128).
11. Turner, 'Liminality and Communitas', p. 96.
12. Victor W. Turner, 'Communitas: Model and Process', in *The Ritual Process*, pp. 131–65 (139).
13. Turner, 'Betwixt and Between', p. 106.
14. Turner, 'Liminality and Communitas', p. 128.
15. The terms 'Axial Age' and 'axis times' were coined by Karl Jaspers, *The Origin and Goal of History* (New Haven: Yale University Press, 1953), and Lewis Mumford, *The Transformation of Man* (New York: Collier Books, 1956). This discussion of the period draws on the work of Shmuel N. Eisenstadt, especially on Eisenstadt, 'The Axial Age Breakthroughs – Their Characteristics and Origins', in Eisenstadt (ed.), *The Origins and Diversity of Axial Age Civilisations* (Albany: SUNY Press, 1986), pp. 1–25; Eisenstadt, 'Cultural Traditions and Political Dynamics: the Origins and Modes of Ideological Politics', *British Journal of Sociology*, 32: 2 (June 1981), pp. 155–81; Eisenstadt, 'Comparative Liminality: Liminality and Dynamics of

Civilization', *Religion*, 15: 3 (July 1985), pp. 315–38; Eisenstadt, 'Frameworks of the Great Revolutions: Culture, Social Structure, History and Human Agency', *International Social Science Journal*, 44: 133 (August 1992), pp. 385–401. See also Benjamin J. Schwartz, 'The Age of Transcendence', *Daedalus*, 104: 2 (Spring 1975), pp. 1–8.

16. See Eric Voegelin, *The World of the Polis* (Volume 2 of *Order and History*) (Baton Rouge: Lousiania State University Press, 1957).
17. Eisenstadt, 'Cultural Traditions and Political Dynamics', pp. 157–8.
18. Shmuel N. Eisenstadt, 'Dissent, Heterodoxy and Civilizational Dynamics: Some Analytical and Comparative Indications', in Eisenstadt (ed.), *Orthodoxy, Heterodoxy, and Dissent in India* (New York: Mouton, 1984), pp. 1–9 (4).
19. Eisenstadt, 'Cultural Traditions and Political Dynamics', p. 170.
20. I am developing the notion of 'lines of meaning' from Eric Voegelin's *Sinnlinien*, which he introduced in his *Über die Form des Amerikanischen Geistes* (Tübingen: J. C. B. Mohr, 1928), p. 15.
21. Karl Bühler, *Sprachtheorie: Die Darstellungsfunktion der Sprache* (Stuttgart: Fischer, second edn, 1965); Niklas Luhmann, *Soziale Systeme* (Frankfurt a.M.: Suhrkamp, fourth edn, 1991), pp. 196–7; Luhmann, 'The Autopoiesis of Social Systems', in Felix Geyer and Johannes van der Zouwen (eds), *Sociocybernetic Paradoxes: Observation, Control and Evolution of Self-steering Systems* (London: Sage, 1986), pp. 172–92 (174); and Luhmann, 'Was ist Kommunikation?', *Information Philosophie*, Vol. 1 (1987), pp. 4–16. The distinction of three 'functions' of communication through language has its parallels in the speech-act theories of John L. Austin and John R. Searle.
22. Quentin Skinner, 'Meaning and Understanding in the History of Ideas', in *History and Theory*, Vol. 8 (1969), pp. 3–53 (49). See also Skinner, 'Some Problems in the Analysis of Political Thought and Action', *Political Theory*, 2: 3 (August 1974), pp. 277–303, for a clarification of Skinner's position.
23. Skinner, 'Meaning and Understanding', p. 47, and for the interpretation itself see Skinner, 'History and Ideology in the English Revolution', *The Historical Journal*, 8: 2 (1965), pp. 151–78.
24. See also Quentin Skinner, 'Conventions and the Understanding of Speech Acts', *Philosophical Quarterly*, 20: 79 (April 1970), pp. 118–38 (136–7).
25. See, for example, Hannah Arendt, 'The Concept of History: Ancient and Modern', in Arendt, *Between Past and Future* (London: Faber & Faber, 1961), pp. 41–90 (69).
26. Skinner, 'Meaning and Understanding', p. 25.
27. Eric Voegelin, *The New Science of Politics: An Introduction* (Chicago: University of Chicago Press, 1952), p. 64.
28. See Leo Strauss, 'What is Political Philosophy?', pp. 9–55, and 'Political Philosophy and History', pp. 56–77, both in Strauss, *What is Political Philosophy?* (Westport: Greenwood, 1977); Strauss, 'On Classical Political Philosophy', in *Social Research*, 12: 1 (February 1945), pp. 98–117. On the complex relationship between the history of philosophy and philosophy itself see J. G. A. Pocock, 'The History of Political Thought: A Methodological Inquiry', in Peter Laslett and W. G. Runciman (eds), *Philosophy, Politics and Society* (second series), (Oxford: Basil Blackwell, 1964), pp. 183–202. Also John Dunn, 'The Identity of the History of Ideas', *Philosophy*, 43: 164 (April 1968), pp. 85–104.
29. Eric Voegelin, *The Ecumenic Age* (Volume 4 of *Order and History*) (Baton Rouge: Louisiana State University Press, 1974), p. 6.
30. See, for example, Eric Voegelin, 'Äquivalenz von Erfahrungen und Symbolen in der Geschichte', in Eric Voegelin, *Ordnung, Bewußtsein, Geschichte* (ed. Peter J. Opitz), (Stuttgart: Klett, 1988), pp. 99–126.
31. From Eric Voegelin, 'Eternal Being in Time', in Voegelin, *Anamnesis*, (trans. and ed. Gerhart Niemeyer), (Notre Dame: University of Notre Dame Press, 1978), pp. 116–40 (132–3).
32. Cf. Strauss, 'Political Philosophy and History', p. 57.

2
Liminality in Platonic philosophy and early Christian thought

In a book dealing with Manichaean spirituality, a chapter on Plato and early Christianity must be considered a digression. Yet, apart from chronology, there is an important reason why this is a useful, and indeed necessary, excursion at this stage.

I intend to use Plato's spirituality as a contrast medium. The contours of Manichaeism, and indeed any belief, will gain in sharpness when compared to alternatives. Selecting Plato for this purpose does not reflect a personal preference. After all, the history of philosophy itself uses his philosophy for similar ends. Rare is the political philosopher who felt he could afford to not comment on the author of the *Republic*. For the investigation of lines of meaning, this practice proves to be of great value. Whenever a thinker writes about Plato, he locates himself in relation to the Greek, and thereby reveals important information about his self-understanding. The history of the heterodox threads in Western thought, for example, contains numerous references to the various manifestations of 'Neo-Platonism'. My use of such information will not be comprehensible unless I give my own account of Plato first. A similar argument justifies the brief discussion of *metanoia* and early Christian spirituality in the second part of this chapter.

PLATO'S *METAXY*

The 'Allegory of the Cave' in the *Republic* provides a suitable starting point for a discussion of Platonic spirituality. The scenario is well known. Human beings are chained in a cave, their necks fastened so that they can only look straight ahead of them and cannot turn their heads. Behind them the cave rises towards an opening, with a blazing fire at a distance. Between fire and prisoners is a low wall, behind which people pass, holding up vessels, statues and figures of animals so that they project above the wall. All the prisoners can see are the shadows produced in this way on the cave's wall in front of them. If the prisoners had been in this situation since they were children, and if they were able to talk to each other about what they see so as to confirm each other's perceptions, then they could not but assume that the shadows are indeed real things and the only 'real things' that exist.

If one of the prisoners is then released from his bonds and forced to stand up suddenly, to turn around and walk, and to lift his eyes towards the light, he will undergo a painful experience. The light will burn his eyes, which are not used to its brightness. He will consider the shadows as the true reality if only because they are less painful to look at; whereas the light and the real objects it made visible appear as distortions. When the prisoner eventually leaves the cave and has to face the upper world and the light itself, he finally recognises the sun as lord of the visible world and as the ultimate creator of all things which he saw in his prison.

The members in the cave-society perhaps had some code of honour and glory to be won among them for keen-sightedness. Prizes were given to those who could remember the order of sequence among the passing shadows and predict their future appearances. The released prisoner, however, will not envy this power of honour. He will be reluctant to return to his fellow prisoners whose life he must now regard as miserable. Should he decide to return, his fate would be predictable. His eyes would be blinded by the darkness in the cave because he came in suddenly out of the daylight. Because he is at first unable to discriminate between the shadows, the other prisoners would laugh at him, and say that he in fact *lost* his sight during his visit to the upper world. The ascent would not only seem not worth attempting but would even appear dangerous. Reflecting on the reception of the returning prisoners among his fellow-prisoners, Plato lets Socrates allude to his own fate in the corrupt *polis* of Athens: 'And if anyone tried to release them and lead them up, they would kill him if they could lay hands on him'.[1]

The 'Allegory of the Cave' introduces the themes of liminality and *communitas* encountered earlier. The ordinary existence of the cave-dwellers which is interrupted by the 'separation' of one of the prisoners and his subsequent exposure to a force which the other prisoners refuse to acknowledge seem to portray the basic features of a *failed* rite of passage. The cave society denies the returning prisoner his reaggregation; the social significance of his liminal experience is rejected. Hence, the 'Allegory of the Cave' sketches a society in a crisis caused by the complete absence of *communitas*.

In order to substantiate this interpretation, three questions need to be answered. First, Plato's presentation of the two layers of reality distinguished in the allegory needs to be elaborated. What symbols does he use to contemplate transcendence and how does transcendence relate to the temporal sphere? Second, what is the nature of the prisoner's experience as he leaves the visible reality of the cave? And finally, why and how should the cave-dwellers pay attention to the insights he gains on his journey? What, in other words, is the *moral* significance of insights concerning transcendence?

Plato distinguishes two layers of reality in his well-known symbolism of the 'forms' or 'ideas' whose existence he 'extracts', in a process of abstraction, from the 'composite' beings and appearances of the temporal world. Plato assumes the existence of 'Beauty in itself and Goodness and Largeness and all the rest of them'. *The* Beautiful, *the* Good and *the* Large are examples of 'forms' or 'ideas'. They are his answer to the problem of conceptualising unity in multiplicity. Thus, 'whatever else is beautiful apart from Beauty itself is beautiful because it partakes of that Beauty, and for no other reason.'[2] The same applies to Goodness, Largeness and all the other forms. Particulars thus obtain their attributes by participating – *methexis* – in the forms; these, in turn, correspond to the 'pure' manifestations of such attributes. For Plato, to know what a thing is is to know in what forms it participates. The task of the philosopher is precisely to avoid logical confusion by separating the form – *eidos, idea* – from that which participates in it.

As part of the intelligible realm, the realm of the forms exists separately (*chorismos*) from the visible world of appearances. Ever since Aristotle's criticisms, the nature of this separation has been the focus of much controversy. Though they exist on their own, the forms do not exist for themselves. They are always forms *of* appearances. In this sense, it would indeed be absurd to assume that the two layers of reality are completely separate so that one could exist without the other.[3] The form is what allows the appearances to be recognised for *what* they are. Of course, to think of 'this here' as 'what' entails a differentiation between the 'this' and the 'what';[4] but this distinction does not imply that the 'what' is not *in* the 'this here'.

Most importantly, to say that the forms exist independently does not imply that they exist literally as objects or entities amongst other entities. The forms express and symbolise a tension, an intuition of the possibility of movement towards true being. Things in the visible world become beautiful by moving towards the form of Beauty, where 'moving towards' corresponds to a more intense 'participation'. Plato occasionally described such participation as a 'coming into being', compared to the 'being' of the forms.[5] There is a sense in which the visible world of appearances is 'incomplete' and movement towards the forms is a longing for 'completion'. It could be said that the realm of forms is therefore 'higher' than that of appearances but the two are clearly not opposed. In particular, one cannot be left in order to move to the other. The theoretical life which contemplates the forms is clearly the best life for Plato but human beings are not gods. While they are always under way towards the divine – the true being of the forms – they are never absolved from the task of living well in the practical world. The best they can achieve is *philosophia*, the striving for or love of wisdom, but not wisdom itself. As a result, even the theoretical life entails practical functions.

There is one form which Plato sometimes places above the others. This is the form of the Good – the *agathon*. When Socrates is asked in the *Republic* to give an account of the Good, he hesitates at first. Giving such an account, he says, is beyond him; he does not even want to try because he is sure that, by doing so, he would only make a fool of himself. In fact, he then gives up the idea of explaining the Good in itself and instead offers to present the effects, the offspring, of the form of the Good. The effects too cannot be described in a direct manner but only through metaphors and allegories: the metaphor of the sun, the metaphor of the 'Divided Line', and the 'Allegory of the Cave'. Hence, although Socrates asserts the existence of the form of the Good, he cannot say anything about its contents, about *what* it is. Earlier (*Republic*, 505a), however, he implicitly acknowledged that knowledge of the Good was possible when he claimed that the 'highest kind of knowledge' pertains to the form of the Good. This ostensible contradiction requires clarification.

In the metaphor of the sun Plato compares the relationship between *agathon* and the human soul – *psyche* – to the relation between the sun and the eye.[6] Sight needs light in order to function, and in this sense, the sun is the 'cause' of sight: 'the eye's power of sight is a kind of infusion dispensed to it by the sun'. Things become visible to the eye when the light dispensed by the sun enters the relationship as a third factor. Moreover, the sun can be seen by the sight it causes. The light coming from the sun stands to the eye and the visible world just as the *agathon* stands to intelligence and the intelligible world. It gives 'the objects of knowledge their truth and the soul the power of knowing'. However, the *agathon* is 'something other than, and even more splendid (*kalos*) than, knowledge and truth, splendid as they are'. In fact, the sun's light also causes 'the processes of generation, growth and nourishment, without itself being such a process'. The *agathon* must also therefore be seen as not only the source of the 'intelligibility of the objects of knowledge, but also of their being and reality; yet it is not itself that reality but is beyond it, and superior to it in dignity and power'.

The meaning of this dramatic account is further elaborated at 511d, where the form of the Good is presented as the 'starting point' or 'first principle' of everything. Hence, it is the Good from which the multiplicity of forms originates. The forms exist *meta arches*, by virtue of the starting point; they derive their intelligibility from the presuppositionless *arche*. There is a sense, then, in which the forms themselves participate in the form of the Good.

A form's proximity to the *agathon* determines its position in the overall order of the realm of forms. Thus, the form of the Good is the *arche* of the forms because it represents precisely this order; as such, it *is* the ultimate ground of being, the Platonic version of the Heraclidean *logos*. It symbolises the experience of a reality that is not a disordered, indifferent chaos but a *cosmos*, a coherent, harmonious wholeness which deserved respect, awe and reverence. The *cosmos* is the space where the order of being applies and therefore shares in its divinity.[7]

If, therefore, it is possible to obtain knowledge of the form of the Good, it is clear that this knowledge must be the 'highest' knowledge that can be gained – just as the sun, in the 'Allegory of the Cave', is the 'final thing to be perceived in the intelligible region', 'the brightest of all realities'.[8] However, the nature of the knowledge humans can obtain of the form of the Good does not depend only on the form itself but also on the faculty which receives and, perhaps, carries this knowledge. Indeed, the metaphor of the sun portrayed the *agathon* in terms of its effects on the soul. And the 'Allegory of the Cave' presents the prisoner's vision of the *agathon* as a *periagoge*, a 'turning around' of the soul. An inquiry into the nature of the 'highest knowledge' thus concurs with an inquiry into the prisoner's experience and leads over to the second of the three questions asked above: what is the nature of this experience?

The *periagoge* is the moment where an individual experiences himself as open towards transcendence. He leaves the world of human conventions, of appearances and shadows, in order to experience a higher stratum of reality which does not owe its existence to human actions or thought. Accordingly, the 'turning around' is not evoked by the soul itself; on the contrary, the soul is passive in that it allows itself to be ordered by the formative force of the *agathon*. The turning around is the climax of a process of attunement. By sharing in the *agathon*, by 'becoming good', the soul's order is attuned to the harmonious order of being. The *periagoge* is the classic example of 'apperception': instead of imprinting its order on to the world, the soul *gives in* to the order of being. It thereby accepts its embeddedness and its place in an order – that is, the *cosmic* order – which is not of its own making.

The *psyche* is the great symbol introduced by the Greek philosophers for the experience of transcendence – now expressed as the experience of the soul's movement in response to a tensional pull towards an order which is beyond visible reality.[9] The movement's momentum is 'compelling' in that its ultimate cause is felt to be beyond the realm of human action. As a sensorium of transcendence, the soul is the very centre of the human being. It differentiates a human being as an *individual* being, not just as a member of a species. The individual is constituted, therefore, through his relationship to the divine, and he succeeds in being human to the extent that he is able to make his participation in the *agathon* sufficiently important so that it becomes an influence on the development of his soul, of his character.[10] Accordingly, one can succeed in being human to varying degrees; an individual brings to the fore his full potential as a human being as he attunes his life to the insights gained in the *periagoge*.

During the *periagoge*, the soul obtains 'knowledge' in three different ways. First and foremost, it obtains self-awareness and self-knowledge. For the soul, the *periagoge* is a moment of truth, for it finds itself outside the structured positions and conventional beliefs of society. As the mundane order is appraised in terms of its proximity to the order of being, the appraiser's soul itself is implicated.

The second important result of the 'turning around' is a reflective tension towards visible reality. After the *periagoge*, the prisoner does not know only that the shadows are shadows but also how it was possible that he mistook the shadows for reality. The significance of this latter insight is twofold. On the one hand, it allows the prisoner to experience his change as an advance; he has gained a new perspective on reality without losing the one he had followed earlier. On the other hand, although the *periagoge* marks a genuine discontinuity which involves the prisoner's soul in full, he will still be able to relate to his fellow-prisoners and to follow their practices. In fact, this ability gives the prisoner the choice to resume his old place in an unchanged society after a brief readjustment to the cave's darkness; and yet it may also provide meaningful starting points for a constructive and reflective involvement in the ordering of society which is neither patronising nor incomprehensible. Moreover, if the prisoner decides to act upon his experience he will be aware of the risk such action involves because he will speak to the members of the cave society after having once been one of them. As he appeals – explicitly or implicitly – to his fellow prisoners to 'turn around', he will know that he may well be the only example that they have of what it means to do as he asks. In these circumstances, he will have to speak up, if he does, in the mode of *parrhesia*.

The third effect of the *periagoge* on the soul incorporates the previous two. Having been 'in between' the mundane and the transcendent increases the soul's ability to discriminate, to differentiate and to distinguish. After the 'turning around', the prisoner's vision has improved in that he can see the world with what may be called a 'higher resolution'. Having become aware of a layer of reality 'behind' the shadows, the prisoner no longer has to accept them at face value, as being what they pretend to be. And because confusion is always the result of a failure to make appropriate distinctions, the prisoner will be less prone to confusion.

By failing to define things properly, to mark off one thing from another, and by separating forms falsely, one gives oneself over to the play of opinions and shadows posing as reality. It is at this point, of course, where 'knowledge' and 'ignorance' of the Good have an immediate bearing on the order of society. If confusion prevails, members of society are at liberty to succumb to the particular urgings of their self-interest. They manipulate, deceive and pretend to be more than they are so as to exploit the lack of orientation for their own advantage. However, before I turn to the moral and practical significance of the insights gained in the *periagoge*, a few more words need to be devoted to their characterisation in order to avoid some popular misunderstandings.

The prisoner's 'knowledge' of reality increases as he leaves the cave and 'turns around' but the advance cannot be compared to a revelation of secrets which remain true forever. The insights gained are neither propositions or statements about how the world works nor blueprints for the organisation of society. As explained above, the progress consists in a refinement of abilities which have as yet to be used and tested in practice. No absolutes and no doctrines can be extracted from the experience of the *periagoge*. The turning around is not an endpoint, not the final actualisation of a state of perfection. On the contrary, the *periagoge* can only be the beginning of a new life, of a new perspective on reality based on an awareness that there is more to reality than can be seen at any moment in time. The *periagoge* divides the prisoner's personal history into a 'before' and an 'after', and the very fact that there once was a 'before' will remind him that the reflective distance and discriminating powers gained cannot be taken for granted but need to be trained and cultivated. The prisoner will learn, therefore, that he must take care of his soul. It is in this context that there emerged in Greek antiquity various practices and guidelines for the 'care of the soul' – *epimelesthai sautou* – which often included provisions for good health. In his *Apology*, Socrates presents himself as a master of the care of the soul and reproaches his judges for caring not for their souls but rather for the acquisition of wealth, reputation and honour.[11]

Sharing in the *agathon* does not imprint the form of the Good on to the prisoner's soul. Although the open soul is being ordered by the *agathon*, it remains far from absorbing the order of being in full. The ascent to the sun always begins from a particular situation with particular assumptions, and the subsequent 'turning around' places the soul in between *this* situation and the realm of forms. The ascent is a quest, and the soul cannot but experience the *periagoge* as a response or answer to *this* specific quest. Insights into the form of the Good are consequently always bound to a context. Therefore, although it becomes aware of an order which truly and comprehensively transcends the temporal realm, the soul cannot possess full knowledge of the contents of the form of the Good. A philosopher like Socrates who has undergone the *periagoge* and who cares for his soul 'acquires the characteristics of order and divinity *so far as a man may*'; and even the philosopher 'will have his detractors'.[12] The *chorismos* cannot be overcome because the truth is known only to the gods.[13]

In Plato's presentation, Socrates knows the experience he describes in the 'Allegory of the Cave' but he cannot talk about it directly. The elusiveness of the form of the Good is a recurring theme in Plato which finds a particularly striking expression in a passage in the *Seventh Letter*.[14] The context of the passage is Dionysius's attempt to convince Plato to return to his court at Syracuse. Plato's first visit had been a disaster with Dion, his disciple, forced into exile and Plato, caught up in the power struggle between the two, kept at Dionysius's court against his will. Thus, Plato had good reason to be reluctant to return to Syracuse. He eventually decided to follow Dionysius's call when the latter promised that 'Dion's affairs shall be settled to your [Plato's] satisfaction'. Moreover, friends assured him that Dionysius had made great progress in philosophy. Upon arrival, Plato proceeds to test Dionysius's progress. The fact that Dionysius even wrote a book about what he had learned from Plato during their first encounter is then taken by Plato as evidence that Dionysius had not properly understood philosophy. Knowledge of the matter with which the philosopher concerns himself is not 'something that can be put into words like other branches of learning'. Remarkably, Plato admits that 'no treatise by me concerning it exists or ever will exist'. He even doubts that it would be to humanity's advantage to put these matters into words for such words are bound to be misunderstood.

Plato is adamant that the wisdom gained in the *periagoge* cannot be implanted in the soul by reading books or by listening to speeches.[15] For this reason, he designed his own texts as *dialogues*; that is, his literary form corresponds to his teaching. The dialogues are not intended to convey the contents of a message but to demonstrate how a particular kind of wisdom could be obtained through the personal involvement of the seekers of wisdom. Typically, the truth is not with the speakers at the beginning of the dialogue but emerges, if at all, only as a result of the dialogue. The good conversation is a model for the search for truth but it cannot offer the contents of the truth. Those who claim to be able to put the vision of the *agathon* into words and those who believe themselves able to obtain the wisdom flowing from this vision passively by mere reading or listening will be filled 'either with an unjustifiable and quite improper contempt for their fellows or with a lofty and vain expectation, based on the belief that they were in possession of some mighty secret'.[16]

One of the important implications of the elusiveness of the form of the Good is that it cannot be taught. The 'turning around' of the soul cannot itself be made a subject of professional skill (*techne*). Although Socrates makes some concessions to the Sophists by accepting that cardinal virtues (*arete*) such as courage (*andreia*) and temperance (*sophrosyne*) can be taught by habituation (*ethesi*) and training (*askesesin*) just like the excellences of the body, he insists that the highest knowledge cannot be put into the soul. In making these assertions, Plato takes transcendence seriously. In the *periagoge* the soul becomes aware of a 'higher' layer of reality and neither the experience nor the layer experienced is the result of human action. Teaching, in contrast, is always an encounter between human beings, an event that takes place in the mundane order.

Because of the transcendence of the *agathon*, the soul's capacity for recognising it for what it is during the 'turning around' cannot have originated within the temporal realm. Accordingly, Socrates is bound to acknowledge that this capacity must be innate. In the 'Allegory of the Cave', the prisoners have had sight all along. The problem is not, therefore, to make blind people see but to make eyes which can see turn away from darkness to light – a manoeuvre, as Plato explains, which requires the whole body to turn. The soul's 'vision' is thus 'something which never loses its power, but whose effects are useful and salutary or again useless and harmful according to the direction in which it is turned'.[17]

Moreover, the problem of transcendence also makes it very difficult to think of souls as 'created' or 'emerging'. Whatever causes the being of souls as sensors of transcendence must be closely related to the *agathon* itself, but to propose that the soul in some way emanated from the *agathon* would clearly have blurred the separate existence of the forms, the *chorismos*. Instead, Plato opted for the symbol of the immortality of the soul. Both the innateness of the capacity to know and the soul's immortality turn the vision of the *agathon* into an experience of remembrance, the Platonic *anamnesis*.

Education cannot place the vision of the *agathon* into the soul but it can prepare the soul for the event. Plato does not dismiss the importance of the traditional virtues (*arete*) but relativises them as habituations of the soul which attune the life of man towards the *agathon*. However, the principal means of preparation is *dialectics*, training in the art of differentiating, for in order to advance towards the form of the Good one needs to be able to distinguish it from everything else. In general, *dialectics* proceeds by the 'destruction of assumptions' which – because they are misleading or simply unnecessary – obscure the true essence of a thing; that is, the form in which it participates. Hence, the *dialectician* is one 'who can take account of the essential nature of each thing'. Plato compares the dialectical method to 'the progress of sight from shadows to the real creatures themselves, and then to the stars themselves, and finally to the sun itself' as shown in the 'Allegory of the Cave'.[18]

Plato is fully aware of the dangers that lie in the 'destruction of assumptions'. If the dialectical method leads the questioner away from the beliefs that tradition has taught him, he may be driven to think that all assumptions are equally vulnerable and the whole method nothing but an arbitrary shifting – rather than a methodical sifting – of opinions. Youth especially, Socrates observes, likes to contradict 'just for the fun of it'. Accordingly, the educational scheme discussed in the *Republic* introduces only mature students to the dialectical method.[19]

Plato's cautions about the dangers of dialectics lead me back, finally, to the third and last question I asked at the beginning of this inquiry into the Platonic symbolism for the experience of transcendence. What is the *moral* significance of this experience? In other words, why should the cave-dwellers pay attention to the truth-telling of their returning comrade? The answer is, simply, that the 'just' or 'good' order of the *polis* must be in harmony with the order of being. In small communities, this harmony may develop naturally in that everyone will find the place and task he is most suited for. In larger societies, those which Socrates calls 'feverish', not everyone can be expected to know his place; not everyone will know who he is. Accordingly, Plato proposes that the *polis* should be ruled by the philosophers, the souls of whom have been ordered by the *agathon*.

It is instructive at this stage to compare Plato's design again with Turner's observations regarding liminality, *communitas* and the ordering of society. Plato's philosophers are defined as those members of society who have undergone the 'turning around'; hence, they are the ones who are capable of liminal experiences. It is through these experiences, through the philosophers' souls, that the order of society is brought into harmony with the order of being. The dangers of liminality are acknowledged by Plato's hints at the dangers involved in dialectics. Analogous to the role of the instructors in Turner's rites of passage, an elaborate educational system both selects and then accompanies the philosophers on their route towards leadership for fifty years.

Plato is also aware that liminal beings tend to form a community of a special kind, the *communitas*. In the *Republic*, he attests that the same applies to the group of philosopher-rulers. They are to live a life of austere simplicity without private property. Among them, 'all the women should be common to all men' and their children will be looked after in nurseries. Plato models the *communitas* of his philosophers as a family.[20]

However, he knows that society is bound to disintegrate unless the *communitas* somehow extends to the other parts of the population. He makes appropriate provisions, for example, in his famous 'Phoenician Tale'. Shortly after dividing society into three groups – the philosopher-rulers, the 'auxiliaries' who perform military, police and executive duties under the order of the rulers, and the ordinary citizens – Plato suggests introducing a 'magnificent myth', a *gennaion pseudos* in order to counter the danger of fragmentation which society's division evokes. Ideally, both citizens and philosopher-rulers should be able to believe in the myth. Its story, in short, explains that the processes of upbringing and education which separated the three groups happened to them only in a dream. In reality, they were all 'fashioned and reared ... in the depths of the earth, and Earth herself, their mother, brought them up, when they were complete, into the light of the day'. Accordingly, the myth opens with the sentence: 'You are, all of you in this polis, brothers'.[21] Balancing community and *communitas*, it then proceeds to confirm both society's division into three groups and the mobility that must exist between the groups.

The myth neatly portrays the purpose of the *polis* as a means of attuning human existence to the transcendent order of being. As I noted earlier, in a small community of farmers, workers and traders – a society which Socrates calls 'healthy' – this attunement occurs naturally. Everyone will know everyone else and it will be impossible for anyone to pose as someone or something that he is not. Larger, 'civilised' societies provide far more opportunities for the game of opinions and shadows. Self-knowledge will be hard to come by. Unless society finds ways of sharing in the order of being through liminality and *communitas* it will inevitably move from an order in harmony with the form of the Good to the unreality of the cave. Citizens will find themselves struggling in positions they are not suited for while erratic mistakes of unqualified rulers inflict misery on everyone. The balancing of community and *communitas* is thus meant to let every soul participate in the *agathon* – if not directly then at least through the mediation of the philosophers. Life in the *polis* will flourish if the jobs that need to be done are done by those who can do them best.

For Plato, then, disorder and corruption in society are an immediate consequence of a lack of the art of differentiating. As members of society fail to distinguish one thing from another they lose sight of the form of the Good and thus their ability to apperceive, to appreciate the limits of their existence. In the *Philebus* Plato speaks of the Good as the structure of a 'mixture' or a 'potion' which has as its ingredients various kinds of pleasure and intellect.[22] What characterises the Good is that these ingredients are mixed well and in the right proportions, rather than indiscriminately thrown together. The 'good' mixture is one that has limits set to it; the Good itself is characterised by 'limitedness', 'measuredness' (*metriotes*) in the midst of the troublesome limitlessness, indeterminacy and confusion which reign in a corrupt society. Without a sense of limits, there is nothing to prevent the citizens from succumbing to the urgings of their self-interests or passions, and from becoming a play-ball in the game of opinions. For Plato, therefore, giving in to the order of being rather than to one's particular self-interests is an accomplishment of *reason*; the opposite, a life unable to set limits to itself, is the result of ignorance.

The strong link between matters of perception and ethical concerns is illustrated in Plato's intellectualisation of 'courage'. As he explains in Book 4 in the *Republic*, Socrates rejects the traditional understanding of courage as virtuous behaviour in the face of physical threats and dangers. Courage is the ability to distinguish in all circumstances what is to be feared from what is not. Since, as Socrates emphasises, the greatest danger to be feared is the seductive power contained in pleasure, courage appears to be a kind of 'steadfastness', an ability to stay on course in spite of the temptations and anxieties waiting along the way. True courage is thus only with those who have seen the *agathon* because only the *periagoge* induces in the soul the capacity to make *eidetic* distinctions. Plato lets Socrates use metaphors from military battle when he confirms that the dialectician who has the form of the Good in front of his eyes can withstand the tests of life.[23]

The nature of Platonic moral reasoning is to a large extent determined by the elusiveness of the *agathon*. The wisdom gained in the vision of the form of the Good cannot be translated into propositions, theorems, doctrines or general rules. It is characteristic of professional knowledge, of *techne*, that it can be taught in the form of axioms and rules so that its application is essentially the result of deductive reasoning. However, as shown above, the wisdom that flows from the 'turning around' cannot be summarised in this manner. Consequently, Platonic moral reasoning emphasises the need to ascend towards, rather than to descend from, the 'highest form of knowledge'. The task is not to consider a specific case or question as an instance of a universal rule that could be known apart from the situation within which the question arose but to define – and distinguish – *from within the situation* the rule of which the situation represents a particular case. This kind of pragmatic moral reasoning Plato calls *phronesis*.

Because of the transcendence of the form of the Good – because of the *chorismos* – the question of true and just human behaviour ultimately transcends any question of public acceptance. This observation is simply a reformulation of the fact that, in Plato's symbolism, the *agathon* transcends all human conventions. The individual who wants to act with a view to the Good must therefore be prepared to act, after careful consideration, *against* the consensus of others. Establishing what is just is not a matter that could be decided democratically because the Good does not necessarily coincide with what is currently accepted in society. Even though the Good remains elusive, and even though it can therefore never be fully implemented and will never display itself to humanity's moral consciousness as a norm held to be incontestably and unalterably true and right, the true essence of justice is different from what is held to be socially acceptable. To equate justice and consensus is a conflation of categories.

Plato lived some two hundred years after the Axial Age proper but he can still be considered an Axial Age thinker in a broader sense. He criticises the traditional poets, including Homer, for having blurred the distinction between the mundane and the transcendent. The poets were wrong, he argues, in presenting the gods as if they were prone to corruption like humans. He emphatically absolved the divine from any responsibility for evil.[24] This insight, in turn, is precisely the reason why Plato embarked on an inquiry into the causes of confusion and disorder as *the* manifestation of evil in society. The *Republic* especially shows how the whole of society is implicated in this search for the causes of disorder. Plato not only declines to shift responsibility away from humans to the transcendent; he also declines to identify particular groups, 'classes', or even individuals as the primary loci of evil. In this sense, the Platonic symbolism does not allow for an externalisation of evil. Those who want to restore the order of society must first of all restore the order of their own souls. Plato's analysis does not separate victims from victimisers but instead looks for the underlying dynamics which turns everyone into a victim.

Plato's return to Axial Age concerns was deliberate. He wanted to return to a wisdom which, as he saw it, stood at the very beginning of the formation and greatness of the Athenian *polis*: the wisdom of Solon. Reflecting on the causes of the Athenian crisis prior to his reforms, Solon had realised that the responsibility for crisis rests not with the gods, but with the folly of human beings. The right order was given, external to humanity, but human actions could be the cause of disorder in the *polis*. The problem was exacerbated by the fact that the divine order was elusive: 'It is very hard to know the unseen measure of right judgement; and yet it alone contains the right boundaries of all things'.[25]

Plato felt that Solon had formed the order of the Athenian *polis* in the sixth century BC according to the order of his soul. Solon had, in other words, done what Plato expected his philosopher-rulers to do. In fact, in the *Timaeus*, Plato reflects on his *Republic* as his effort to repeat the Solonic undertaking,[26] but it may well be possible that he was able to summarise the essence of the Solonic *polis* in such a lucid manner only because he witnessed its dissolution.

PERIAGOGE AND *METANOIA*

Towards the end of his life, Plato witnessed the rise of Macedonia under Philip II. After Philip's victory over the Greeks, his son, Alexander the Great, continued to expand Macedonia into an empire. The times of the *polis* were replaced by the times of Alexander's and, later, the Roman empire. The collapse of the ancient empires of the East, the loss of independence for Israel and the Hellenic and Phoenician city-states, the resulting population shifts, deportations and enslavements, and the interpenetration of cultures in the wave of the imperial conquests must have produced extreme states of forlornness in the turmoil of the world. If the empires were able to create order, they were unable to restore or preserve a genuine community spirit – *communitas* – which could have sustained social and political structures.

For Plato, the size of the *polis* was a central concern. Even the 'healthy' community of farmers, merchants and retailers had to exert some kind of birth control policy so as to 'keep the numbers of their families within their means'. If the *polis* had to nurture too many families, the pressures on resources would inevitably bring either war or poverty.[27] The society proposed in the *Laws* was to have exactly 5,040 citizens who were householders and owned a portion of land.[28] The number was chosen for symbolic and technical reasons: 5,040 can be divided by all numbers from one to twelve except eleven and thus society could easily be subdivided into equal administrative and religious units. The key divisor is twelve – the population consisted of twelve tribes – which shows that the numerical relations governing these subdivision were modelled after the sun symbolism. However, Plato could have chosen a larger number with the same mathematical properties. I assume, therefore, that the number 5,040 reflects roughly what Plato thought was a 'good' size for a society.

In theory, then, the *polis* was a relatively small, close-knit and yet autonomous community. Government was relatively intimate, and the people were comparatively homogenous. Empires, however, are very different political entities. A distant emperor rules over a seemingly limitless expanse of peoples who have very little in common apart from their shared government. While the experience of displacement and exodus dissolves the ordered existence of the community in some parts of the empire, the imperial politics of intrigue and factionalism, together with the artificiality of the political structures, atomise the last remains of *communitas* in others.

The absence of balance between community and *communitas* is thus also an important feature of the historical context from which Christianity arose. In fact, the extent to which the order of the ancient world was renewed by Christianity is often overlooked – not least by the Christian Church itself. Attempting to claim a monopoly on revelation, Christianity overlooked the fact that the Greek thinkers had a 'revelation' when they discovered the *logos*, *agathon* or the *nous*. The purpose of this present section is to draw attention to some fundamental equivalences among elements of Platonic and Christian symbolism which partly stem from the structural correspondence between the situations and experiences to which they responded.

The Platonic *periagoge*, for example, clearly expresses a kind of 'conversion' experience and thus lends itself to a comparison with the Christian *metanoia*. Matthew 4:17 describes how Jesus demanded that his listeners 'turn around'. Jesus's preaching was a call to *metanoia*, and calling for *metanoia* was the purpose of his sending.[29] In classical as well as in Hellenic Greek, the noun *metanoia* and its corresponding verb were comparatively rare. The term usually meant 'to adopt another view', 'to change one's feeling'. When that was derived from the recognition that earlier views were foolish, improper or evil, the change of view would be accompanied by a sense of regret. The word became somewhat more frequent in the *koine*, the popular form of Greek spoken in the biblical regions from the fourth century BC onwards, but did not significantly alter its meaning. Referring to 'later knowledge', it expressed a dissatisfaction with thoughts cherished, plans followed and acts performed, but did not entail more than the wish that these things had not been thought, willed or done.[30] *Metanoia* did not, however, refer to any specific knowledge.

The necessity to 'turn around' is also emphasised in the prophetic tradition in the Old Testament. The prophets questioned whether the cultic and ritual penitence could sufficiently involve the individual person. What was required was a personal turning away from sinful life as such and a turning to Yahweh with all one's being. In the *Septuagint*, the earliest translation of the Old Testament into Greek (from the first half of the third century BC), the noun *metanoia* is still as rare as it was in the secular Greek of the time. However, the use of the corresponding verb shows some conceptual development. Related in the meaning to the verb *epistrephomai*, it is used to translate the 'turning around' of the Hebrew original and thus assumes a religious and ethical sense. At stake is an alteration in total attitude leading to a relation to God which embraces the whole of life. The emphasis seems to be laid on the turning away from any sin as compared with turning towards God.

In the New Testament, the meaning of *metanoia* is further differentiated. It involves a final and unconditional decision on the part of an individual human being, a change from within. *Metanoia* refers to a radical conversion which occurs, if at all, once and for all. It is thus a definitive turning away from evil, an unconditional turning from all that is against God, including that which, in a given case, makes total turning to God impossible.[31] In Catholic theology, *metanoia* includes sorrow for sin, confession of sin, amendment and satisfaction for sin. The principle and result of this conversion is faith, by which one comes into contact with the kingdom of God and Jesus.[32] Conversion is not only a negative rejection of past sins but leads to faith – *pistis* – to a positive attitude based on openness towards the divine will.[33] For Paul, the totality of the act is so fundamental that it is impossible to undergo *metanoia* a second time.[34] The uniqueness of the act was important in order to distinguish it from ritual penitence and the usual casuistry towards the Law. Facing divine will rather than static Laws, sophistry was out of place. Divine judgement would wait for those who do not convert.[35]

Certainly, Platonism and Christianity differ significantly in the way in which they envision the divine-human encounter. Plato emphasised the implications of the vision of the *agathon* for the human being, but did not elaborate extensively on the responsiveness of the divine to the human quest for truth.[36] Similarly, the Aristotelian *philia politike*, political friendship, was considered possible only between equals, hence impossible between humans and gods. In contrast, the Christian symbolism is based on the experience of *mutuality* in the divine-human encounter. This is reflected in the symbolisation of the relationship between the creator and his creation as a relationship of 'wills'. The creator is a 'he' and hence a will. The divine-human encounter is presented as a relationship of 'likeness' in which the human being responds to God and vice versa.

As a 'he' the divine is not a thing, a situation, or an order that humanity could eventually 'know' and thus remains unattainable. The individual's relationship to the divine cannot be taken for granted but requires permanent attention. Christianity, in fact, radicalises this experience. The mutuality and likeness between humans and God is not a daring and pretentious gesture but, on the contrary, reinforces the insight that the divine cannot be conquered. If divine truth comes in the form of a will, then no mere logical methods of arguing and reasoning can make the human mind understand this will. God must reveal himself, he must speak to humanity, he must make known his commandments.

These symbols, of course, were taken over from Judaism. The Beyond of the Old Testament is not a transcendent world that could invite human intentions, but the Beyond is a will who speaks to humans. For both Judaism and Christianity, the source of salvation is a 'who', not a 'what'. The personality of God is neither a 'something' nor the culmination of 'something' but its own incommensurable 'I'. The 'I' of God cannot be reached via an inverse gradual emanation; it cannot become the *telos* of a morphogenetic process nor is it a suitable object of speculation. Christian faith excludes any direct, self-evoked intention towards a state that is divine in itself. What is open to humans is the design of their relationships to God.

Although strikingly different from Platonic symbolism, the Christian symbols reveal a famliar concern: the separateness of the mundane and the transcendent. The separation of wills is the Judeo-Christian version of the *chorismos*. While the concern is the same, the tension expressed in the symbols has increased as separateness is now combined with mutuality and 'likeness'. To the extent that 'likeness' suggests closeness, the gap between the mundane and the transcendent appears to have narrowed – but this only brings the unbridgeable nature of the gap into sharper focus. This, tragic, version of the *chorismos* requires a more complex mediation between the temporal and the transcendent. Not only must the human being ascend to the light, but the light is a will and hence must want to descend towards humanity in order to reveal, again, its presence. Accordingly, the divine-human encounter must become a concurrence of 'acts'. *Metanoia* is the human act of penitence *and* the divine act of salvation; it is both a human task and a divine gift.

Once the experience of transcendence in reality became a 'problem', the answer could only be 'salvation', an act of God by which human awareness of *two* distinct and yet related orders is restored. The Judeo-Christian religion is *gospel*, good news, because it announces how God saved mankind out of love and mercy. As the Old Testament reports, humans were created in a state of right order towards God and his fellow creatures. Elevated to the divine order by grace, he was destined, after a trial on earth, to the eternal enjoyment of union with God in heaven. Through Adam's disobedience, this state was lost. God promised to restore mankind to the state from which it had fallen by the sin of Adam. He prepared humans for their Saviour by choosing the Hebrews as the people of God. By rescuing his people from Egypt under Moses, God gave them the conviction that he alone saves by raising up a human leader. This leader would be a king of David's line, who would save a faithful remnant of the people through suffering, yet be a mysterious Son of Man come from heaven with miraculous power.[37]

Jesus established a strong link to the Mosaic tradition precisely because he saw his work as the fulfilment of the prophecies and of the whole hope of salvation. He placed himself at the end of the salvation history of the Old Testament.[38] 'Do not imagine that I have come to abolish the Law or the Prophets. I have not come to abolish but to complete them.'[39] The Gospels portray Jesus as a man who was conscious of his mission, of goals from which he refused to be turned aside. He was cautious when others applied the title 'messiah' to him because it had been a popular conception that the messiah was to establish the political domination of Israel over the whole world. Jesus knew that this was not his mission; Jesus was not talking about 'politics' in this sense. He modified the messianic role by stressing the need for his suffering.[40]

The title that Jesus uses most often to describe his own role is 'Son of Man'; it is used approximately eighty times in the Gospel, and mostly by himself. In the Old Testament the Aramaic expression *bar nasa* for son of man, or its Hebrew equivalent, is used to mean 'human being' with special emphasis on human weakness and proneness to suffering, in contrast to the strength of God. However, in Daniel 7:13 the term is applied to a transcendent figure descending on the clouds of heaven surrounded by the exalted symbols of divine majesty. This figure was to represent the messianic kingdom of God. Jesus preferred this term not only because it did not arouse mistaken political hopes but also because it captured the paradox of his relationship to divinity. The early Christians professed their faith in the divinity of Jesus by the confession, 'Jesus is the son of God'. And according to Matthew, Luke and John, Jesus depicted his unique relationship to God by the way he referred to him as 'my father'.

In Christian symbolism, Jesus represents a mode of existence which is determined by a transcendent will and is worldly-temporal as 'human'. The paradox of incarnation, of the living presence of the divine word in Jesus, was the answer to two problems. First, salvation could only be granted by God's will. Second, for the honour of mankind as much as for his own glory, God willed that one of the human race should offer condign satisfaction for sin, for his disobeyence of divine order. Jesus's suffering and his death as a 'human', was 'necessary' for humanity's redemption. Jesus could do what only a human being can do: to suffer and die and take up the penalty of sin – *and thereby* he did what only divine grace could do: to restore humanity in essentials to its original state. From spiritual death and disinheritance human beings were reborn as children of God and heirs of heaven.[41] By dying,

Jesus killed death. He rose from the dead and so shall those he died for.

In that Jesus did not draw on divine modes of existence which could have transcended his temporal-worldly existence, he showed how the relationship to the Father had to be *lived* in a 'how' of being and not anticipated as a divine status.[42] Just like Jesus, the Christian had to live his temporal existence in his world in the modes of *pistis*, hope and love. Paradoxically, only life and death in this world led to the overcoming of death. Socrates' refusal to escape from prison exemplified a related if not similar message. The human being can share in immortality not by escaping death but through the practice of *athanatizein* – the activity of 'immortalising' by attuning his soul to the divine *logos* while alive.[43] Because an escape would have run counter to everything he had taught during his life, Socrates knew that, as a *parrhesiast*, he could not escape without destroying the authority of his voice. He died and therefore became immortal.

In fact, the crucial elements in Plato's 'Allegory of the Cave' – divine vision and *parrhesia* – are also present in Jesus's human experience. When Jesus applied to himself the saying, 'A prophet is despised only in his own country, among his own relations and in his own house' he showed that he knew of the difficult situation of the one who talks about light in a corrupt society which sees only shadows.[44] The human knowledge of Jesus includes the beatific, or intuitive, vision of God. 'Not that anybody has seen the Father, except him who has his being from God; he has seen the Father.'[45] The paradox of incarnation has made it difficult for the Church to clarify precisely what this vision consisted of. It is generally agreed, though, that Jesus's beatific vision had distinct limitations. As his human intellect is a created thing and therefore finite, he could not comprehend God to the extent that God comprehends himself. As a human, Jesus could not grasp God totally and at once in a single act. Moreover, his knowledge of God was non-conceptual. As much as the philosopher could not give an account of contents of the form of the Good, Jesus's vision could not be expressed in terms of concepts.

In the *Septuagint*, it is stated that God gives the people *parrhesia* and that divine *sophia* has *parrhesia*. At Job, 22:23–7, *parrhesia* refers to a form of 'freedom', a 'free and joyful standing before God', including open access to him with no more let or hindrance. In the New Testament, especially in the Johannine writings, *parrhesia* is distinctly linked with the work of Jesus. Indeed, at John 16:25, Jesus implies that he will use *parrhesia* after resurrection. In the Pauline writings, the emphasis is on apostolic *parrhesia*. It occurs in connection with preaching the Gospel and presupposes openness towards God. The one who lives in Christ has again found freedom towards God and can approach God with confidence. He can stand before the Ruler and Judge free and erect, not lowering his head, able to bear his presence.[46]

The Gospels present the act of salvation as a moment in time, a historical fact. The Christians of the first decade after Jesus continued to live as good Jews, but Jews who were convinced that the day of the Lord had arrived and that the spirit of God had been poured out on the world.[47] Jewish contemporaries found their God and their identity in God's great acts of the past and in the hope for future restoration of their life and character. The present was a time of preservation of what God had done, and of waiting for the fulfilment of the promises. The past and the future were loaded with meaning, but not the present. Jesus's proclamation restored the significance of the present because 'the time is fulfilled, and the kingdom of God is close at hand'.[48] Because God and his will were inescapable present realities in the person, teaching and activity of Jesus, the present again deserved full attention. The preservation of this attentive state became the concern of a new community – the Christian *ekklesia*.

If, as Eric Voegelin points out, Jesus had been the messiah according to the older Israelite tradition, his death would have been the proof of his failure and the community of his disciples would have dissolved soon afterwards.[49] The vision of the resurrection turns therefore into a touchstone for a new community of believers. What distinguishes the members of the community is that they believe in the reality of an event which to those outside transcends visible reality. The importance of the issue is confirmed in Jesus's encounter with Thomas at John 20:29. Thomas had been unable to be with the other disciples when Jesus appeared to them. When he heard of Jesus's resurrection from their reports he said he could not believe unless he saw Jesus himself. Eight days later, Jesus again called upon his disciples, and this time Thomas was among them. He turned to Thomas and delimited the measure for the coherence of the Christian community by saying: 'Because you have seen me, you have believed; blessed are those who have not seen and yet have believed.'

The actual constitution of the new community occurred with the Descent of the Spirit on Pentecost day. Acts 2:1–36 clearly depicts the event as a liminal experience for those involved. The Apostles gathered in a house which was suddenly filled by 'a sound like the blowing of a violent wind' which came from heaven. 'All of them were filled with the Holy Spirit and began to speak in other tongues as the Spirit enabled them.' As the *communitas* of the group of Apostles radiated into society, social divisions and language boundaries were momentarily dissolved. Acts emphasises that there lived in Jerusalem 'God-fearing Jews from every nation under heaven'. As the people approached the scene, they were amazed that each of them could understand what was being said in his own native language. 'Parthians, Medes and Elamites; residents of Mesopotamia, Judea and Cappadocia, Pontus and Asia, Phrygia and Pamphylia, Egypt and the parts of Libya near Cyrene; visitors from Rome (both Jews and converts to Judaism); Cretans and Arabs – we hear them declaring the wonders of God in our own tongues!' Peter then stood up to address the crowd, explaining that the men were not drunk from wine but filled with the Spirit as prophesied by Joel (2:28–32). He proclaimed the truth of Jesus's resurrection as a fulfilment of what God had announced to David: 'God has raised this Jesus to life, and we are all witnesses of the fact. Exalted to the right hand of God, he has received from the Father the promised Holy Spirit and has poured out what you now see and hear.' Under the guidance of the Spirit of the Resurrected, the community continued to exist as it did when Jesus was present in the flesh. The Acts report that more than three thousand people were baptised on that day.

NOTES

1. Plato, *Republic*, 517a.
2. Plato, *Phaedo*, 100b.
3. This reading of Plato was influenced by Eric Voegelin, *Plato and Aristotle* (Volume 3 of *Order and History*), (Baton Rouge: Louisiana State University Press, 1957), and Hans-Georg Gadamer, *The Idea of the Good in Platonic-Aristotelian Philosophy*, (trans. by P. Christopher Smith), (New Haven: Yale University Press, 1986).
4. Gadamer, *The Idea of the Good*, p. 88.
5. For example, Plato, *Philebus*, 26d.
6. *Republic*, 507b–509d.
7. On the Greek conception of the cosmos see Hans Jonas's discussion in *Gnosis und Spätantiker Geist – Erster Teil: Die mythologische Gnosis* (Göttingen: Vandenhoeck & Ruprecht, third edn, 1964), pp. 146–8.
8. *Republic*, 517c, 518d.
9. See also Eric Voegelin, *In Search of Order* (Volume 5 of *Order and History*), (Baton Rouge: Louisiana State University Press, 1987), p. 97.
10. This is how Eric Voegelin defines the 'life of reason'. See Voegelin, 'Industrial Society in Search of Reason', in Raymond Aron (ed.), *World Technology and Human Destiny* (Ann Arbor: University of Michigan Press, 1963), pp. 31–46 (34).
11. Plato, *Apology*, 29d. The significance of the 'care of the soul' is elaborated in the work of Michel Foucault. See Foucault, 'Technologies of the Self', in Luther H. Martin, Huck Gutman and Patrick H. Hutton (eds), *Technologies of the Self: A Seminar with Michel Foucault* (London: Tavistock, 1988), pp. 16–49; Foucault, 'Hermeneutik des Subjekts', in Helmut Becker and Lothar Wolfstetter (eds), *Freiheit und Selbstsorge* (Frankfurt a.M.: Materialis, 1985), pp. 32–60; Foucault, *The Care of the Self* (New York: Pantheon, 1986); Foucault, 'The Ethics of Care for the Self as a Practice of Freedom', in James Bernauer and David Rasmussen (eds), *The Final Foucault* (Cambridge, MA: MIT Press, 1988), pp. 1–20.
12. *Republic*, 500d, my emphasis.
13. *Republic*, 517b.
14. Plato, *Seventh Letter*, 341–2. On the debate on the letter's authenticity see, for example, J. E. Raven, *Plato's Thought in the Making* (Cambridge: Cambridge University Press, 1965), pp. 19–26.
15. See also Plato, *Phaedrus*, 277–9.

16. *Seventh Letter*, end of line 341.
17. *Republic*, 519a.
18. *Republic*, 531d–534e.
19. *Republic*, 538d–539d.
20. *Republic*, 415d–421d, 457b–461e.
21. *Republic*, 414c–d.
22. *Philebus*, 61a–d; see also P. Christopher Smith in his Introduction to Gadamer, *The Idea of the Good*, p. xx.
23. *Republic*, 534c.
24. *Republic*, 379c, 380c, 381b, 382e; *Laws*, §21.
25. Solon, 'Elegiac Poems', no. 16, in J. M. Edmonds (trans. and ed.), *Elegy and Iambus with the Anacreontea. Part I: Elegiac Poets from Callinus to Critias* (London: Heinemann (Loeb Classical Library), 1931), pp. 114–44 (133).
26. *Timaeus*, Introductory Conversation (b).
27. *Republic*, 372c.
28. *Laws*, 738.
29. Luke 5:32.
30. For this discussion see the entry by J. Behm and E. Würthwein on '*metanoia*' in Gerhard Kittel (ed.), *Theological Dictionary of the New Testament*, Volume 4 (Grand Rapids: Eerdmans, 1967), pp. 975–1008.
31. Matthew 10:32–9, Luke 14:33.
32. G. F. Kirwin, 'Metanoia', in *The New Catholic Encyclopedia*, Volume 9 (New York: McGraw-Hill, 1967), p. 724.
33. Mark 1:15.
34. Hebrews 6:4–6.
35. Matthew 18:3.
36. He did point out though that the gods are concerned about the world and the human race. See *Laws*, 900.
37. Isaiah 10:20–2, 52:12–15, 53.
38. Matthew 11:4–5, 13:16–17, 23:37–8.
39. Matthew 5:17.
40. Mark 8:27–33.
41. Romans 8:17.
42. Hans Jonas, *Gnosis und Spätantiker Geist – Zweiter Teil: Von der Mythologie zur mystischen Philosophie* (Göttingen: Vandenhoeck & Ruprecht, second edn, 1966), pp. 48–9.
43. See Eric Voegelin, *Autobiographical Reflections* (Baton Rouge: Louisiana State University Press, 1989), p. 120.
44. Mark 6:4.
45. John 6:46.
46. Heinrich Schlier on 'parrhesia', in Gerhard Kittel (ed.), *The Theological Dictionary of the New Testament*, Volume 5 (Grand Rapids, Michigan: Eerdmans, 1967), pp. 875–6, 879, 881–3.
47. Acts 2:1–11.
48. Mark 1:15.
49. Eric Voegelin, *History of Political Ideas Volume I: Hellenism, Rome, and Early Christianity* (The Collected Works of Eric Voegelin, vol. 9), (ed. Athanasios Moulakis), (Columbia: University of Missouri Press, 1997), pp. 163–6.

3

Issues in 'Gnostic Studies'

Perhaps the most controversial issue in the study of Gnosticism is the definition of the subject matter itself. There is no generally accepted definition of 'Gnosticism'. The 1966 Messina Conference on the Origins of Gnosticism drew a distinction between 'gnosis' and 'Gnosticism'. 'Gnosis', from Greek 'knowledge', was defined as 'knowledge of the divine mysteries, reserved for an elite'. By implication, all kinds of esoteric doctrines and mystic experiences involve 'gnosis'. The term 'Gnosticism' was reserved for the 'Gnostic' systems of the second and third centuries AD, particularly for the systems of Basilides, Valentinus and Mani.[1] Yet this convention, which characterises 'Gnosticism' in strictly historical terms, has not stood the test of time. The crucial question is whether the systems of late antiquity which are often taken as the paradigmatic manifestations of 'Gnosticism' are sufficiently uniform to place them in one single category.

While Greek words like *Christianos*, *Christianikos*, *Christianismos* began to appear in ancient texts a few generations after Jesus, no such words existed for 'Gnosticism' or a 'Gnostic religion'. However, Christian heresiologists do report that the members of at least some groups which later came to be called 'Gnostic' referred to themselves as *gnostikos*. As the heresiologists then began to compile catalogues of heresies, the temptation was to generalise such sporadic self-designations into one single category. There are instances in Irenaeus's writings in which the term 'Gnostics' is already used as a generalising label for all heretics.[2] In fact, for a long time the main sources available on 'Gnostic' sects and movements were the writings of Christian heresiologists writing explicitly against the heretics: Dionysius at Corinth, Irenaeus at Lyons, Theophilus at Antioch, Philip of Gortyna in Crete, Tertullian at Carthage, and Hippolytus and Rhodon in Rome. When it was coined in eighteenth-century France, the term 'Gnosticism' still had a pejorative connotation.

In spite of the more scholarly tone of twentieth-century writings on 'Gnosticism', and in spite of the concept's increasing popularity in a number of disciplines, the confusion surrounding its definition remained unresolved. According to an early reviewer, the most important treatment of 'Gnosticism' by a philosopher, Hans Jonas's classic

Gnosis und Spätantiker Geist (1934, first edition), left its readers 'in a terminological fog'.[3] And the sensational discovery in 1947 of a 'Gnostic' library at Nag Hammadi further blurred the borderline between 'Gnostic' and 'non-Gnostic' treatises. The inflationary and often still polemic use of the term makes even late twentieth-century students of early Christianity and religions of the Greco-Roman world complain how they learned 'from very authoritative interpreters of Gnosis' that 'science is Gnostic and superstition is Gnostic; power, counter-power, and lack of power are Gnostic; left is Gnostic and right is Gnostic; Hegel is Gnostic and Marx is Gnostic; Freud is Gnostic and Jung is Gnostic; all things and their opposites are equally Gnostic'.[4]

These problems of definition, of grasping the common 'essence' of phenomena which often appear to be associated, seem to be the consequence of asking the wrong question. 'Gnosticism' cannot be defined as a category which exists outside history. Attempts to delineate its margins through lists of characteristic features and symbols against which concrete historical manifestations are 'checked' have been shown to encompass either too much or too little. Yet, while these may be good reasons for dismantling the 'dubious category' (Williams, 1996), they do not absolve students from the task of identifying those experiences to which the various systems once nominated as 'Gnostic' responded. Real affinities among mythological or philosophical systems are often concealed by an apparent incompatibility of symbols. For example, both sexual excess and asceticism may come from the same desire to overcome the constraints of the cosmic and social orders by rebelling against what appears to be one of their cornerstones: the institution of the family.

The question of how mythologies or philosophies relate to each other cannot be decided at the level of symbols alone. The underlying experiences, however, can only be investigated historically. Thus, the debate about the 'proper' definition of 'Gnosticism' leads me back to my earlier remarks about method, remarks which are confirmed rather than undermined by Williams's criticism. The historical analysis of lines of meaning does not begin with definitions; and if it deals with 'categories', these categories will have to emerge from the historical material itself.

It is also important, however, to acknowledge that studies in 'Gnosticism', even if they ultimately fail to resolve issues of definition, have not been fruitless. Jonas's work in particular offers much more than a mere exercise in categorisation. Because the uniformity of the phenomena he studied can be doubted to some extent, one must be careful not to generalise his results beyond the actual mythological systems they were derived from, but Jonas strove to go beneath the symbols to the analysis of the experiences which evoked them. As part of this process, he delineated a number of problems, questions or concerns to which the systems he studied responded. While none of these responses can be taken as a *generic* 'Gnostic' response, the problems themselves define the dimensions of a semantic space within which all these systems 'moved'. In other words, Jonas defines a list of issues in such a way that each of the systems under investigation *activates* some, or indeed all, elements of this list in a more or less coherent manner. As long as it is understood that it cannot be used for purposes of definition, Jonas's list is relevant to my study because some of his systems form starting points for my historical inquiries in later parts of this work. The following summary of his understanding of 'Gnosticism' will therefore introduce some of the key issues which are explicated and refined in lines of meaning which, as I will argue in subsequent chapters, extend from at least some of the religious movements studied by Jonas right up to the present.

ASPECTS OF HANS JONAS'S ANALYSIS OF 'GNOSTICISM'

It is common to relate 'Gnosticism' to a negative view of the visible world and its creator and the assumption of a 'divine spark' at the centre of the human being, which had become enclosed within the material body because of a tragic accident in the pre-cosmic world. But the individual was able to reverse this tragic turn of cosmic history and to release the divine substance within him by means of a saving knowledge, *gnosis*. According to Roelof van den Broek, this outlook is fundamental for the 'greater part' of the Nag Hammadi Library and the systems described by the Christian heresiologists Irenaeus, Hippolytus and Epiphanius.[5] Jonas recognises the same scheme in his systems and then proceeds to analyse in greater detail the various aspects of which it is composed.

Cosmology: Anticosmic dualism

As Jonas's 'Gnostics' reject the cosmos, they place themselves in opposition to, and therefore out of, it. They do not belong to the cosmos; their home is elsewhere. This 'elsewhere' is the Beyond, a divine world which is radically opposed to the cosmos, to 'this' world. The cosmos is devalued relative to this Beyond and a *second* principle is necessary to account for its existence. For example, many Gnostics considered the God of Israel, who reigns as king and lord over creation, makes the law and judges those who violate it, as a lesser deity, a demiurge. Those who had knowledge, *gnosis*, had learned to reject the false claims to power made by this jealous deity and to reserve their worship for a purely spiritual principle that transcends the material creation. The demiurge of these mythologies is, if not directly evil, at the least indifferent and ignorant.

In other versions of anticosmic dualism, the second principle does not coexist with the first, but is produced by it in an unwanted accident, a fall, a catastrophe. In some variants, the demiurge of the world is ejected by a deity in doubt, the other-worldly 'mother', in an episode of unwilling maternity.[6] More common variants are scenarios in which Satan is a fallen angel or a son of God who out of pride, envy or concupiscence rebels against his Father. The creation of the material visible world is a consequence of this fall or rebellion. Everything unfolding from this unfortunate event needs to be reversed so that the original state is restored. Versions of dualism which assume two opposed, coeternal, independent principles are called 'absolute' or 'radical'; whereas versions which derive the second principle from the first and thereby preserve the superiority of the latter are labelled 'monistic' or 'moderate'. In practice the two views would hardly disagree on the depravity of the evil creator or the malignancy of the world he created. However, radical dualists tend to be more deterministic in their cosmologies while for moderates the idea of a 'fall' involves an element of volition. Because the purpose of history is a return to some 'original' state, the different starting points of the two forms of dualism may also imply different eschatological visions.

Before the cosmos, there was a divine sphere of uniformity and light, called the *pleroma*, the 'fullness' of God. The divine world is understood as an extension and actualisation of the nature of God. Its powers are called *aeons* and represent the various levels of being in the divine world. *Aeonic* speculation is a hallmark of 'Gnostic' systems. Although there is some variation with regard to the number, gender, names and ranks of the *aeons*, it is usually the female *sophia*, Wisdom, who is the last and least of them. She is often the one who disturbs the calmness of the *pleroma* and becomes the cause of the cosmic tragedy.

The creation of the cosmos is the result of an accident rather than of a meaningful, deliberate divine act. The relationship between the first and second principle, or between the true world and the cosmos, is almost by necessity a dialectical one. Jonas gives the example of Simon Magus, who thought of the original schism as a movement by which the divine spirit leads itself out of itself by objectifying its own 'thought'. This 'thought' recognises the spirit as its 'father'. The two principles oppose each other as much as they form a problematic pair. The space between them is the space in which the superfluous drama of creation is staged.[7]

Humanity's place in the cosmic drama and the problem of evil

Human beings are created as part of the cosmos; they are created by the same demiurge who created the world. However, as part of a divine scheme to restore the original pre-cosmic state of perfection, they were given a divine spark, a flash of the divine light or substance, the *pneuma*, which renders them superior to their creator. Although their temporary 'home' is the cosmos, they belong to the divine world, the *pleroma*. The *pleroma* is mostly envisioned as a space, an 'it' rather than a 'he', open to be conquered and hence a suitable object of human intentions.

The details of this story of human divinisation are complex and vary from system to system. In the 'Script without Title' of the Nag Hammadi codices, the demiurge is initially ignorant of the divine world of light which ejected him. He creates powers below him, the *archons*, and boasts 'I am God. There is no God above me.' But the world of light interferes. For a brief moment, the 'Adam of Light' appears at the horizon of the lower world in order to make it aware of the existence of the *pleroma*. The demiurge and the *archons*, however, conspire against the upper world and decide to create a human being as the defender of *their* creation, the cosmos. The plan is to create the human being as the image of the Adam of Light so that the divine Adam, should he return, will fall in love with the human and become a servant of the lower world.

The powers of light, however, succeed in using this plan for their own purposes. The *archons* create *their* own Adam, but leave him unattended for forty days, during which period the upper world sends its *pneuma* to him. Because of the divine inspiration, Adam is now able to move, but he cannot stand up and walk. When the *archons* return, they are so pleased with their creation that they place Adam in paradise. In a second step, Adam becomes aware of his links to the world of light. The *pleroma* uses its powers to send the divine Eve in order to awake Adam. When she calls him, 'Adam! Live! Rise from the earth', Adam gets up and recognises her as the mother of life. Horrified by Eve's intervention, the *archons* send seven angels to prevent her from fulfilling her mission. She, in turn, leaves a worldly copy of herself with Adam and turns into a tree. The *archons* return to paradise and warn Adam and the worldly Eve not to eat from this 'Tree of Knowledge', the tree of *gnosis*.

However, the world of light interferes again by sending the snake to convince first Eve and then Adam that they would become like the gods and learn to know how to distinguish between good and evil if they eat from the 'forbidden fruit'. The snake is here a representative of the divine sphere, who reveals to the humans the evil purposes of their creators. They want to keep Adam from eating the forbidden fruit only in order to preserve his state of ignorance. Adam, of course, eats from the forbidden fruit and thereby obtains knowledge, *gnosis*, of his divinity. Full of envy and anger, the *archons* expel Adam and Eve from paradise and send them to earth. Witnessing the spark of light glowing in Adam, they become fully aware of his superiority and decide to make him forever a prisoner of matter. They curse Adam and Eve and everything that exists in the cosmos. The demiurge and the *archons* remain masters of the matter, *hyle*, and the cosmos, but the divine plan to overcome creation and hence to deprive them of their power now has powerful assistants in the men and women of knowledge.

The episode which places humanity above its creator is essentially an inversion of the Christian reading of Genesis.[8] Adam actually obtains knowledge by eating the forbidden fruit. This act is an act of liberation, of awareness, of awaking from the sleep of ignorance.[9] Eating the fruit was humanity's first revolution against its oppressive creators, the beginning of its emancipation. Through knowledge, humans realise that they have to turn away from their creators.[10] In this outlook, the Christian exegesis appears as the continuation of the *archonic* attempt to keep humans in a state of ignorance about their real powers.

The dualism described by Jonas entails an answer to the problem of theodicy, the problem of reconciling the assumption of a good, omnipotent creator with the existence of evil and the imperfections of human existence. As the divine is absolved from any deliberate involvement with the creation, and as humans are firmly associated with the divine, a second principle must be called upon in order to locate the responsibility of evil somewhere.

'This' world

Jonas's 'Gnostics' tend to consider the relationship between cosmos and God as a radical opposition of a world of darkness and a world of light. The divine light does not illuminate human existence in the cosmos but rather annuls the darkness which *is* the cosmos. This approach differs dramatically from Plato's distinction of two layers of reality – the noetic realm of forms and the visible reality. Certainly for Plato, the body represented a lower form of 'being-in-the-world' than the soul, but the soul does not provide an alternative 'being-in-the-world'. As a sensorium towards the *agathon*, the soul only allows a clearer, purer, more appropriate existence in the cosmos. More so than the body, it ensures the individual's attunement to the order of being, to the cosmic order. Similarly, the relationship between matter and forms is complementary. Matter is the possibility of the concretisation of form. Where Jonas's dualists see the workings of the powers of darkness, the Platonist begins his search for the *eidos*. The Platonic forms are more substantial than their concretisations in the visible world but this difference in substance does not deprive the cosmos of meaning. On the contrary, this slope of substance turns reality into a movement towards the Good.

For some of the systems studied by Jonas, in contrast, the cosmos is the world of death. However, the world is not simply a negation of life, it is actively evil, a positive force, an enemy of divinity; but if humans are more powerful than the creator of the cosmos, then their acceptance of the terms and conditions of cosmic existence requires their ignorance. The world itself is a force of darkness which is actively trying to prevent humans from obtaining knowledge of their divine nature. Ignorance, *agnoia*, is the *causa prima* for the continued existence of a lower world. Especially with their main weapon of love, *eros*, the cosmic powers know how to lead humans into their earthly involvement, which is possible only because of their numbness, ignorance, unawareness, sleep and drunkenness. Jonas observes how, in this kind of mythology, human existence has adopted all those characteristics which were once ascribed to the existence of the souls of the dead in the *hades*.[11]

Humanity's position in this world is characterised as a state of alienation. The human being exists here, in this world, but because of the divine spark he carries within him, he should be elsewhere. The true life, the spirit, ended up in this world in a process of 'falling' and of 'being thrown' into the body. All symbols used in this context share elements of passivity, of an involuntary fate. They all refer to an event of the past, to something that happened to 'life' as an object. Since then, the cosmos has made life forget its roots.

The cosmic forces to which humans are exposed in his pitiful existence on earth are the *heimarmene*, the law-like fate. In late antiquity, the *heimarmene* were mostly understood in astrological terms, but whereas for the Greeks the regularity of the movements of celestial bodies confirmed the non-arbitrariness of the cosmic processes and hence the governance of the *logos*, the 'Gnostic' systems accepted the symbolism but reversed its meaning. The non-arbitrariness turns into a symbol for the cosmic constraints. The sphere of the fixed stars is the wall that demarcated the cosmos as a prison, and the seven planets represent the seven *archons* who, employed by the demiurge, reign over the cosmos. The constellations of heaven appear here as the merciless and cruel administrators of the inescapable prison of the world. The sphere of the stars embodies the extreme opposite of everything that is divine.[12]

The Beyond of Jonas's 'Gnostics' – the 'new and unknown God' – was the perpetual opposite to everything that was familiar. Not only was the cosmos thereby deprived of its supreme divinity, of its uniqueness as the totality of being, it also became a confined space, beyond which there was another world. The cosmos was bracketed by the mere existence of the 'other' world. Moreover, to propose a world without constraints beyond the cosmos required an enormous expansion of the realm of necessity until it filled the entire cosmos. In contrast to the necessities determined by the *heimarmene*, the world of light was the world of freedom.

In comparison, for the Greeks there was only one cosmos. There was not 'this' world as opposed to 'another' world. There was 'cosmos' and no further specification, numerical or pronominal, was required. In the symbolisms examined by Jonas, 'world' became 'this world', and the world external to 'this' world was the place where the true life resided. The pronominal specification is more than a minor change. If there is a plurality of worlds, 'being-in-this-world' becomes 'lodging', the world becomes a 'house' or 'apartment', which is replaceable especially if it is a dark and decrepit home. At the same time, it is only through the plurality of worlds that there is a possibility of escape from 'this' world.[13]

The soul

Jonas's 'Gnosticism' adopts the Greek symbol of the soul, *psyche*, as the sensorium for attuning human existence to the cosmic order. But as the cosmic order has now been placed on the negative side of the dualism, the soul turns into a symbol for human interwovenness with this world. The soul is the principle organ through which the cosmic powers confine humans to their earthly existence. Through the soul they reach into the interior of an individual in order to chain him to the world. The soul provides them with a battlefield on which they fight out their rivalries and struggles at the expense of the fools who believe they must follow their souls. Just like the body, the soul forms another layer which veils the divine spark at the centre of human beings. The *pneuma* is chained to the world by both soul and body. Thus, the soul too must be left behind when the divine humans return to their origin.[14]

It is not the soul which links human beings to divinity; instead, it is the *pneuma* within them that *makes* them divine. The human being's spiritual centre and the transcendent divine space are consubstantial. In 'Gnostic' mythology the *pneuma* is the non-material matter that filled the *pleroma*, the divine sphere. Hence, *pneuma* is the divine substance, the divine light, the pure spirit. It is supernatural and transpsychic. Until the tragic moment that led to the creation of the cosmos, the *pleroma* was the totality of *pneuma*. But the unity of the *pleroma* had to be given up by disseminating *pneumatic* sparks over mankind in order to counter the plans of the cosmic powers.

Humanity's return to the divine world is therefore a restoration of unity, sameness and fullness.

The negation of the soul is a departure and separation rather than a transformation. Although the groups studied by Jonas might use the words *metanoia* and *epistrophe* in this context, their members are leaving rather than accepting the world as they 'turn around'. Leaving the soul behind means in practice to reject everything that individuates a human being. Overcoming the cosmos means precisely to repudiate even the very last residual of an 'I', of the unity of the soul. This repudiation is the second of a 'double negation'. Out of ignorance, the demiurge created the cosmos as a negation of the divine *pleroma*. And out of knowledge, humans negate the previous negation.

While still in the cosmos, the sense of equality which identifies all human beings as carriers of the same *pneuma* is the basis for a *common* experience of alienation, for a collective loneliness in the cosmos. Still, the 'Gnostic' community does not play an instrumental role comparable to the *polis* or the *ekklesia*. For the philosophers, the *polis* was a means for the soul's attunement to the order of being. Its educational function stemmed from the incompleteness of human existence, its 'lack' of divinity. In contrast, Jonas's 'Gnostics' possess the divine substance. They *are* divine and hence not in need of community as an ordered form of being-in-the-world. For the *pneumatic* individual, there is nothing external to himself that would be worthwhile relating to. On the contrary, to the extent that he does maintain a relationship to what is external to him, to the cosmos, he remains a prisoner of the cosmic powers. It is not surprising, therefore, that many 'Gnostic' sects shared a general antipathy towards philosophy.[15]

The self-objectification of being and the literary form of the 'system'

One of the most important characteristics of the 'Gnostic' mythology as investigated by Jonas is the peculiar way in which the obtainment of knowledge and the contents of knowledge are linked. The contents of the myth explain how humans became entrapped in this world, how they were thrown into their psychic and material prisons, and how they differ from their surroundings. At the same time, the knowledge of humanity's route into alienation is the precondition for the reversal of the very same process. 'Salvation' corresponds to a 'return' on the same route which brought human beings to their current position. Hence, within the history of humanity, the very knowing of that history plays a crucial part in shaping humankind's history. The obtainment of knowledge of humanity's true history – of 'who we were and what we have become, where we were and into what we have been thrown, whither we hasten and from what we are redeemed, what is birth and rebirth'[16] – is at the same time the decisive moment, the turning point, in the very same history. 'Gnostic' myth belongs to its own contents. The narration refers back to itself, re-enters itself. Narration of the myth opens a new phase in the myth. In this sense, the *gnosis* of Jonas's 'Gnosticism' is more than just 'knowledge'. The myth does not simply denote but actually implements a turning point. *Gnosis* is both recital and effectuation of salvation.[17]

According to Jonas, *gnosis* is not a mere passive devotion to mythical themes. By knowing humanity's history, the knowing person is directly and prominently involved in the drama that is the history of humankind. The theoretical appropriation of the myth is already the practical suspension of its contents. Each act of individual enlightenment forms an immediate contribution to the restoration of the divine fullness. Therefore, the myth incorporates the knower's presence, his knowing, into the myth. The narration of the myth ends with an individual becoming aware of his divine origin. Hence, it ends with the myth becoming known and then continues as the history of the knower, who is on his route towards certain salvation. This certainty is definite precisely because it no longer depends on cosmic reality; it cannot be questioned from within the cosmos.

The 'Gnostic' mythology studied by Jonas explained, retrospectively, the history of the cosmos, and thereby showed its readers and listeners the way they needed to go in order to return to their place of origin. A history of the past was implicitly an anticipation of their future. The more comprehensively the first task was solved, the more evident were goal and route, necessity and feasibility of the knowing person's return to the *pleroma*. The more detailed, elaborate, meticulous and encompassing the myth became, the more obvious and immediate was the path to be taken. 'Gnostic' mythology thus amounted to the attempt to comprehend the whole of being as a context, to deduct creation and human existence from one particular event: the loss of unity and uniformity in the *pleroma*. Accordingly, the myth comes in the literary form of the 'system', an all-encompassing totality, a 'fullness' in itself that memorises the loss of *pneumatic* fullness and thereby contributes to its restoration.

The 'system' is more than just a stylistic form. The 'systems' of Jonas's 'Gnostics' are descriptive, logical or 'ordering' systems. They were not used as analytical devices to simplify what is otherwise a chaotic reality. Instead, reality *is* systematic. Reality as presented in the myth has a direction which leads from a problematic beginning to the end which annuls the beginning. Moreover, because the myth cannot 'accept' the existence of the cosmos, it cannot 'accept' cosmic structures as given, as structures *sui generis*. The myth as 'system' must provide its own account of the things in this world. It thereby formulates a 'second reality' which is the ultimate answer to all questions for everyone. Hans Jonas described the second century AD as a 'hothouse' for universal 'systems' of this kind.[18]

Antinomian tendencies

It is often argued, and not only by Jonas, that 'Gnostic' groups were counter-cultural, counter-traditional movements, protesting against society. As an accidental deviation from the unity of the divine world of light, the cosmos is a conglomerate of divisions, separations and individuations. Divisions based on property, however, were the primary target of such movements because pride of one's cosmic possessions seemed the most vulgar and unashamed expression of cosmic involvement. Similarly, social divisions between the rich and the poor, between freedom and slavery, between the rulers and the ruled could be considered arbitrary. At the same time, however, cosmic existence was beyond redemption. There was little point, therefore, in taking these divisions as starting points for social reforms. 'Gnostic' groups could disregard social conventions not because they were 'unjust' but because they were pointless. Belonging to the world of light, members of such groups stand outside of any commitment, obligation or institutional bonds based on criteria of this world. In extreme cases, *pneumatic* beings are not liable to the law; they are representatives of a species above which there is no authority.[19]

The ultimate root of such antinomian tendencies is the absence of moral imperatives, of indications of how the divine-human relation is to be designed as a form of conduct in this life.[20] There are, in other words, no *aretai* or virtues which determine the appropriate way of 'being-in-this-world'. The reasons for this absence have already been mentioned. First, because of the radical depravation of the cosmos, the route towards the divine could never lead through the cosmos. Hence, little attention had to be paid to the question of how cosmic existence is to be designed. Second, humans themselves are consubstantial with the divine. It is not through *praxis* that *pneumatic* beings achieve salvation, rather it is through their very *pneumatic* nature.[21] According to Irenaeus, the 'Gnostics' believed their *pneumatic* nature remained undamaged regardless of the actions they were involved in – just like gold that does not lose its beauty when it falls into the mud.[22]

Because the escape from the cosmos still takes place within it, many groups designed imperatives which would guide humans away from the world while they were still living a worldly life. Some of these imperatives could also aim at an anticipation of an exit from reality which would occur, however, only with or after death. For the groups commonly called 'Gnostic' such guidelines varied greatly. The cosmic bonds can be disregarded in many different ways ranging from libertinism to asceticism. Some groups, including the Manichaeans, had internal structures which distinguished between élite and ordinary members with different standards applying to them. The *pneumatic* élite may either reserve the right to libertinism to themselves or may become the model of ascetic perfection.

Many 'Gnostics' called themselves 'Christians'. Their Christologies would typically deny that Jesus was a human being. The anticosmic dualism made it impossible to conceive of the paradox of incarnation. Incarnation was impossible because light cannot use darkness as a camouflage; instead, light destroys darkness. Jesus was pure spirit who represented himself to human perception in the illusory form of a human being. Accordingly, he was never affected by what was done to him as a human. Such views are commonly referred to as 'Docetism', from the Greek *dokein*, to seem.[23] Christ's appearance as human was an illusion, as is human existence in general. In fact, Christ came to crucify this world. He was the 'stranger' from the world of light who came to this world in order to call back what was a part of him before it was left behind in the cosmos: the *pneuma*. To the extent that his mission is successful, he restores the unity of the *pleroma* rather than the dignity of humanity. As he therefore restores his own unity, he becomes the 'saved saviour'.[24]

Other self-descriptions of 'Gnostic' groups are 'the selected', 'children of light', 'spirits', 'possessors of spirit', the 'wakeful', 'the perfected', 'the truthful', 'the saints', 'the strangers', 'the free'. They tended to understand themselves as the true, non-wavering, perfect species.[25] They were mostly conscious of a break which they performed with the traditions of society. Scorn and hatred for the 'old world' and its wisdom prevail in the respective mythologies. In 'Gnostic' myth, the validity of this old world is already overcome, its perspectives on being replaced by a different perspective, and its monopoly broken from within a new interior.

At the same time, however, Jonas's 'Gnostics' are permanently in danger of being seduced by the cosmic powers and of losing themselves again in ignorance and sleep. There are treatises among the Nag Hammadi texts which compare the situation of those who know with the life of fish which are hunted by a fisherman, explicitly referred to as the 'opponent', who uses a net as well as a fishing-hook to catch them.[26] It was best, therefore, to keep secret the saving knowledge. Irenaeus describes how the 'Gnostics' would tell their dying comrades secret verses which they were asked to recite before the cosmic powers in order to bypass them on their return to the *pleroma*.[27] Secrecy becomes the key to the superiority of these 'Gnostics' over the *archons* as well as over the ignorant part of mankind – for only they possessed the secret knowledge necessary in order to not miss salvation.

THE DEBATE ABOUT ORIGINS

Once it became a matter of routine to assume that 'Gnosticism' formed a relatively coherent historical force, it seemed obvious enough to inquire into its beginnings and ancestry.[28] Not surprisingly, perhaps, the debate about its origins reflects the confusion that went into the initial definition of 'Gnosticism'. A popular theory asserts that 'Gnosticism' was a 'parasitic' movement that emerged together with Christianity. Other viewpoints consider 'Gnosticism' older than Christianity but confirm its 'parasitic' nature; they do not treat it as a separate religion but rather as a phenomenon which typically develops at the fringes of other religious movements.[29] Christianity is considered to be particularly vulnerable to the kind of 'parasitic' growth which 'Gnosticism' is thought to express. The tension and uncertainty of faith which Christians were supposed to endure rather than to resolve seemed to invite speculation on what it might take to move beyond 'faith'. Why, in fact, should one be content with faith?

From the point of view of the Christian heresiologists, the notion that there existed a secret knowledge which, once possessed, would guarantee salvation entailed a number of obvious dangers. Most importantly, it seemed to suggest that the tension of faith could eventually be supplanted by the certainty of knowledge. The complex mythological systems which promised such knowledge appealed especially to wealthy, well-educated Christian gentiles. However, the challenge posed by these 'Gnostic' movements was not numerical: Couliano assumes that 'Gnostics' in Rome should not be imagined in excess of a few hundred.[30] Edward Gibbon reports that during the second century AD approximately fifty such 'Gnostic' groups were known.[31] The real challenge represented by these groups was intellectual. In a delicate process of self-organisation, the young Christian Church had to differentiate its own symbols and practices in a complex interaction with a great number of other religious movements. For the sensitive person in late Antiquity, it might have been far from trivial to distinguish one from the other, especially since many of the competing groups called themselves 'Christians'.

In a classic work, Walter Bauer suggested that, in earliest Christianity, orthodoxy and heresy did not always stand in relation to one another as primary and secondary. In some quarters, 'heresy' might well have been understood as the original manifestation of the new 'Christian' religion. According to Bauer, in Edessa Christianity was more recent that Marcionism, and in Egypt he found its first certain traces in the person of Basilides during the reign of Hadrian.[32] Bauer's thesis has been much debated and contested; but it does highlight the historical complexity behind the distinction between orthodoxy and heresy. Celsus, a second-century pagan critic, considered sectarian diversity the great weakness of Christianity.[33]

There are many other, equally contested theories of the origins of 'Gnosticism'. Adolf von Harnack characterised the 'Gnostics' as the result of a 'Hellenisation of Christianity', and Wilhelm Bousset explained their success as a composite of Persian dualism and the spirit of late Greek antiquity. Hans Jonas suggested that 'Gnosticism' emerged and spread roughly from the times of the wars of the *diadochai* after Alexander's death up to the times of Manichaeism; hence, it developed from *c.* 330 BC to AD 350. Its breakthrough occurred around the times of Jesus. According to Jonas, Egypt was the western boundary of the regions where 'Gnosticism' emerged, and then the 'Gnostic' outlook spread from the East to the West. All the major preachers of 'Gnosticism' came from the East even if they taught in the West. At the beginning, 'Gnosticism' was a distinct non-Christian phenomenon.[34] Eric Voegelin also links the rise of 'Gnosticism' with the disorder caused by imperial expansion, but cannot find a convincing proof for the oriental (Iranian or Babylonian) origin of the movements.[35] Ioan Couliano, in contrast, considers a birthdate after AD 70 to be more probable and relates the beginnings of 'Gnosticism' to the fall of the Jerusalem temple.[36] Both Zoroastrian and Zurvanite dualism were unlikely to have provided an inspirational basis for 'Gnostic' thought because the former was essentially procosmic and the latter arose much too late. And since 'Gnostic' thought arose mostly in the form of full-blown comprehensive 'systems', Couliano concludes that its emergence must have been a revolution rather than the outcome of a gradual evolution.[37] In Kurt Rudolph's account, the 'Gnostic' sects grew out of a non-Christian movement which gradually incorporated elements of Christian symbolism and thereby mutated from a distinct religion in late antiquity to a 'Christian heresy'.[38]

MARCION, VALENTINUS, MANI

Among the teachers commonly mentioned as representatives of 'Gnosticism' are Marcion, Valentinus and Mani. Marcion's case is particularly controversial because his anthropology differs crucially from what the Messina Conference would consider as being typically 'Gnostic'. Marcion was born at the end of the first century into a Christian family in Sinope at the Black Sea. When he moved to Rome in AD 139 or 140, he became an active member of the Christian community there. Influenced by the Syrian preacher Cerdo, Marcion tried to use a synod in Rome in order to introduce a dualistic opposition between the Creator God of the Old Testament and the Christian God into a Christian canon. He maintained that the Church had been mistaken in retaining the Old Testament by regarding Jesus as the 'messiah' foretold by the prophets. The date of his rejection and excommunication, July AD 144, became the date of the foundation of his own sect, which developed into an extensive religious network.

There are no surviving texts from Marcion directly and so his teachings have to be reconstructed from the criticisms of his enemies, especially the five-volume attack on his teaching by Tertullian of Carthage. Central to Marcion's view is the distinction between the divine Father announced by Christ and the God of the Old Testament who created the cosmos. According to Marcion, the God of the Jewish Scriptures is constantly swearing or threatening, he is often angry and jealous and shows humanlike emotions. Creation itself evinced the imperfection of its maker in abundance. This demiurge was unaware that another God existed above himself, and proclaimed that he alone existed. But the transcendent, forgiving and loving God announced by Jesus and Paul was clearly another and superior deity. The true Father, the hidden, remote God, had nothing to do with the creation of the cosmos.

Marcion insisted that Jesus had been sent by the true God. In fact, the appearance of Jesus was the *only* evidence of the existence of an unknown God, the Kind Stranger. Jesus was not, therefore, a messiah who came to fulfil the Old Testament prophecies. Jewish Scripture referred only to a messiah whom the demiurge planned to send. As the true God's messenger, Christ appeared on earth in the 'likeness of humans' so that he could be seen by those he addressed. But his body was not really of flesh. He came to reveal to humankind how their souls could escape death in the created world. Faith in the 'cross of Christ' was the key to salvation. According to Tertullian, Marcion promised those who accepted the gospel of grace that their souls would be carried to the 'heavenly bossom and harbor' of the unknown God. Sexuality and procreation were rejected as instruments serving the intentions of the Creator God.

While these beliefs may qualify as 'anticosmic dualism', Marcion did not uphold the idea that the human being was divine. On the contrary, humans were entirely created by the God of the Old Testament; they had no privileged relationship to the nameless God who sends Christ to earth. For salvation, therefore, the human being depends entirely on God's grace. Moreover, Marcion was fixated on the Scriptures; hence, his teaching lacks the *aeonic* speculation which characterises Jonas's 'Gnosticism'.

Tertullian considered Marcionism as the greatest threat to the Christian Church in the second century AD. Its branches can be traced not only in Italy and Egypt but also in Mesopotamia and particularly in Armenia. However, most of the Marcionite communities seem to have dissolved in the fourth century. Some of them might have returned to Christianity, while others were absorbed by Manichaeism. In this way, sections of Marcion's religious organisation provided prefabricated modules for the Manichaean network. Of Marcion's disciples, Apelles is considered to be the most important. He brought Marcionism closer to modern stereotypes of 'Gnosticism' by ascribing to the souls a precosmic existence during which they were joined with the true God. The demiurge emerged as a fallen angel. Apelles eventually had to leave the Marcionite Church and founded in Rome his own movement, which spread in parallel with Marcionism to the East but disappeared somewhat earlier in the third century.[39]

Valentinus was born in Egypt. He converted to Christianity in Alexandria, and then moved to Rome around AD 140 where he had great success as a teacher. Tertullian reports that Valentinus was briefly considered a candidate for bishop in Rome, but, at a time when his own school had already been established, Valentinus broke with the Roman Church (or vice versa). He continued teaching in the city until about AD 160 when he either moved eastwards or died in Rome. As with Marcion, the sources for Valentinus's teaching are difficult and contradictory, rendering it a matter of dispute. About a handful of quotations of his writings have survived; the heresiologists Irenaeus, Hippolytus, Origen, Clement of Alexandria and Epiphanius provide more than five different accounts of the Valentinian system. Moreover, Irenaeus's account seems to be based on the system of Ptolemy, one of Valentinus's more famous students. Yet, it is this latter account which is typically considered as an exemplar of 'Gnosticism'.

Ptolemy's system portrays two primordial principles, a male and a female principle called Pre-Father (*bythos*) and Silence or Thought (*sige*, *ennoia*). Union between male and female creates Mind and Truth, and further pairings generate a total of thirty *aeons* which constitute the *pleroma*. The last of the *aeons*, Wisdom (*sophia*), 'rushes forward' in her longing after the Pre-Father. Although she is restrained by a divine power called Limit (*horos*), her passionate speculation gives birth to a spiritual essence. This essence was, however, imperfect because *sophia* was unable to understand the Pre-Father. While she eventually resumed her place in the *pleroma*, the imperfect essence was excluded from perfection by Limit. It formed *achamoth*, a lower level of wisdom.

Mind then creates Christ and Holy Spirit. The former teaches the *aeons* that the Pre-father is incomprehensible and brings them to order. The latter erases all distinctions among them. The *aeons* are now so harmonious that they co-ordinate all their qualities and create one single perfect being, Jesus, who reaches out from the *pleroma* and gives *achamoth* a certain formation. Helped by a second Saviour sent by Christ, *achamoth*'s passions are gathered and turned into the foundation of the material element in creation. In addition, two further 'elements' are created in this process. *Achamoth* cannot pass by Limit and must 'turn back' (*epistrophe*). It is from this 'turning back' and remorse that the *psychic* element is introduced. Finally, the purification caused by the second Saviour is the origin of the *pneumatic* element.

Achamoth then proceeds to create a *demiurge* from the *psychic* element. This *demiurge* is the creator of all things outside the *pleroma*. He is ignorant and pretentious, proclaiming that there is no god above him. With the cosmos created, the *demiurge* fashions human beings from fluid matter into which he breathes the *psychic* element. But when the *demiurge* himself was created *achamoth* secretly injected the *pneuma* into him so that he would breathe it into the humans. Thus, humans have the *pneuma* from *achamoth*, their souls from the *demiurge* and their flesh from matter. One of the purposes of the cosmos is to convey the knowledge that the *pneumatic* element is in the world, chained to the soul. The drama will end when the *pneuma* in the cosmos has been recognised and properly cultivated. At this point, *achamoth* and *pneumatic* beings, the perfect Christians, will rejoin the *pleroma*. The Valentinians understood themselves as such *pneumatic* beings.

Valentinus's school is considered the largest and most influential representative of 'Gnosticism' prior to Manichaeism. After Valentinus's death, the school split into two branches. Hippolytus mentions an 'Italian school' which was active in Italy and in Gaul, the most famous members of which were Ptolemy and Heracleon. The other 'oriental school' had its centres in Egypt, Syria and Asia Minor with Marcus and Theodotus as major representatives. The history of Valentinian schools extends into the fifth century AD. Origen travelled to Athens in AD 229 for a discussion with a Valentinian named Candidus. In Edessa, the fourth century AD still witnessed debates between Arians and Valentinians.[40]

It is no exaggeration to consider Manichaeism as one of the four world religions next to Buddhism, Christianity and Islam. For a long time, scholars believed that Manichaeism originated in the ancient Zoroastrian tradition of Persia on the grounds that both had dualist tendencies. This view has been replaced, however, by one which emphasises influences by Marcion and Bardaisan, a Syrian eclectic whose school had some influence, especially in the Edessa of the late second and early third centuries AD. Bardaisan is sometimes introduced as a representative of a 'Christian-hellenistic' *gnosis* and is said to have provided the basis of Mani's cosmogony;[41] while Marcion was the source not only of the principles of the Manichean Church organisation but also of Mani's opposition between the Old and the New Testament. One of Mani's greatest disciples, Addas (Adda, Adimantus), compiled a treatise against the Old Testament based on Marcion's teaching.

Mani was born on 14 April AD 216, near the southern Mesopotamian town of Seleucia-Ctesiphon. According to the account of Mohammed Ibn al-Nadim, a Muslim writer of the late tenth century, he was the son of Futtuq – in other accounts his name is Patik or Patticius – and his wife Mays, or Marmaryam. One day, Futtuq heard a loud voice urging him not to eat meat, drink wine or have sexual intercourse. Futtuq eventually gave in to the voice and joined an ascetic Judaic-Christian sect, the Mughtasilah. By that time his wife was already pregnant with Mani, who was raised among the members of his father's sect.[42]

Mani had his first vision at the age of twelve, and a second at the age of twenty-four. The second vision especially he interpreted as his calling to be the 'Apostle of the Light'. As a result, he distanced himself from society and fell out with the leaders of the Mughtasilah. He soon attracted a large number of followers as he began his own missionary project. In AD 241 Mani travelled to India and managed to persuade the King of his convictions. In Persia, after the death of King Ardashir I, he won the favours of the successor, Shapur I, who might have considered Manichaeism a suitable ideology for the Persian Empire precisely because it allowed him to exclude the powerful cast of the Zoroastrian priests. For three decades Mani was free to teach his gospel, which subsequently spread to Syria, Egypt and eastern Iran. By the times of Bahram I, however, the balance of influence at the court shifted against Mani; he was imprisoned and died in chains in AD 276. His disciples saw him as a martyr.

From then on the Manichaean Church went through a difficult period marked by persecution and factionalism. However, enforced emigration also led to its spreading further. At the end of the fourth century, Manichaeism reached northern Africa, where Augustine became one of its auditors. From Syria, it spread to Palestine, Asia Minor and Armenia. From the early fourth century onwards, Rome too sheltered Manichaeans. In AD 372 their presence in the Holy City was attested by a decree of the Emperor Valentinian. Mani's Church lost influence in the West during the sixth century, but aspects of the Manichaean system would later resurface in the symbolisms of the medieval heretics – the Paulicians, the Bogomils and the Cathars. With the beginning of the Arabian conquests, Manichaeism regained its foothold in Persia, but its centre was to become central Asia. In 762, it became the official religion of the Uighur empire, and remained influential in the area even after the collapse of the empire in 840.

Manichaeism came to an end in the region only with the Mongol conquests of the thirteenth century.

Mani's disciples reached China in the late seventh century via the Silk Road. Manichaeism was heavily combated by the Confucian literati. We know of a violent persecution in 843/4, but the emperors of the Ming dynasty in the fourteenth century were still fighting the Manichaeans. According to Portuguese reports, Manichaean tradition persisted in southern China up to the seventeenth century. Its influence in Tibet has also been acknowledged. The history of Manichaean *gnosis* thus extends over more than one thousand years and covers an area reaching from Spain to China.

Mani's teaching begins with the dualism of the realms of Light and Darkness, which are the two primary elements or principles. The word 'God' is reserved for the world of Light; its fullness, the entire world of Light, forms the highest Godhead, the Father of Greatness. The realm of Light is unlimited and infinite to the North, West and East, but to the South it has a boundary with the realm of Darkness. In their own internal struggles, the powers of Darkness sometimes approach the boundary and, on one occasion, catch sight of the Light. Amazed by what they have seen, they begin to attack the Light, to break into it from below, in order to share in its beauty. As a result, a conflict ensues and Light and Darkness begin to mix. The purpose of the subsequent drama which includes the history of the cosmos and of humanity is the restoration of the original separation between the two realms.

In defence of his realm, the Father of Greatness 'creates' or, as Mani preferred to say, 'calls' into being three 'powers', 'entities' or 'evocations'. First, he 'calls' the Mother of Life who gives birth to Primal Man. The latter descends to the world of Darkness in order to do battle against its cohorts but is defeated. His defeat causes the second evocation. The Father of Greatness 'calls' forth the Friend of Light or, in his other names, the Great Builder or Living Spirit. The Living Spirit sends a call of salvation to the perishing Primal Man, who responds with a resounding hail. Living Spirit then extends his right hand into the Darkness and succeeds in rescuing Primal Man. However, in the struggle, Primal Man has to leave behind his soul. The particles of Light, of which his soul consisted, are devoured by the powers of Darkness. What looks like another defeat is in fact just an ingenious element in Light's overall strategy. As Darkness devours the particles of Light from Primal Man's soul, it introduces into itself a substance of essential difference which it cannot support.

The third evocation is the Third Messenger, who proceeds to 'seduce' the *archons*, the powers of Darkness. As he shows himself to them in his feminity (to the male *archons*) and his masculinity (to the female *archons*), he provokes violent sexual excitement among them. The male *archons* discharge particles of Light as sperms on to the earth, which had been created in foresight by the Great Builder. From these particles the world of plants and vegetation emerges. The female demons, already pregnant, lose their offspring prematurely at the sight of the Messenger's beauty. The abortions fall to earth, where they begin to eat from the plants, assimilate the Light particles contained in them, and turn into animals and demons.

In order to retain that portion of Light which still remained to it, the world of Darkness creates living containers of Light – human beings. The *archons* concentrate the remaining Light into two demons who, through intercourse, create Adam and Eve as a counterweight to the heavenly creation. In Darkness's interest, Adam was created deaf, blind and totally unaware of the Light he was carrying. However, the world of Light interferes and sends a manifestation of the Third Messenger, Jesus the Luminous, in order to rise Adam from his sleep, shake him, open his eyes, and show him the soul of Light imprisoned and suffering in his body and in all of matter. Jesus the Luminous instructs Adam in redemptive knowledge, which explains what was, what is, and what will be. Adam learns of his twofold origin, how his body was derived from the powers of Darkness and how his spirit or soul originated in the world of Light. From then on, the human being becomes an ally in the struggle for the restoration of the fullness of Light.

In order to return the particles of Light from Darkness to Light, the Third Messenger 'calls forth' an ingenious device, a cosmic wheel which, like a waterwheel, draws up the particles to the moon and from there to the sun where he lives. During the first half of the month, the Light particles rise through a pillar of Light, called the Column of Glory, towards the moon, which becomes full by the middle of the month (full moon); it is then emptied during the second half as the particles travel on to the sun and then to the world of Light whence they came from. The process is assisted by the Apostles of Light, called forth by Jesus the Luminous, who include Buddha, Zoroaster, Jesus, Paulus and, finally, Mani himself. Mani is the promised Paraclete, the fulfilment of all religions.

The drama ends shortly before all particles of Light have been separated from the world of Darkness. At this stage the end of the world will come. The event will be heralded by a series of catastrophes similar to those announced in the apocalyptic speculations which were popular in Iran and the Middle East, and in late Judaism and Christianity. During the end, Jesus the King will reign on earth for a short time before he and the elect leave the world and return to the realm of Light. A last purification will follow; those particles still possible to rescue will be collected. Afterwards, the terrestrial globe will be annihilated. Light and Darkness are separated again; but this time, they will be prevented from mixing.

The mission and purpose of Mani's Church was to look after the remaining Light in the cosmos. By ensuring that Light particles were not immersed into matter even further and by dissipating Mani's teaching as redemptive knowledge, the Manichaeans were actively accelerating cosmic history towards its inevitable end. The doctrine that Light must not be maltreated was translated into an extreme asceticism aimed at minimalising involvement with cosmic existence. Practically, this kind of life was sustainable only for few members of the community. Accordingly, the Church was divided into two parts. The *electi*, who were also called 'the perfect', 'the just', or 'the true', formed the kernel of the group. They lived the ascetic life *for* the other Church members, the 'hearers' or 'auditors' (*auditores*). Although their ethical guidelines were far less austere, the auditors participated in the 'true life' of the *electi* by providing for the subsistance which even their minimal life required.

In the larger cities, the Manichaean *electi* brought with them an air of mystery which proved irresistible especially to students and intellectuals. Complicated secret prayers, the writings of Mani himself contained in masterfully crafted parchment volumes, and the hint of some deeper and secret knowledge veiled beneath sophisticated cosmologies gave the Manichaeans the aura of a secret society in possession of a powerful truth about the fate of humankind. The Manichaeans appealed to younger educated men and women because they were trendy, cliquish, different, dashing and illegal. Peter Brown compared the Manichaeans in fourth century Carthage with the Bolsheviks of the twentieth century: 'a fifth column of foreign origin bent on infiltrating the Christian Church, the bearers of a uniquely radical solution to the religious problem of their age.' And 'like Communism in England in the 1930s', the exotic and highly doctrinaire core of Mani's system did not keep its secrets from spreading rapidly. Church leaders, like Faustus of Milevis, travelled along the Manichaean network of 'cells' as 'top party members'.[43] Fluent in the details of Mani's systems, they were looked at as the scientists who could answer all questions. In fact, Mani's system was meant to be 'scientifically' convincing; it entailed an 'objective' description of the physical universe. The waxing and waning of the moon, for example, was caused by the influx of released particles of Light flowing upwards from the world; and the Milky Way was visible proof that the Column of Glory was already in operation.

According to Steven Runciman, 'Gnostic dualism reached its height of eminence' with Manichaeism. Mani's religion 'absorbed the bulk of the Gnostically-minded public'.[44] Similarly, Robert Haardt argued that

Mani's system represented the 'conclusive and logical systematisation of the *gnosis* of late antiquity in the form of a universal, revealed religion with missionary purpose'.[45] Although Manichaeism does not easily fit into the modern stereotypes of 'Gnosticism' – Mani's cosmos has a 'positive' purpose and both the Living Spirit and the Third Messenger are involved in the creation of the world – such comments still capture an important aspect of the attraction of Mani's system: its totality and comprehensiveness. If there were unanswered questions, the system was flexible enough to allow for *ad hoc* modifications or additions of details which would close apparent gaps. The Manichaeans were also famous for their ability to adapt Mani's teaching to the existing beliefs and religious symbols of the peoples they wished to convert. There exists an account by the Patriarch Photius of a Manichaean treatise by a writer named Agapius. It is believed that Agapius lived in the fifth century in either western Asia Minor or Egypt. In the twenty-three chapters of his work, Agapius combined his Manichaean creed with the Christian symbols of the Trinity, the incarnation, the baptism, and the crucifixion and resurrection of Christ. According to Photius, he was able to do this by 'altering and translating almost all the terms of piety and of the Christian religion into other meanings, either strange and abominable, or monstrous and foolish' and by teaching 'perversely behind the names of our dogmas quite different things'.[46] Manichaeism seemed superior because, instead of having to reject competing symbolisms in debates about doctrine, it was able to reinterpret them from within its own system.

'GNOSTICISM' AND CLASSICAL CULTURE

Regardless of whether they can be meaningfully placed in one category labelled 'Gnostic', both Mani's and Valentinus's teaching represent clear departures from key features of classic philosophy and Christianity. As I have explained in the previous chapter, both Platonic philosophy and Christianity celebrate humanity's participation in the order of being, the cosmic order. The cosmos is the place for humans to dwell and to advance towards a measure that, ultimately, remains transcendent, 'unseen'. The Christian exegesis of Genesis 1 largely adheres to this comprehension of human life by making humanity's history a continuation of, and element in, the creational process of order in reality.

Certainly, the soul's rebellion against the order of the cosmos, hatred of the gods and the revolt of the Titans are popular in Hellenic myth as well. But in the end, as Eric Voegelin points out, Prometheus is fettered. The revolutionary reversal of the symbols – the dethronement of the gods, the victory of Prometheus – lies beyond classical culture.[47] In both Valentinus's and Mani's account of creation, humans are 'emancipated' from their immediate creators through knowledge.

The same cannot be said about Marcion, but he too sees human participation in the created cosmos as problematic because Jesus's 'Father' and the Creator God are not the same. Jesus is the *only* emissary and revealer of the Redeemer God who, with his infinite and incomprehensible compassion, is prepared to liberate mankind from this world of sorrow and imperfection, and from the stern but not always impartial rule of the Creator God. For Marcion, faith meant trusting the mercy of the Kind Stranger, who had given no evidence of his existence or love except in the appearance and work of Christ. While for Mani Jesus was just one of a series of Apostles of Light, Marcion dramatises the newness and incomparableness of the revelation given by Christ. But the result is, similarly, that the revelation makes humans turn away from the cosmos. The sudden and entirely unexpected interventions by the hitherto unknown God who is beyond everything does not lead to an ordering of the human soul, or to a more 'appropriate' and refined being-in-this-world, but dramatically exhausts the meaningfulness of cosmic existence; it manifests a 'transvaluation of all values', a new dispensation in complete contrast with the old dispensation of the Creator.[48]

As I pointed out in the previous chapter, Plato's political philosophy emphasises the need to balance community and *communitas* in human efforts to attune the order of individual souls and the order of the *polis* to the form of the Good. His own efforts were directed towards a restoration of this balance. By comparing important elements of Platonic and Christian symbolism I argued furthermore that the balance between community and *communitas* was equally important for Jesus and the early Christians. In both cases, attempts at the restoration of this balance required an act of faith in the 'unseen measure' of the Divine.

In Manichaeism and Marcionism I have presented two examples of symbolisms where the loss and absence of balance has been declared a 'normality' or even an 'objective'. Manichaeism in particular develops the quest for *communitas* and permanent liminality in all three dimensions: it is a universal (space) and final (time) revealed religion in which the true essence of humanity consists of particles of Light which, although imprisoned in the souls of individual human beings, are entirely devoid of any aspect of individuation (abstraction). Marcionism, too, opposes community and *communitas* but says very little on how humans could move from one to the other. In fact, humans do not seem to have any means of experiencing *communitas*. The singularity of Christ's revelation gives humans an awareness of another layer of reality which is, however, too remote to have any positive bearing on their lives in the cosmos. On the contrary, knowing of the Kind Stranger without being able to experience his presence in the world makes worldly existence all the more miserable.

Perhaps it was this insight into the existence of religious symbolisms which present the relationship between community and liminality in other than symbiotic terms which led scholars of religious movements in late Antiquity to define – unsuccessfully – the category 'Gnosticism'. I do not mean, however, to revive debates about definitions. The purpose of this chapter was merely to introduce some of the key issues around which the debates about 'Gnosticism' revolve. Moreover, as I will argue in subsequent chapters, many of these issues are explored and explicated in the lines of meaning which unfold from the religions of Marcion and Mani.

NOTES

1. Roelof van den Broek, 'Gnosticism and Hermetism in Antiquity: Two Roads to Salvation', in Roelof van den Broek and Wouter J. Hanegraaff (eds), *Gnosis and Hermeticism: From Antiquity to Modern Times* (New York: SUNY Press, 1998), pp. 1–20 (4).
2. Michael Allen Williams, *Rethinking 'Gnosticism': An Argument for Dismantling a Dubious Category* (Princeton: Princeton University Press, 1996), pp. 33–43.
3. A. D. Nock in his review of the first volume, quoted in van den Broeck and Hanegraaff, *Gnosis and Hermeticism*, p. 4.
4. Ioan P. Couliano quoted in Williams, *Rethinking 'Gnosticism'*, p. 4.
5. Van den Broek, 'Gnosticism and Hermetism in Antiquity', p. 4.
6. Cf. Ioan P. Couliano, *The Tree of Gnosis: Gnostic Mythology from Early Christianity to Modern Nihilism* (San Francisco: Harper, 1990), p. 93.
7. Hans Jonas, *Gnosis und Spätantiker Geist – Erster Teil: Die mythologische Gnosis* (Göttingen: Vandenhoeck & Ruprecht, third edn, 1964), p. 354.
8. Couliano, *The Tree of Gnosis*, p. 121.
9. Jonas, *Die mythologische Gnosis*, p. 285.
10. Jonas, *Die mythologische Gnosis*, p. 222.
11. Jonas, *Die mythologische Gnosis*, p. 113.
12. Jonas, *Die mythologische Gnosis*, pp. 156–61, and Kurt Rudolph, *Die Gnosis: Wesen und Geschichte einer spätantiken Religion* (Göttingen: Vandenhoeck & Ruprecht, third edn, 1994), pp. 76–81, 88–90, 196–7.
13. Jonas, *Die mythologische Gnosis*, pp. 101, 165.
14. Jonas, *Die mythologische Gnosis*, pp. 145–6, 181; Jonas, *Gnosis und Spätantiker Geist – Zweiter Teil: Von der Mythologie zur mystischen Philosophie* (Göttingen: Vandenhoeck & Ruprecht, second edn, 1966), pp. 10–11.
15. R. McLachlan Wilson, *Gnosis and the New Testament* (Oxford: Basil Blackwell, 1968), p. 133.
16. From Theodotus, a second-century follower of Valentinus, quoted in Jonas, *Die mythologische Gnosis*, p. 261, and in Jean-Pierre Mahé, 'Gnostic and Hermetic Ethics', in van den Broek and Hanegraaff (eds), *Gnosis and Hermeticism*, pp. 21–36 (30).
17. Jonas, *Die mythologische Gnosis*, pp. 258–9, 374–5, and *Von der Mythologie zur mystischen Philosophie*, pp. 14–19.
18. Jonas, *Von der Mythologie zur mystischen Philosophie*, p. 173.
19. See Christopher Lasch, 'Gnosticism, Ancient and Modern: The Religion of the Future?', in *Salmagundi*, No. 96 (Fall 1992), pp. 27–42 (39).

20. Jonas, *Von der Mythologie zur mystischen Philosophie*, p. 24.
21. Cf. Rudolph, *Die Gnosis*, p. 265.
22. Quoted in Jonas, *Die mythologische Gnosis*, p. 235.
23. It is sometimes argued that the alleged originator of Docetism, Julius Cassianus, was a follower of Valentinus. See Mahé, 'Gnostic and Hermetic Ethics', p. 32.
24. Jonas, *Die mythologische Gnosis*, p. 125.
25. Rudolph, *Die Gnosis*, pp. 222–3.
26. Rudolph, *Die Gnosis*, p. 159.
27. Rudolph, *Die Gnosis*, pp. 188–9.
28. For the debate on definitions and origins see also Robert Haardt's survey in his Introduction to his anthology *Gnosis: Character and Testimony* (trans. J. F. Hendry), (Leiden: Brill, 1971), pp. 1–28.
29. See the overview in Williams, *Rethinking 'Gnosticism'*, pp. 80–95.
30. Couliano, *The Tree of Gnosis*, p. 30.
31. Edward Gibbon, *The Decline and Fall of the Roman Empire* (London: Encyclopaedia Britannica, 1978), chapter 15, p. 184.
32. Walter Bauer, *Orthodoxy and Heresy in Earliest Christianity* (London: SCM Press, 1972 (1935)), p. 232.
33. Williams, *Rethinking Gnosticism*, p. 41.
34. Jonas, *Die mythologische Gnosis*, pp. 1, 70. See also Jules Lebreton and Jacques Zeiller, *Heresy and Orthodoxy* (trans. Ernest C. Messenger), (New York: Collier, 1962), p. 23.
35. Eric Voegelin, *The Ecumenic Age* (Volume 4 of *Order and History*), (Baton Rouge: Louisiana State University Press, 1974), pp. 22–3.
36. Couliano, *The Tree of Gnosis*, p. 29.
37. Couliano, *The Tree of Gnosis*, pp. 53, 62.
38. Rudolph, *Die Gnosis*, p. 296.
39. Rudolph, *Die Gnosis*, pp. 339–42; Williams, *Rethinking Gnosticism*, pp. 23–6. Also, E. C. Blackman, *Marcion and his Influence* (London: SPCK, 1948).
40. See Rudolph, *Die Gnosis*, pp. 342–52; Williams, *Rethinking Gnosticism*, pp. 14–18.
41. On Bardaisan see Han J. W. Drijvers, *Bardaisan of Edessa* (trans. G. E. van Baaren-Pape), (Assen: VanGorcum, 1966).
42. See Otakar Klíma, *Manis Zeit und Leben* (Prag: Tschechoslowakische Akademie der Wissenschaften, 1962); Samuel N. C. Lieu, *Manichaeism* (Tübingen: Mohr, second edn, 1992); Rudolph, *Die Gnosis*, pp. 352–79; Johannes van Oort, 'Manichaeism', in van den Broek and Hanegraaff (eds), *Gnosis and Hermeticism*, pp. 37–51; Geo Widengren, *Mani and Manichaeism* (trans. Charles Kessler), (London: Weidenfeld and Nicolson, 1965).
43. Peter Brown, *Augustine of Hippo: A Biography* (Berkeley: University of California Press, 1967), pp. 46, 55–6.
44. Steven Runciman, *The Medieval Manichee: A Study of the Christian Dualist Heresy* (Cambridge: Cambridge University Press, 1960), p. 18.
45. Quoted in Rudolph, *Die Gnosis*, p. 352. My translation.
46. Quoted in Dmitri Obolensky, *The Bogomils: A Study in Balkan Neo-Manichaeism* (Cambridge: Cambridge University Press, 1948), p. 26.
47. See Eric Voegelin, *Science, Politics and Gnosticism* (Chicago: Regnery Gateway, 1968), p. 37. However, the tragedy *Prometheus Bound*, which is attributed to Aeschylus, was probably the second part of a trilogy, and was supposed to be followed by *Prometheus Unbound*. The author might have thought of a reconciliation between Prometheus and Zeus, but it is impossible to say how he devised it. It remained to Percy Shelley to compose a 'Prometheus Unbound' in which Prometheus is released and Jupiter (Zeus) punished.
48. Blackman, *Marcion and his Influence*, p. 109.

4

Lines of meaning I: From Manichaeism to 'Neo-Manichaeism'

The Middle Ages are bracketed by a number of interrelated phenomena. First, late Antiquity and the late Middle Ages witness the diffusion of Manichaeism and 'Neo-Manichaeism' respectively. Between the third and the seventh centuries Mani's religion was able to find millions of followers over the whole of the Mediterranean world, extending from Syria, Asia Minor, Judaea to Egypt, northern Africa, Spain, southern Gaul and Italy, and penetrated into the two centres of Roman Christian civilisation, Rome and Byzantium. A few centuries later, between the dawn of the Middle Ages and the fourteenth century, a number of heretical movements sometimes subsumed under the label 'Neo-Manichaeans' swept over all of southern and part of central Europe, from the Black Sea to the Atlantic and the Rhine.

The doctrinal and historical continuity from the original Manichaeism of the fourth century to the heretical movements of the late Middle Ages and early Renaissance is the concern of a long-standing debate. Already Edward Gibbon, in chapter 54 of his *The History of the Decline and Fall of the Roman Empire*, saw a line of direct continuity beginning with the Paulicians in seventh century Syria and Armenia, to their resettlement in the Balkans, their ramification into the Bogomils, the migration of both Bogomils and Paulicians into Northern Italy, and the emergence of the Cathars in southern France in the eleventh century. From the Cathars he saw links to the Waldenses and Spiritual Franciscans and the later sectarian movements, which spread all over Europe with climaxes in the Lollard movement in England and the Hussite movement in Bohemia in the fourteenth and fifteenth centuries. By the time of the Reformation, these protest movements had grown into mass movements with manifestations in the Peasant Wars in Germany and the Anabaptist movement, which continued to diffuse into the Netherlands and Moravia. While some segments of Gibbon's genealogy have been confirmed by subsequent scholarship, the relationship between the earliest entry in his list, the Paulicians, and the Manichaeans remains somewhat controversial. The circumstances allow for some informed conjectures but incomplete evidence makes it difficult to resolve the issue conclusively.

The second phenomena which might be used to delineate the beginning and end of the Middle Ages is the rise of monasticism in late Antiquity and its revival during the high and late Middle Ages. Christian monasticism emerged in Egypt and Palestine towards the end of the third century AD and spread rapidly to the West. In the eleventh century the monastic reform movement reached its climax with the Investiture Contest, which became the forum in which Western monasticism for the first time put forward the claim to pose as the only Christian life for all adult believers and attempted to ensure the general recognition of this claim. The early thirteenth century witnessed the tremendous success of the mendicant orders, the Franciscans and the Dominicans.

Moreover, late Antiquity and early Renaissance also seem connected by the emergence of Neo-Platonism in Plotinus and his school and its revival and celebration in Marsilio Ficino's 'Academy' in fifteenth-century Florence. To Ficino, significantly, Plotinus was a more truthful interpreter of Platonism than Plato himself. Finally, both late Antiquity and the late Middle Ages were times of high eschatological excitement. The Montanist movement was just one of many groups of religious enthusiasts who acted upon the belief that the Kingdom of God was close; and the apocalyptic beliefs of the Crusaders as well as the popularity of Joachimite speculations about the imminent arrival of a 'third status' testify to the widespread diffusion of similar expectations during the later Middle Ages.

Monasticism, Neo-Platonism, and millenarianism are highly complex and diverse historical phenomena – lines of meaning in their own right which run across the whole Middle Ages. But they are drawn into, and then intertwined with, the line of meaning which extends through Mani's religion into subsequent centuries. Given the complexity of these developments, this chapter can only provide a very schematic overview of the main links and continuities as they pertain to my inquiry.

MANICHAEANS, PAULICIANS, BOGOMILS AND CATHARS

From its birthplace in Babylonia, Manichaeism spread eastwards to Persia, Turkestan, India and China and westwards to the Roman Empire. According to legendary accounts, Mani had sent his personal disciples to preach in Egypt and Syria. By the later fourth century AD, Manichaeism had firmly established itself in Syria and Asia Minor, where it became a powerful rival to the Christian Church. The Armenian historian Samuel of Ani reports the arrival in Armenia in 588 of heretics from Syria, 'men with words like honey', who brought a library of 'false books' with them which contained Mani's *Living Gospel* and two other apocryphal scriptures which are known to have been used by Manichaeans.[1] This evidence seems to confirm the presence of Manichaeans in Armenia in the late sixth century. Some fifty years later, Armenia became the geographic centre of the Paulicians.

The evidence linking the Manichaeans with the Paulicians is partly circumstancial and partly based on the report of Peter of Sicily who in 869 spent nine months in Tephrice, the capital of the by then powerful Paulician organisation. There does not seem to be any contemporary historical evidence of a direct involvement of Manichaeans in the foundation of the Paulician sect, but there are a number of reasons why such contacts are likely. First, I have already mentioned that by the fourth century AD Manichaeism had successfully penetrated into Asia Minor; a region known to be the home of numerous movements and sects which propagated an extreme form of asceticism. Although absolute in theory, the boundaries between Christian asceticism and a dualistic conception of matter were probably blurred in practice. In these circumstances, such movements could well have functioned as a medium for the preservation and transmission of Manichaean doctrines in the region right up to the formation of the Paulicians. Second, a thirteenth-century Syriac writer mentions a new influx of heretics from Persia to Armenia and Syria during the reign of Justinian II (685–95). He describes them as offshoots of the Manichaeans.[2] The Manichaeans were frequently persecuted by the Sassanian rulers in Persia and it is likely that many of them looked for refuge in the neighbouring territories of the Roman Empire. From there they could have extended their influence over Syria, Armenia and Asia Minor.

Protestant writers often tended to regard the Paulicians as ancestors – via the Cathars to whom I will turn below – of the Protestant Churches. It was therefore important to them to absolve the Paulicians from Manichaean influences. Edward Gibbon's account is a good example of such theories. He considered the Paulicians as non-Manichaean 'Gnostics'. However, there are more recent attempts at explaining the rise of the Paulicians and the development of their doctrine without references to Manichaeism. According to Nina Garsoïan, Paulicianism by the middle of the ninth century consisted of at least two traditions. Armenian Paulicianism, which she traces back to the sixth century, was essentially an outgrowth of the earlier Syriac Christianity of Armenia, which had advocated Adoptionism, the doctrine that Jesus was born as a man and later adopted as Son of God in reward for his virtue. The doctrine became heretical when the Armenian Apostolic Church shifted to the leadership of Caesarea and accepted the anti-Nestorian resolutions of the Council of Ephesus.

This tradition of Paulicianism believed in the unity of God, the humanity of Jesus and the importance of baptism; it accepted the Old Testament and adhered to a rather inflexible iconoclasm. Garsoïan also conjectures that an influence of Paul of Samosata, a contemporary of Mani, and his adoptionist heresy was probable. The second tradition developed somewhat later in the eighth and ninth centuries in Byzantium, where contact with the more radical Iconoclasts might have pushed the Paulician doctrine towards dualism and Docetism.[3]

Garsoïan acknowledges that it was likely that Machinaeans reached Armenia from Persia in an early epoch, but in the absence of any contemporary corroboration of direct contacts between Manichaeans and Paulicians, she prefers an account which does not assume that such contacts existed. The Paulicians were called 'Manichaeans' partly because it was common, for polemical purposes, to equate Manichaeism with Iconoclasm; and partly because of the dualism of the later Paulicians. Garsoïan's explanation, however, is at least equally controversial. Neither the contacts with late followers of Paul of Samosata nor with Iconoclasts are generally considered plausible. Paul never succeeded in founding a lasting school, and it is assumed that the 'Samosatean sect' was extinct by the fifth century. The alleged interaction between Paulicianism and Iconoclasm, finally, would have been hindered by the fact that the Byzantine Iconoclasts were not Adoptionists but, on the contrary, Monophysites.[4] Hence, most scholars still assume that the Paulician heresy (in its dualist version) originated in late Antiquity with direct or indirect links to Manichaeism, Marcionism and possibly other 'Gnostic' groups, and thus forms a crucial link in a continuity of 'dualist' teaching from Antiquity to the late Middle Ages.

By the late ninth century the Paulicians were a powerful religious and military force. In alliance with the Saracen Emir of Melitene they made frequent raids into the territory of the Byzantine Empire. Paulician communities were war-like and well-organised. They held fortified towns near the western borders of Armenia with their capital, Tephrice, as the most important. In 867 they captured and plundered Ephesus. When the Emperor made a peace proposal, the Paulician leaders demanded that the provinces east of the Bosporus should be given to the Paulicians. The Byzantine armies responded to such requests with the campaign of 871/2 which destroyed Tephrice and the military power of the Armenian Paulicians.

Peter of Sicily was an imperial ambassador who was sent to the Paulicians to negotiate peace and arrange an exchange of prisoners. When he learned that the Paulicians were planning to send missionaries to Bulgaria he decided to write his report not just for the authorities in Constantinople but also for the Bulgarian Church. Peter as well as all subsequent Byzantine historians and theologians considered the Paulicians direct descendants of the Manichaeans; the two groups were the same heresy. Accordingly, he entitled his work *Historia Manichaeorum*. The last twenty-two chapters are devoted to a history of the sect from 668 to 868, in which he gives an extremely vague account of the origins of the Paulician sect. Paulicianism, he explains, first appeared in Samosata, where a Manichaean woman named Callinice educated her two sons, Paul and John, in the Manichaean faith and sent them as missionaries to adjacent regions. The name of the new sect of the Paulicians was derived from the names of these two Manichaean teachers.

Peter's account does not give dates and is possibly unreliable. He becomes more concrete in his reports of the Armenian Constantine, who lived during the reign of Constans II (641–68). Constantine was originally a follower of Mani's religion but attempted to bring his religion into apparent agreement with Christianity. He is therefore considered one of the instigators of the distinction between an exoteric teaching consisting of the New Testament and St Paul in particular and between an esoteric teaching, reserved for the Paulician élite, which interpreted the Scriptures allegorically so that they would conform with the sect's dualist tradition. Constantine also seems to have initiated a veneration for St Paul which became typical of Paulicianism. He even assumed the name of Silvanus, the Saint's companion.[5] Constantine-Silvanus was arrested and stoned to death during the first general persecution of the Paulicians. The Paulicians persevered and, in the ninth century, developed into a strong religious and military organisation under the leadership of Sergius and, after his death in 835, Carbeas and Chrysochir.

Peter recounts that the Paulicians believed in two principles which were opposed as good and evil. The evil principle corresponded to the creator and ruler of the visible world; the good principle was the creator and ruler of the world to come. In accordance with their anticosmic attitude, the Paulicians were advocating Docetism. But Peter also observed during his visit that Paulicians could openly anathematise Mani and Manichaean heresiarchs. The disapproval of Mani might have been part of Constantine-Silvanus's strategy of making Paulician beliefs appear closer to Christianity; or it might have been incorporated in the sect's exoteric teaching in an attempt to avoid interference and persecution. There are even *Manichaean* writings which refer to Mani as a 'wicked man'.[6]

Constantine's reforms seem to have simplified the Manichaean doctrine. In the course of this change, the asceticism of the Manichaeans mutated into the antinomianism of the Paulicians. It is sometimes suggested that the modification Manichaeism underwent as it became

Paulicianism were due to an influence of Marcionism. This view presupposes that Marcionite groups survived in the mountains and high valleys of Armenia until at least the seventh century. There are certainly definite reports attesting their existence for as late as the fifth century. The eight Marcionite communities which Theodoret of Cyrus claimed to have converted were located precisely in the area which would later become the home of the Paulicians. Marcionite influence could also explain how the Paulicians came to embrace St Paul for it was above all Marcion who considered St Paul as the pillar of the true faith, second only to Christ.

As Peter of Sicily learned during his stay at Tephrice, the Paulicians were considering sending missionaries to Bulgaria. But at that time, probably unknown to Peter, Paulicianism had already gained a hold in the country. The beginnings of Paulicianism in Bulgaria lie in the second half of the eighth century, when the Emperor Constantine Copronymus relocated heretics from Syria and Armenia in Thrace. The purpose of these resettling programmes might have been related to the Emperor's anti-orthodox stance in the Iconoclastic Controversy. In addition, he might have hoped that war-like groups like the Paulicians could operate as buffers between Bulgaria and Byzantium, which, throughout the century, was subject to invasions from the north. In fact, the borderland between Bulgaria and the Empire was continually changing hands between the eighth and tenth centuries.

The Paulician heresy was already a powerful force in Bulgaria in the third quarter of the ninth century. Its teachers came from Armenian colonies in Thrace or directly from Asia Minor. Moreover, during the thirty years of peace between Bulgaria and Byzantium from 816 to 846, Armenian merchants profited from a lively trade between the two sides so that Paulicians may have arrived in Bulgaria on trading routes. This influx increased further when Bulgaria annexed Thracian cities like Sardica, Philippopolis, and indeed Macedonia in 864.

There are three main reasons why Bulgaria and Macedonia provided a fertile ground for the diffusion of the heresy. The first relates to the confusion caused by the variety of religious beliefs entering Bulgaria at roughly the same time. Because Christianity and Paulicianism arrived simultaneously in the country, the Paulicians may well have been the first in some areas to introduce the Gospel to pagan Bulgarians. The confusion did not end once Bulgaria became a Christian country in 864. In that year, the Emperor Michael sent a military force into Bulgaria in order to counter a Franko-Bulgarian pact which threatened to open the region to Carolingian influence. Khan Boris had to capitulate and was forced to admit Greek missionaries into the country. Representing the whole of Bulgaria, Boris himself was baptised, with Emperor Michael as his Godfather. Two years later, however, Boris requested instruction in the Christian faith from Rome in the hope of obtaining independence for his Church, which the Byzantine patriarch had been unwilling to grant. For a few years, while the Greek clergy was expelled, Latin priests and bishops taught in Bulgaria of papal primacy and the inferior position of the Eastern Church. Not much later, during the council held in Constantinople in 869/70, it was decided that Bulgaria was to return to the Byzantine Church and the situation was reversed again. The struggle between the Byzantine and Roman Churches clearly did not help the Christian cause against paganism and heresy.

The second reason for the success of the Paulicians and their offshoot, the Bogomils, in Bulgaria is that Christianisation tended to be seen as a manifestation of Byzantine imperialism. After all, Christianisation had been enforced. The desire for self-assertion found powerful expression in the early tenth century, when the Bulgarian ruler Symeon, a son of Boris, raised the archbishop of Bulgaria to the rank of patriarch and had himself crowned as Tsar of all Bulgarians. But, ironically, the newly established Bulgarian Church had as a model its Byzantine rival and thereby initiated the Byzantinisation of Bulgaria. Symeon's successor, Peter, officially entered an alliance with Byzantium by marrying the Emperor's granddaughter. The Empire, in turn, formally recognised Peter's status and the independence of Bulgaria's Church. But resistance movements against Byzantine domination erupted on several occasions, often in open or coincidental alliance with heretical groups with antinomian tendencies. When the Byzantine–Russian war of 969/72 was fought over the remains of Bulgaria, only Macedonia could escape complete Byzantine domination. For almost half a century it resisted imperial pressure until Bulgaria lost its independence completely and became a Byzantine province. Not accidentally, Macedonia was also the cradle and stronghold of the Bogomils.

Finally, the economic conditions of the ninth and tenth centuries led to extreme forms of social inequality with quasi-feudal features. Frequent wars with the Empire increased the influence of provincial lords who acted as military commanders while, at the same time, increased taxation and economic misery destroyed the small peasant holdings. Many peasants had to exchange subsistence and protection for their labour and economic dependence. Because of their antinomian tendencies, heretics like the Bogomils opposed such relationships of inequality and therefore could appear as defenders of the people against their oppressors.

The Bogomils take their name from a village priest named Bogomil who appeared in Bulgaria in the late 930s or early 940s as the first teacher of the 'new' heresy.[7] Sources from the mid-tenth century describe the new movement as an amalgamation of Manichaeism and Paulicianism. Because it is highly unlikely that 'real' Manichaeans existed at that time in the Balkans such statements are often taken to be a reference to the Massalians (or Messalians). The Massalians – from a Syriac word meaning 'those who pray' – were religious enthusiasts who believed that continual prayer could purify the soul from its demons and thereby evoke a visionary and prophetic state of impassivity in which one could enter into union with the Holy Spirit and behold God. Reaching this state required the strictest abstinence but once the union with God was complete, sin was no longer possible. As a *pneumatikos*, the initiate was now part of God and salvation was assured regardless of his behaviour. The Massalians are thought to have originated in the area around Edessa but spread rapidly to Syria and Asia Minor in the second half of the fourth century. They were numerous in Armenia between the sixth and tenth century, where they were sometimes identified with the Paulicians; but in contrast to the latter, the Massalians demanded asceticism and, accordingly, were usually found in or near Orthodox monasteries.

The Massalians were dualists. For them, Satan was the elder son of God – Christ being the younger son – who rebelled against his Father and fell. The created, material world is the result of this fall and, therefore, a wicked place. The Bogomils too adhered to an anticosmic dualism. Yet, while Paulician dualism was 'absolute', at least some Bogomil groups seem to have advocated the 'moderate' type. It is sometimes argued that Bogomil doctrine evolved from a predominantly moderate to an absolute version of dualism during the later stages of its history although again the evidence is not conclusive.[8]

The Bogomils rejected the Mosaic Law and the Old Testament. For them, too, dualism implied Docetism. Massalian influences may explain why the Bogomils, in contrast to the Paulicians, were ascetics. Their asceticism rejected lawful marriage; the reproduction of the human species was the law of the demon. They considered themselves the 'true Christians' and claimed that they alone lived 'according to the Spirit' and were 'inhabitants of heaven'. As such they refused to obey any external authority through a policy of passive resistance. As Bogomilism expanded into Byzantium in the eleventh century it came into contact with the more educated layers of society and was thereby transformed into a more coherent, mythological system. Byzantine Bogomilism was also known for a division among its adherents between a spiritual and ascetic élite and the mere auditors as it was known from the Manichaeans. The Bogomils flourished, however, mainly in Macedonia from the tenth century to the fourteenth. From there it spread westwards into Serbia, Bosnia and Herzegovina. The sect disintegrated with the Turkish conquests. There is indirect evidence that some Bogomils became Muslims, probably even prior to Turkish rule, while others may have converted to Orthodox Christianity.

The most powerful heresy in the thirteenth century, however, was Catharism. The degree of alarm and hostility the Cathar heresy provoked within the ranks of the Roman Church found its clearest expression in the practice of the Inquisition. The Cathars were different from the many other movements which strove to reform the Church of Rome at that time in that they presented themselves not as a reformed Church but as a *new* one, the Church of the Spirit. The Cathars were conscious that their religion had eastern roots. In 1143/4 Cathars exposed in Cologne claimed that they had fellow adherents in 'Greece' (Byzantium) and 'certain other lands'. In 1190 Nazarius, bishop of the Ecclesia de Concoresso, an Italian Cathar Church in Lombardy, brought from the Bogomils in Bulgaria the *Interrogatio Johannis*, or *Secret Supper*, which became one of only two non-canonical writings accepted by the Cathars. In the early thirteenth century members of Nazarius's church claimed to have learned their religious doctrines from the Slavs and the Bulgars. There was a general awareness among the Cathars and their enemies that, in the twelfth and thirteenth centuries, Bulgaria and Macedonia were the schools where dualism was learned. Morover, the Cathars honoured Eastern heresiarchs such as Nicetas, who presided over the Cathar council at Saint-Félix-de-Caraman, near Toulouse. Nicetas represented the Ordo of Drugunthia (Dugunthia, Drugutia, Drugonthia), which professed a radical dualism, and was bishop of the Bogomil Church in Constantinople. During the council he succeeded in persuading most of the Cathar Churches to adopt his own absolute dualism, an episode with important consequences to which I will return later.[9]

Bogomil missionaries came to Western Europe through Bosnia via the Danube–Rhine route to the Rhineland, from where their teaching spread – along routes taken by merchants and pilgrims – to Flanders, England and Champagne. But their strongholds became southern France and Italy. For over half a century Languedoc was dominated by the Cathars and seemed permanently lost to the Roman Church. The name 'Cathar' derives from the Greek word for 'pure' and was given by the heretics to their spiritual and ascetic élite. The Cathars, like the Manichaeans and Byzantine Bogomils, distinguished between an élite – the 'perfect', 'elect' or simply the 'pure' – and the mere 'believers' or *credentes*. In Italy they were also known as *patarenes*, a name which probably came from the *pataria*, a lay reform movement named after a quarter in Milan where the group was active in the eleventh century.

In the later twelfth century, the Cathars of the Albigeois were also called 'Albigenses'.

The *Interrogatio Johannis* presents the creation of the cosmos in the familar framework of a moderate dualism. Originally, Satan held a very high position in heaven, close to the Invisible Father, who was the lord and governor of everything, but Satan wanted to be equal to the Father and revolted, seducing many angels of the first five heavens to join him. The Father eventually expels him from the divine realm, and Satan begins to create his own realm, the visible world. By imprisoning the fallen angels in clay bodies Satan creates human beings. But at the fall, the angels that form human souls have left behind their spirits in heaven. For the Cathars, the Holy Spirit was the collective of all such individual spirits but in heaven all spirits were the same and all were one. Salvation means to reunite the soul with its spirit, whereby the soul passes out of the power of Satan.

Catharism was a sacramental religion. The crucial turning point for the believer, the union of his soul and its original spirit, was not evoked by the obtainment of knowledge but effected through the baptism of the Spirit by the imposition of hands, without the use of water. This procedure was called *consolamentum* and was adopted from the Bogomils. The *consolamentum* expressed a spiritual transformation and the renunciation of the world. Through 'having been consoled', the believer became a member of the spiritual Cathar élite. He was now expected to live a strictly ascetic life. He was not allowed to eat meat, eggs, cheese or any other products which came from coition because sexual desire was implanted into the world by Satan. In addition, the 'perfect' was not permitted to kill, lie, take an oath, or have sex. Any of these acts would amount to a mortal sin and entail the immediate revocation of the *consolamentum*. In that case, all those consoled by the sinning 'perfect' lose their status as well. One sin could instigate a chain reaction, undermining the foundation of an entire Cathar community. Therefore, the ascetic discipline of candidates was thoroughly tested during a probation period of at least one year.

The Cathar who was able to maintain his ascetic way of life after baptism was assured that, at his death, his restored soul would return to its heavenly origin. The unconsoled soul, however, would continue to wander from body to body until it arrived at a body of a 'perfect'. The souls of *credentes* would be rewarded for their affiliation with the 'perfect' by advancing one step in a ranking of possible incarnations from humble creatures to distinguished and noble human beings. An evil life, however, resulted in slipping back down the chain to a lower creature.

After a period of feudal fragmentation following the demise of the Carolingian organisation in France, and amidst a number of reform movements which appealed to monastic ideals as a means to the regeneration of a papal Church which seemed increasingly involved in secular power struggles and corruption, Western Europe provided a fertile ground for the diffusion of heretical movements. Celibacy, abstinence from meat, and extensive fasting gave the Cathars a position of respect, set apart from the surrounding tediousness and vicissitudes of everyday life. Because their élite's capacity to live a life of apostolic liminality seemed unquestionable, they could make a convincing case that they, rather than the Christian monks, were the true 'athletes of God'.

In Southern France, the local nobility tended to favour the heretics against the papacy in their struggle to maintain control over the area. As efforts failed to resolve the problem through missionaries, Pope Innocent III appealed first to the King and then to the feudatories of the North for support. The Northerners began to listen once the Pope put forward the idea of a crusade against the heretics. He offered the same indulgences to anyone who went on such a war as were given to the Crusaders going to the East. Thus was launched the Albigensian Crusade (1209–29).[10] In the course of the fighting, the religious issue soon became blurred in territorial issues; in the end, the Albigensian Wars served the suppression of heresy as much as the unification of France under Louis VIII and Louis IX. Once the struggle for control over the South was decided, it was no longer opportune for the rural nobility to lend support to the heretics; and once the Cathars were without important defenders, the Inquisition was able to work much more efficiently. The 1240s became the turning-point in Cathar history, leading to their ultimate demise in the first half of the fourteenth century.

In Italy too the Cathars profited for a long time from political circumstances, particularly from the struggles between the Popes and Frederick II. They enjoyed quasi-immunity in places where Ghibelline forces were in control. Moroever, Rome was reluctant to exert pressure on cities to accept the statutes of support for the introduction of the Inquisition for fear of losing allies. The communes were suspicious of the Inquisition as an infringement of their rights. Frederick's attitude was opportunistic. However, after his death and the decline of the imperial party in Italy, the victory of Charles of Anjou over Frederick's successors, and the success of the Guelf party in the cities, the balance shifted against the heretics. The last major trials were held in Bologna from 1291 to 1309; in Languedoc, the last Cathar was burnt in 1330.

The Albigensian Crusade and the increasing efficiency of the Inquisition were not the only reason for the ultimate extinction of Catharism in Europe. Internal fragmentation set in with Nicetas's visit to the Cathar council at Saint-Félix-de-Caraman mentioned above. The debate about the adoption of absolute dualism not only showed that the original concern with evangelical life had been replaced with problems of belief, doctrine and symbols, but also antagonised the fervent moderates. Some years after Nicetas's return to the East, another visitor arrived in Italy, Petracius of the Church of Bulgaria which, in contrast to Nicetas's Church of Drugunthia, adhered to a moderate dualism. He told the Lombard Cathars that Simon, who had administered the *consolamentum* to Nicetas, had been found guilty of moral lapses. The implication was that, as Simon lost his *consolamentum*, so would Nicetas and the entire Lombard church because they were reconsoled by Nicetas when they accepted his order. It took the Cathars some time before they agreed on a unified response to the news. Eventually they decided to send a bishop to the East in search for an undoubted *consolamentum*. Shortly before the candidate's departure, he too became suspected of having been in contact with a woman. After that, all attempts at restoring unity failed.

The most important factor, perhaps, in the disintegration and disappearance of Catharism was the fact that the mendicant orders succeeded in providing effective alternatives to the Cathar way of life. When Francis came to Pope Innocent III in 1209 to seek approval for the unconventional way of life of his group of followers, the response was initially hostile. On the condition that Francis promised to remain obedient to the Holy See the Pope gave recognition to the Franciscans – a move which was meant to harness rather than reject the zeal for evangelical poverty. In order to evoke the spirit of apostolic liminality, Francis appealed to the *Imitatio Christi*, the participation in the sufferings of Jesus. This new piety, which focused on the incidents of Jesus's life, was entirely foreign to the Cathars. Their dualism did not allow them to think of Jesus as a man.

Dominic started teaching in poverty in accord with the gospel texts in the very centre of the Cathar heresy in Southern France, and fought the heretics on their own terms. He established himself in Fanjeaux and founded a house at Prouille for women and girls 'rescued' from the Cathars. The Cathars themselves had established houses in which poor girls and widows lived with women 'perfect'. In 1215 Dominic moved to Toulouse. One year later, he obtained recognition for his order of preachers, the Dominicans.[11] Alhough the confutation of heresy was their explicit aim, they nevertheless profited and flourished on the very same grounds and in response to the same quest which had sustained the heretical movements.

Finally, Joachimism contributed to popular religious feeling by promising a further dispensation of the Spirit in the not too distant future, leading to spiritual fulfilment on earth after a profound struggle with evil. In a sense, Joachimite prophecies appeared more 'positive' than Catharist visions of a return of one's angelic soul to heaven after death because they seemed to reaffirm the suitability of the cosmos as a place for the Spirit to dwell. However, as the papal Church was soon to learn, Joachimism channelled the quest for liminality into different directions but did little to help contain it, thereby nourishing new forms of heresy. The Cathar religion came to an end not only because it was suppressed by the Inquisition but also because it was supplanted by radical movements within the Christian Church.

MONASTICISM AND HERESY

With the exception of the Paulicians, the lineage presented in the previous section connects movements which all share a concern with an ascetic form of life. With regard to their outer appearance, a member of the spiritual élite of the Manichaeans, the Massalians, the Bogomils or the Cathars could not readily be distinguished from a good monk or nun. When in the early thirteenth century Cistercian missionaries tried to combat the Cathar heresy in Languedoc, they concluded from their lack of success that only by adopting complete poverty, by showing equal austerity and purity of life, could their arguments stand a chance of being heard. Just a few years later, this insight was implemented with the foundation of the Dominican Order.

As I noted earlier, the distinction between Christian and Manichaean asceticism is absolute. In the Christian outlook, the flesh is 'contrary' to the Spirit only in so far as it is not subjected to a reasonable discipline.[12] The sacramental character of nature is expressed in the symbol of incarnation. The whole of nature can be used sacramentally provided that it is used with discipline and renunciation. For Manichaeans, in contrast, the cosmos including the body is intrinsically evil. Nevertheless, in practice monasticism and heresy often appear together, continually provoking suspicions that the former might be infiltrated by the latter. This proximity in terms of time and space – rather than doctrine – is attested for both the beginnings of monasticism in the fourth century AD and its revival in the monastic reform movement of the tenth and eleventh centuries.

St Antony (Anthony) the Hermit and St Pachomius the Abbot are often considered the founders of two different traditions in monasticism. Antony (*c.* 251–356) was a Coptic-speaking Christian of the Alexandrian region. He lived as a 'hermit', from Greek *eremos*, 'desert'. St Pachomius (*c.* 292–346) is regarded as the founder of the Christian tradition of communal monastic life. To the Greek-speaking Christians, the monastery was known as the *coenobium*, from Greek *koinos* 'common'. In contrast to the hermits, the monks of the *coenobium* lived in a community.

It was not uncommon in the West to group the first monks with the Manichaeans. In his biography *The Life of St Antony*, which was instrumental in bringing the hermit tradition to the West, Athanasius felt it necessary to mention that Antony avoided contact with Manichaeans during his sojourn in the desert in order to ensure that his ascetic endeavours were not misconstrued as a form of Manichaeism. Fears that the Manichaeans could seize the new movement were not unfounded. Patriarch Timothy of Alexandria (380–5) was so horrified by the extent of Manichaean infiltration into the ranks of the clergy and monastics that he introduced food-tests by allowing monks to eat meat on Sundays and thereby singling out the Manichaeans among them.[13] The monks could be made to eat meat but the Manichaeans could not. When Bishop Serapion of Thmuis in the Delta, a friend of Antony and Athanasius, wrote a pamphlet against the Manichaeans, he emphasised that these heretics were particularly dangerous because they were not a set of visibly different rivals, but were hidden within his Church.[14]

The relationship between the Pachomian communities and Manichaean and other ascetics is a matter of controversy amongst experts. The codices from Nag Hammadi – of which many exhibit anticosmic dualism – were found very close to Chenoboskian in Upper Egypt, which was Pachomius's native village and the site of one of his later monasteries. The gradual extraction, unfolding and eventual publication of the paper used to stiffen and thicken the leather bindings of eight of the twelve codices brought to light a number of letters and other documents from a monastic setting. There were thought to be references to known Pachomian personalities. John Barns, who was involved in editing the Facsimile edition of the cartonnage, suggested that one letter was addressed to Pachomius himself.[15] Barns also suggested that the Nag Hammadi 'library' might have been collected by the Pachomian monks themselves and then later, after Athanasius's declared anxiety, buried as either redundant or too embarrassing to retain.[16]

For some time, scholars took for granted that the codices from Nag Hammadi all came from the same source, and that this source was a Pachomian monastery. A number of theories were proposed which explained their actual use inside a monastic library. The most obvious suggestions, that the texts were collected as documentation for heresiological purposes, was questioned by Frederik Wisse because the doctrines which were later to prevail as orthodox were not unchallenged within the Pachomian movement during the fourth century.

Wisse observes that the Egyptian schools of 'Gnosticism' – he has no hesitation in using the category – was on the decline at the same time as Christian monasticism was gaining momentum. He concludes that many 'Gnostics' must have joined the Christian anchoritic and cenobitic movements. Because the monastic movement lacked the organisation and political power to be a threat to the 'Gnostic' groups, only assimilation through 'osmosis' could account for the rise of the former and the decline of the latter. For the monks the main issue was not orthodoxy but 'orthopraxy' (Wisse, 1978), which consisted of asceticism as demanded in the monastic rules. As Christianity was narrowed down to the question of asceticism, the movement became indiscriminately open to outside influences which, regardless of differences in other aspects, supported this theme so that, as Wisse observes, 'single-mindedness played into the hands of syncretism'.

Wisse proposes that the texts from the leather bindings of the Nag Hammadi codices pointed to the presence within Pachomius's monastery itself of 'Gnostics' who had ultimately been reconciled with the Christian Church by their incorporation in a community not inimical to their ideas and not dissimilar to their former associations. There was at least one purge of heretical books under Abbot Theodore, Pachomius's successor, in response to Athanasius's anti-heretical paschal letter of AD 367. On this occasion, the codices were probably collected and buried in a jar away from the monasteries.[17] In this way, early monasticism in Egypt could have functioned as a 'half-way house' for a variety of ascetic sectarians to enter or return to the Church.

The main problem with Wisse's theory is, however, that all the other available sources on Pachomian monasticism are far from suggesting that heretical, 'Gnostic' doctrines were ever present in the movement. Tito Orlandi concluded from his work on Shenute that the communities in which the Nag Hammadi codices circulated might have been Evagrian monks, ascetic disciples of Evagrius Ponticus (*c*. 346–99). Evagrius, a friend of Basil the Great and a student of Gregory the Theologian, believed that conquering the flesh would allow the souls to return to their primordial oneness with God. Apart from the circumstancial evidence provided by Orlandi, the Evagrian connection is also attractive on doctrinal grounds. As I will explain below in the next section on mysticism and heresy, the spirituality of the codices would have appealed to the Evagrian disciples.[18]

More generally, it is not implausible that early ascetic communities in Egypt included members who had been drawn to asceticism from a variety of theological backgrounds and they might have continued to draw their ascetical inspiration from works which were later regarded as heretical. In the Manichaean writings, Mani's father is often referred to as a 'house-steward' although he is not known to have held any important rank among the Mughtasilah. This title or office is sometimes taken as an indication of monastic functions. There is also evidence that Addas, who had founded ascetic Manichaean communities especially in the Thebaid half a century before the first Christian monastic communities, travelled as far as Egypt.[19] Addas was a personal emissary of Mani and one of the most skilful debaters among the Manichaeans. All this gives a measure of plausibility to the suggestion that Manichaeism played some part in the early history of monasticism in Egypt.

The success of the monastic movement in late Antiquity can be understood as the result of two kinds of developments. First, monastic communities provide a reasonably safe sanctuary during times when society disintegrates because of war, civil unrest, or economic and social decline. Similarly, the early anchorites were probably refugees seeking safety in the desert from persecution under Decius and Diocletian. A second important driving force of the movement was the social success of Christianity. In the latter half of the second century the Church still had to decide whether it should remain, as it had been at first, a congregation of religious enthusiasts, separate and distinct from the routines of society, or whether it should begin a world mission on a grand scale by effectively entering the Roman social system. Already by the third century, the decision was made. The Christian Church became a well-established organisation, influencing all areas of life. Especially after Constantine gave peace to the Church in AD 313, many Christians might have felt that the moral fibre of the Church was softening because of its success. Once Christianity became the official religion of the Empire, it inevitably attracted people who were more concerned about their career in the imperial hierarchy than in leading a Christian life. In this context, monasticism was both an escape from the increasing worldliness of the Church and an attempt at reform.[20]

The relationship between monasticism and heresy became apparent when the monasteries themselves were absorbed by worldly concerns. In tenth century Bulgaria, during the 'monastic reign' of Tsar Peter, monasticism developed rapidly. The economic exhaustion after the wars with the Empire, and the recurring chaos that followed the invasions from the north by Magyars and Russians, made the monasteries the only stable places of retreat and peace. However, as the number of monks increased, the standards and ideals of monasticism were increasingly distorted. If even the monasteries are filled with hypocrites, the asceticism of the heretics appears as the only refuge left. That there was an immediate link between the sorry state of Orthodox monasticism in Bulgaria and Bogomilism is attested by contemporaries.

Comparable circumstances link the medieval monastic reformers and the Cathars. The reform movement pursued a variety of aims: renewal of asceticism, strict organisation of the monks, and the restoration of the autonomy of the monasteries *vis-à-vis* local princes. It then extended gradually to the Episcopal Church and strove for the moral reform of the secular clergy, for centralisation of the whole Church, for its emancipation from the state, and finally for the domination of the state. At all levels, both the original movement and its extension aimed at a purification of the Church, a restoration of 'old' discipline, an enhancement of the clerical vocation and status in Christendom, and dominion of the whole spirituality, as regulated by the monks, over the laity.

The gradual decline of state power and the rise of feudalism after and during the demise of the Carolingians provided the occasion for the monastic reformers to claim a hold on social life. The 'Peace of God' movement illustrates how the lay world became responsive to monastic ideals in the later tenth century. In a society in which general insecurity was the immediate consequence of the withdrawal of royal protection, real authority moved from the King to the great magnates in their provinces, and then further down to even smaller units, with castles as their centres from which castellans and their knights with no effective authority above them terrorised their neigbourhoods.

Largely of ecclesiastical inspiration, the idea behind a 'Peace of God' was originally to protect Church property by using the 'spiritual resources' of the Church. At a council of the archbishop of Bordeaux and his suffragans at Chassoux in 989, excommunications were pronounced against violators of churches, aggressors of unarmed clerics, and despoilers of the livestock of the poor. Local bishops tried to impose a 'peace pact' on their subjects. With the consent of the King of France, a Council of Peace was established by the bishop of Aquitaine at Bourges in 1031. The peace movement eventually tried to ban all violence at certain times of the year and days of the week. Such bans were usually imposed in collective oaths. If the castellans and knights refused to accept peace provisions, the movement itself could call on 'Christian warriors' to engender military actions against the peace-breakers. The monastic reformers were actively involved in the 'Peace of God' arrangements, and the growing piety expressed in new church buildings, new monasteries and the growing number of pilgrimages testify to its influence on society.

The spiritual climate in which the movement could flourish was prepared and sustained by the Cluniacs. Founded in 909, the monastery at Cluny became the head of an impressive monastic empire containing many hundreds of dependencies and associated houses spread throughout Western Europe. Cluniac abbots were prominent counsellors at the courts of Popes and Emperors. The Cluniac monk was not confined to a contemplative life but applied his strong impulse of ethical piety to the lay world. At the core of his mission was the attempt to monasticise the world.

In 1048 the reform movement found its centre in Rome with the election of Pope Leo IX, who initiated a new style of papal government. Prelates were examined on the circumstances of their appointment, and those who had paid money for their offices were disciplined. Leo's attack on simony was a first challenge to lay control of ecclesiastical offices. His reign marks the beginning of the liberation of the papal Church from both the Roman nobility and German imperial entanglements. The challenge was based on a notion of 'liberty' which first emerged in the great exempt abbeys such as Cluny. Cluny had been accustomed to enjoying 'liberties' granted by the popes, which freed them from the power of bishops and kings. Since St Odilo, abbot at Cluny from 994 to 1048, had secured from Pope John XIX a grant of complete exemption from the bishop of Mâcon, Cluny stood under the direct authority of Rome, but was autonomous towards other authorities.

The dismissal of the sacral character of kingship was the logical implication of such claims. The reform project aimed at the autonomy and superiority of a group of people, inspired by monastic ideals, who were in charge of the 'spiritual resources' (Pizzorno) of society.[21] Such claims led Gregory VII, himself a monk and admirer of Cluniac ideals, into a war in Germany with the King and Emperor-designate Henry IV. During the conflict, known as Investiture Contest, Western monasticism fought for the general recognition of its self-understanding as the only Christian life for all adult believers, marking the only period in the history of the papacy when the popes found themselves in the position of being the leaders of a radical party in the Church.[22]

The implications of the success of the reform movement cannot be overestimated. Many of them, however, were unforeseen by its protagonists. As the reforms and the victory in the Investiture Contest increased its political power, the Church became more and more involved in precisely those worldly affairs the original strive for purification had attempted to exclude. Ultimately, entering the ceaseless pettiness of business and litigation could only lead to a loss of the monopoly in the control of devotion and liminality. It is thus after the Gregorian revolution that the heretical movements exploded in the West.

These examples show that the social relevance of monasticism lies in its ability to counter the atomisation of society by providing a symbol and sanctuary for *communitas*, for a common spirit in the midst of the unrestrained selfishness which feeds on chaos. But as the monasteries partake in the reorganisation of society they are in danger of becoming indistinguishable from the other political forces which fight over the corpse of communal life. The quest for pure *communitas* and permanent liminality which might have inspired the monks originally must then move on to other, more radical parties which exclude any reconciliation with society and cosmos as a matter of doctrine. According to Hans Jonas, monastic asceticism *always* appears as a preliminary stage of what he calls 'Gnosticism'.[23]

NEO-PLATONISM, MYSTICISM AND HERESY

Mysticism is the complement to a life of withdrawal and quietism and as such is often located on the borderline between orthodoxy and heresy. Medieval mysticism drew heavily on the translations of Plotinus, Proclus and the Pseudo-Dionysius and thereby tapped into one of the main streams of unorthodoxy. The search for God in the soul with its emphasis on inner experience tended to undermine the importance of the sacraments and the mediation of the priesthood even where it was not meant to lead to the identification of the soul with God.

The history of Neo-Platonism begins with Ammonius Saccas's school in the early third century AD. Saccas, who, like Socrates, never wrote a single treatise, was the teacher of Plotinus and Origen. When he was teaching in Rome, Plotinus was astonished that some of his friends and students had 'Gnostic' leanings. Plotinus's disciple and biographer, Porphyry, mentions that they believed that 'Plato had not penetrated to the depth of the intelligible reality'.[24] Eventually Plotinus turned against these students and wrote *Against the Gnostics*, in which he outlined his main objections against their teaching. He disapproved of their anticosmic outlook and criticised them for introducing too many 'levels of being' – *hypostases* – whereas he accepted only three: the One, Mind (*nous*) and Soul (*psyche*). Still, the episode reveals that at least for the 'Gnostics' mentioned by Plotinus there must have been something about his philosophy which caught their attention.

Plotinus's Neo-Platonism departed in crucial points from Plato's philosophy. To Plotinus, reality appeared as a continuum expanding outwards from its centre, the One. The centre linked, formed and animated the various *hypostases* of the cosmos: *nous*, *psyche* and matter. While the One, *nous* and *psyche* qualify as 'being', matter forms the lowest grade of reality, 'non-being'. As such it was like darkness, the furthest removed from the light of the One. The relation of the One to that which proceeded from it was conceived as an 'emanation' in which the unity of the One brings forth the plurality of things in the world. The One, however, remained in its place; it animates without lessening itself. The One emanates *nous*, which is the realm of forms. *Psyche* is an intermediate level between *nous* and matter; it relates to *nous* in the same way in which a spoken word relates to an idea. *Psyche* comprehends individual souls which combine with matter to form 'ensouled' bodies. The cosmos itself possesses such a soul, the World-Soul, which gives the cosmos its harmony. Human souls are divided into parts, the highest of which is directly linked to Mind. The human soul can ascent to the One in a practice of purification; its goal is *ekstasis*, complete liberation through the contemplation of the One.

Plotinus relates the soul to the One in a manner which appealed to his 'Gnostic' students. The principle of 'emanation' makes it possible to think of the soul's ascent towards the One as a return to its origin. Moreover, if the various categories and levels of being all emanated from one origin, the boundaries which separate them must be 'softer' than they might appear to the ignorant. That being the case, the union of soul and God becomes a distinct possibility. Hence, operating within a Neo-Platonic framework, medieval mystics found it extremely difficult, if not impossible, to describe their experience of *ekstasis* in terms which did not invite accusations of heresy. There seemed to be nothing in this framework that could prevent them from obtaining beatific vision – according to orthodox teaching, the prerogative of Jesus.

The fluidity of gradations of being is even more visible in Origen's system, large parts of which are known to us only through Rufin's Latin translation. For Origen, the ultimate centre of being is the absolute Oneness which does not contain distinctions. Within this Oneness, God created pure Intelligences (*noes*), all equal, vested with ethereal bodies, who spend their being in contemplation of God. Because they were nameless and numberless their existence did not contradict the absolute Oneness. However, all except one grew cold in their fervour and became Souls (*psyche*). The degree of their fall differentiated them into angels, human beings and demons, categories that were not separated by impassable limits. The material world is still a creation of God, because God gives bodies to the fallen Intelligences in accordance with the vertical ranking of all being some time after the fall from the divine unity. Still, this creation is only the visible expression of a process which has its own dynamics. Origen skilfully combines the view that the cosmos is the product of a fall with the biblical postulate that God created the world.

Origen also maintained the doctrine of the *liberum arbitrium*, the doctrine of freedom of will. All Intelligences decide for themselves whether they turn towards or away from God. The gradation of being is not, then, a gradation of knowledge but a hypostatisation of *liberi arbitrii potestas in utroque* and divine *justitia*. However, as a consequence of the fall away from God and the subsequent materialisation, the ranking of being also becomes a ranking of knowledge.

The unity and uniformity of the Oneness is not lost after the fall. It remains the background of the subsequent cosmological evolution. As all beings have a common origin not just in time but also in substance, everything can become everything else. Indeed, Origen proposes a rotation and circulation of beings and worlds. The permanent up and down of individual beings is interrupted by divine judgements which determine a being's rank in the next world. Even if some beings may continue to fall during the transition from one world to the next, the overall direction of the process points towards a restoration of the original unity. If End and Beginning are the same, however, then the End does indeed mark another Beginning. The circle of worlds continues with another fall.

Within these worlds, the human being stands between angels and demons. To be 'human' is thus a transitional stage for a being that is either ascending or descending. In Origen's Christology, we find Christ as the one Intelligence which did not turn away from God at the moment of the fall. This particular being is thus able to descend through all the various ranks until it becomes human in order to lead the other humans back to their origin. Since the doctrine of free will makes it impossible to predict which of the Intelligences will manage to maintain its original divine rank, 'Christ' is here only a name for a being which is, however, essentially replaceable.

Origen's work was widely circulated and read in the early desert monasteries. He continued to exert a profound influence even after his teaching was declared heretical at the Fifth Ecumenical Council in 553. In the fourth century AD Evagrius Ponticus offered a variation of Origen's system which became one of the cornerstones of the spiritual tradition of the Byzantine Church. The centre of Evagrius's system is again a Oneness, *henade*, formed by the universe of equal Intelligences. Following a fault, the latter were separated from God, each experiencing a fate in accordance with the degree of the fall. The fallen Intelligences, called 'souls', were joined to bodies. By asceticism and contemplation, the souls can progressively return to God, and there will be a time when all make this return and the original *henade* will be restored. This process is called *apocatastasis*, from Acts 3:21. Evagrius's use of the term shows that the mystic's vision, as it was embedded in Neo-Platonic cosmology, was not simply a 'private' affair but was an effective element in the history of the cosmos.

For Evagrius, the return to God is accomplished in two steps; the ascetic (*praktike*) and the contemplative (*gnostike*). The former aims at removing obstacles to contemplation, delivering the human mind from its passions, and purifying the intellect of sense reactions. Its goal is *apatheia* or impassibility. The contemplative life is developed in two degrees: natural contemplation (*physike*), which is subdivided into a contemplation of the body and a contemplation of the *logoi*; and progressive contemplation in which the intellect, by emptying itself of all forms, comes to see in itself the light of God. The true vision of God is a formless light in the 'naked intellect' contemplating itself. Evagrius, too, was condemned at the Fifth Ecumenical Council in 553. When they came under suspicion of heresy, the later Hesychasts would defend such claims by arguing that the experience was indeed of God, but of his energies, not his essence.

Ernst Topitsch suggests that the enormous popularity of Fichte, Hegel and Schelling among the Russian *intelligentsia* of the ninteenth century must be explained with reference to the Neo-Platonic foundation of the contemplative spirituality of the Eastern Church.[25] Both Origen and Evagrius believed that their teaching was accessible and appropriate only for a spiritual élite; Origen distinguished between the *simpliciores* and the 'perfect'. The members of the *intelligentsia* understood themselves exactly in these terms as a 'secular priesthood', devoted to the spreading of a 'specific attitude to life, something like a gospel'.[26] Many of them found life on earth, material existence and, above all, politics both repulsive and unimportant. What mattered was the evolution of the World-Soul, of which concrete realities were just moments, aspects, or expressions. For the second generation of the *intelligentsia*, their ancestors were 'men of knowledge without will'.[27] The subsequent attempt to turn mysticism into activism set the tone for the talk and action which culminated in the Russian Revolution. To Hegel and Marx's position in this tradition I will return later.

Given significant similarities in mythology and doctrine, it is perhaps not surprising that Hans Jonas lists Neo-Platonism as a manifestation of 'Gnosticism', as an epi-phenomenon of a development which had its centre in the East.[28] Origen appears in Jonas's account as the typical representative of a 'Christianised Gnosis'.[29] Ioan Couliano finds the Cathar teaching of the transmigration of souls so similar to Origenism that he concludes that it must have been concocted in Byzantine ascetic religious circles with 'an intense nostalgia for Origenism'.[30] Because I do not approach 'Gnosticism' as a category, I cannot contribute to the debate on whether Neo-Platonism is 'Gnostic'.[31] I have instead referred to Neo-Platonism here as a line of meaning of its own which is historically intertwined, in a complex manner, with the line of meaning considered at the beginning of this chapter, running through Manichaeism in late Antiquity to the medieval revival of heresy. The proximity of these lines of meaning will be confirmed in the next chapter when I turn to Renaissance Neo-Platonism.

APOCALYPTICISM

Eschatological expectations are among the most important driving forces behind ascetic movements. If the end of the world is near, possessions, wealth and vanity do not matter. On the contrary, they distract from what must be the ultimate tasks for human beings who are about to confront God: reflection, conversion and repentance. For the Gospels the poor were 'blessed' not because they were to become the carriers of a new social order that was meant to last but, on the contrary, because they were the least distracted by a world that was about to end.

While this liminal impulse was certainly part of early Christianity's attraction, it developed into a problem once it had become clear that the Second Coming of Christ was not as imminent as was thought. The Church had to prepare itself for the possibility that the world could endure for an unspecified period. In these circumstances, the emphasis had to shift from *communitas* and liminality to community and organisation. The original impulse, however, did not fade away easily. In AD 156, a certain Montanus in Phrygia declared himself to be the incarnation of the Holy Ghost, that 'spirit of truth' who, according to the Fourth Gospel, was to reveal things to come. Montanism aimed at representing the true Christian doctrine, and this in its entirety. At first only a movement of religious enthusiasts, it eventually presented itself as the rule of the Paraclete foretold by Jesus in the Gospel according to John. Montanism desired to group all Christians together, to separate them from the world, and prepare them for the imminent Kingdom of God. Montanists would renounce their belongings and gather in the desert to await the apocalypse.

In order to counteract Montanism the Church insisted that the New Covenant was completed by Christ and the Apostles. The age of pure liminality was past, and the Spirit now spoke with final authority through a book, the collection of writings which originated in the age of the Apostles. The threat of Montanism lay behind the growth of the New Testament canon. Accordingly, many of the Christian apocalypses which had hitherto enjoyed canonical authority were now deprived of it. The *Apocalypse of John*, also known as the Book of Revelation, survived only because it was mistakenly attributed to St John the Apostle. As a part of the New Testament, however, it became something like the 'magna charta' for what came to be known as Christian 'millenarianiism'.[32]

The Book of Revelation was probably written in times of disturbance and persecution during the second half of the first century AD in order to increase the hope and determination of the infant Church. The persecuting Roman Empire with its emperor worship is referred to symbolically as 'the beast from the sea', which is a tool wielded by Satan (Revelation, 13:1–10). It is assumed that the author, John the Divine, was a member of a 'Johannine' school, community or circle which also brought forward the author of the Fourth Gospel. Both are therefore considered as representatives of the same 'Johannine' spirituality.

The Book of Revelation introduces the symbol of the 'Millennium' as the time period between the two great battles between good and evil which precede the end of the world. Revelation announces that the devil will be chained up for one thousand years in the abyss as a result of Christ's triumph in the first battle. During this 'Millennium', Christ and the newly-risen martyrs will reign on earth. After this period of blessedness, however, Satan will 'be released from his prison and will come out to deceive all the nations in the four quarters of the earth' (Revelation, 20:7–9). But in the final struggle, which coincides with the climax of history and paves the way for the descent of the Heavenly Jerusalem, God himself will interfere and secure the ultimate victory of good over evil. The annihilation of the enemy is followed by the resurrection and judgement of the dead. Those who are not found written in the book of life are cast out into the 'burning lake of sulphur' (Revelation, 21:8); the New Jerusalem will be let down from heaven to be the dwelling-place for the elect. The New Jerusalem represents a 'second' creation which replaces the world of the past. It forms a kingdom of perfect happiness which does not know mourning, sadness or death (Revelation, 21:3–5).

Although apocalyptic enthusiasm continued to lose support in official Church doctrine, the canonisation of Revelation left the door open to movements who preached the imminent return of the Spirit at the onset of a period of permanent liminality prior to the end of the world. Such movements are called 'millenarian movements' and their doctrine 'millenarianism' or 'chiliasm'. They are inspired by the – literal or allegorical – belief in the imminent beginning of a (thousand-year) period of blessedness as the last stage before the culmination of history. In the following I will distinguish the 'Millennium' of Revelation 20 from its everyday meaning through capitalisation.

St Augustine eventually provided the Church with an orthodox interpretation of the Millennium. According to Augustine, the apocalyptic Millennium meant the *present* reign of Christ in the Christian Church. Moreover, the symbol 'Millennium' was not meant in a literal sense as representing a thousand years but was a symbol for a totality. It represented the whole duration of this world. In order to substantiate his interpretation, Augustine refers to other biblical texts which use the term 'millennium' in this symbolic way. He concludes that the Second Coming of Christ will coincide with the end of this world.[32] But the quest for the concluding instauration of *communitas* was not to be contained on intellectual grounds alone. Apocalyptic anxiety was effectively contained once it found an institutional outlet, and this outlet was provided by the monasteries.[34] Monastic mysticism deflected the more destructive implications of millenarianism by transforming it into the disciplined, mystical contemplation of an *individual* eschatology.[35] But, as part of the Evagrian *apocatastasis*, this contemplation still had cosmological significance. It is not surprising, therefore, that it was from amidst the monastic reform movement that millenarian expectations re-erupted with violent consequences.

The apocalyptic enthusiasm of the First Crusade must be seen as an outflow of the monastic reforms of the eleventh century. The ideas of the world-ruling monk of Cluny led the van of the Crusades. Certainly, the First Crusade had a concrete *casus belli*. In March 1095, Urban II presided over a Council at Piacenza, which was also attended by an embassy sent by the Byzantine emperor Alexius to ask for help against the Seldjuk Turks. The Turkish advance across Asia Minor had brought the Turks within striking distance of Constantinople. Urban had been in touch with the Byzantine emperor since the beginning of his pontificate with the aim of improving relations between the Latin and Greek Churches and restoring Latin superiority. However, as Jonathan Riley-Smith observed, the first Crusade hardly needed a *casus belli* because 'the inner momentum of the reform movement would probably have led to it sooner or later'.[36] Urban himself was a former Grand Prior of Cluny. Monks responded enthusiastically to his appeal and typically functioned as recruiting-officers. The more wealthy and influential monasteries such as Cluny itself served as important fundraisers. The time period as a whole witnessed a phenomenal growth of monasticism.

Monks themselves were not allowed to join the Crusade – Urban proposed the Crusade as 'way of the Cross' for laymen. As a contemporary observed, the Crusade allowed 'knights and the crowd' to 'attain in some measure God's grace while pursuing their own careers, with the liberty and in the dress to which they are accustomed'. Divine grace was attainable without 'abandoning secular affairs completely by choosing the monastic life or any religious profession, as used to be the custom'.[37] When he preached the Crusade at the Council of Clermont in 1095, Urban placed the Crusader's person and property under the protection of the Church's 'Peace of God' until he returned. Moreover, he declared a plenary indulgence for all participants of the Crusade. The venture was thought to be so arduous and unpleasant that it would make good all penance owed to God by individual sinners. As such it paralleled the ascetic efforts of the monks. Hence, the Crusade became an instrument in the larger project of monasticising the world – the formal exclusion of monks did not keep later writers from describing the Crusade as a 'monastery on the move'.[38] The surprising success of the campaign must have convinced the reformers that their goal, the infusion of the outside world with monastic values, was attainable at last.

The success of Urban's appeal and the enthusiastic response of lay people was to a large extent due to the fact that Urban, contrary to all military logic, proposed the conquest of Jerusalem and the liberation of the Holy Sepulchre as the second aim of the Crusade in addition to the provision of the military assistance requested by the Byzantine Emperor. It was the goal of Jerusalem that made the Crusade a pilgrimage and therefore guaranteed popular support. The mystical conception of the Heavenly Jerusalem from the Book of Revelation cast a shimmer of unreality upon the earthly Jerusalem. As the centre of the world, the focus of God's intervention in history, the place where Christ had walked, the ground which had soaked up Christ's blood and where he had been laid to rest, but especially as the place where, at the end of time, the last events leading to Doomsday would be enacted, Jerusalem was elevated from the everyday world. In many charters of departing Crusaders, the holy city was closely and uniformly at the centre of the stage. Hardly any mention was made of Christian people in the East.

The apocalyptic significance of Jerusalem was increased by the popular belief that Babylon was the mystical capital of the infidel, the birthplace of the Antichrist. And during the victorious advance of Islam in the ninth century, a few clerics had decided that Mohammed must have been the 'precursor' of a Saracen Antichrist. The ferment of such ideas together with the predictions of Revelation made many Crusaders believe that they were part and expression of providential history which would end with the Second Coming of Christ. And as the end was approaching the Crusade was all the more welcomed as a means for self-purification before the Last Judgement.

If eschatological excitement is one of the driving forces behind asceticism, and if monastic asceticism tends to become a prelude to dualist heresy, then there must be corresponding points of intersection between apocalypticism and the line of meaning which unfolded from Manichaeism. At the level of doctrine and mythology, the proximity of these two lines of meaning is obvious. Both involve dualist teaching. At the core of apocalyptic writings lies the doctrine of the two ages. The current age is definitely detached from the age to come. The two ages are not only separated in terms of time but also in terms of quality and significance. This age is temporary and perishable; the next age is eternal and imperishable. The new age is illuminated by transcendence; it breaks in from beyond in supernatural fashion, through divine intervention, and puts an end to this world-era.[39]

The doctrine of the two ages recognises no continuity between the time of this world and of that which is to come. The old must pass away entirely before the new, the holy, can be established as the final state. In light of the future age, the meaning of the present is devalued. The real baseness and transitoriness of this world-era can be expressed in the symbol of Satanic powers which hold dominion over this world. The influence of Satan and evil forces leads to moral degeneration and an increase of godlessness, culminating in a final conflict between the hostile powers and the Saints, and finally with God himself. Apocalyptic writers typically devote their special interest to this last evil era which is usually their own time. The history of the past is presented in the form of fulfilled prophecies, lending further credibility to the prediction of the End. The present of the actual (not always the fictional) author is always the last time.

The apocalypticist sees history as closed, complete, exhausted in meaning. The movements of history are levelled out and become of no interest. Instead, apocalyptic texts develop fantastic pictures of the after-life, the glory of the blessed and the torments of the impious. Their authors claim to know the Last Things and the conditions of the age to come. The initiated were thus able to receive assurance about existence through knowledge of the world above and a proleptic glance of eschatological bliss.

However, although the contents of apocalyptic knowledge can be quite similar to the *gnosis* of the Valentinians or Manichaeans, it does not have the latter's saving power. Knowledge of the apocalypse – of what is past and what is still to come – is not in itself a means of salvation. For example, in the Book of Revelation, the elect who are destined to inhabit the Heavenly Jerusalem are what they are, not because of an innate pneumatic purity which they discovered through reading Revelation, but because they have washed their robes and made them white in the blood of the lamb (Revelation, 7:14). Apocalyptic knowledge is neither exhortation like Jewish prophecy nor salvation in the sense of *gnosis* but a mere hypostatisation.

The analogy of a duality of ages and a duality of worlds has long been a matter of contention among experts in 'Gnosticism'.[40] Those who accept the category 'Gnosticism' point out that the literary form of the apocalypse flourished in 'Gnostic' communities. Among the texts found in the 'library' at Nag Hammadi, five works were described in their titles as apocalyptic. Many assume an influence of Jewish apocalyptic thought on the development of 'Gnosticism'.[41] More specifically, Burkitt and Grant interpret the advent of 'Gnosticism' as a response to disappointed apocalypticism.[42] When his predictions did not become reality, the Judaic apocalypticist of the first century could postpone the time of fulfilment and rewrite his apocalypse; but he could also claim that the apocalyptic revelation had been misunderstood: the cosmos is doomed but, after all, there will be *no new creation*.

If the climax of history and the end of the world are felt to be near, antinomian asceticism may easily appear as the appropriate form of preparation. But if the vision of the end has to be postponed and the ascetic impulse turns into a new normality, the quest for *communitas* must turn to more radical forms of expression. I have argued in this chapter that the historical developments in both late Antiquity and the later Middle Ages confirm the proximity of lines of meaning which underlie phenomena as diverse as monasticism, Neo-Platonist mysticism, apocalyptic beliefs and the rise of Catharism or its predecessors. For contemporaries, the boundaries between these phenomena were not always clear. At the edges of apocalypticism and monasticism, symbols and outlooks deriving from Manichaeism could look surprisingly attractive and conclusive.

In late Antiquity, however, the Christian Church was still in a process of self-organisation. The notions of 'orthodoxy' and 'heresy' developed together for each is implicated in the definition of the other. The memory of the Spirit that dwelled among Jesus and the Apostles was still relatively fresh, and the Church's success seemed to confirm the universal significance of the Apostolic experience. In the later Middle Ages and early Renaissance, the position of the Church was different. After a history marked by expansion, power and indeed corruption, the various attempts at reform grew more intense. Ironically, the fate of the monastic reform movement only reinforced the suspicion that reform from within is either unlikely or counterproductive. The Cathars drew the ultimate conclusion by establishing their own Church as a new alternative.

The heretical movements had their ups and downs, but they would not fade until the great breakdown in the unity of the Christian Church in the West. The Reformation is again a major point of intersection of various lines of meaning. There is clear evidence that from the very beginning of the movement Luther's Reformation was thought to have apocalyptic significance. Popular texts celebrated Luther as the angel of Revelation 14:6, who announces the eternal gospel to every nation on earth, and warns that the hour of Judgement has come.[43] Further confirmation of the importance of the changes was found in the Hermetic and Cabalistic texts and practices to which I will turn in the next chapter. And once the apocalyptic excitement began to wane among Germans influenced by the Lutheran tradition, they turned to the inner, mystic spirituality of Pietism – which also forms the spiritual climate in which Hegel was brought up.

NOTES

1. Dimitri Obolensky, *The Bogomils: A Study in Balkan Neo-Manichaeism* (Cambridge: Cambridge University Press, 1948), p. 19.
2. Obolensky, *The Bogomils*, p. 27.
3. Nina G. Garsoïan, *The Paulician Heresy: A Study of the Origin and Development of Paulicianism in Armenia and the Eastern Provinces of the Byzantine Empire* (The Hague: Mouton, 1967).
4. See Obolensky, *The Bogomils*, pp. 53–8, for the alleged Samosatean link, and Edward James Martin, *A History of the Iconoclastic Controversy* (New York: AMS Press, 1978), pp. 275–8, for the relationship between Iconoclasm and Paulicianism.
5. 2 Corinthians 1:19.
6. Obolensky, *The Bogomils*, p. 43.
7. For a brief introduction to Bogomilism see also Dimiter Angelov, *The Bogomil Movement* (Sofia: Sofia Press, 1987).
8. For an account of these developments see Bernard Hamilton, 'The Origins of the Dualist Church of Drugunthia', in Hamilton, *Monastic Reform, Catharism and the Crusades* (London: Variorum, 1979), Chapter VII.
9. On the Cathars see Steven Runciman, *The Medieval Manichee: A Study of the Christian Dualist Heresy* (Cambridge: Cambridge University Press, 1960), pp. 116–70; Roelof van den Broek, 'The Cathars: Medieval Gnostics?', in Roelof van den Broek and Wouter J. Hanegraaff (eds), *Gnosis and Hermeticism: From Antiquity to Modern Times* (New York: SUNY Press, 1998), pp. 87–108; Malcolm Lambert, *Medieval Heresy: Popular Movements from the Gregorian Reform to the Reformation* (Oxford: Blackwell, 1992), pp. 105–46; Gordon Leff, *Heresy in the Later Middle Ages* (Manchester: Manchester University Press, 1967), pp. 445–93; R. I. Moore, *The Origins of European Dissent* (Oxford: Basil Blackwell, 1985), pp. 168–240.
10. See Bernard Hamilton, 'The Albigensian Crusade', in Hamilton, *Monastic Reform, Catharism and the Crusades*, Chapter VIII, for a summary of the events and their background.
11. Details in C. H. Lawrence, *The Friars: The Impact of the Early Mendicant Movement on Western Society* (London: Longman, 1994).
12. Galatians 5:17.
13. Samuel N. C. Lieu, *Manichaeism* (Tübingen: Mohr, second end, 1992), pp. 183–4.
14. Quoted in Philip Rousseau, *Pachomius: The Making of a Community in Fourth-century Egypt* (Berkeley: University of California Press, 1985), p. 35.
15. See the review of the Facsimile edition by C. H. Roberts in *The Journal of Theological Studies*, New Series Volume 32 (1981), pp. 265–6.
16. J. W. B. Barns, 'Greek and Coptic Papyri from the Covers of the Nag Hammadi Codices', in M. Krause (ed.), *Essays on the Nag Hammadi Texts in Honour of Pahor Labib* (Leiden: Brill, 1975), pp. 9–17.
17. Frederik Wisse, 'Gnosticism and Early Monasticism in Egypt', in Barbara Aland (ed.), *Gnosis: Festschrift für Hans Jonas* (Göttingen: Vandenhoeck & Ruprecht, 1978), pp. 431–40.
18. Tito Orlandi, 'A Catechesis against Apocryphal Texts by Shenute and the Gnostic Texts of Nag Hammadi', in *Harvard Theological Review*, 75: 1 (January 1982), pp. 85–95.
19. Lieu, *Manichaeism*, p. 182.
20. On these issues see Adolf Harnack, 'Monasticism: Its Ideals and History', in Harnack, *Monasticism: Its Ideals and History, and: The Confessions of St Augustine. Two Lectures* (trans. E. E. Kellett and F. H. Marseille), (London: Williams and Norgate, 1913); and C. H. Lawrence, *Medieval Monasticism: Forms of Religious Life in Western Europe in the Middle Ages* (London: Longman, second edn, 1989).
21. Alessandro Pizzorno, 'Politics Unbound', in Charles S. Maier (ed.), *Changing Boundaries of the Political: Essays on the Evolving Balance between the State and Society, Public and Private in Europe* (Cambridge: Cambridge University Press, 1987), pp. 27–62.
22. For a general account of the Investiture Contest and its context see Uta-Renate

Blumenthal, *The Investiture Controversy: Church and Monarchy from the Ninth to the Twelfth Century* (Philadelphia: University of Pennsylvania Press, 1991).

23. Hans Jonas, *Gnosis und Spätantiker Geist – Erster Teil: Die mythologische Gnosis* (Göttingen: Vandenhoeck & Ruprecht, third edn, 1964), pp. 87–8n.
24. Quoted in Roelof van den Broek, 'Gnosticism and Hermetism in Antiquity', in van den Broek and Wouter J. Hanegraaff (eds), *Gnosis and Hermeticism: From Antiquity to Modern Times* (New York: SUNY Press, 1998), p. 2.
25. Ernst Topitsch, 'Marxismus und Gnosis', in Topitsch, *Sozialphilosophie zwischen Ideologie und Wissenschaft* (Berlin: Luchterhand, third edn, 1971), pp. 261–96 (264).
26. From Isaiah Berlin, 'A Remarkable Decade', in Berlin, *Russian Thinkers* (ed. Henry Hardy and Aileen Kelly), (London: Hogarth Press, 1978), pp. 114–209 (117).
27. Ronald Hingley, *Nihilists: Russian Radicals and Revolutionaries in the Reign of Alexander II* (New York: Delacorte Press, 1967), p. 40.
28. Jonas, *Die mythologische Gnosis*, p. 43.
29. Hans Jonas, *Gnosis und Spätantiker Geist – Zweiter Teil: Von der Mythologie zur mystischen Philosophie* (Göttingen, Vandenhoeck & Ruprecht, second edn, 1966), pp. 175–223.
30. Ioan P. Couliano, *The Tree of Gnosis: Gnostic Mythology from Early Christianity to Modern Nihilism* (trans. H. S. Wiesner and Ioan P. Couliano), (San Francisco: Harper, 1990), pp. 214, 229.
31. For a critical assessment of Jonas' interpretation see A. H. Armstrong, 'Gnosis and Greek Philosophy', in Armstrong, *Plotinian and Christian Gnosis* (London: Variorum, 1979), Chapter XXI.
32. On Revelation see also Norman Cohn, *The Pursuit of the Millennium: Revolutionary Millenarians and Mystical Anarchists of the Middle Ages* (London: Paladin, 1970), pp. 24–5, and Norman Cohn, *Cosmos, Chaos and the World to Come: The Ancient Roots of Apocalyptic Faith* (New Haven: Yale University Press, 1993), pp. 212–19.
33. Augustine, *The City of God* (trans. Henri Bettenson), (Harmondsworth: Penguin, 1984), Book XX, 6–9.
34. On this point see also Harnack, 'Monasticism', p. 69, and Michael J. St. Clair, *Millenarian Movements in Historical Context* (New York: Garland, 1992), pp. 75–94.
35. Cf. Jakob Taubes, *Abendländische Eschatologie* (Bern: Francke, 1947), p. 76.
36. Jonathan Riley-Smith, *The Crusades: A Short History* (London: Athlone Press, 1987), p. 6. On monastic reform and the idea of crusade see also Carl Erdmann, *The Origin of the Idea of Crusade* (trans. by M. W. Baldwin and W. Goffart), (Princeton: Princeton University Press, 1977), and Jonathan Riley-Smith, *The First Crusade and the Idea of Crusading* (London: Athlone, 1995).
37. Riley-Smith, *The Crusades*, pp. 8–9.
38. Riley-Smith, *The First Crusade*, pp. 154–5.
39. See P. Vielhauer, 'Apocalypses and Related Subjects: Introduction', in E. Hennecke and W. Schneemelcher (eds), *New Testament Apocrypha: Volume Two* (London: SCM Press, 1975), pp. 581–607, for an overview and Christopher Rowland, *The Open Heaven: A Study of Apocalyptic in Judaism and Early Christianity* (London: SPCK, 1982), and Cohn, *Cosmos, Chaos and the World To Come*, for comprehensive treatments.
40. See, for example, Carl-A. Keller, 'Das Problem des Bösen in der Apokalyptik und Gnostik', in Martin Krause (ed.), *Gnosis and Gnosticism* (Papers read at the seventh International Conference on Patristic Studies, Oxford 1975), (Leiden: Brill, 1977), pp. 70–90; George MacRae, 'Apocalyptic Eschatology in Gnosticism', in David Hellholm (ed.), *Apocalypticism in the Mediterranean World and the Near East* (Tübingen: Mohr, 1983), pp. 317–25; C. K. Barret, 'Gnosis and the Apocalypse of John', in A. H. B. Logan and A. J. M. Wedderburn (eds), *The New Testament and Gnosis* (Edinburgh: Clark, 1983), pp. 125–37.
41. R. McLachlan Wilson, *Gnosis and the New Testament* (Oxford: Basil Blackwell, 1968), p. 132.
42. Francis Crawford Burkitt, *Church and Gnosis: A Study of Christian Thought and*

Speculation in the Second Century (Cambridge: Cambridge University Press, 1932); R. M. Grant, *Gnosticism and Early Christianity* (New York: Harper and Row, 1966).

42. See Robin Bruce Barnes, *Prophecy and Gnosis: Apocalypticism in the Wake of the Lutheran Reformation* (Stanford: Stanford University Press, 1988).

5

Intersections: Renaissance syncretism

Catharism died out partly because it was effectively suppressed, partly because its adherents were absorbed by movements within the Christian Church. For some time, the mendicant orders successfully absorbed the prevailing quest for liminality and channelled it into orthodox forms of expression. It is not surprising, therefore, that the question of *communitas* would arise again from amidst the Franciscans, now inspired by the prophecies of Joachim of Fiore.

Joachim's originality and relevance lies in his departure from the Augustinian interpretation of Revelation. As I mentioned earlier, Augustine effectively diffused radical eschatological expectations by understanding the Millennium as a symbol for the present reign of Christ in the Church. Thus, the Second Coming would coincide with the end of the world. Accordingly, the present age was an age of waiting for the eschatological events, an age of awaiting God's judgement, an age that grows old – a *saeculum senescens*. The appearance of Antichrist would be a prelude and thus a part of the end. In contrast, Joachim's 'third status' was a period between the defeat of Antichrist and the Second Coming. The victory against Antichrist was to be won *before* the apotheosis of history. At the heart of Joachim's teaching lies the affirmation of a real achievement of peace and beatitude *within* history. The characteristic feature of 'Joachimism' is thus the third historical dispensation of the Spirit, to be distinguished clearly from the Final Advent at the end of history.

Speculation about the time after Antichrist as a station for earthly progress did not originate with Joachim. And even after Joachim, such speculation continued sometimes independently of his prophecies. However, there is little doubt that Joachim was the most influential thinker on these matters of the Middle Ages.[1] The insertion of a third age into the Augustinian conception of history opened up all kinds of speculative questions. Who or what would instigate the transition from the second to the third status, and what would be the nature of human interrelatedness in the third status? These questions expressed a new eschatological hope and expectation in which the value of the cosmos is restored as the place to which the Spirit will return, as the forum in which salvation history will run its full course and reach its fulfilment. For Augustine, the end of salvation history was the restoration of human dignity through Christ. But in this vision, the human being seemed to remain little more than a criminal who was granted amnesty, and God's role in this drama appeared far from glorious: his own creation turned against him and the whole effort of salvation history had no other goal than to repair the damage. The alternative – chosen by Montanists and other early religious enthusiasts as much as by Joachimites – is the assumption of a progressive unfolding of the Spirit within history culminating in the creation of a new spiritual human being.

Joachim redirects the quest for *communitas* back to the cosmos. As a result the quest loses its anticosmic harshness. The great transfiguration that is about to occur is a transformation of life in the cosmos, not its destruction. The result, however, is still the *pneumatisation* of humanity. Therefore, the fundamentals of Joachim's vision could easily be incorporated within more elaborate and systematic cosmologies in which the future arrival of the third status was celebrated as a rediscovery of the individual's divine powers – his *pneuma* —whereby he would regain control over his cosmic fate.

Hermeticism and Cabalist mysticism provided fifteenth-century thinkers with precisely such a framework within which Joachim's books obtained a new meaning. Renaissance concerns such as the expectation of an imminent 'Golden Age', the celebration of the human being as a terrestrial god, as a co-creator and *magus* who, through alchemy, magic and science, acts upon the world to shape it according to his liking, derived from the amalgamation of these three ingredients: Joachimism, Hermeticism and Cabalist mysticism. Their intersection marks the beginning of the modern epoch. In the following, I will summarise the concerns of all three as continuations of lines of meaning presented in the previous chapter.

JOACHIM OF FIORE

Joachim of Fiore (Flora, Floris) was born in Celico, near Cosenza in Calabria around 1135. It is difficult to reconstruct the main events and turning-points in his life as sources are scanty and surrounded by legend. According to the more popular accounts of his life, Joachim withdrew as a young man to the Cistercian monastery at Curazzo after his return from a pilgrimage to the Holy Land. En route he witnessed the horrors of an epidemic. This event, as well as his visit to the Thebaid anchorites, and a Lenten retreat in Jerusalem are said to have provoked his conversion. Although he embraced a monastic way of life by giving away all his money and rich clothing, he did not initially take the habit. He remained a lay preacher until ecclesiastical disapproval led him to formally enter the Order. He was ordained in 1171 and elected Abbot in 1177 or 1178.

Cistercianism, named after its first establishment in Cîteaux, Burgundy, was in many ways a continuation of the attempts at monastic reform launched by Cluny. By the later twelfth century, however, the Cluniac organisation was in a state of decline which, as I explained in the previous chapter, was partly due to its success and subsequent involvement in the affairs of the world. However, the Cistercians too became involved in activities beyond the scope of a purely contemplative life. Abbots and monks of Cistercian houses, led by the example of their famous leader, Bernard, served as papal diplomats, fought the Albigensians, supported the Crusades and served as missionaries in Eastern Europe and the Baltic lands.

Joachim shared the original Cistercian concern with monastic reform because, as he observed, there had been too many monks who 'under the rule of poverty strove for worldly riches' but he was unsure whether he could live up to his vocation within the Cistercian movement. Moreover, the administrative duties of an abbot threatened the solitude Joachim needed to penetrate the meaning of the Scriptures in his meditations and studies. After several years of frustration, he broke away and escaped to a Cistercian sister house at Casamari, where he was able to spend time meditating and dictating to his friend and scribe, Luke, later Archbishop of Cosenza. Finally, however, in search of a more perfect realisation of monastic life, he left the monastery to found his own order at Fiore in Calabria. The order received papal approval in 1196.[2]

In his writings, Joachim mentions two visions or illuminations which he, as a mature thinker and experienced abbot, was able to channel into great productivity. His accounts present these crucial moments as rewards after long and ardous periods of studies during which he had reached an impasse. The first one followed a study of the Book of Revelation around Easter 1190; the second of these visions came upon him during his sojourn at Casamari. He admits that, at this time, he was terrified by doubts about the Trinity. He went into the chapel in a state of terror and turned to the discipline of repeating the set psalms. During this practice, he had a vision of a psaltery, in clear visual form, which resolved all his doubts. According to his own accounts, Joachim's visions did not provide answers to specific questions but freed his mind from doubts or intellectual barriers and thus allowed him to work out the problems.

All of Joachim's works are grounded in Sacred Scripture. Like many other medieval thinkers, he tried to advance from a literal reading of the Scripture to its inner spiritual meaning. Yet Joachim's exegesis was different from traditional methods. The search for a concealed meaning and the resulting allegorical interpretations of the sacred texts was not only applied for moral and dogmatic purposes, but was also meant to reveal the underlying patterns of concrete history. Joachim believed that the correct understanding of the Old and New Testament would enable him to forecast the development of history. He was convinced – and managed to convince many of his contemporaries – that he had found a pattern in the events and personages of the two Testaments which made it possible to perceive meaning in history and to prophesy in detail its future stages. In the same way in which prophecies and patterns in the Old Testament could have been used to anticipate the fulfilment of the New Testament, the pattern underlying the harmony between the two could be used to forecast a third dispensation.

Joachim suggested that, in the history of the human race, the mysteries of the Trinity were expressed within time. Thus, in somewhat simplified terms, the history of mankind consisted of three periods which corresponded to the three persons of the Trinity. The first age was the age of the Father or of the Law. The second period was the age of the Son or of the Gospel, and the third age *would be* the age of the Spirit. Each distinct age marks an advancement to the previous age so that history progresses in terms of an intelligible increase of spiritual fulfilment. For Joachim, Spirit is neither the ordering principle of a transcendent realm of forms nor the power of creation and restoration which calls humanity into existence and restores human dignity after the fall. Instead, Spirit is the principle of the concrete realisation of salvation history. The Kingdom of God is not, then, a transcendent *civitas platonica* but the concrete goal of the development of human society within the course of salvation history.

According to Joachim, each age in this process must be preceded by a period of incubation. For the first age, the incubation had lasted from Adam to Abraham; for the second, it lasted from Elijah to Christ; and for the third age, it began with St Benedict and was nearing its close when Joachim composed his works. According to Matthew, forty-two generations lay between Abraham and Christ. Because Joachim assumed that the internal structures of the various ages were comparable, he concluded that the period between the birth of Christ and the fulfilment of the third age must also last for forty-two generations. With one generation lasting roughly thirty years, the culmination of human history would have to take place around 1260. Contemporary accounts do indeed show a concentration of hopes and fears on the decade between 1250 and 1260.

Moreover, each epoch has its own spiritual leader, who introduces the next stage of history: Abraham belongs to the age of the Father, which lasted from the creation until Christ. Jesus introduced the second age, the age of the Son. Thus, shortly before 1260, the appearance of a new leader, a supreme teacher, was to be expected. He would lead the people away from their obsession with earthly things and prepare them for the love of the things of the Spirit. Joachim's symbol of the leader of the third age was later transformed, probably in the later thirteenth century, into the prophecy of the Angelic Pope, the *beatissimus papa*, who would reform the Church.

Antichrist enters history three and a half years immediately preceding the fulfilment of the third age. This time period corresponds roughly to the 1,290 (and 1,335) days mentioned in the twelfth chapter of Daniel, and to the forty-two months of Revelation 13:5. The age of the Spirit would come in its fullness after the overthrow of Antichrist. Joachim shocked his contemporaries with the thought that, at the time when he wrote, Antichrist had already been born.

The division of history into three ages is a derivation of Joachim's trinitarian doctrine, not its basis: the Three are One in his theology. Thus, all persons of the Trinity are active in history at all times. In some sense, then, history was still the work of the *Unus Deus*. Yet, each person in the Trinity has its own distinctive work. Moreover, although he insisted on the equality of the Three, he considered the work of the Third Person, of the Holy Spirit, as the culmination of history in the third *status* – just as the obtainment of *spiritus intelligentsiae* marked the crowning illumination in the life of an individual. In fact, his own illumination, which he understood as a divine gift enabling him to understand *clarissime* all the mysteries of the Scriptures, was not a gift that he alone would enjoy. It was only a foretaste of the spiritual intelligence which would be poured out on the whole of humanity before the end of history. Just as his own mind had proceeded from the meditation of the Old and the New Testament to one spiritual intelligence which combined all truth into one understanding, so would the history of mankind proceed from the work of God the Father, to the work of God the Son, and to the work of God the Holy Spirit.

Each status is characterised by a particular order of men. The primary works of these orders depend on the person of the Trinity to whom they belonged. The Father creates, the Son teaches and the Spirit exults. Thus, the activities of the corresponding three orders are *operatio*, *doctrina* and *iubilatio*. There seems to be no specific description of the third order in Joachim's writings, but its general character can be derived from the many labels he assigns to it. He speaks of an *ordo monachorum*, of the *ordo* or *ecclesia contemplantium* or *quiescentium*, and sometimes of the *ecclesia spiritualis* or *populus ille spiritualis*. Thus, the order of the imminent third status consists of new spiritual men. Their lives are marked by liberty and spiritual understanding, by *iubilatio* and *laetitia*, and by a kind of 'spiritual drunkenness' – *ebrietas* – which gives immediate vision of the *res sacramenti*. In other words, the new spiritual men live a life of permanent liminality and *communitas* which is contrasted to a life of organised activity and labour.

The new order of spiritual men was not intended to be a narrow circle of hermits who practised what Joachim saw as a supreme way of life. It was not, in other words, an esoteric sect. The *ecclesia laycorum* had its place in the divine scheme. Joachim's concern was to bring all believers into the new religious life; he was concerned with the general body of Christian people. The *ordo contemplantium* had a sevenfold form, of which five divisions belong to monastic life, the sixth to the clergy, and the seventh to pious (married) men. Only the first five belong to the centre of the new order; the last two divisions are located on the periphery of the centre. At some places in his writings Joachim envisions the conversion of all peoples, including the Tartars and Jews, to a new spiritual intelligence. The Greek Church would return to Roman obedience, wars were to cease and universal love would reign. The third status was not only one of spiritual understanding and liberty, but also of ecumenism.

A spiritual élite was necessary, however, to lead the papal Church into the third status. Joachim prophesied that, just as Moses and Aaron, and then Joshua and Caleb led the Israelites, so two new orders of spiritual men must lead the Church of the second status into the third. The need for *two* orders comes from the many concords of pairs in the Old and New Testament, such as the raven and dove of Noah, two angels sent to rescue Lot from Sodom, Moses and Aaron, Paul and Barnabas, etc. The members of the two preaching orders were the evangelistic agents, the *viri spirituales*, who already embodied the new life, but whose task was to prepare the Church of the second status for the transition into the third status. Thus, the two orders were active in the second age; they had to be distinguished from the new order of men which would mark the third status. Originally, Joachim envisioned two different tasks for the two orders. They were not meant to be parallel orders. The members of one were to lead a hermit life, praying for the world and gathering vision for its needs on the mountain-top of contemplation; the second order was to be an active preaching order which would carry the visions downwards to the people. Its members would live a contemplative life in comparison with the world's, and an active life in comparison with the hermit's.

Joachim's prophecy later became inextricably associated with the two mendicant orders, the Franciscans and the Dominicans. When the orders of Francis and Dominic emerged in the early thirteenth century, they were inevitably seen as the two orders of spiritual men who would lead the Church through the passage of the River Jordan into the

Promised Land. The emergence of the mendicants was widely accepted as a confirmation of Joachim's philosophy of history. When the first Dominicans approached Joachim's order in Fiore the monks went out to hail them as one of the two orders which their founder had expected. In turn, Joachim's expectations also found resonance among the mendicants as at least some of them claimed for their orders the role of the carriers of the meaning of history. By the 1240s, the advent of the mendicants had prompted a renewed interest in Joachim's third status. His original conception of two bodies of men fulfilling different functions was soon lost and replaced by the reality of two active preaching orders.

Joachim was well-known and respected during his lifetime. In 1184 Pope Lucius III consulted him at Veroli on how to interpret the Sibylline Prophecies. And in the winter of 1190/1 Richard Cœur de Lion met him in Messina while en route to the Third Crusade. It was Richard's wish to see Joachim and ask him questions about the fate of Jerusalem. On this occasion Joachim proclaimed that Antichrist had already been born *in urbe Romana* around 1175. In 1191 Joachim is reported to have met the Emperor Henry VI when the latter came to South Italy to claim the kingdom. Joachim saw Tyrus Nebuchadrezzar's destruction of Tyre from Ezekiel 26:7 mirrored in Henry's campaign. These episodes show Joachim as a political adviser in the midst of the European political arena. Soon after 1200 his reputation had spread to north Italy and then north of the Alps. Before his works were re-edited in the early sixteenth century, the impact of Joachimism was most visible in the development of the Franciscan order.[3]

The self-understanding of the Franciscans explains their emotional response to Joachim's texts. The person of Francis had eschatological significance. To his followers, his stigmata identified him as the Angel of the Apocalypse who carries the seal of the living God. In his self-understanding, Francis was heralding things to come rather than fulfilling past prophecies; he was not, therefore, a second Christ. The awareness of an imminent end was at least part of his refusal to plan for the social security of his order. Francis also considered his foundation as being directly willed and inspired by God. The Franciscans formed a new covenant which was valid next to, and separately from, the Gospel of the second era.

Dissension arose early among the Franciscans about the issue of poverty. The early Franciscan way of life was harder to bear than that of most ascetic monastic orders because Francis aimed to renounce not only individual but also common property. The monk was supposed to leave behind even the normal framework of collective (material) security, but as the order grew in size and attracted more and more men from diverse backgrounds, practical and organisational problems made it difficult to uphold the original standards of simplicity, strictness and poverty. Francis's last testament added further dynamics to the situation by implying that the order had departed from the original impulse of its creation. After years of semi-eremitical life in resignation from the active government of his order, Francis looked back with nostalgia to the simple early days of his brotherhood. He ordered his deathbed statement to be kept with the rule of the order and to be read with it. In the aftermath of his death, the issue of poverty continued to divide his disciples. When in 1230 a moderate majority appealed to the Holy See to settle the controversy, Pope Gregory IX issued the bull *Quo elongati*, which declared that Francis's testament did not have the force of law, that the friars were bound to observe only those counsels which were expressly mentioned in the final rule of 1223, that ownership of the goods used by the friars remained with the donors, and that trustees could hold and administer money for the order. The bull preserved the vow of poverty as a fiction, but allowed for its practical circumvention. A further clarification issued by Innocent IV in 1245 reserved ownership of goods used to the Holy See and allowed recourse to money through the trustees, not only for the care of the sick and other pressing needs, but also for the 'convenience' of the friars.

The radicals among the Franciscans, the *zelanti*, openly rebelled against such laxity, and it is to them that Joachim's prophecies offered the proper sectarian consciousness. Soon after Joachim's texts had entered the convents in the early 1240s, the *zelanti* or Spirituals, as they came to be known, applied the prophecies of the third status to themselves and their dead leader. Francis was the spiritual leader, the *novus dux*, who stood at the beginning of the third age just as Christ stood at the beginning of the second. Many found it irresistible to give the rule and testament of Francis the authority of a Third Testament. It was to Francis and his order that the final eschatological task of converting the world was assigned. But if the meaning of history rested on the shoulders of the Franciscans, then strict observance of the principles designed by Francis himself was more than an obligation. Through the rejection of compromise the Joachimite Franciscan would serve for the benefit of mankind. The Joachimite conception of history drove the extremists towards the persuasion that they alone, in their separation from the order, represented the true order of new spiritual men and the true Church of the third status.

As a result of the fusion of Franciscan eschatology and Joachimism, the consciousness of a Spiritual Franciscan was characterised by: a sense that the extreme crisis of history is about to break upon the world; a belief in the supreme mission of the order to match this moment; and the conviction that disobedience towards the papacy and ecclesiastical hierarchy could be justified by the fact that the order held the key to the future. As the new spiritual men who would lead the Church into the imminent third status, the Spiritual Franciscans were driven by a sense of certainty and urgency, a mood which Marjorie Reeves compares to that of an early Marxist.[4]

The subversive potential of Joachim's teaching became obvious for the first time in the Scandal of the Eternal Evangel which erupted in Paris in 1254/5. Five years prior to the expected beginning of the third age, Gerard of Borgo San Donnino, a fanatical Franciscan Joachimite and companion of John of Parma, the General of the Franciscan order from 1247 to 1257, announced in Paris the imminent advent of the third status in a book which was to be the Eternal Evangel, the Everlasting Gospel, superseding the Old and New Testaments. The title 'Eternal Evangel' is from Revelation 14:6. Gerard's book consisted of Joachim's main works and a *Liber Introductorius* written by Gerard himself in which he argued that Joachim's writings are indeed the *evangelium aeternum*.[5]

Joachim never envisaged a Third Testament, least of all one composed of his own writings. However, the masters of Paris University, who had always been hostile to the Mendicants, seized on Gerard's text and compiled a set of excerpts which they sent to the Pope for examination. The result was a condemnation (1256) of Gerard's introduction; Joachim's work was carefully excluded. However, at least one of the members of the commission which examined the *Eternal Evangel* must have been convinced that the real source of the problems was Joachim's doctrine of the third status. In 1263, Florentinus, Bishop of Arles, secured at the provincial council of Arles a full condemnation of the doctrine and of the writings of Joachim on which it was founded.

In the context of the reception of Joachim's work, the Scandal of the Eternal Evangel highlighted what has been a point of contention ever since: the problematic nature of the transition from the second to the third status and, in particular, the fate of the Roman Church. Was the third status supposed to supersede the second in such a way as to undermine the once-and-for-all character of the revelation of Christ and to substitute a new spiritual order for that of the Church as Christ founded it? Joachim is ambiguous on this point and thus invited radical readings and misreadings. On the one hand, he remained firm in his belief in the reality of two historical dispensations, of two Testaments, and of two Churches (the Synagogue and the Church of Christ). However he envisioned the transition to the third status, the historical reality of the two dispensations remained. Moreover, he occasionally emphasises how the *Ecclesia Petri* stood alone, like a monument, and would go transformed but immovable through the great transition. On the other hand, there are passages where Joachim gives the impression that something does pass away as humanity moves into the third status. He refers to the 'church' or the 'life' designated in Peter which will be replaced by the life designated in John, leaving the life in John to endure to the end. Such remarks were bound to create trouble because, at other places in Joachim's writing, St Peter often stands for the papacy.

The Scandal of the Eternal Evangel demonstrated that the Spirituals had fused their beliefs with Joachimism and thereby sharpened the antagonism towards the moderate Franciscans. John of Parma, the General of the Order, was known to have tolerated the radicals and, as a friend of Gerard, was implicated in the scandal of 1254. According to a later leader of the Spirituals, Angelo Clareno, John did in fact declare Francis's testament to be the embodiment of the *spiritualis intelligentia* of Joachim's third status. After their examination by the new General of the order, Bonaventura, John was allowed to retire quietly while Gerard was kept in detention by the order for the remaining eighteen years of his life.

The first direct evidence from a Franciscan group of Joachimites comes from Hugh de Digne, a friend of John of Parma, and his disciples at Hyères in Provence in the 1240s. However, the main representative of Joachimism in the area was Jean d'Olivi. He was born in 1248 in Languedoc and studied at Paris. His formative period fell into the time just after the first generation of Franciscans had died and the disputes on poverty became more intense. Olivi's most influential text is his *Postilla* on the Apocalypse in which he presents the typical Joachimite expectations with St Francis as the initiator of the new age. His thought can be summarised in three key ideas. First, he acknowledged the importance of the Roman Church for the protection of the Franciscan order but insisted that only the latter was the legitimate successor of the *ordo* of the old epoch. Second, the work of the Spirit will be fulfilled through suffering in a period of transition. This suffering was effectively a re-evocation of the persecution and crucifixion of Christ. Finally, the transition into the third era was a period of reformation in which the Church and mankind are formed according to the rule of Francis.

Just like Gerard, Olivi failed to obtain approval for Joachim's idea of a 'spiritual Church' in a third age. His writings were condemned at the Chapter General at Lyons in 1299, one year after his death. Possession of his works was prohibited under pain of excommunication. His disciples were persecuted and some were burned by the Inquisition. From 1317 onwards, many of his followers joined a heretical sect known as the Beguins. The Beguins are first officially mentioned in 1299, the year Olivi's writings were defined as heretical. At the council of Béziers, they were condemned for preaching without authorisation. However, especially after the burning of four Spirituals in Marseilles in 1318, one year after the papal bull *Quorumdam exigit* had declared obedience a greater good than poverty, the Beguins turned to Olivi for authority and guidance. From then on, the cult of Olivi gave the Beguins their distinctive character as a religious group. Belief in the sanctity of his person and teachings provided them with a focal point for their tribulations. For both Spirituals and Beguins, Olivi could sometimes be elevated above Francis in terms of eschatological significance and his tomb became a place of pilgrimage where sick children were taken to be healed.

The Beguins were a Languedocian heresy, and thus affected regions in which Catharism was strong, even if the old Cathar centres lay somewhat further to the east. Olivi himself opposed the Cathars as members of Antichrist but the Franciscan Spirituals were not, in externals, wholly unlike the Cathar perfect. There is evidence that Beguins were attracted to the strict life of poverty of the Cathar élite. Like the Cathars, the Spirituals profited from the protection they were granted by municipalities opposed to the activity of the Inquisition and its implications in secular politics. The experience of the Albigensian Crusade and the subsequent hatred of the Dominican Inquisitors made the region especially susceptible to anti-ecclesiastical feeling.

Towards the end of the thirteenth century, many Spirituals in Italy believed that the days of persecution would come to an end with the election of the hermit Pope, Celestine V, who was celebrated as the figure of the Angelic Pope derived from Joachim's prophecies. Shortly after his election in 1294, two radical Franciscan Spirituals, Peter of Macerata and Peter of Fossombrone, obtained from Celestine an authorisation for their group of disciples to separate from the Franciscan Order and become hermits directly under the rule of St Francis. The new group was called the Poor Hermits of the Lord Celestine. Macerata was thereafter called Liberato, and Fossombrone, Angelo Clareno. For Clareno, Francis and Olivi had equal eschatological relevance.

After the renunciation of Celestine V, only five months after his election, Boniface VIII annulled Celestine's concessions to the Spirituals. The group, now also called 'Clareni', fled to Greece, but returned after Boniface's death. The group apparently hoped for a revolution in the papacy itself but were disappointed in the papal election of 1304/5, when, instead of an Angelic Pope, Clement V, who would remove the Holy See to Avignon, was elected. After Liberato's death, Clareno was at first able to exercise a constraining influence on them. However, in the aftermath of his own death in 1337, competing claims to authority within the group led to fragmentation. From the Clarenists, and probably as well as from other remnants of the Spirituals, there sprang many of the groups known as the *fraticelli*. Other groups of *Clareni* were later united to the Franciscan Observants.

The *fraticelli* were widely scattered throughout Italy. There were communities in the March of Ancona, Naples, Rome and Umbria, especially Todi, Rieti and Amelia, as well as in the regions of Perugia, Narni and Tuscany. The *fraticelli* declared openly their separation from the Roman Church and attacked the Pope fiercely. They were, in the Joachimite framework, the few to whom the perfection of the future status was entrusted. They were the saving remnant gathered into Noah's ark of the last age. In the sixth age of the Church and at the end of the second era, Christ had sent St Francis to build a new ark, the Ark of the Evangelical Rule, in which only the elect would be saved from the flood that would come over the unfaithful. The navigators of the voyage included Joachim, who had foretold all these things. Although the Inquisition struck hard at these groups, there were some political and social situations which favoured them. In Florence, where Olivi had lectured in Santa Croce with Ubertino da Casale and possibly Dante in the audience, they had a particularly long influence.

Florence was one of those cities in which local politics favoured heretical groups.[6] With the formation of the popular government in 1343, the communal authorities changed their attitudes towards the Church courts and the Inquisitor. The new government no longer co-operated with the Inquisitor and permitted a wider diffusion of the teachings of the *fraticelli*. The change of attitude was not entirely based on sympathy for the Spirituals, but was also a consequence of the city's changing relationship with the papal Church. Approximately half of the members of the Florentine government were international traders and bankers who had maintained a close and good relationship with the Pope (in Avignon) in matters pertaining to finance and foreign policy. However, in the 1340s the Florentine banking system went through a severe crisis. Frictions arose between the two sides because the Florentine bankers felt that the disastrous financial situation had been worsened by the uncooperative attitude of Avignon. Clement VI had shown ignorance and indifference towards the companies in their hour of need and, in addition, demanded that ecclesiastical creditors be granted preferential treatment. Avignon tried to back up such demands by utilising the Church courts and the Inquisition to press these claims.

In their efforts to constrain the power of the Inquisitor, the Florentine upper classes could draw on the active support of the *gente nuova*, the middle classes who, without representation among the upper clergy and the nobility, were striving for recognition. And with the

Inquisitorial powers effectively curbed, the *fraticelli* groups were left in peace. The lower social classes, the *populo minuti*, turned out to be especially receptive to their teaching, if only for the reason that the Spirituals ascribed the highest virtue to the poor. Since, in addition, the Spirituals had always been hostile to the papacy, the further diffusion of the heresy was congruent with the general politics of the city. It is likely that the ruling patricians believed that they could control the economic, social and political manifestations of the heresy among *il populo minuti*.

Although relations between city and papacy became more cordial later on, the various priorates ruling the city from the Black Death until the aftermath of the *Ciompi* rebellion (1348–82) maintained an attitude of tolerance towards the *fraticelli*. In the 1370s the Florentines became increasingly concerned about papal attempts to re-establish temporal authority in the papal States. When, by 1375, the tensions accumulated in the War of the *Otto Santi*, the War of the Eight Saints, between the republic and Gregory XI, the Florentine government recognised the need for popular support to sustain the war. Again, the Spiritual Franciscans were permitted to spread their doctrine without fear of reprisal. For the purposes of the war, they were the ideal mobilisers of support; and their efforts were crowned with success. The artisan and shopkeeper class seemed most receptive to their teaching. Public enthusiasm for the war suggests that the *fraticelli* did have a significant influence on the citizenry.[7]

This influence is also visible in the *Ciompi* revolution of 1378. Gaspare di Ricco, one of the principal leaders of the revolutionaries, wore the yellow cross of the heretic upon his sleeve; the post-revolution government tolerated and protected the *fraticelli*. The revolutionaries, who called themselves *il populo di Dio*, were not ungrateful to the debt they owed to the Spirituals. Joachimite prophecies taught by the *fraticelli* exalted the cause of the common people as the inheritors of the 'true' religion. When the urban patriciate regained political control in 1382, they acknowledged the link between heresy and rebellion by proposing legislation that was meant to expel the *fraticelli* from Florentine territory. Interestingly, there was sufficient opposition to bring about the proposal's defeat. The same measures were proposed again the following day and only barely attracted enough votes to ensure acceptance. From then on, the government co-operated with the Inquisitor in suppressing the heresy.

According to the eighteenth-century annalist of the Franciscan order Luke Wadding, the *pestifera secta Fraticellorum* was still growing like a hydra in Italy in the fifteenth century.[8] However, under pressure from the Inquisition, the *fraticelli* groups eventually dissolved. The last recorded trial against a *fraticelli* was at Rome in 1466. However, their Joachimite hopes lived on, especially in Florence. The troubled decade of the 1490s – with the French invasion of 1494 and the brief rule of the Dominican Girolamo Savonarola – saw another outpouring of prophecies in the city and, by then, these prophecies could draw on a rich tradition. In 1498, Giuliano de Gondi expressed his fear that Savonarola had founded 'a new sect of *fraticelli* like that one that formerly existed in this city' and that he, Savonarola, aspired to make himself its Angelic Pope.[9]

Joachimist beliefs are present in the beginnings of most reformatory or revolutionary movements in the modern period. Joachimism is a visible element of Reformation spirituality;[10] it forms a source of inspiration for Thomas Müntzer; and it had an impact on the Taborites in Bohemia, on the Anabaptists in Germany, and on the Rosicrucian movement.[11] For the English Puritans, the effective abolition of the monarchy signified the entry into the Third Age, in which the Holy Spirit was coming into all human hearts to free them from existing forms and ordinances.[12] Similarly, the myth of the Eternal Evangel had its adherents during the French Revolution.[13] Joachim was also an acknowledged influence on the philosophy of religion and social metaphysics of German Idealism and Romanticism, notably on Lessing and Schelling, as well as on Auguste Comte's three stages of history. Schelling did not know Joachim when he worked out his doctrine of the three ages and was surprised and delighted to find out that this notion had been anticipated and developed 'in the writings of a man so significant and so prominent in the history of the Church'.[14]

According to Erich Frank, the most 'consequential literary revival' of Joachimism in the twentieth century was to be found in the writings of the Russian author D. S. Merezhkovsky (1865–1941), who, living in exile in Paris from 1905 to 1941, prophesied a third empire of the Spirit which would finally unify *logos* and *cosmos*. In Paris, the Russo-German literary critic Moeller van den Bruck was closely connected with Mereshovsky, with whom he edited the German translation of Dostoevsky. Moeller van den Bruck returned to Germany after the First World War and wrote, under the influence of his Russian friend, *Das Dritte Reich*, translated into English in 1934 as *Germany's Third Empire*. The title of the book provided Hitler with the term *Drittes Reich*.[15] It must be pointed out, however, that in spite of obvious agreements between their understanding of the Trinity as the key to human existence, Merezhkovsky never refers to Joachim directly and there is no other evidence that he knew of the Calabrian abbot.[16]

MARSILIO FICINO'S HERMETICISM

The foundation of a Platonic Academy in Florence in the second half of the fifteenth century is often mentioned as the clearest expression of a renewed interest in Plato during the Renaissance. The Academy was not institutionalised as a university or school but formed an informal coterie of scholars and students, united by an interest in Platonic philosophy as well as by the friendship and patronage of the ruling Medici family. It had a geographical focus in Marsilio Ficino's villa at Careggi outside Florence, but its only scheduled events were irregular lectures by Ficino and occasional banquets and symposia. The group of people who would meet at Careggi consisted of artists, poets, men of letters, and professional and civic dignitaries.[17]

The main figure in this group was Ficino himself. Born in 1433 as the son of Cosimo de Medici's physician, his promise as a student was detected by Cosimo, who then supplied him with the means and opportunities of study. Ficino spent all his life in Florence, where he enjoyed increasing popularity. He was first the tutor, and later trusted adviser, of Lorenzo de Medici, Cosimo's grandson, when Lorenzo became ruler of Florence. Until 1463 Ficino wrote a number of short philosophical essays and some translations of minor importance; only a few of these early works have survived. He is best known for his translation of the Platonic dialogues.

At the request of Cosimo de Medici, Ficino started to translate Plato into Latin in 1463; the work being completed more than twenty years later in 1484. Ficino's translation soon entirely superseded all earlier attempts and remained for centuries *the* Plato of the Western world. With the help of the newly-invented printing technology, Plato's texts, in Ficino's translation, began to circulate widely in fifteenth-century Europe.

Ficino considered himself a restorer of Platonism and was regarded as such by his contemporaries. Members of the Florentine Academy would call him 'alter Plato', and he liked to be known as 'Platonist'.[18] After having published all the Platonic writings – authentic as well as spurious – into Latin, Ficino translated Plotinus's *Enneads* (1492), works by Iamblichus, Proclus, Porphyry, Synesius, Albinus and other Neo-Platonists (1497), as well as commentaries on Plato (1496) and the Pseudo-Dionysius (1496). Ficino's interest in Neo-Platonism is based on his admiration of Plotinus as a 'second Plato', indeed as an even 'truer' expression of Platonism than the original.

The version of 'Platonism' which re-entered the West in the fifteenth century was therefore closer to Plotinus than to Plato. These developments, however, were not only the result of Ficino's personal preferences. Throughout the Middle Ages, the West had access to Plato only through the Neo-Platonists of the last century BC and the first two centuries AD. In this sense, medieval Platonism had always been Neo-Platonism. The two main pillars of medieval Platonism in the West – Calcidius's commentary (*c.* 400 AD) on *Timaeus*, lines 17A–53C and

Macrobius's contemporary commentary on Cicero's *Somnium Scipionis* – were both entirely dependent on Middle-Platonic as well as Neo-Platonic interpretations of Plato. Calcidius's partial translation of the *Timaeus* was the only Platonic text available in the West for many centuries. Around 1156, Henricus Aristippus, archdeacon of Catania, translated into Latin the *Meno* and the *Phaedo*, but the translations were clumsy and apparently not widely read.

The first time a Greek manuscript of Plato is mentioned in the West after Aristippus is in a work by Petrarch of 1367, in which the author accuses his adversaries – in his attack on Averroistic Aristotelianism – of ignorance about Plato. He claims to be in possession of more than sixteen manuscripts, most of them in Greek. However, Petrarch could not read Greek, and thus his own writings do not show a profound knowledge of Plato. The situation only changed when, in 1396, Manuel Chrysoloras, a Byzantine nobleman and scholar, began to teach Greek in Florence. Chrysoloras had been invited to become professor of Greek in Florence by one of Petrarch's disciples, Coluccio Salutati, the famous Chancellor of the Florentine Republic. During the first three years of the fifteenth century, Chrysoloras together with Uberto Decembrio translated the *Republic* into Latin. This translation initiated a series of Plato translations, culminating in the Ficinian edition of 1484.

Given this history of Plato interpretations the fifteenth-century bias towards Plotinus is perhaps not surprising, and yet Renaissance Platonism was not a mere return to the Neo-Platonism of late Antiquity. There are some new elements involved which, just like the Platonic texts themselves, came to Florence through the Byzantine connections.[19] In contrast to the situation in the West, the original works of Plato and the Neo-Platonists were always available in the East, where Michael Psellos revived the interest in Platonic philosophy in the eleventh century. Psellos was a man of considerable learning and influence. His attempt to combine Platonic philosophy with the *Chaldaean Oracles*, at that time often attributed to Zoroaster and highly valued by Porphyry and later Neo-Platonists, and the *Corpus Hermeticum* found many successors among Byzantine scholars and marked an important precedent for Renaissance Platonists like Ficino. Kristeller assumes that the *Corpus Hermeticum* as it arrived in Florence was probably an edition or anthology prepared by Psellos. The collection of *Chaldaean Oracles* too goes back to him. Psellos's commentary on the *Oracles* was known to Ficino, who also translated Psellos's treatise *On Demons*.[20]

An important intermediary between Psellos and Ficino is Georgios Gemistus Plethon. Plethon lived approximately from 1360 to 1452 and spent most of his later life in Mistra, the capital of the despots of

Morea, and served as a counsellor to the reigning princes and as a private tutor. He envisioned a strengthening of the Byzantine Empire by a political and philosophical reform based on ancient Greek models. The proposed revival of Plato was meant to be based on Proclus and Psellos. Like Psellos, Plethon was convinced that Plato and his followers were representatives of an old pagan theology whose written testimonies were attributed to Hermes Trismegistus, Zoroaster, Orpheus and Pythagoras, and which paralleled both in age and content the revelation of the Hebrew and Christian Scriptures.

Plethon visited the Council of Ferrara as well as Florence in the years 1438 and 1439. In his preface to his version of Plotinus (1492), Ficino states that Cosimo de Medici, during the Council of Florence, had had several occasions to listen to Plethon's lectures. Apparently, he was so deeply impressed by them that he conceived the idea of founding a Platonic Academy in Florence, a task for which he later chose Ficino when the latter was still young. There is some doubt whether this account is authentic but, even as a fiction, it still shows that Ficino intended to establish a historical link between his own work and that of Plethon. Ficino refers to Plethon at least four times in his writings. In an early preface to ten Platonic dialogues to Cosimo (1464), Ficino remarked that the spirit of Plato had flown from Byzantium to Florence.[21]

The fact that the Byzantine thinkers read Plato together with the *Corpus Hermeticum* explains Cosimo's interest in the Hermetic texts. In 1463, when Ficino had finally collected all the necessary manuscripts of Plato and was ready to start work on the translations, Cosimo urged him to wait with Plato and translate the *Corpus* first and at once. The collection of texts which Cosimo forwarded to Ficino had been brought from Macedonia to Florence in 1460 by a monk named Leonardo da Pistoia. It contained fourteen treatises and a commentary in which Hermes Trismegistus, an Egyptian monk, philosopher and sage was introduced as their author. Hermes was hailed as *priscus theologus*, a contemporary if not predecessor of Moses, possessing knowledge of things divine surpassing that of the Hebrew prophets and in certain respects comparable to the Evangelists. Ficino spent a few months translating the texts in 1463 and then moved on to the Platonic dialogues. Thus, he began to translate and interpret Plato with the *Hermetica* still fresh in his mind, and it is clear from Ficino's own accounts that he read Plato through *Hermetic* eyes. He understood Plato as a mere confirmation of the Hermetic wisdom. The fact that the *Corpus* was thought to have been written in pre-Mosaic times made Plato appear to be a derivation of the more ancient, and thus purer, wisdom of Hermes Trismegistus. The veneration of Hermes is an important aspect of Renaissance Neo-Platonism which distinguishes it from the original Neo-Platonism of Plotinus. While they embraced the *Chaldaean Oracles*, pagan philosophers until Iamblichus, a student of Porphyry, were relatively silent on the writings attributed to Hermes because they connected Hermetic writings with the Manichaeans and the 'Gnostics' attacked by Plotinus.[22]

Ficino's collection of Hermetic texts seems to have been a truncated version of a *Corpus Hermeticum* which originally comprised at least seventeen treatises. Some versions of the collection, which circulated between the fourteenth and seventeenth centuries, contain seventeen texts with a comment by Psellos in which he criticises the passages which discuss occult topics like astrology and magic. Because such passages are much rarer in the first fourteen treatises than in the last three, it is often assumed that the truncation was a response to Psellos's reservations.[23] Ficino named his edition after the first and most widely known text in the collection, the *Pimander* (or *Poimandres*). Another text, the *Asclepius*, is usually considered to be part of the Hermetic heritage. A Greek version of the *Asclepius* was known to Lactantius; a Latin text is referred to in Augustine's *City of God*, and a Coptic section of it was found in the 'library' of Nag Hammadi. A first printed edition of the *Asclepius* appeared in 1470, one year before the publication of Ficino's translation of the first fourteen Hermetic treatises. Later editions of the *Corpus* sometimes included all seventeen treatises and the *Asclepius*, but Ficino's *Book on the Power and Wisdom of God, Whose Title is Pimander* remained the most influential presentation of the *Corpus Hermeticum* until the nineteenth century. By the mid-sixteenth century, it had seen at least two dozen more editions and had stimulated vernacular versions in French, Dutch, Spanish and Italian.

The texts of the *Corpus Hermeticum* deal mainly with theological issues. They reveal knowledge of the origin and nature of divine, human and material being so that readers can use this knowledge to save themselves. The Hermeticists' answer to the problem of salvation is that the human individual, as the most glorious of God's creations, is animated by a divine spark and is therefore divine himself. Only very few humans have knowledge of their own divinity. The highest aspiration of all the others must be, therefore, to overcome their ignorance, to know God and to assert their own divinity. The key to salvation is to know the stages of the creative process for, taken in reverse order, they delineate the route back to the root of all existence.

The *Pimander* presents the stages of creation in a dialogue between Trismegistus and Pimander, who reveals himself as the divine *nous*, and is seen by Trismegistus as a limitless vision which is all light. When Hermes asks Pimander, 'The elements of nature – whence have they arisen?', Pimander explains how the *nous*-God, existing as life and light, brought forth a second *nous*-Demiurge, who fashioned the seven Governors, who 'envelop with their circles the sensible world'. The Demiurge together with the luminous Word issued by the *nous*-God move the seven Governors on which all the lower elemental world depends. Man was created by the *nous*-God as a being similar to himself in image and form.

When the Man saw how the Demiurge had created a world out of fire, he wished to be able to produce a work of his own, and permission to do this was given to him by the *nous*-God. This is how he entered the Demiurgic sphere. Yet, having received participation in the nature and works of the Governors, Man wished to break through the periphery of the seven circles and to know the power of the *nous*-Father who reigns above the fire. Once he broke through the spheres, Nature below was able to see the beautiful form of God. She realised that she had in Man the beauty and all the energy of the Governors, joined to the form of God, and she 'smiled for love'. And Man, having seen this form like to himself in Nature, reflected in the water, loved Nature and wished to dwell with her. 'Nature took hold of her beloved, hugged him all about and embraced him, for they were lovers.'[24] Taking on a mortal body in order to live with Nature, Man becomes the only being on earth which has a double nature.

At this stage, Pimander promises to reveal to Hermes a 'mystery that has been kept hidden until this very day'. From her union with Man, Nature brought forth the first seven men, who corresponded to the nature of the seven Governors. In this transition from Man to men, Man changed from life and light, which he had been, to soul and intellect. Thereafter, Pimander continues, 'all things in the cosmos of the senses remained thus until a cycle ended ...'. At the end of the cycle, 'the bond among all things was sundered by the counsel of God'. All living things, which had been androgyne, were then sundered into two parts, male and female. And God spoke: 'Increase in increasing and multiply in multitude ...'

Pimander then turns to Hermes and says: 'So if you learn that you are from light and life and that you happen to come from them, you shall advance to life once again'. As Hermes wishes to learn about the 'ascension' after death, Pimander explains that at death the mortal body dissolves into its elements but the spiritual human goes up through the seven spheres and loses at each sphere a part of his mortal nature and the evil it contains. Once he is only spirit, he enters into the *ogdoadic* nature and becomes mingled with the Powers. Pimander leaves Trismegistus after having invested him with power and instructed him 'on the nature of the universe and on the supreme vision'. Hermes begins to appeal to his people, asking them how they could have surrendered themselves to 'drunkenness and sleep and ignorance' when, in fact, they have 'the right to share in immortality'.

The vision Hermes receives in his dialogue with Pimander allows him to perceive his inalienable kinship with the divine world; he acquires true self-knowledge as a human being capable of moving beyond the natural conditions of human life as he rediscovers the originally independent divine element at the centre of the human being. Some treatises in the *Corpus* – such as those numbered IV and XIII – envisage this emancipating experience as taking place within the span of mortal life, while the *Pimander* holds that it may occur only after death. Choosing the 'way of Hermes', Fowden emphasises, was a 'deeply private' decision, the reward of a conscious effort and therefore not a rite of passage.[25] These efforts are driven by the Hermetist's desire for release from this world of flux and materiality.

Equating ignorance with worldly existence, some of the Hermetic texts in the *Corpus* advocate an anticosmic dualism not unlike Hans Jonas's 'Gnosticism'. However, the *Corpus* as a whole is not consistent in this regard. This lack of consistency has led some scholars to distinguish between 'monist' and 'dualist', 'optimist' and 'pessimist', 'positive' and 'negative' Hermeticism. The 'positive' version asserts that humanity's divinity manifests itself in the control humans exert over their own destiny within the cosmos. Ficino's Hermeticism was certainly of this latter kind, which celebrates the human being as a *terrestrial* god. Fowden suggested that such variations among the treatises should be considered as sequential rather than contradictory. A 'positive' view of the cosmos as good and worthy of understanding would correspond to an earlier stage of initiation when the body's needs are still great. A 'negative' treatment would suit later stages closer to the culmination of *gnosis* and liberation from the body.

The *Asclepius* gives a similar account of the divine nature of humans. Pico della Mirandola's famous *Oration on the Dignity of Man* opens with a quotation taken directly from the *Asclepius*, celebrating man as a '*magnum miraculum*, a living thing to be worshipped and honored'.[26] Man was to be worshipped because 'he changes his nature into a god's, as if he were a god; he knows the demonic kind inasmuch as he recognizes that he originated among them.' According to the *Asclepius*, man despises that part of him that is human nature for he has placed his hope in the divinity of his other part. The text also contains a striking passage in which man is presented as being capable of creating gods. The symbolism refers to the Egyptian religious practice of worshipping statues which were animated by the *sensus* and *spiritus*. The statues, 'ensouled and conscious', were filled with spirit and able to 'foreknow the future and predict it by lots, by prophecy, by dreams …', to 'make people ill and cure them, bringing them pain and pleasure as each deserves'.

The issue of magic was quite important for the reception of the *Hermetica*. Augustine, for example, acknowledged that Hermes said 'much that corresponds to the teaching of the truth' and confirmed that Hermes lived only three generations after Moses but was highly condemnatory of Egyptian magic, which for him was nothing but idolatry and superstition. He refers explicitly to the passage in the *Asclepius* in which it is claimed that spirits can be drawn into statues.[27] Augustine's censorship weighed heavily against Hermes and is partly responsible for the fact that the Latin West showed little interest in the Hermetic texts until the twelfth century. Ficino was aware of Augustine's condemnation of Hermes but was convinced that humans were able to 'draw down the life of heaven' through the *spiritus mundi* which is infused throughout the universe and to place it into statues and idols. Frances A. Yates calls this practice 'pneumatic magic'.[28] When challenged, Ficino introduced the distinction between 'demonic' and 'natural' magic. He admitted that there might have been Egyptian priests who used demonic magic, which was illicit and wicked as it invoked the demons of the stars, but Hermes Trismegistus was not one of them. From such demonic magic one had to distinguish 'world' or 'natural' magic, *magia naturalis*, which was addressed to the gods as the powers of the world. Such magic was useful and necessary, in medicine, for example. Ficino explained that, in ancient times, priests always practised medicine. Christ himself, after all, was a healer. The implicit suggestion that Christ did his wonderful works by means of magic was taken up by later Renaissance *magi*.

The *Asclepius* contains another section which provoked a hostile response from Augustine. One apocalyptic passage predicts that the glorious Egyptian religion will decline at some point. As a consequence, the gods will leave the earth and abandon Egypt, the former home of religion. The common order will be reversed. Laws will prevent acts of piety or cults of the gods. Egypt will be polluted with crimes. Darkness will be preferred to light; the pious believer will be thought mad and the impious, wise; the frenzied will be thought brave and the worst criminal, a good man. The gods will separate themselves from humanity, and only the evil angels will remain. However, the age of irreligion, disorder and confusion will end when the Lord and Father annihilates all malice, either in a deluge or in a fire. He will bring back the world to its first beauty. A renewal of all good things, a holy restoration of Nature, imposed by force in the course of time will follow.

The first one who, on the basis of the apocalypse of the *Asclepius*, honoured Hermes as a pagan prophet who supported Christian revelation was Lactantius, a Christian of the late third and early fourth centuries. To Lactantius, Hermes foresaw the ruin of the early religion, the birth of a new faith and the coming of Christ. Augustine, too, read the *Asclepius* as a prophecy of the advent of Christianity but he could not accept, of course, that Christianity was a revival of Egyptian religious magic as implied in the text. The opposite was true: Christianity was a departure from the superstition which underlay such practices. Thus, Augustine concluded, Hermes was a prophet but he owed his prophetic knowledge to the devil. He then contrasted Hermes to a true prophet, to Isaiah, who pronounced: 'The idols of Egypt shall be moved at His presence, and the heart of Egypt shall melt in the midst of her.'[29]

Ficino, finally, again ignored Augustine's reservations and read the Hermetic texts as a confirmation of rather than a rival to the Scriptures. In the introduction to his edition of the *Corpus*, Ficino writes that there are two 'divine' works by Hermes, the *Pimander* and the *Asclepius*. He was particularly impressed by the account of creation in the *Pimander* because it reminded him of Genesis. In later years, he wondered whether Hermes Trismegistus was indeed Moses. Ficino's reading of the *Pimander* is remarkable because the differences between the biblical account and the Egyptian Genesis are fundamental. According to the Old Testament, humans were indeed made in the image of God and they were given dominion over all creatures – but Adam was not created as a divine being; he did not have the divine creative power, not even in the Garden of Eden before the fall. Moreover, eating the forbidden fruit from the tree of *gnosis* was the sin of disobedience which led to Adam's expulsion from Paradise. In the *Pimander*, Man is welcomed in the Demiurgic sphere; he is allowed to be a creator, and to move beyond the seven spheres of the seven Governors. Pimander's Adam is more than human; he is divine, consubstantial with God. God's will to break the 'bond among all things' seems to evoke a sense of a loss or fall, but there is no question that the immortal parts of human's, originating from Man, remain divine and creative.

What purified the Hermetic treatises in the eyes of their readers in spite of their unorthodoxy was their alleged antiquity. If Hermes wrote the texts before or around the times of Moses – and even Augustine did not question such estimates – then they must stem from an even purer source of revealed wisdom than the Old Testament. By placing the *Hermetica* at the very beginning of a fountain of illumination flowing from the divine *nous*, Ficino was able to proclaim that an unbroken chain of wisdom and illumination led from Hermes, to Orpheus, Aglaophemus, Pythagoras, Philolaus and Plato. The idea of a theological genealogy incorporating Hermes and Plato remained influential among European intellectuals for the next two centuries.

Renaissance syncretism which thought it possible to combine Hermeticism, Platonism, Neo-Platonism, Christianity and, as I will explain below, Cabalist mysticism thus depended on the *misdating* of crucial texts. It was not before 1614 that the *Corpus Hermeticum* was shown to have been composed in the post-Christian era. Isaac Casaubon (1559–1614), one of the most brilliant Greek scholars of his time, was invited to England in 1610 by James I to comment on Cesare Baronius's *Annales Ecclesiastici*. Baronius's twelve volumes, published between 1588 and 1607, presented a Counter-Reformation view on Church history. In his polemic against Baronius, the Protestant Casaubon also attacked the notion that pagan prophets had predicted Christ's coming. In this context, Hermes was an obvious target. Although Casaubon did not deny the existence of an Egyptian sage called Hermes (Mercurius) Trismegistus who had lived before Moses, he did argue convincingly that this person could not possibly have written the texts of the *Corpus*. As he pointed out, the texts contained biblical, Jewish and Christian language and ideas. The Greek diction was too abstract to be early, and Greek etymologies and puns, he observed, were impossible in a text that was thought to be a translation from Egyptian. Moreover, the texts contained historical references and doctrines which required a much later date than the assumed date of the composition of the *Corpus*.

A similarly colossal misdating gave the writings of the Neo-Platonist Pseudo-Dionysius, a fifth-century Syrian disciple of Proclus, an almost Scriptural veneration throughout the Middle Ages and the Renaissance. Pseudo-Dionysius, who borrowed some basic elements of his theological system from Evagrius, successfully convinced his medieval readers that he was Dionysius the Areopagite mentioned in the New Testament at Acts 17:34. Taking for granted that the Areopagite wrote Neo-Platonic texts, the Renaissance philosophy must have felt confirmed in their belief in the compatibility of Christianity and Neo-Platonism. The alleged antiquity of these texts – and the fact that their presumed authors were a pagan prophet who foresaw the coming of Christ and a disciple of Paul – was important to Ficino and Pico as a justification for their attempted synthesis.

Modern Hermetic studies began with the work of Reitzenstein in the twentieth century.[30] His assertion that the religious context of the *Corpus* was Egyptian was for a long time controversial but seems to have been confirmed in more recent scholarship. According to Fowden, Hermeticism was a product of the 'Greek-speaking milieu' in the Egypt of the late second century AD. But, he adds, Hermeticism was also part of a 'wider Mediterranean whole' and enjoyed wide dissemination in the Roman empire.[31] Coptic translations made the texts available to Egyptians who did not speak Greek. Originally, many more Hermetica – that is, texts which identify Hermes as their author – circulated in the Empire. Experts sometimes distinguish between the more 'technical' or 'popular' and the 'philosophical' or 'theoretical' Hermetica. The former deal with the technical details of astrological, magical and alchemical practices which were thought to promise deliverance from disease, poverty and even social strife; the latter deal with 'salvation' in a more abstract sense, through knowledge of God and self. In addition to the *Corpus Hermeticum*, other Hermetic collections have survived until today: the Hermetic texts and fragments in the *Anthology* of Stobaeus, the three Hermetica found in the Nag Hammadi 'library', the Armenian *Definitions*, and the so-called Vienna fragments. Why and when the seventeen treatises of the *Corpus* came to be considered as forming a distinct body of writing is not clear. It is not impossible that the *Corpus* obtained its present form in eleventh-century Byzantium for purely accidental reasons after a complicated history of textual transmission.

I have already mentioned that pagan philosophers prior to Iamblichus remained silent on Hermes because they associated Hermeticism with the ideas propagated by Manichaeans and the 'Gnostics' identified by Plotinus. Indeed, the contents of the treatises in the *Corpus*, especially of the *Pimander*, resembles closely Jonas's definition of 'Gnosticism'. Jonas classifies the *Corpus Hermeticum* as 'mythological *gnosis*', as the Greek-pagan expression of the 'Syrian-Egyptian type of Gnosticism'.[32] Fowden accepts this classification not only because of an obvious affinity at the level of ideas but also because of his comparison of the 'socio-intellectual milieus' of Hermeticism and 'Gnosticism'.[33]

This affinity between Hermeticism, Manichaeism and, for example, the Valentinian school is not, however, a mere issue in the classification of ideas. There are concrete historical links which support this affinity. There are contemporary reports that Valentinus himself used Hermes as one of his sources. A sixth-century source refers to a sect called the 'Hermaioi' associated with Valentinus.[34] Bardaisan too was familiar with, and almost certainly influenced by, Hermetica, and it is probably through Bardaisan's work – or through direct contacts with Egypt – that Hermeticism reached Mani.[35] Ephraem the Syrian reports that Mani claimed Hermes as a herald of his message, next to Plato, Buddha, Zoroaster and Jesus. Fowden suggests that Manichaeism, which spread rapidly throughout the Mediterranean, played some role in the dissemination of Hermetic ideas.[36] In the late fourth century, the Manichaean functionary Faustus of Milevis argued that Hermes's supposed prophecies of Christ were of greater value than those of the Hebrew prophets.

Of some importance for the dissemination of Hermeticism in the world of Islam were the Harranians, from the city of Harran in northwestern Mesopotamia. The Harranians were pagans who resisted conversion first to Christianity and then, after the city had fallen to the armies of the Prophet by the mid-seventh century, to Islam. Following a visit by the caliph al-Ma'mun to the region, the Harranians claimed to be followers of *sabi'a*, a prophetic religion which the Quran tolerates as a religion of the book.[37] The Harranians chose Hermes as their prophet, and identified him with the Quranic Idris and the biblical Enoch. They were astrolators, worshippers of heavenly bodies, and the history of their cults may well go back to the second century AD. Drijvers assumes that the planetary sanctuary in Sumatar – situated 50km southeast of Edessa and 30km northeast of Harran – provides a link between Bardaisan and the Hermeticists of Harran.[38] In spite of the intensification of forced conversion during the ninth century, the Hermetic *Sabi'ans* held out until the eleventh century. It has been suggested that the Hermetic revival in Byzantium represented by Psellus was inspired by the dispersal of the *Sabi'ans*. *Sabi'an* sources nourished the *Goal of the Wise*, a manual of talismanic astrology better known by the name of its Latin translation, *Picatrix*. Drawing on the authority of Hermes, the *Picatrix* was notorious in Europe for its magic as interest in Hermetic practices increased during the Renaissance.[39]

The fascination with Hermeticism did not fade with Casaubon's revision of the date of composition of the *Corpus Hermeticum*. The Hermetic outlook and its practices informed Rosicrucianism and Freemasonry, and proved popular among most representatives of what Margaret Jacob called 'Radical Enlightenment'.[40] More importantly, perhaps, is its involvement in the early history of modern science. While the precise nature of this involvement remains hotly debated amongst experts, there is little doubt that the boundaries between mysticism and 'science' were far more blurred in the seventeenth and eighteenth centuries than they might be today. As is well known, Copernicus himself, in his *De revolutionibus orbium caelestium*, quoted Hermes Trismegistus in the *Asclepius* on the sun as the visible God immediately after he presented a diagram with the new sun-centred system. The sun is among the list of Egyptian gods given in the *Asclepius*, and treatises V and X in the *Corpus* contain passages on the divinity of the sun.

The scientists of the early modern period believed that they were on the verge of the (re-)discovery of a wisdom which would place humans (back) in control of their fate. The great reform proclaimed in Francis Bacon's *Great Instauration* of the sciences was meant to be a return to, and a restauration of, an ancient, innocent empiricism; scientific progress was progress *back* towards the state of Adam.[41] Descartes's scientific system was literally the result of a mystical experience. According to his own account, his *scientia mirabilis* was revealed to him in a daytime vision on 10 November 1619, and in three dreams which he had the following night. The original title of what later became the *Discours de la Méthode* promised a 'universal science capable of raising human nature to its highest degree of perfection', and thus mirrors the millenarian tinge of Bacon's 'great instauration'. Yet, while Bacon rejected Hermeticism as speculative, Descartes tried repeatedly to get in contact with the secret brotherhood of the Rosicrucians who, drawing on Hermetic and Cabalist ideas, prophesied a general reformation in which God would reveal to humanity a more perfect knowledge so that humans might understand their own 'nobleness'.[42]

Even Isaac Newton, the epitome of modern science, is not free from Hermetic influences. His unpublished manuscripts reveal that he believed that his discovery of the law of gravity and the cosmic system associated with it was a mere rediscovery of an ancient truth, presumably known to Pythagoras, and hidden in the myth of Apollo with his seven-stringed lyre. Newton ignored Casaubon's late dating of the *Corpus* and continued to study Hermetic writings such as the *Emerald Tablet*, the bible of the alchemists of his time, over a period of at least twenty years. However, in his comments on the *Tablet*, Newton interprets the Hermetic cosmogony in terms of historical sequence which places God's creation first and alchemical processes second. Hence, Newton was interested in alchemy not because he thought that humans were divine and creators by themselves, but because God utilised alchemy when he created and shaped the world. Alchemy, to Newton, could be a means of fully partaking in God's creation. Those who claimed more he attacked as the 'Gnosticks' of his times, and he included Leibnizians and Cartesians in this assault.[43]

The idea of a reformation of society through science entered the centre stage of European politics during the Puritan Revolution in England. John Hartlib, one of the leading activists in the Puritan movement, was working towards the realisation of Francis Bacon's utopia, the *New Atlantis*, in England – a project which soon attracted like-minded reformers such as John Dury from Scotland and John Amos Comenius from Moravia. Comenius (1592–1670) was a well-known reformer in Europe. He was a member and later a bishop of the Bohemian Unity of Brethren, a mystical brotherhood attached to the teaching of Jan Hus. His *pansophia* is essentially a fusion of Baconianism and Hermeticism. In Comenius's Hermetic framework, Bacon's educational reforms mutated into *the* means of universal salvation, of an inner-worldly *apocatastasis*.

Comenius contended that the novelty of his project lay precisely in its 'universal range', that it amounted to 'nothing in fact less than the improvement of all human affairs, in all persons and everywhere'. The universal provisions of schools was a necessary precondition for the 'extension of light over all men universally'. Through *pansophic* education the individual could achieve full faith, unity and knowledge; he could approach the stature of Christ and be a child no longer as in Isaiah 65:20.[44] Evans calls Comenius's vision a 'totalitarian pedagogy' because its universalism was based not on generosity but on the fact that the reform's success depended on it affecting and involving everyone. One single sick limb could easily affect another and thus endanger the whole human race. Comenius considered a reformed papacy an important instrument for the realisation of his project. Cajoling them into accepting *pansophic* principles was important because 'if we win them we win the whole world'.[45]

A first step towards the implementation of the universal reformation was the establishment of a 'universal college', in which instructors 'chosen from the whole world', 'of quick and industrious temper, of piety, warmly devoted to the welfare of the people', must be set, 'as it were, in a watch-tower to look out for the well-being of mankind'. The college had to represent and affect all levels of human existence. As the institutional realisation of Comenius' college appeared increasingly unlikely, Hartlib replaced it with a vision of a 'virtual' and 'invisible' college. The 'Correspondencie and Agencie for the Advancement of Universal Learning', or 'Office of Address', was meant to become a network of correspondences among scholars from all over the world.

The enthusiasm of the early 1640s, of course, turned out to be a false dawn. In 1660 the restoration of the monarchy passed off with remarkable smoothness. Many of the Hermetic reformers and proponents of Comenius and Hartlib's *pansophic* visions subsequently found a new intellectual and institutional home in the Royal Society of London for Improving of Natural Knowledge, which was founded in a climate of reconciliation with Charles II as its patron. Although Thomas Sprat and other apologists and historians of the Society later downplayed its links to the intellectual movement of the Puritan Revolution in order to legitimise the Society after the Restoration, there is plenty of evidence of continuity. Elias Ashmole, a well-known Hermeticist and alchemist, was invited to join the Royal Society in 1660 as one of its foundation members. Comenius dedicated his *Via Lucis* to the Society in 1668, in the hope of encouraging its members to direct their efforts towards the ultimate goal of world reformation.

In fact, the extremely rapid consolidation of the Royal Society between 1660 and 1663 indicates that a sound organisational basis must already have existed in London before the formal charters were granted. According to the account of the mathematician John Wallis, the Royal Society started around 1645 with a number of meetings in

London among scholars interested in 'natural philosophy' and other parts of human learning, and were initiated by Theodore Haak. Haak was German, from the Palatinate, and a friend of Comenius, Hartlib and Dury. Through Haak, Comenius's vision of the 'universal college' and Hartlib's notion of the 'invisible college' stand at the beginning of the meetings which were later institutionalised in the form of the Society.

The rise of the scientific movement in England therefore correlates 'extremely closely' (Webster, 1975) with the growth in strength of the Puritan movement.[46] There is a sense in which the establishment of the Royal Society *deflected* the revolutionary impulse of Comenius and Hartlib's Hermetic *pansophism*, thereby allowing for a remarkable degree of continuity from Hermeticism and *pansophia* to the 'modern' science of the Society.[47] These developments were not just an English but a European phenomenon. The Royal Society established its first charter in 1662; the Académie des Sciences in France was inaugurated in 1666, and the Berlin Society of Sciences, the Societas Regia Scientiarum, followed in 1700. For the analysis of the lines of meaning which pass through the Hermetic revival in Renaissance Europe, the role played by scientific institutions and theories in the seventeenth century thus appears broadly comparable to the role played by monasteries and monastic mysticism in deflecting the more destructive implications of millenarianism and antinomian asceticism in late Antiquity. And just as it was from amidst the monasteries that apocalypticism reappeared in the late Middle Ages, it was in the name of 'science' that *pansophic* eschatologies regained social significance through Positivism and Marxism in the nineteenth and twentieth centuries.

PICO DELLA MIRANDOLA'S 'CHRISTIAN CABALA'

The Renaissance fascination with Hermeticism was in many ways complemented, and eventually surpassed, by the attention devoted to the Jewish mysticism of the Cabala. The term 'Cabala' (kabbalah, kabbala) comes from the Hebrew *qabbalâ*, meaning 'receiving, accepting'. The word indicates that those who practised Cabala understood themselves as members of a mystical tradition which was handed down orally from Moses himself. As a technical term in Jewish mysticism 'Cabala' refers to a system of occult theosophy which uses techniques for the manipulation of numbers, figures, names, symbols and letters from the Hebrew alphabet in order to reveal the esoteric meaning and secret messages hidden in the Holy Scriptures. Hebrew, after all, was the divine language of creation, the language of the Old Testament. And the Holy Scriptures contained all grammar, all knowledge. Thus, the Cabala pronounced that its function was to hand down to its own disciples the secrets of God's revelation to Adam or that it represented the esoteric part of the Oral Law given to Moses at Sinai. It was meant to be an auxiliary science which could unfold the mysteries which were not fully or directly explained in the Scriptures.[48]

The medieval Cabala is a derivation of earlier forms of Jewish mysticism. *Merkabah* mysticism, the earliest expression of a mystical tradition within Judaism, emerged in Palestine and Egypt in the first centuries AD. According to Gershom Scholem, the growth of *Merkabah* mysticism among rabbis 'constitutes an inner Jewish concomitant to Gnosis, and it may be termed 'Jewish and rabbinic Gnosticism'. This earliest mysticism is throne-mysticism; its name derives from the vision of God's throne-chariot – the *merkabah* – from the first chapter of Ezekiel. God's pre-existing throne embodies and exemplifies all forms of creation. The celestial throne-world, Scholem explains, is to the Jewish mystic what the *pleroma* is to 'Gnosticism'.[49] Experts generally assume that there was some interaction between the early Jewish mystics and groups commonly categorised as 'Gnostic'. The documents which come from some of these groups seem to presuppose a Jewish *gnosis* in which the figure of the Redeemer has not yet acquired a central place.[50]

However, in *Merkabah* mysticism, the emphasis was still placed on the order of the cosmos rather than on the drama of its creation. Stronger speculative tendencies in its fringes came to the forefront in the medieval Cabala, and especially in the sixteenth-century Lurianic Cabala. The origins of Cabalist mysticism lie in the twelfth century in Provence in southern France. From Provence it spread to Burgos, Gerona and Toledo and from these cities to the rest of Spain. Given that Cabala originated at a time and in a region in which Cathars were active, the question of the relationship between Jewish mystics and Cathars has fascinated scholars for some time, leading some of them to make far-reaching assertions concerning Jewish involvement in the Cathar movement and Cathar influences on Jewish mysticism. Unfortunately, the scarcity of sources yet again precludes a conclusive analysis.

Because of the situation in southern France it is inconceivable that the Provençal Jews had observed nothing of the profound agitation between Catharism and Catholicism that shook the land. Narbonne and Toulouse, two important Jewish centres of the time, witnessed stormy disputes and clashes between the hostile camps, and it is precisely in these regions that the Cabala made its first appearence. However, the Cathar heresy was unable to establish itself firmly in Jewish centres such as Narbonne and Montpellier. The assumption of direct mutual influences appears unlikely mainly for two reasons.

First, Catharism entails a 'metaphysical anti-Semitism' (Scholem) in that the Old and New Testament were considered mutually exclusive. The Cathars rejected the world as the creation of Satan and the Torah as the law of Satan. Second, Jewish scholars of Provence seemed fully aware at that time of the gulf separating their conception of the world from that of the Cathars. On the other hand, given that both groups were adversaries of Catholicism, their antagonism did not necessarily prevent them from exchanging ideas on occasion. There are some significant similarities between Cathar and Cabalist doctrines but Scholem, the foremost expert on Jewish mysticism, prefers to explain them in terms of their common source in ancient *gnosis* rather than through immediate influence. While the situation made contacts between the two movements unavoidable, the question of whether the very emergence of the Cabala – as expressed in the redaction of the central text in Provençal Cabala, the *Bahir* – was due to Cathar influence must remain unresolved. Although the possibility of such a connection cannot be excluded, it cannot be demonstrated at present.[51]

Cabalistic systems distinguish between two different ways of thinking of God. One can think of God himself and of God in relation to his creation. For the Cabalist, God in himself is beyond cognition. Every cognition of God is based on his manifestation in something else, on his relationship to his creation, and not on a relationship between him and himself. The God of the Cabala is thus the hidden, unknown God, not unlike the Neo-Platonist God.

The two central texts of Cabala are the *Bahir* and the *Zohar*. The *Bahir* appeared in Provence in the second half of the twelfth century. It is an edited collection of treatises of oriental origin, though many of them had at least passed through circles of German Hasidim, an ascetic-mystic movement with ideals akin to the monastic-Christian environment in which it grew in medieval Germany. The *Bahir* uses the Scriptures not simply as a source of what happened in the created world but also as a guide to events and developments in the divine realm. At the centre of this speculation is the symbolism of the ten *sefiroth* which are divine attributes, lights and powers, each fulfilling a particular function in the work of the creation. The emanation of the *sefiroth* is a process that takes place *within* the unknown God, symbolising a wider *aeonic* realm of divinity.

For a long time, the *Zohar* was believed to be the final edition of a collection of texts composed over a long period, possibly still containing rudiments of the original mystical thought of the legendary rabbi Simeon ben Yohai from the second century AD. Scholem, however, argues convincingly that the work had just one author, Moses de Leon from Guadalajara, and that it was written between 1280 and 1286. Hence, the *Zohar* is a product of the Spanish Cabala.

The *Zohar* calls the *sefiroth* the 'ten names most common to God'. They form the various stages of God's self-revelation and self-representation: 'He is they, and they are He.'[52] The hidden God is called the *Ên Sôph* – 'the infinite', 'Him who has no end', or 'That which has no end'. Both forms, the personal 'him' and the neutral 'that', were in use. The latter, in fact, was often thought more appropriate as it imposed less attributes to the Unknown than the former. The *Ên Sôph* is the realm of absolute perfection in which there are no distinctions and no differentiations, and according to some authors, even no volition. The ultimate conclusion of such ideas was that neither Scriptures nor Oral Law could contain any reference to the hidden *Ên Sôph,* and that only mystics had received some hint of it. The mystic vision shows that the *Ên Sôph* reveals itself through the *sefiroth,* which also occur as doorways of gates through which humans can enter into the understanding of the divine mysterium. Humans are capable of this because they, like the rest of creation, are images of the divine essence.

According to the *Zohar*, the fundamental causes of evil do not lie in human sin but in developments within the realm of the *sefiroth*. The totality of *sefiroth* forms a harmonious whole which is sacred and good as long as they maintain a certain equilibrium among themselves. Evil originates in a loss of balance between the fourth *sefirah*, the mercy of God (*hesed),* and the fifth, God's power of stern judgement (*gevurah* or *din*). Once the latter is no longer tempered by the former and the quality of stern judgement tears itself loose from the quality of mercy, it breaks away from God altogether and becomes the radically evil, the dark world of Satan.

The *Zohar*'s understanding of human sin is based on its conception of the human soul as comprising three faculties: life, spirit and soul proper (*nefesh, ruah, neshamah*). *Neshama* is the deepest intuitive power leading to the divine secrets; as such it is a spark of the divine intellect itself which appears as the *binah*, the third *sefirah*. However, it can be 'realised' or 'actualised' only by the perfect devotee, the Cabalist. *Neshama*, the divine part of the soul, is beyond sin. In his other writings, Moses de Leon asked how it was possible for the soul to suffer in Hell if parts of the soul are in fact the same as God. His solution was that, during the act of sin, the divine element abandons the human being and is replaced by an impure spirit who alone suffers the torments of retribution.

Such ideas were later radicalised in the 'new' Cabala of Isaac Luria (1534–72). The experience of the expulsion of the Jews from Spain in 1492 altered the Cabalist mysticism in a significant manner. The earlier versions of the Cabala did not yet focus on the closing stages of the unfolding universe and if they did, they did so in the spirit of supererogation. However, 1492 did not bring a redemption from above but rather a most horrifying exile on earth. In response to the material and spiritual crisis of the period, Cabalism established its claim to spiritual domination in Judaism and developed from an esoteric into a popular doctrine. In this process, the consciousness that redemption and catastrophe belonged together unfolded in the messiaism and apocalypticism of the Lurianic Cabala.

According to Scholem, the 'Gnostical character' of Luria's psychology and anthropology is self-evident.[53] At the centre of Luria's system is the doctrine of the *tsimtsum*, a term which means 'concentration' or 'contraction' in normal usage but in Cabalistic parlance comes close in meaning to 'withdrawal' or 'retreat'. Luria's *tsimtsum* is an inversion of sayings from the *Midrash* which refer to God as having concentrated his divine presence at the place of the *cherubim*, the holiest of holies, so that his whole power is contracted into a single point. To the Cabalists of Luria's school, the *tsimtsum* describes the opposite process: God's retreat *away* from a point. According to Luria, God – the *Ên Sôph* – was compelled to make room for the world by abandoning a region within himself. He withdrew from this space in order to return to it in the act of creation and revelation. The first act is therefore one of limitation; God unfolds as the creator only in a second act, in which he sends out a ray of his light into the primordial space. All subsequent acts of emanation and revelation are preceeded by acts of concentration and retraction, turning the whole cosmic process into a pulsation of light which streams back into God and flows out from him. The world exists only because of God's repeated effort to hold himself back.

The first configuration of the divine light which bursts into the primordial space is *Adam Kadmon*, the 'primordial man'. From his eyes, mouth, ears and nose, the lights of the *sefiroth* come forth, although without any initial differentiation. The lights coming from his eyes, however, emanate in form of isolated points, 'punctiform lights', which are caught and preserved in special 'bowls' evoked for this particular purpose. These vessels together with their contents correspond to the first three *sefiroth*. But the light for the following six *sefiroth* – the last *sefirah* is again a special case – breaks forth all at once and through its impact shatters the vessels which were prepared to receive it. This 'breaking of the vessels' (*shevirath ha-kelim*) forms the beginning of the cosmic drama.

The drama itself has a cleansing effect – the forces of evil were mixed up with the light of the *sefiroth*, and the breaking of the vessels initiates a process whereby the power of evil can be given real existence and separate identity. When the bowls are broken the light either diffuses or returns to its source, or flows downwards where it mixes again with the vicious powers which, from then on, continue to contaminate all stages of the cosmological process. The purpose of the process is, however, to restore the original ideal order. Salvation means restitution, reintegration of the original whole.

Luria's system emphasises humanity's essential role in bringing about the end of the historical process as a return to God. The process in which God conceives, brings forth and develops himself, does not reach its final conclusion in God without human agency. Not all the divine sparks which are held in captivity by the powers of darkness are able to free themselves by their own efforts. Human beings have to complete the enthronement of God; they have to perfect the Maker of all things. Emanation and contraction are combined, via human agency, into a closed system, the *tikkun*. For the earlier versions of Jewish mysticism, *tikkun* denoted the striving for the perfection of the world; but the new Cabala considered it as a means for the ultimate destruction of the forces of evil, a process which was tantamount to redemption. The task of the Jew was to reassemble the divine sparks which were scattered in all directions and diffused into matter, and to lift them to their proper place and to restore the original splendour of human nature as God conceived it. The doctrine of *tikkun* 'raised every Jew to the rank of a protagonist in the great process of restitution'.[54]

Luria left no written legacy. When he was asked by one of his disciples why he did not set out his ideas and teaching in book form, he is said to have replied: 'It is impossible, because all things are interrelated. I can hardly open my mouth to speak without feeling as though the sea burst its dams and overflowed'.[55] There exists a written comment by Luria on a section of the *Zohar* but it does not reveal much that is specific to his thoughts. Most of what we know today about his system is based on his conversations with his disciples. The spread of Lurianic Cabalism is almost entirely the world of Israel Sarug, who between 1592 and 1598 had a tremendous impact on the Cabalists in Italy. Sarug inserted aspects of Neo-Platonism into Luria's teaching and thereby made the system attractive to the Renaissance syncretists.

By the time of Luria and Sarug, however, pre-Lurianic Cabala had already become an integral element of the syncretistic canon of Renaissance thinking. Ficino had understood the texts of Hermes Trismegistus as manifestations of the same divinely revealed and inspired truth flowing through Moses, Orpheus, Pythagoras, Plato, Plotinus and the Renaissance Neo-Platonists themselves. It was his friend and disciple Pico della Mirandola who included the Cabala in this illustrious tradition of the *prisci theologi*. Thus, Pico was not interested in pure Cabala in historic isolation, but as only one manifestation of one spiritual truth.[56]

After studies in Bologna, Padua, Florence (under Ficino) and Paris, Pico embarked on his research into the Cabala in 1486. He had a number of passages from Cabalistic texts translated into Latin by Flavious Mithridates, a converted Spanish Cabalist who also provided him with manuscripts. Mithridates, who was also known under different names, followed a common practice among Jewish converts by inserting into his translations interpolations which pointed into Christian directions, thus encouraging Pico to combine not only Neo-Platonism and Hermeticism but also Christianity with the mysticism and magic of the Cabala.[57]

The greatest expression of Pico's desire to synthesise all knowledge into one true religion was his plan to hold a public disputation in Rome in 1486 in which he would present nine hundred theses on philosophy, theology and science, which he had put together from Hermetic, Platonic, Neo-Platonic, Orphic, Chaldaean and Cabalist texts, and many other sources. His plan was to prove that these theses were all reconcilable with each other. Forty-seven of his propositions were directly taken from Cabalistic sources, and seventy-two more reflected his own conclusions from his research on the Cabala. Most striking among these 119 theses was his claim that 'no science can better convince us of the divinity of Jesus Christ than magic and the Cabala'. In the fourteenth Cabalist conclusion, Pico uses Cabalist techniques of manipulating the Hebrew alphabet in order to prove that 'Jesus' is indeed the name of the messiah.

In advancing such claims, Pico was much bolder than Ficino. His defence, taken over from Ficino, that there were two different kinds of magic, a 'natural magic' of which Cabalist magic was an indispensable part, and a 'wicked and false magic' which had to be condemned, seemed less convincing in his case than in Ficino's. For Pico also insisted that pure Cabala could go beyond Ficino's natural magic. It could go immediately to the first principle, to God himself. In his eleventh thesis, Pico described how the Cabalist, in a supreme trance, can communicate with God through the archangels in an ecstasy which was so intense that it could lead, accidentally, to the death of the body. This way of dying was called the 'Death of the Kiss'.

Rumours soon spread in Rome that Pico's theses were heretical. In response, Pope Innocent VIII appointed a commission to investigate Pico's views. In the end, a number of his theses, which were displayed in Rome but never publicly disputed, were condemned, including the proposition that Cabala was a science essential for proving the truth of Christianity. Pico replied by publishing an *Apology* together with part of the *Oration*. But, as I mentioned before, the *Oration* draws on the *Asclepius* and, moreover, contains a homage to natural magic and the secret Mosaic tradition which deals with the mysteries of the

Hebrews. His defence only reinforced suspicion. A new commission, now with Inquisitorial powers, was appointed, to which Pico, in July 1487, made a formal submission and retraction. One month later, the Pope issued a condemnation of all the nine hundred theses and their publication was forbidden. Because of his earlier retraction, Pico was exculpated. With papal nuncios still trying to arrest him, he fled to France where he was welcomed on the grounds of the reputation he had gained during his earlier stay in the city. With French royal letters in his favour, as well as with Lorenzo de Medici's continuous support, he was eventually allowed to return to Florence, where he died in 1494 at the age of thirty-one.

Two years before his death, Pico was rehabilitated. Pope Alexander VI, the successor of Innocent VIII, was greatly interested in astrology and magic and thus looked favourably at Pico's writings. In June 1493, Alexander proclaimed Pico's absolution. In addition, he wrote a personal letter to Pico in which he reviewed the entire history of Pico's case. Alexander ends by absolving Pico and his works from all heretic corruptions and addresses him as a faithful son of the Church. In fact, Pico is described as being illuminated by a *divina largitas*. The papal letter was reprinted in all subsequent editions of Pico's work. Readers were thus led to believe that Pico's Hermeticism and Cabala were perfectly compatible, as attested by the highest authority, with Christian doctrine. With Pico's rehabilitation the Holy See accepted his Cabala as a science which would elucidate and prove the truth of Christianity.

Pico thus became, largely in retrospect, the founder of a tradition which referred to itself as 'Christian Cabala'. Mainly due to the great influence of Johannes Reuchlin (1455–1522), Swabia, and the Tübinger Stift in particular, soon developed into one of the centres of this tradition in Europe. During his travels to Italy, Reuchlin met Ficino and Pico, and became the most important representative of their syncretistic Neo-Platonism north of the Alps. Because of Pico's encouragement, Reuchlin also became the first German scholar to embark on intense Cabalistic studies, drawing directly on Pico – so much so in fact that his *De Arte Cabalistica* (1517) eventually appeared in the *Opera Omnia* of Pico. For Reuchlin as well as for his many disciples, the Cabala was the residue of an ancient revelatory wisdom which, prior to the birth of Christ, introduced humanity to the secrets of divine Being.[58] It was with Christ, however, that this wisdom found its most perfect climax and expression. Hence, Reuchlin, like Pico, understood the Cabala as one of the earliest entries in the *prisca theologia*.

The ideas of Luria's 'new' Cabala were widely disseminated through Knorr von Rosenroth's (1636–89) three-volume work *Cabbala Denudata*, written as a commentary on the *Zohar*. For Rosenroth, the Cabala contained the *intelligentia spiritualis* which unlocks the hidden, esoteric truth of the entire Holy Scriptures. The presumed antiquity of the texts – like most readers of the *Zohar*, Rosenroth accepted the theory that Simeon ben Yohai was its author – seemed to underline that the Cabala was one of the oldest philosophies flowing from the same source as the Scriptures. As such it was, historically and intellectually, prior to the religious divisions so characteristic of the seventeenth century. Cabalistic studies, therefore, entailed an ecumenic mission, a return to the one and only religious truth. Rosenroth had intensified his inquiries into the Cabala after a visit to England, where he met the two leading figures of Cambridge Neo-Platonism, Henry More (1614–87) and his friend Franciscus Mercurius van Helmont (1618–99). More and van Helmont still worked in the tradition of Pico but incorporated the novelties of Luria's Cabala. The third volume of *Cabbala Denudata* was entitled 'Pneumatica Cabbalistica' and contained texts from Luria's school in van Helmont's translation together with the latter's commentary. It is in van Helmont's commentary that the term 'Christian Cabala' (*Kabbalae Christianae*) appeared for the first time in print.

In the 18th century, Reuchlin's tradition was continued by Friedrich Christoph Oetinger (1702–82), a student of Johann Albrecht Bengel in Tübingen. Oetinger would become the leading figure of the Christian theosophy of early Pietism in Germany. The Pietist movement provided the framework for a renaissance of Cabalistic studies in the eighteenth and nineteenth centuries. Like his teacher, Bengel, who had famously predicted the Second Coming and the onset of the Millennium for 1836, Oetinger was convinced that the *tikkun* had reached or was about to reach its final shape, leading to an age of messianic action which, in turn, would inaugurate the *güldene Zeit*, the Golden Age, within just a few decades. Oetinger admired and – at great risk – publicly defended both Jacob Boehme (1575–1624) and Emanuel Swedenborg (1688–1772). In Boehme, he found the Cabala in its 'highest form', while in Swedenborg, he discovered an updated version of Luria's system.

NOTES

1. Cf. Robert E. Lerner, 'Refreshment of the Saints: The Time After Antichrist as a Station for Earthly Progress in Medieval Thought', *Traditio*, Vol. 32 (1976), pp. 97–144; and Marjorie Reeves, 'The Originality and Influence of Joachim of Fiore', *Traditio*, Vol. 36 (1980), pp. 269–316.
2. My account of Joachim follows Ernst Benz, 'Creator Spiritus: Die Geistlehre des Joachim von Fiore', in Olga Fröbe-Kapteyn (ed.), *Der Mensch und das Schöpferische* (Zürich: Rhein-Verlag, 1957), pp. 285–355; Ernst Bloch, *Das Prinzip Hoffnung*, 'Freiheit und Ordnung: Abriss der Sozialutopien', in Bloch, *Gesamtausgabe* (Frank-

furt a.M.: Suhrkamp, 1977), Vol. 5, pp. 590–8; M. Bloomfield, 'Joachim of Flora: A Critical Survey of his Canon, Teachings, Sources, Biography, and Influence', in Delno C. West (ed.), *Joachim of Fiore in Christian Thought: Essays on the Influence of the Calabrian Prophet*, Vol. 1 (New York: Burt Franklin, 1975), pp. 29–91; Bernard McGinn, *The Calabrian Abbot: Joachim of Fiore in the History of Western Thought* (London: Collier Macmillan, 1985); Marjorie Reeves, *Joachim of Fiore and the Prophetic Future* (London: SPCK, 1976); Reeves, *The Influence of Prophecy in the Later Middle Ages: A Study in Joachimism* (Oxford: Clarendon, 1969).

3. See Ernst Benz, *Ecclesia Spiritualis: Kirchenidee und Geschichtstheologie der Franziskanischen Reformation* (Stuttgart: Kohlhammer, 1934); Malcolm Lambert, *Medieval Heresy: Popular Movements from the Gregorian Reform to the Reformation* (Oxford: Blackwell, second edn, 1992), pp. 189–214; Gordon Leff, *Heresy in the Later Middle Ages* (Manchester: Manchester University Press, 1967), pp. 51–255.
4. Reeves, *The Influence of Prophecy*, p. 174.
5. On the scandal of the Eternal Evangel see also Marjorie Reeves and Warwick Gould, *Joachim of Fiore and the Myth of the Eternal Evangel in the Nineteenth Century* (Oxford: Clarendon, 1987), pp. 7–42.
6. Marvin B. Becker, 'Florentine Politics and the Diffusion of Heresy in the Trecento: A Socioeconomic Inquiry', *Speculum*, Vol. 34 (1959), pp. 60–75.
7. See also Donald Weinstein, *Savonarola and Florence: Prophecy and Patriotism in the Renaissance* (Princeton, NJ: Princeton University Press, 1970), pp. 43–50.
8. Quoted in Reeves, *The Influence of Prophecy*, p. 224.
9. Quoted in Weinstein, *Savonarola and Florence*, p. 230.
10. Robin Bruce Barnes, *Prophecy and Gnosis: Apocalypticism in the Wake of the Lutheran Reformation* (Stanford: Stanford University Press, 1988), p. 56; and Reeves, *Joachim of Fiore and the Prophetic Future*, pp. 136–65.
11. Reeves, *The Influence of Prophecy*, pp. 475–6, 490, 492, 501; Reeves, *Joachim of Fiore and the Prophetic Future*, pp. 149–50; Frances A. Yates, *The Rosicrucian Enlightenment* (London: ARK Paperbacks, 1986), pp. 35, 37–9.
12. Cristopher Hill, *The World Turned Upside Down: Radical Ideas During the English Revolution* (London: Temple Smith, 1973), p. 118.
13. Reeves and Gould, *Joachim of Fiore and the Myth of the Eternal Evangel*, p. 56.
14. Reeves and Gould, *Joachim of Fiore and the Myth of the Eternal Evangel*, pp. 59–65.
15. Erich Frank, *Philosophical Understanding and Religious Truth* (New York: Oxford University Press, seventh printing 1963), p. 171.
16. Reeves and Gould, *Joachim of Fiore and the Myth of the Eternal Evangel*, pp. 2–4, 306–7.
17. Nesca A. Robb, *Neoplatonism of the Italian Renaissance* (New York: Octagon, 1968), pp. 57–89.
18. Robb, *Neoplatonism*, p. 57; E. N. Tigerstedt, *The Decline and Fall of the Neoplatonic Interpretation of Plato: An Outline and Some Observations* (Helsinki: Societas Scientiarum Fennica, 1974), p. 18.
19. On the link between Renaissance humanism and the Byzantine didactic tradition see Paul Oskar Kristeller, 'Italian Humanism and Byzantium', in Kristeller, *Renaissance Thought and its Sources* (ed. Michael Mooney), (New York: Columbia University Press, 1979), pp. 137–50.
20. Paul Oskar Kristeller, 'Renaissance Platonism', in Kristeller, *Renaissance Thought and its Sources*, pp. 50–65 (53–8) .
21. Paul Oskar Kristeller, 'Byzantine and Western Platonism in the 15th Century', in Kristeller, *Renaissance Thought and its Sources*, pp. 150–63 (151–61). See also Daniel P. Walker, *Spiritual and Demonic Magic from Ficino to Campanella* (Notre Dame: University of Notre Dame Press, 1975), pp. 60–3.
22. See Garth Fowden, *The Egyptian Hermes: A Historical Approach to the Late Pagan Mind* (Cambridge: Cambridge University Press, 1986), pp. 202–3.
23. See, in addition to Fowden, the very useful philological report in Brian P. Copenhaver's Introduction to his edition of the Hermetica in *Hermetica: The Greek* Corpus Hermeticum *and the Latin* Asclepius *in a new English translation* (Cambridge: Cambridge University Press, 1992), pp. xiii–lix (xl–xli).

24. All quotations are from the translation in Copenhaver (ed.), *Hermetica*, pp. 1–7.
25. Fowden, *The Egyptian Hermes*, p. 111.
26. The phrase 'on the dignity of man' was apparently not used by Pico but was added by later editors. See Paul Oskar Kristeller, 'The Dignity of Man', in Kristeller, *Renaissance Thought and its Sources*, pp. 169–81 (173). The quote is from the *Asclepius* in Copenhaver's translation, pp. 67–92 (69).
27. Augustine, *The City of God*, Book VIII, Chapters 23–4.
28. Frances A. Yates, *Giordano Bruno and the Hermetic Tradition* (Chicago: The University of Chicago Press, 1991 [1964]), p. 69.
29. Isaiah 19:1.
30. Richard Reitzenstein, *Poimandres: Studien zur griechisch-ägyptischen und frühchristlichen Literatur* (Leipzig: Teubner, 1904).
31. Fowden, *The Egyptian Hermes*, p. 213.
32. Hans Jonas, *Gnosis und Spätantiker Geist – Erster Teil: Die mythologische Gnosis* (Göttingen: Vandenhoeck & Ruprecht, third edn, 1964), pp. 328ff. See also Kurt Rudolph, *Die Gnosis: Wesen und Geschichte einer spätantiken Religion* (Göttingen: Vandenhoeck & Ruprecht, third edn, 1994), pp. 30–1.
33. Fowden, *The Egyptian Hermes*, pp. 186–93.
34. Fowden, *The Egyptian Hermes*, p. 173.
35. Han J. W. Drijvers, 'Bardaisan of Edessa and the Hermetica: The Aramaic Philosopher and the Philosophy of his Time', in Drijvers, *East of Antioch: Studies in Early Syriac Christianity* (London: Variorum Reprints, 1984), Chapter XI.
36. Fowden, *The Egyptian Hermes*, p. 204.
37. The Holy Quran, II, 62; V, 69; XXII, 17.
38. Drijvers, 'Bardaisan of Edessa and the Hermetica', pp. 193–5.
39. See Yates, *Giordano Bruno*, pp. 49–56, on the *Picatrix*.
40. Margaret C. Jacob, *The Radical Enlightenment: Pantheists, Freemasons and Republicans* (London: Allen & Unwin, 1981).
41. See Paolo Rossi, *Francis Bacon: From Magic to Science* (Chicago: The University of Chicago Press, 1978). Also, Moody E. Prior, 'Bacon's Man of Science', in Brian Vickers (ed.), *Essential Articles for the Study of Francis Bacon* (Hamden, CT: Archon Books, 1968), pp. 140–63.
42. On the Rosicrucian message see Yates, *Rosicrucian Enlightenment*, pp. 41–58. On Descartes's interest in this message see William R. Shea, *The Magic of Numbers and Motion: The Scientific Career of René Descartes* (Canton, MA: Science History Publications, 1991), especially pp. 101ff.
43. Frances A. Yates, 'Did Newton connect his Maths with Alchemy?', in Yates, *Ideas and Ideals in the North European Renaissance. Collected Essays Vol. 2* (London: Routledge & Kegan Paul, 1984), pp. 269–72. For details see Betty J. T. Dobbs, *The Janus faces of genius: The role of alchemy in Newton's thought* (Cambridge: Cambridge University Press, 1991), especially pp. 66–73. This work supersedes Dobbs's earlier *The Foundations of Newton's Alchemy or, 'The Hunting of the Greene Lyon'* (Cambridge: Cambridge University Press, 1975). For a summary see Dobbs, 'Newton's *Commentary* on the *Emerald Tablet* of Hermes Trismegistus: Its Scientific and Theological Significance', in Ingrid Merkel and Allen G. Debus (eds), *Hermeticism and the Renaissance: Intellectual History and the Occult in Early Modern Europe* (Cranbury, NJ: Associated University Presses, 1988), pp. 182–91. See also Frank E. Manuel, *The Religion of Isaac Newton* (Oxford: Clarendon, 1974).
44. Comenius quoted in Charles Webster, *The Great Instauration: Science, Medicine and Reform 1626–1660* (London: Duckworth, 1975), pp. 50, 114.
45. R. J. W. Evans, *Rudolf II and his World: A Study in Intellectual History 1576–1612* (Oxford: Clarendon Press, 1984), pp. 283–4; Comenius is quoted from Frank E. Manuel and Fritzie P. Manuel, *Utopian Thought in the Western World* (Oxford: Basil Blackwell, 1979), Chapter 12, 'Comenius and his Disciples', p. 316.
46. Webster, *The Great Instauration*, p. 503. To suggest a correlation between Puritanism and the rise of modern science has become known as the 'Merton Thesis', following Robert K. Merton's seminal *Science, Technology and Society in Seventeenth Century England* (New York: Howard Fertig, 1970), originally published in 1938.

Merton's work has provoked a stream of scholarship and debate. For an overview see I. Bernard Cohen (ed.), *Puritanism and the Rise of Modern Science: The Merton Thesis* (New Brunswick: Rutgers University Press, 1990). The argument suggested here, however, is quite different from Merton's. Merton argued that Puritanism provided a context of values within which modern science was allowed to flourish. In a sense, I suggest the reverse: that science, as an institution, functioned as a sanctuary for Puritan designs of a *renovatio mundi* leading to the realisation of the Kingdom of God in the form of the earthly paradise.

47. See also Karin Johannisson, 'Magic, Science, and Institutionalization in the Seventeenth and Eighteenth Centuries', in Merkel and Debus (eds), *Hermeticism and the Renaissance*, pp. 251–61.
48. For the following see Ernst Benz, *Die Christliche Kabbala: Ein Stiefkind der Theologie* (Zürich: Rhein-Verlag, 1958); G. Mallary Masters, 'Renaissance Kabbalah', in Antoine Faivre and Jacob Needleman (eds), *Modern Esoteric Spirituality* (London: SCM Press, 1993), pp. 132–53; Gershom G. Scholem, *Major Trends in Jewish Mysticism* (New York: Schocken, 1961); Scholem, *Jewish Gnosticism, Merkabah Mysticism, and Talmudic Tradition* (New York: The Jewish Theological Seminar of America, 1965); Scholem, 'Kabbalah', in *Encyclopedia Judaica* (Jerusalem: Keter Publishing, 1973), Vol. 10, pp. 490–654; Scholem, *Origins of the Kabbalah* (Princeton: Princeton University Press, 1990 [1962]).
49. Scholem, 'Kabbalah', p. 498.
50. Scholem, *Jewish Gnosticism*, p. 4.
51. For this discussion see especially Scholem, *Origins*, pp. 16–17, 197, 234–8.
52. Quotation from Scholem, *Major Trends*, pp. 213–14.
53. Scholem, *Major Trends*, p. 279.
54. Scholem, *Major Trends*, p. 284.
55. Quoted in Scholem, *Major Trends*, p. 254.
56. On the notion of the *prisca theologia* and its revival during the Renaissance see Stephen A. McKnight, *The Modern Age and the Recovery of Ancient Widsom: A Reconsideration of Historical Consciousness 1450–1650* (Columbia: University of Missouri Press, 1991), pp. 27–59.
57. Ch. Wirszubski, 'Giovanni Pico's Companion to Kabbalistic Symbolism', in E. E. Urbach, R. J. Zwi Werblowsky and Ch. Wirszubski (eds), *Studies in Mysticism and Religion presented to Gershom Scholem* (Jerusalem: Magnes Press, 1967), pp. 353–62. On Pico see also Frances A. Yates, *The Occult Philosophy in the Elizabethan Age* (London: Routledge & Kegan Paul, 1979), pp. 17–22, and the relevant chapters in Yates, *Giordano Bruno and the Hermetic Tradition*.
58. Lewis W. Spitz, *The Religious Renaissance of the German Humanists* (Cambridge, MA: Harvard University Press, 1963), pp. 61–80.

6
Lines of meaning II: Boehme, Hegel, Marx

Ferdinand Christian Baur, one of the most important historians and philosophers of religion of the nineteenth century, was the first, to my knowledge, who argued that, with the Enlightenment and German Idealism, 'Gnosticism' had acquired great social significance. In his *Die Christliche Gnosis*, published in 1835, he discusses under the heading 'Ancient Gnosticism and modern philosophy of religion' the theosophy of Jacob Boehme, Schelling's philosophy of nature, Schleiermacher's doctrine of faith and Hegel's philosophy of religion.[1] Given Boehme's influence on Hegel, and Hegel's influence on Marx, it is surprising that intellectual genealogies of Soviet Communism do not follow the route suggested by Baur more often. Eric Voegelin's work on the 'Gnostic mass movements of our time' is in many ways an exception;[2] as is Alain Besançon's *The Intellectual Origins of Leninism* (1977), which argues that 'ideology', in its various guises, is the form the 'Gnostic attitude' takes in the presence of modern science. Besançon observes how, in sixteenth and seventeenth century Germany, among the disciples of Paracelsus, Valentin Weigel and Jacob Boehme, a 'new Gnosticism' flourished 'no less luxuriously than the old Gnosticism of Alexandria'.[3] Ernst Topitsch, too, pursued Baur's lead.[4] However, these efforts remain exceptions confirming a rule. The otherwise apparent lack of interest in Baur's work in the late twentieth century reflects the relative neglect in Western political philosophy of its own powerful mystical tradition and of the manifold ways in which the latter informed modern Western philosophy and science.

JACOB BOEHME

In its own language, Boehme's mysticism anticipates the Hegelian system. At the centre of his cosmic history stands an eternal tendency towards self-realisation and self-consciousness. All life is at first dark life seeking itself; it becomes luminous only when it finds itself. Applying this notion to God, Boehme postulates an intrinsic drive in the divine towards differentiation in order to reveal itself. Boehme's God –

like Hegel's – is a *Deus revelatus*. Yet, something is revealed as what it is only in the presence of something that it is not. Accordingly, the Absolute remains hidden unless it introduces distinctions and oppositions. On these grounds, Boehme's mysticism is sometimes considered the original form of the modern understanding of 'dialectics' as the fundamental principle of cosmogony.[5]

For Boehme, God's will to reveal himself stands at the root of creation. 'Revelation' however, only occurs in relation to a knowing subject. And in the mind of the subject, revelation must be a passage from darkness to light. Accordingly, Boehme's system begins with darkness manifesting the hiddenness of God. The pure, unrevealed deity is not a fullness, but an infinite, undifferentiated nothingness, the *Ungrund*. There is no knowledge in the *Ungrund*. God must obtain being in order to become discernible. At the beginning, the Absolute is nothing but an undifferentiated totality of potentialities. As God reveals himself, these potentialities are activated, and light shines forth from darkness.[6]

Even if God revealed himself only to himself, in order to contemplate himself, he would still have to call into existence something that he is not. In other words, he would need something that could function like a mirror which, although inhabited by him, is distinct from him. This mirror is the body of angels. The hidden God begins to become the revealed God at the very moment the angels are there to contemplate him.

Thus, before creating the cosmos, God emanates a primordial heaven, a celestial earth, the realm of angels, which Boehme calls 'eternal nature'. This realm is the true abode of God, the body through which God will be born in several stages. As God desires to communicate himself, he implants into eternal nature the desire to receive him. Nature emanates from God as that which needs his love and grace. With the strength of its own desire, however, eternal nature begins to separate itself from God and hence stabilises into a body which, disconnected from the divine source of being, is extremely hard and opaque. This first body must be broken so that light may reign. A second body is then formed which has light as its substance, as its flesh. This body is the temple of God; it is a human body, the figure of the Eternal Man.

Eternal nature's disconnection from the divine is exemplified in the fate of Lucifer. As the realisation of the full measure of creation, Lucifer is the most beautiful of all the angels. But he is not satisfied with his splendour. Driven by the desire to affirm himself, he attempts to recreate himself in order to be born equal to the supreme God. However, as he returns to the dark roots of life, he plunges into darkness which closes about him, enclosing him forever. But Lucifer subdues the darkness and becomes its prince. The darkness itself is now called 'hell'.

The fallen angel occupied a space in eternal nature which, after his fall, is devastated and must be restored. This is the space where the cosmos – with Adam as its inhabitant – will come into being. But the world which God creates in order to restore Lucifer's dwelling place is not of the same quality as that which it replaces. The cosmos is a lower nature for it does not know the fullness of light which pre-existed Lucifer's fall. Still, it participates in the supreme light thanks to the sun. However, for eternal nature to become visible again in all its splendour, the cosmos must disappear.

Adam has an angel's body, representing eternal nature, but he also has another body in which earthly nature is incarnated. With his two bodies, Adam is in fact superior to the angels because he embraces the totality of God's manifestation. If angels fall and lose their bodies of light – as Lucifer did – they are plunged forever into darkness. If Adam turns away from the light, he will not plunge into darkness but will become captivated by his earthly nature without losing his angelic nature.

All developments in eternal nature are anticipations of processes in the cosmos. Lucifer's fall, for example, is mirrored in Adam's story. Adam's fall occurs through sleep. While he was awake, the brightness of his angelic nature covered his earthly body; yet, as soon as he gave in to sleep, he discovered the latter in his imagination and thereby crystallised into a mere image of his earthly nature. In his angelic body, Adam was without gender but when he awoke from his sleep, he was no more than a half, a male, and woman was born.

Humanity will, however, be restored by God's will. It is in humanity that God's works are realised. Long before they were created, humans were present in God's thought. Following Adam's fall, God places a seed in Eve's womb. This is the seed of light which is to bear fruit in the womb of Mary, who will give birth to Christ. Humanity will be restored when Christ, the model of the angelic human being, shines forth in his body of light after his resurrection. Reminded of their angelic natures, humans convert and bodies of light will multiply. The body of Christ will embrace the totality of all these bodies, each of which will be identified with him. During the last age of the cosmic world, the fullness of light will be realised on earth.

Boehme's disciples were quick to compare his work with the wisdom of the Cabala. Oetinger became aware of Boehme's work during his visit to Frankfurt in 1729. Staying at the house of Councillor Fende, who was the centre of a Cabalist group in the city, Oetinger met Koppel Hecht, who told him of a book written by a Christian and which dealt far more explicitly and directly with the Cabala than even the *Zohar*. When he asked which book this was, Hecht explained that its author was Boehme. There is also the famous case of Johann Jakob Spaeth, a Protestant Boehme disciple who assisted von Rosenroth in compiling the *Cabala Denudata*, who converted to Judaism under the influence of Boehme and van Helmont. In fact, both van Helmont and Henry More embraced Boehme's work in their studies. And for a minority of devotees it was the voice of Mani rather than Simeon ben Yohai that spoke through Boehme. His first great disciple, Johann Georg Gichtel (1638–1710), who edited all his works in 1682, accentuated the dualism inherent in Boehme's system and ended up defending Manichaeism.

Although his admirers established such links with great ease, it is difficult to reconstruct Boehme's actual sources. He was not a scholar like Ficino, Pico or Reuchlin; he was a shoemaker and claimed that his writings flowed from two revelatory experiences which initiated him into the secrets of the divine world and creation. The origins of his fame were somewhat involuntary. After his second illumination, he began to write about his experiences. In 1612 he gave his work to a visitor, Karl Ender of Sercha, who in conversation had shown an interest in religious questions. Without Boehme's knowledge, Ender had the manuscript copied and circulated. When a copy reached the chief pastor of Görlitz, Boehme was subjected to hostile questioning, censored and forced to agree to write no more. Other copies of his first work, *Aurora*, continued to circulate. For several years he kept his word and remained silent until, in 1618, friends urged him to resume writing. There then followed an unceasing stream of works, which were copied and circulated by hand amongst a rapidly expanding circle of readers and disciples. Towards the end of his life, Boehme came increasingly to accept that he had a mission. He travelled in order to look for further contacts and distributors who could support his campaign for what he called a 'new reformation'.

Boehme's writings were not only intuitive; they were openly hostile towards theologians, philosophers, lawyers and 'scholarly know-it-alls' (Weeks, 1991). Their disputes were presented as interminable, always threatening to escalate from insults and accusations of 'heresy' to bloodshed and murder. Not without pride, Boehme called himself the *Philosophus der Einfältigen,* 'the philosopher of the simple folk'. Boehme's illumination took place in an age of competition between rival theologies, philosophies and cosmologies. The universe of Aristotle, Ptolemy and Galen had lost its power to convince while the outline of a new universe was as yet uncertain. At the same time, the forces of the Counter-Reformation were gaining momentum against a bitterly divided Protestant world. The area where Boehme came from – Upper Lusatia, situated between Bohemia to the south, Silesia to the east, Brandenburg to the north and Saxony and Meissen to the west – had been exposed to religious upheaval ever since the Hussite Wars of the fifteenth century. Engaged by the new theories of nature and by issues emerging from the confessional quarrels of the time, the layman Boehme inquired into the secrets of the divine in the hope of finding grounds for reconciling conflicting beliefs. His ecumenism paralleled the syncretism of the Neo-Platonists, Hermeticists and Cabalists.

Given his disdain for the scholars, Boehme rejects their literary conventions. He does not reveal his sources or formative influences. At the same time, his life is clouded by legend. According to his devoted disciple and first biographer, Abraham von Franckenberg, Boehme acquired contemporary knowledge of science, alchemy, theology and philosophy in conversations with 'learned friends'. This is probably as accurate as one can be in this context. Görlitz was known as a breeding ground of heterodox theories and doctrines. The medical doctors of the city were mainly adherents of Paracelsian medicine. The city's mayor, Bartolomäus Scultetus was himself a Paracelsian. A renowned mathematician and scholar, Scultetus dominated the intellectual life of Görlitz. He was acquainted with Tycho Brahe and Johannes Kepler, and met the illustrious scholar and Cabalist rabbi Jehudah Löw on at least two occasions as the latter was travelling through the city. It was in Görlitz that the writings of Paracelsus (1493–1541) were collected and edited. Boehme seems to have been familiar with some of his doctrines, as is demonstrated by some analogies between the Boehmian and the Paracelsian systems. Unfortunately, although contemporaries as well as modern scholarship emphasise parallels to Hermeticism, Cabala and even 'Gnosticism', Paracelsus's sources are no less opaque than Boehme's.[7]

Abraham Behem, Scultetus's brother-in-law, was perhaps the most important mentor of the young Boehme. He corresponded with the heretical Valentin Weigel (1533–88) in 1579, when Boehme was four years old. Weigel's writings did not circulate before 1609, although Boehme might already have been familiar with their contents at an earlier date. A Lutheran pastor in the Saxon town of Zschopau, Weigel wrote a number of treatises criticising the repressiveness of the new Lutheran orthodoxy. His mysticism, not unlike Boehme's, had an anti-authoritarian tinge to it.

In his later life, after 1612, Boehme developed a close friendship with Balthasar Walter, who, according to Franckenberg, had travelled to Arabia, Syria and Egypt in order to learn the wisdom of the Cabala, magic and alchemy. In 1619 or 1620, Walter is said to have spent three months with Boehme, conferring with him at great length. In fact, in his later works, Boehme refers to Cabala twice. Apart from his conversations with Walter and possibly others – during this period knowledge of the Cabala was not unusual – Boehme could also have learned about Cabala through the works of Reuchlin, which were available to those unable to read Hebrew.

Boehme's influence cannot be overestimated. Of the four thinkers placed by Baur in the tradition of 'Gnosticism' – Boehme, Schelling, Schleiermacher and Hegel – Boehme may well be the most important. All important philosophers and scientists of the seventeenth and eighteenth centuries knew of Boehme and most of them read him. Isaac Newton read Boehme in his youth, and Oetinger compared the two, suggesting the laws of gravity derived from Boehme's *Aurora*, in which the so-called 'source-spirit' (*Quell-Geist*) represented the power of attraction and coagulation, or the self-centredness which produces rigidity. Hegel considered the shoemaker the first German philosopher.[8] After his death, Boehme's reputation soon spread to Holland, England, France and America. During the Puritan Revolution, Boehme was popular with both sides. John Sparrow (1615–65) translated and published all his works between 1645 and 1662. In 1653 Samuel Hering urged the Long Parliament to set aside two colleges for the teaching of Boehme's theosophy. Alongside Paracelsus, Bacon and Comenius, Boehme's work was found to accord with the religious, philosophical and social objectives of the Puritan reformers. Indirect links existed between Comenius's circle and the followers of Boehme.

HEGEL

Schelling was among the first to accuse Hegel of borrowing from Boehme. The accusation does not simply claim that Hegel's philosophy drew on Boehme as a source but that, in fact, there is little in Hegel's work that could not also be found in Boehme's. While the polemical intentions of Schelling's claims seem to question their validity, the recent work of Cyril O'Regan has in fact confirmed and further clarified the heterodox nature of Hegel's sources. Much of what follows in this section draws on O'Regan's findings, which clearly and convincingly identify Boehme as the single most important modern precedent of the Hegelian religio-philosophical system.[9]

Hegel came into contact with heterodox thought no later than 1795 when Schelling sent him a copy of his dissertation on Marcion. Hegel's response was enthusiastic. In his thank-you letter to Schelling, Hegel remarked that, by reading about Marcion, he had found confirmation of a suspicion he had harboured for a long time, namely that 'it would perhaps have done more credit to us and mankind if no matter what heresy ... had risen to become the public system of belief, instead of the orthodox system maintaining the upper hand'.[10] Hegel finds much to recommend in Neo-Platonist thought, especially in Proclus, and in the Christian mysticism which it inspired, especially in Meister Eckhart.

Hegel also knew of 'Gnosticism' and the 'Gnostics' to whom he refers on a number of occasions. It is striking that he refers to 'Gnosticism' – together with Philo and Neo-Platonism (Proclus) – in an attempt to establish the basic credentials for Christian trinitarian dogma. He must have felt that the revelatory dynamics of the divine sphere are much more explicit in 'Gnosticism' than in orthodox symbols. Although the overall approval rating of the 'Gnostics' is high, there are also some critical observations. Hegel objects to the way in which the divine self-revelation within the immanent divine sphere is hypostatised and therefore reified into entities – the *aeons*. Moreover, 'Gnostic' myth tends to present the opposition between the infinite and finite as irreconcilable so that it becomes impossible for the divine realm to be fully constituted totality. Hegel approves of the opposition as such because the dialectical self-revelation of the Spirit requires the material order and finitude as the antithetical counter to the infinite. But what is simply asserted in 'Gnosticism' as an ontological fact is no more (and no less) than a temporary episode in the narrative of the Absolute in Hegel. The same problem underlies Hegel's criticism of 'Gnostic' Christology, which he understands as docetic. This position is unacceptable to Hegel because he sees the human as the alienated form of the divine, with suffering and death as the extreme of such alienation. Yet, because divine knowledge is not fully actual unless it has travelled the route of finite cognition, alienation is a necessary step towards the self-revelation of the divine. For Hegel, therefore, Jesus's suffering had to be real.

Hegel's vague familiarity with 'Gnosticism' comes from August Neander's *Genetische Entwicklung der vornehmsten gnostischen Systeme* (1818). His occasional evocations of the 'Gnostics' thus refer to the thought of Basilides and the Valentinian school as presented by Neander. Just like Baur's account of 'Gnosticism', Neander's presentation does not distinguish Valentinian 'Gnosticism' from Neo-Platonism or Hermeticism so that the meaning of the word 'Gnostic' comes close to 'esoteric'.

On the grounds of both Hegel's references to Boehme and obvious structural correspondencies between their systems, however, Boehme clearly figures as the most important, if not constitutive, heterodox influence on Hegel. Hegel bought Boehme's collected works in 1811 but already had some knowledge of their contents in the mid-1790s. In his lectures on the History of Philosophy, Hegel devotes as much space to 'the first German philosopher' as to Spinoza. In these lectures Boehme's *Aurora* is cited more than a dozen times. Throughout his work, Hegel's attitude towards Boehme is positive. Even if he rejects Boehme's 'wilde and phantastic' mythological mode of expression, Hegel is fully aware that at least two cornerstones of his system were anticipated in Boehme's thought: the idea that the divine engendered the non-divine and the notion that the non-divine manifests the divine by being its dialectical counter.

At the centre of Hegel's system and his appreciation of Christianity is his vision of the self-revelatory God, the *Deus revelatus*. Already in his essay 'Faith and Knowledge', published in 1802, Hegel dismissed modern theological positions which emphasised the absolute transcendence and radical unknowability of the divine. During subsequent years, Jacobi, Schelling and Schleiermacher crystallised as the main targets of Hegel's criticism for they, in Hegel's reading, expound the view that no positive knowledge of God is either actual or possible. But according to Hegel, the Christian doctrine of revelation implies that the divine bridges the gap between infinite and finite and makes itself known. Hence, revelation is not accidental but is central to God. Hence, God is not pure, static Being or Goodness; he is movement, life, reconciliation, process. 'Spirit' is the adequate expression for a God who reveals himself in a movement from potential to actual, a God who reveals himself through process and narrative.

'Self-revelation' thus amounts to a 'narrative elaboration' (O'Regan, 1994) from an initial state of indetermination – Boehme's *Ungrund* – to a state of full determination. In this sense, Hegel is envisioning God in Aristotelian terms of potency and actuality although Aristotle himself, and the Scholastics after him, never applied this distinction to the divine. Creation therefore becomes manifestation, and although both Boehme and Hegel paid lip service to the doctrine of *creatio ex nihilo* – Boehme by speaking of the *Ungrund* as nothingness, Hegel by speaking of creation from the abyss of the Father – the actual position adopted is one of *creatio ex Deo*.

Hegel confirms Boehme's insight that 'mere light is mere darkness'.[11] Hence, revelation demands contrast and opposition of light and darkness. Differentiation within the divine – an 'immanent Trinity' – is not sufficient because, for the divine to become visible, it must distinguish itself from something that poses as non-divine, and thus follows the need for a realm of finitude, embedded in a divine history of creation, fall, incarnation, redemption and salvation. Finitude is essential as the true antithesis of the infinite, as the indispensable element of true dialectics. If the realm of the finite is supposed to be the true other or other-being of the divine infinite, it must be capable of executing refusal, of responding No to the eternal Yes of God. The Spirit reveals itself, then, in an encounter and struggle with, and through its ultimate victory and ultimate appropriation of, the initially alien world of finitude. The Absolute obtains 'personhood' in an antagonism between its (virtual) self and the world. The world is the 'narrative field' (O'Regan, 1994) for divine self-elaboration.

Hegel endorses Boehme's vision of creation as the result of a fall: 'Nature is negative because it is the negative of the idea. Jacob Boehme says that God's first born is Lucifer, and this son of Light centred his imagination on himself and became evil; that is the moment of difference, of otherness held fast against the Son, who is otherness within the divine love.'[12] The self-centring activity of Lucifer is responsible for the materialisation of the cosmos, which emerges as the 'independent' finite antithesis to the infinite. Simplifying Boehme's subtlety somewhat, Hegel considers Lucifer's involution – the othering of God – as *coinciding* with the creation of the world rather than as preceding it. As a result, the order of finitude is most definitely evil for if God is the absolutely positive, what differs from him must be negative. 'This negative appears on the side of worldly essence, of human being. This negative of God is evil, or wickedness in general.'[13]

Because Lucifer's fall is underlined with Adam's fall from grace, evil comes into being through a 'double fall'. However, in both Boehme and Hegel, the duality of good and evil is never radicalised. When viewed not as it is in itself but in the context of its purpose and place in the overall narrative of divine self-revelation, evil appears as a pre-condition of the realisation of the infinite. All dualities and opposition which occur within the narrative of this process cannot be but 'relative' in that there is always an underlying unity whereby they are bridged. Words that denote opposites do not refer to different realities but to different aspects or manifestations of a single, unfolding reality. In this context, O'Regan speaks of the 'bilingualism of the divine'.[14] Thus, because evil has a purpose, humanity's fall or the Original Sin is in effect a fall *upwards*; it is part of 'the eternal myth' of man's becoming man.[15] Adam had to eat from the Tree of Knowledge in order to become what he is.[16] Thinking this through to the end, Hegel notes that the Serpent is not a symbol of Satan, the father of lies, but a discloser of the unrecognised truth.[17]

No event in history, however negative, can therefore constitute a rupture of meaning; history does not know accidents. Even finitude and evil are authentic manifestations of God's plan. There is no suffering that is not a step towards a higher order of being and enjoyment, and no sacrifice which does not bring benefit. On these grounds, Hegel was able to proclaim that '[w]hat is rational is actual, and what is actual is rational'.[18]

The endpoint of the process is reached once the divine returns into itself. It returns to itself as the divine selfhood which unfolded in its encounter with what it is not, that is, finitude; it returns as the divine goodness which was made determinate in its struggle with evil; it returns, finally, as divine love which was rendered concrete by its partaking in the pain and suffering of its other, that is, the created world.[19] This self-encounter occurs in the thought of the philosopher who is the locus of recollection of the entire trajectory of finite experience. At that stage, the philosopher ceases to be a mere 'lover of wisdom' and becomes coincident with wisdom itself. In that Spirit meets itself in human consciousness, Hegel follows Meister Eckhart rather than Boehme. The latter believed that knowledge of the transcendent was possible but did not imply salvation. Divine selfhood requires mediation through human existence but constitutes itself independently of human knowledge. Eckhart, in contrast, was able to formulate the position later adopted by Hegel so succinctly that Hegel quotes him directly: 'the eye with which God sees me is the eye with which I see him; my eye and God's eye are one and the same'.[20]

The *Phenomenology of the Spirit* is thus Hegel's demonstration that he had reached the state of absolute knowledge – a claim whereby he, in his self-understanding, simultaneously exemplifies and confirms his philosophy. The very existence of his philosophy is therefore evidence that the Spirit is about to fully realise itself. Hegel's philosophy, in other words, entails an apocalyptic note. It is only at the end of history, Hegel explains, that 'the ill that is found in the world may be comprehended and the thinking spirit reconciled with the fact of the existence of evil'.[21] In the lectures on the Philosophy of History, Hegel uses Joachimite language as he distinguishes the age of the Father, of the Son and of the Spirit. The latter, the eschatological age, is characterised by 'reconciliation' in which faith and knowledge coincide.[22]

Although the use of trinitarian symbols for the periodisation of history does not in itself prove contact with Joachimism – especially since Hegel does not cite the Calabrian abbot anywhere in his work – there are circumstances which support the proposition that Hegel's apocalypticism has Joachimite features. Hegel may well have had direct contact with apocalyptic literature. One of the courses taken by Hegel during his studies at the Tübinger Stift concerned the Book of Revelation. It seems likely that he encountered contemporary commentaries on Revelation in Tübingen, especially as the school had recently hosted in Bengel and Oetinger a teacher and student who became famous for their exposition of apocalyptic expectations. As I mentioned earlier, Bengel in particular applied Revelation to his own times, expecting the Second Coming for the year 1836.

More important, perhaps, is that Joachimite beliefs and symbols remained popular even after the radical wing of the Reformation had died out. Lutheran Christianity as a whole tended to think of the Reformation as the entrance to a new, unsurpassable age. Boehme, who came to advocate a 'new reformation' in his later life, knew of the texts written by radicals like Weigel whose hopes for spiritual reform were disappointed by Lutheran orthodoxy. Interacting with the German mystical tradition, this apocalyptic theme survived and regained currency in eighteenth-century Pietism, where it finds Hegel. However, both Boehme and Hegel, if they can be placed in this tradition, transform the Joachimite tradition in significant ways. Joachim's trinitarian scheme concerned epochs of divine acts in the world; Boehme and Hegel's scheme is more directly about various stages of the divine as such. Joachim's scheme of history is subsumed, therefore, in German Idealism in its Hegelian variant.

MARX

For Karl Marx, the failure of the mid-nineteenth-century revolutions demonstrated that Hegel could not provide the answers to the problems of his, Marx's, times. Once further suffering could no longer be explained as the 'cunning of reason', as the price to be paid for the advancement of the Spirit, the Hegelian system itself was in danger of becoming a contemplative prison. The completeness of the system – its closure – was an achievement for Hegel but turned into a problem for Marx as soon as reality, as he perceived it, demanded more than contemplation. For Marx and the Young Hegelians, then, Hegel's total philosophy posed a serious question: how can philosophy continue after Hegel? In fact, how could people live after a total philosophy? Like many of his contemporaries, Marx compared the post-Hegelian to the post-Aristotelian phase in the history of philosophy and, accordingly, began his own philosophical endeavours with studies in Stoic, Epicurean and Sceptic post-Aristotelian philosophy. He wrote his doctoral dissertation on Epicurean philosophy and throughout his life continued to express his admiration for Epicur as 'the genuine radically-enlightened mind of antiquity'.[23]

In order to overcome the completeness and abstract perfection of Hegel's system, Marx transformed Hegel's contemplative *gnosis* into an activist mysticism.[24] For Hegel, history was the actual unfolding of the Spirit through reality, but this unfolding could not be made the concrete intention of human action even if the Spirit could use individual action as a means of advancing towards self-realisation. Marx transformed the system in such a way that humans now carried immediate responsibility for accelerating the historical dynamics. This transformation had three aspects which I call *inversion*, *demotion* and *contraction*.

The *inversion* of Hegel's system was mediated by Ludwig Feuerbach's 'anthropological' interpretation of religion as presented in his *The Essence of Christianity*. As I explained above, human consciousness was the place where, according to Hegel, Spirit would meet itself. In a sense, then, humanity represented God in his state of self-alienation and it was within human consciousness that God's self-alienation was overcome. Feuerbach reversed this relationship: *the idea of God reflects man's state of self-alienation.* 'God' was a human projection, an idealised generic human being: 'The divine being is nothing else than the human being, or, rather, the human nature purified, freed from the limits of the individual man, made objective – i.e., contemplated and revered as another, distinct being. All the attributes of the divine nature are, therefore, attributes of the human nature'.[25]

Accordingly, Feuerbach insisted,

> [T]he true statement is this: man's knowledge of God is man's knowledge of himself, of his own nature. ... Where the consciousness of God is, there is the being of God – in man, therefore; in the being of God it is only thy own being which is an object to thee, and what presents itself before thy consciousness is simply what lies behind it.[26]

In other words, human beings externalise their own nature and then deny to themselves what they attribute to God. Moreover, humans believe that they know nothing of what is ultimately their own projection. Feuerbach concludes that 'in religion man denies reason'.[27]

Looked at from this angle, Hegel's system appeared as a grandiose expression of human self-alienation. It started from and ended with the Absolute. The finite – the human being – was only a transitory phase in the development of the Spirit. Hegel's system was the most perfect, and therefore the last, expression of 'religion' as humanity's traditional symbol for human self-alienation. In the preface to *The Essence*, Feuerbach attached himself to what he called 'realism' or 'materialism'. He intended to found his ideas 'on materials which can be appropriated only through the activity of the senses', and he placed his approach 'in direct opposition to the Hegelian philosophy'. As a critique of Hegel, he called his approach 'transformational criticism'.[28] According to Feuerbach, 'philosophy' was the one true activity of the post-religious thinker. As such, it would have to start and then remain within the realm of the finite, the concrete, the particular, because there was no other realm to consider. Feuerbach thought that this method had first been suggested by 'the French' and concluded that the new true philosopher of the future would have to be of 'Gallo-Germanic blood'.[29]

Feuerbach, of course, was a contemporary of Auguste Comte, whose 'positive philosophy' was meant to supersede the 'theological' and 'metaphysical' stages in the development of mankind. Although Feuerbach was probably not aware of Comte's 'Positivism' – *The Essence* was published in 1841; Comte's project on the 'positive philosophy' was not finished before 1842 – the logical positivists of the Vienna Circle would later count both Feuerbach and Comte as their intellectual predecessors. Just like Comte, Feuerbach sees traditional religion as the residual domain of ignorance, as the realm of the abdication of reason.

Such views were not uncommon. The first half of the nineteenth century as a whole saw a remarkable proliferation of 'systems' which were designed as substitutes for 'religion'. Condorcet, Saint-Simon and his disciples, Comte, Fourier, the Young Hegelians in Germany – all offered their vast and prophetically toned 'doctrine of the age'. The Absolute, Progress, Humanity and the Universal Harmony were only some of the abstractions which were presented in apocalyptic and semi-mystical terms.[30] There was a general expectation, often framed in Joachimite language, that a turning-point in history was imminent and would lead to a further or final stage of progress in human development. The 'systems' which grew in France and Germany reflected a renewed search for the Eternal Evangel. This time, however, the key to the revelation of the new Gospel was science. Both Saint-Simon and Comte believed at some stage that Newton's theory of gravitation was, if not the Eternal Evangel itself, at least a model of what it would look like.

The view that French and German philosophy were complementary, however, seemed more popular among German thinkers than the French. Saint-Simon and Comte were only vaguely aware of Hegel's teaching. During Saint-Simonian discussions, accusing someone of agreeing with Hegel usually meant that he had grown too subtle, that he was uttering metaphysical nonsense. In Comte's new *Calendrier Positiviste*, 'Hegel Day' was the twenty-seventh of 'Descartes', the eleventh month of the year, which was consecrated to the 'modern philosophy'.[31] But there does not seem to be any serious discussion of Hegel in Comte, who, in any case, at some point in his life deliberately decided to not read books written by his contemporaries.

In contrast, French 'utopian socialism' had an important influence on the emergence of socialism in Germany. Some of the Young Hegelians considered themselves a 'new edition of the Encyclopaedists and the heroes of the French Revolution'.[32] Saint-Simon had an important spokesman in Germany in Eduard Gans, whose lectures in Berlin were followed by Marx. Marx's father in law, Ludwig von Westphalen, was an ardent admirer of Saint-Simon. Marx later tended to dismiss Saint-Simon along with Fourier and Owen as 'utopian'. This is also the view which was popularised in the *Communist Manifesto* (3. III.). However, Engels later acknowledged Saint-Simon's original genius as a social philosopher and declared that almost all the ideas of later socialists were contained in embryonic form in his theories. Engels also claimed that Marx eventually changed his negative assessment of the French thinker and spoke with admiration of his 'genius and encyclopaedic brain'.[33]

The view, however, that the French socialists were 'utopian' was widespread. In contrast to their German counterparts, French thinkers seemed to know what they wanted the future to look like, or at least they felt it necessary to contemplate in great detail how ideas were to be implemented in reality. Their social designs often incorporated aspects of social life in a characteristically encyclopaedic manner, right down to the most minute detail. The vagueness of the Germans' ideas is striking in comparison. By the mid-nineteenth century they were using the words 'humanism', 'democracy' and 'communism' almost interchangeably to describe their visions of the society of the future. For reasons I will return to soon, Marx, too, never specified in any detail what Communist society would be like.

For Feuerbach, the French-German philosophy of the future would have to follow his lead. The anthropological deconstruction of religion would turn speculative philosophy 'upside down'.[34] As a consequence, the completeness of Hegel's system becomes a mere symbol for the emptiness of life: 'The more empty life is, the fuller, the more concrete is God. The impoverishing of the real world and the enriching of God is one act'. If humans project into God what is, in truth, their own, and if God is envisioned as the omnipotent creator, then, Feuerbach concluded, the act of creation had to be at the very centre of human nature. Productive activity was thus an attribute of the human species. Indeed, 'in activity man feels himself free, unlimited, happy; in passivity, limited, oppressed, unhappy. Activity is the positive sense of one's personality'.[35]

Marx accepted this conception of humanity as self-creating.

> Men ... begin to distinguish themselves from animals as soon as they begin to produce their means of subsistence, a step which is conditioned by their physical organisation. By producing their means of subsistence men are indirectly producing their actual material life.

Humans are what they are through their work:

> As individuals express their life, so they are. What they are, therefore, coincides with their production, both with what they produce and with how they produce. The nature of individuals thus depends on the material conditions determining their production.[36]

In interpreting this insight, however, Marx departed from Feuerbach in a significant way. He was not satisfied with Feuerbach's dissolution of 'the religious essence into human essence' for 'the human essence [was] no abstraction inherent in each single individual'. The real essence of humanity resided in 'the ensemble of the social relations'. There was no 'isolated' individual who was responsible for the illusion of religion; rather 'religious sentiment itself [was] a social product'.[37] Indeed, consciousness was 'from the very beginning a social product, and remain[ed] so as long as men exist at all'.[38] Feuerbach did not see that the sensuous world around him was 'not a thing given direct from all eternity, remaining ever the same, but the product of industry and of the state of society ...'. 'The cherry tree, like almost all fruit trees, was, as is well known, only a few centuries ago transplanted by commerce into our zone, and therefore only by this action of a definite society in a definite age it has become "sensuous certainty" for Feuerbach.'[39]

The addition of history and, if you will, 'sociology' to Feuerbach's interpretation of religion led Marx to redefine the notions of 'alienation' and 'dialectics'. The individual was 'alienated' from himself (from his 'nature') to the extent to which he was unable to create himself through his work. He was alienated as soon as his work and its results ceased to be a means of self-creation and turned into the opposite, into a means of preventing the free self-expression of a human being. Once work was no longer voluntary, it ceased to be a satisfaction of man's wants and became 'a means for satisfying wants outside his work'. The work of an alienated worker resulted in his objectification rather than in his self-affirmation. 'The worker puts his life into the object; but then his life is no longer his but the object's'.[40] In a state of alienation, the work *negated* the worker.

However, such a state of alienation was not the alienation of an individual human being, the worker. Rather, Marx's sociology turned alienation into a condition that affected society as a whole.

> The propertied class and the class of the proletariat present the same self-alienation. But the former class finds in this self-alienation its confirmation and its good, its own power: it has in it a semblance of human existence. The class of the proletariat feels annihilated in its self-alienation; it sees in it its own powerlessness and the reality of an inhuman existence.[41]

The overcoming of the state of alienation was thus inevitably an act of revolution. The very form of society had to be altered. At the same time, however, this revolution entailed a change of human nature, of human consciousness, because consciousness was determined by the condition of society. The revolution was a zero-point in a double sense: it created a new society and a new man, socialist man.

Marx could not therefore nominate a spiritual élite who would guide mankind into the new realm. The revolution must happen first because it is the revolution which engenders the new consciousness. The educators themselves had to be educated, and this education coincided with the revolution. 'The coincidence of the changing of circumstances and of human activity or self-changing can be conceived and rationally understood only as revolutionary practice.'[42] Hence, the historical proof that the overthrow of the bourgeoisie was the proper method for ending society's state of self-alienation would come only after the revolution had occurred. In the meantime, this tautology allowed a tremendous amount of destruction and disturbance.

Thus, in contrast to the French 'utopians', Marx could not provide detailed descriptions of his ideal society. Any design proposed prior to the revolution was still contaminated by both the wrong state of society and the wrong consciousness. Only the revolution would show what Communist society was like. At present, the vision of the future was nothing but the negative of the present. Communism represented the positive in the form of the negation of the negation.[43]

With the inversion of Hegel, the notion of 'dialectics' became problematic. In his *Principles of the Philosophy of the Future* (1843), Feuerbach uses the term 'dialectics' only once: 'The true dialectic is not a monologue of a solitary thinker with himself; it is a dialogue between I and thou.'[44] Human beings were asked to turn their eyes away from their projections, from God, and to make *other* human beings, their neighbours, the object of adoration. Marx, too, occasionally spoke of the alienation that existed *between* members of society.[45] But he did not restrict the realm of dialectics to social relationships. Neither did he transform the Hegelian dialectics into a dialectics of nature. As David McLellan observes, Marx never used the term 'dialectical materialism', which was first used by Joseph Dietzgen in the 1870s and later popularised by Plekhanov, Lenin's teacher.[46] For Marx, dialectics was not the unfolding or activity of a system; rather, it was the interaction *between* two equally real poles within a system. The dialectic of historical praxis was the dialectic between human existence and nature or, in other words, the dialectic of metabolism.

The result of historical praxis was, then, the overcoming of the antagonism between human existence and nature. Communism was 'the true solution of the struggle between existence and essence, between objectification and self-affirmation, between freedom and necessity, between individual and species. It [was] the solution to the riddle of history and knows itself to be this solution'.[47] The realm of freedom would be characterised by a 'rational regulation of [man's] metabolism with nature'. Instead of being dominated by the necessities of metabolism, metabolism would be brought under 'communal control'. The problems of metabolism were to be solved with a minimum of effort and under conditions that would satisfy the dignity of human nature. The realm of freedom therefore still had its necessities, but society would be in control of them. Nevertheless, beyond such necessity, there began 'the unfolding of human forces that can be considered an end in itself.' Only there began 'the true realm of freedom – which however can only blossom out of the realm of necessity as its basis'.[48] The ultimate purpose of the revolution and the ultimate endpoint of dialectical metabolism was to allow humanity to reach this realm of freedom, the realm beyond metabolism.

The realm of freedom was to be inhabited by the 'total individual'. This individual could not be reduced to one and only one mechanistic task, but he could 'become accomplished in any branch he wishes' for

society regulate[d] the general production and thus ma[de] it possible for [him] to do one thing today and another tomorrow, to hunt in the morning, fish in the afternoon, rear cattle in the evening, criticise after dinner, just as [he had] a mind, without ever becoming hunter, fisherman, shepherd or critic.[49]

In the Afterword to the second German edition of the first volume of *Capital*, Marx wrote that his 'dialectical method' not only was different from the Hegelian method, but was 'its direct opposite'. Under the name of 'the Idea', Hegel had transformed the process of thinking into 'an independent subject' and then presented it as 'the demiurgos of the real world', which was only the 'external, phenomenal form of "the Idea"'. Marx praised Hegel for having been the first to present dialectic in a comprehensive manner. The greatness of the *Phenomenology* lay in its 'dialectic of negativity as the moving and creating principle'. However, Hegel had mystified dialectic; with him it was 'standing on its head'. It had to be 'turned right side up again' in order to 'discover the rational kernel within the mystical shell'. With Marx, 'on the contrary, the ideal is nothing else than the material world reflected by the human mind, and translated into forms of thought'.[50]

On the basis of Feuerbach's inversion of Hegel, Marx constructed his system as a *contraction* of Hegel's system. The visible world was not 'just' on one side in the dialectical process, as the negation of the Absolute, but both sides of the process were immanent. The world was not the expression of the dialectics of the Spirit, but it was the place where the whole dialectical process took place as historical praxis. The movement of the intellect in the consciousness of the empirical self became the ultimate source of knowledge for the understanding of the universe. Faith and the Spirit were 'expressly excluded as an independent source of order in the soul'.[51] Ironically, the purpose of Marx's exercise was not altogether different from Hegel's original intention, namely to restore the relevance of reality. Hegel wanted to achieve this by presenting world history as an expression of the development of Absolute Spirit; Marx, in contrast, would not even allow for the devaluation which seemed, at least to him, implicit in the opposition of Spirit and world.

But, arguably, Marx not only misunderstood Hegel's intentions, he also misunderstood Hegel's problem. Hegel wanted to be a philosopher and he knew that the problem of philosophy was the nature of reality. Empirical reality is either a disorderly flux of events or it has a discernible order, an element of non-arbitrariness. If the latter is true, as philosophy assumes, then the philosopher faces the task of giving an account of the relationship between reality and its order, as well as of the source of order and of the status of elements of reality which do not fit into that order. Hegel's 'philosophy' was meant to be the final answer to these questions to conclude the philosophical quest but, in a sense, it still addressed the question. In the way in which he constructs his system, Marx not only inversed Hegel he also denied the meaningfulness of Hegel's problem of reality. Hence, the Marxian position is not anti-Hegelian, it is anti-philosophical.[52]

Marx made this refusal explicit. Questions about the nature of reality were not to be answered but to be rejected as a product of abstraction. Far more important than these questions was to ask how one came to pose them.

> When you inquire about the creation of the world and man, then you abstract from man and the world. ... Do not think, do not ask me questions, for immediately you think and ask, your abstraction from the being of nature and man has no meaning.[53]

It is important to realise that, in spite of inversion and contraction, the Marxian system inherited its architecture from the Hegelian system. Putting a circle 'on its head' still produces a circle. But inversion and contraction placed this architecture in an entirely immanent framework. Hence, where Hegel offered the *Phenomenology*, Marx and Engels offered the *Communist Manifesto*. The *Manifesto* is not an outline of the future Communist society. It does not make concrete programmatic demands for changing the actual state of things. In truly Hegelian fashion, the change is built into actuality. The *Manifesto* claimed to reveal the actual state of society and suggested that the actual tendencies inherent in society are about to be carried to their full realisation.

> The theoretical conclusions of the Communists [were] in no way based on ideas or principles that have been invented, or discovered, by this or that would-be universal reformer. They merely express[ed], in general terms, actual relations springing from ... a historical movement going on under our very eyes.[54]

The *Manifesto* both explained and exemplified the task of those who drafted it. The task of the Communists was to bring the march of history into the consciousness of the people and *thereby* to advance it.

Implicit in the inversion and contraction of Hegel's system was its *demotion* from first to second place in the dialectics of history. Hegel was not, after all, the 'synthesis' and endpoint of the dialectical process. Rather, his system was the most comprehensive 'antithesis'. In its perfection, it opposed and negated human existence and the world. The *Communist Manifesto* could not evoke from one day to the other the great transfiguration envisioned by Marx. It functioned as a call for the organisation of the forces which would eventually execute the inevitable revolution, the great cataclysmic self-transformation of society. Hence, the only reason why Marx could not claim to have reached the endpoint of history was that, according to his system, the ultimate climax was a matter of action and practice rather than theory.

Once the Revolution had taken place and the Communists had seized power in a major country, the system was put to the test of fulfilment. But as the realm of freedom was not forthcoming, emphasis shifted from the ultimate end of the Revolution to the tactical necessities of its preparation. The distinction of the two phases of Communism, of which the first, the actual one, could run indefinitely into the future, belongs in the context of this transition from eschatology to conservation and to the scholasticism that goes with it. Marx's system proved to be very flexible in this game of tactics. As I explained before, the change of consciousness which was to inaugurate the realm of freedom was expected to occur as a side-effect of the experience of the Revolution itself. In this sense, the ultimate end of the Revolution was beyond preparation. Hence, the politics of preparation was not required to promote the end of the Revolution – the realm of freedom – but only to promote the Revolution itself. Everything was possible and all atrocities justifiable, then, on the route towards freedom.[55]

NOTES

1. Ferdinand Christian Baur, *Die Christliche Gnosis oder Die Christliche Religionsphilosophie in ihrer geschichtlichen Entwicklung* (Tübingen: Osiander, 1835), pp. 557–738.
2. Eric Voegelin, 'Religionsersatz: Die Gnostischen Massenbewegungen unserer Zeit', *Wort und Wahrheit*, 15: 1 (1960), pp. 5–18; an English translation by W. J. Fitzpatrick is in Voegelin, *Science, Politics and Gnosticism* (Chicago: Regnery Gateway, 1968). For Voegelin's broader argument see in particular Voegelin, *From Enlightenment to Revolution* (ed. by John H. Hallowell), (Durham, NC: Duke University Press, 1975).
3. Alain Besançon, *The Intellectual Origins of Leninism* (trans. Sarah Matthews), (Oxford: Basil Blackwell, 1981 (1977)), pp. 18, 38.
4. Ernst Topitsch, 'Marxismus und Gnosis' in Topitsch, *Sozialphilosophie zwischen Ideologie und Wissenschaft* (Berlin: Luchterhand, third edn, 1971).
5. See, for example, Józef Piórczynski, 'Jakob Böhme als Vorläufer der Hegelschen Absoluteslehre', in *Reports on Philosophy*, Vol. 9 (1985), pp. 33–9.
6. On Boehme's theosophy and his background see Pierre Deghaye, 'Jacob Boehme and His Followers', in Antoine Faivre and Jacob Needleman (eds), *Modern Esoteric Spirituality* (London: SCM Press, 1993), pp. 210–47; Pierre Deghaye, 'Jakob Böhmes Theosophie: die Theophanie in der ewigen Natur', in Peter Koslowski (ed.), *Gnosis und Mystik in der Geschichte der Philosophie* (Zürich: Artemis, 1988), pp. 151–67; Ingrid Merkel, 'Aurora, or The Rising Sun Allegory: Hermetic Imagery in the Work of Jakob Boehme', in Ingrid Merkel and Allen G. Debus (eds), *Hermeticism and the Renaissance: Intellectual History and the Occult in Early Modern Europe* (Cranbury, NJ: Associated University Presses, 1988), pp. 302–10; Arthur Versluis, 'Christian

Theosophy and Ancient Gnosticism', in *Studies in Spirituality*, Vol. 7 (1997), pp. 228–41; David Walsh, *The Mysticism of Innerworldly Fulfillment: A Study of Jacob Boehme* (Gainesville: University Presses of Florida, 1983); Andrew Weeks, *Boehme: An Intellectual Biography of the Seventeenth-Century Philosopher and Mystic* (New York: SUNY Press, 1991); Gerhard Wehr, *Jakob Böhme* (Reinbek: Rowohlt, 1971).

7. See, for example, Walter Pagel, *Paracelsus: An Introduction to Philosophical Medicine in the Era of the Renaissance* (Basel: Karger, 1985), pp. 203–343; and Andrew Weeks, *Paracelsus: Speculative Theory and the Crisis of the Early Reformation* (New York: SUNY Press, 1997).
8. G. W. F. Hegel, *Lectures on the History of Philosophy Vol. III* (trans. E. S. Haldane and Frances H. Simson), (London: Routledge & Kegan Paul, 1963), pp. 188–216 (188).
9. Cyril O'Regan, *The Heterodox Hegel* (New York: SUNY Press, 1994).
10. Hegel to Schelling [Letter 14], 30 August 1795, *Hegel: The Letters* (trans. Clark Butler and Christine Seiler), (Bloomington: Indiana University Press, 1984), p. 43.
11. Hegel, *Logic (Part One of the Encyclopaedia of the Philosophical Sciences)*, (trans. by William Wallace), (Oxford: Oxford University Press, 1968 (repr. from the second edn, 1892)), §36, p. 74.
12. Hegel, *Philosophy of Nature (Part Two of the Encyclopaedia of the Philosophical Sciences)*, (trans. A. V. Miller), (Oxford: Clarendon, 1970), §248, p. 19.
13. Hegel, *Lectures on the Philosophy of Religion Vol. I* (ed. Peter C. Hodgson), (Berkeley: University of California Press, 1984), p. 194.
14. O'Regan, *Heterodox Hegel*, p. 145.
15. Hegel, *The Philosophy of History* (trans. J. Sibree), (New York: Dover Publications, 1956), pp. 321–2.
16. Hegel, *Philosophy of Nature*, §246, p. 9.
17. Hegel, *Logic*, §24, pp. 54–7.
18. Hegel, *Elements of the Philosophy of Right* (ed. Allen W. Wood, trans. H. B. Nisbet), (Cambridge: Cambridge University Press, 1991), p. 20.
19. See O'Regan, *Heterodox Hegel*, p. 295.
20. Hegel, *Lectures on the Philosophy of Religion Vol. I*, p. 347.
21. Hegel, *The Philosophy of History*, p. 15.
22. Hegel, *The Philosophy of History*, p. 345.
23. Quoted in David McLellan, *Karl Marx: A Biography* (London: Papermac, 1995), p. 31.
24. For the following see Sidney Hook, *From Hegel to Marx* (Ann Arbor: The University of Michigan Press, 1966); Topitsch, 'Marxismus und Gnosis'; Robert Tucker, *Philosophy and Myth in Karl Marx* (Cambridge: Cambridge University Press, second edn, 1972); Eric Voegelin, 'The Formation of the Marxian Revolutionary Idea', *The Review of Politics*, 12: 3 (July 1950), pp. 275–302; Voegelin, 'Marx: Inverted Dialectics', pp. 240–72, and 'The Genesis of Gnostic Socialism', pp. 273–302, both in Voegelin, *From Enlightenment to Revolution*.
25. Ludwig Feuerbach, *The Essence of Christianity* (trans. George Eliot), (New York: Harper Torchbooks, 1957), p. 14.
26. Feuerbach, *The Essence of Christianity*, p. 230.
27. Feuerbach, *The Essence of Christianity*, p. 27.
28. Feuerbach, *The Essence of Christianity*, p. xxxiv.
29. Quoted in McLellan, *Marx*, p. 62.
30. Cf. D. G. Charlton, *Positivist Thought in France During the Second Empire 1852–1870* (Oxford: Clarendon, 1959); Frank E. Manuel, *The New World of Henri Saint-Simon* (Cambridge, MA: Harvard University Press, 1956); Frank E. Manuel, *The Prophets of Paris* (Cambridge, MA: Harvard University Press, 1962); David McLellan, *The Young Hegelians and Karl Marx* (London: Macmillan, 1969).
31. Auguste Comte, *System of Positive Polity or Treatise on Sociology: Instituting the Religion of Humanity*, Vol. 4 (New York: Franklin, 1966), p. 349.
32. McLellan, *Young Hegelians*, pp. 33–4, 37–40.
33. Manuel, *The New World of Saint-Simon*, pp. 2, 371.
34. Quoted in Tucker, *Philosophy and Myth*, p. 86.

35. Feuerbach, *The Essence*, pp. 217–18.
36. From *The German Ideology*, in David McLellan (ed.), *Karl Marx: Selected Writings* (Oxford: Oxford University Press, 1977), pp. 159--91 (160–1).
37. *Theses on Feuerbach*, in McLellan (ed.), *Karl Marx: Selected Writings*, pp. 156–8 (157).
38. *The German Ideology*, in McLellan (ed.), *Selected Writings*, p. 167.
39. *The German Ideology*, in McLellan (ed.), *Selected Writings*, p. 174.
40. For a list of typical quotations from Marx on alienation see Voegelin, 'Marx: The Genesis of Gnostic Socialism', p. 286.
41. Marx, *The Holy Family*, in *Selected Writings*, pp. 131–55 (134).
42. Marx, *Theses on Feuerbach*, in *Selected Writings*, p. 156.
43. Marx, 'Private Property and Communism' (from the 1844 Manuscripts), in *Selected Writings*, pp. 87–96 (96).
44. Ludwig Feuerbach, *Principles of the Philosophy of the Future* (trans. M. H. Vogel), (New York: Bobbs-Merrill, 1966), §62, p. 72.
45. For example, Marx, 'Alienated Labour' (from the 1844 Manuscripts), in *Selected Writings*, pp. 77–87 (84).
46. David McLellan, *The Thought of Karl Marx* (London: Macmillan, third edn, 1995), p. 120n.
47. Marx, 'Private Property and Communism', p. 89.
48. Quoted in Voegelin, 'Marx: Inverted Dialectics', pp. 243–4.
49. Marx, *The German Ideology*, in *Selected Writings*, p. 169.
50. Marx, 'Critique of Hegel's Dialectic and General Philosophy' (from the 1844 Manuscripts), in *Selected Writings*, pp. 96–109 (101); Afterword (1872) to the second edition of *Capital*, in *Selected Writings*, pp. 418–21 (420).
51. Voegelin, 'The Genesis of Gnostic Socialism', p. 273.
52. This is brilliantly discussed in Voegelin, 'Marx: Inverted Dialectics', p. 257. See also Peter Stern, 'Marx's Critique of Philosophy', in *Interpretation*, 5: 3 (Spring 1976), pp. 266–87.
53. Marx, 'Private Property and Communism', p. 95.
54. Marx, *Communist Manifesto*, in *Selected Writings*, pp. 221–46 (231).
55. Cf. Voegelin, 'Marx: Inverted Dialectics', p. 246.

7

Lines of meaning III: The Third Rome against the New World

The previous chapter has brought us to the recent past and the present. The manner, however, in which the 'Manichaean' line of meaning informed the political configuration of the Cold War deserves further exploration. In this chapter, I will therefore present in more detail how the ideas, events and people encountered so far were present in the minds of those who shaped, and participated in, the great ideological conflict of the twentieth century. However, my argument is not that these ideas characterise Soviet and American self-understandings in full. In the United States, especially, rival self-interpretations were occasionally able to find an audience and influence political leaders. Nevertheless, the dynamics of the conflict elevated to the centre stage of world politics an opposition of systemic outlooks on the world which *both* connected to the line of meaning outlined in the preceding chapters. The spiritual underpinnings of these outlooks are largely responsible for their totality, which, in turn, soon evoked the spectre of a man-made 'nuclear apocalypse'. The ensuing drama quickly overshadowed and obscured the conflict's spiritual aspects.

BOEHME IN RUSSIA

Modern Western mysticism and German Idealism influenced Russian spirituality and thought in a profound manner. This influence goes back, again, to Jacob Boehme, who had many followers in the flourishing German community in Moscow in the late seventeenth century. By the second quarter of the eighteenth century, Boehme's theosophy had gained some popularity even amongst ecclesiastical circles in Russia, advancing mainly through the mediation of German Pietism.[1] The latter had one of its most renowned centres at the University of Halle where August Francke and later his son, Gotthilf Francke, embarked on a long-range project of disseminating Pietist beliefs – and especially their foundation in Boehme's mysticism – into the Tsarist Empire.

The impact of German Pietism was strongly felt in Russian monasteries and theological schools. From there, it blossomed out into the intellectual activities of Russian Freemasonry, which became the most effective vehicle for the Pietism and esotericism of the Enlightenment. After the 'quasi-Reformation' (Besançon, 1977) imposed 'from above' by Peter the Great, large parts of the population were increasingly unable to take the official Church seriously. While some simply deserted the patriarchal Church, others joined the growing multitude of anti-hierarchical, illuminist sects, which were not altogether different in their nature from the sects of Protestant Europe. The nobility and the civil service tended to turn to Pietism and esotericism so that Freemasonry eventually counted as its members almost anybody who was anybody in Russia. In the 1780s, after they had followed English and Swedish models for most of the 1770s, the Russian Masons formed a close association with the Berlin lodge of the 'Three Globes', which was devoted to theosophic mysticism.

The movement suffered a brief setback under Catherine the Great, who suppressed Freemasonry in 1792, only in order to re-emerge, now with official backing, in a new wave of mystical study and writing in the epoch of Alexander I. Alexander himself studied Swedenborg, Boehme and his disciples Gottfried Arnold (1666–1714) and Claude de Saint-Martin (1743–1803), and remained for a long time an active supporter of international Pietism. When Alexander turned to a stricter Orthodoxy towards the close of his life, the Holy Synod decreed a suppression and confiscation of the works of Boehme and related mystics. Some of the secret lodges dedicated to the study of Boehmist theosophy, such as Alexander Labzin's 'Dying Sphinx', were closed in 1822. Interest in Boehme and theosophy did not fade, though, even if greater caution had to be exercised in the study of him and the dissemination of his and his disciples' writings.

At the same time, Russian intellectuals were captivated by the new developments in philosophical Idealism in Germany, especially by Hegel and Schelling. This new intellectual current also allowed a more scholarly return to Boehme and his school as its most important spiritual foundation. Vladimir Odoevsky (1804–69), the founder of the 'Society of Wisdom-Lovers', a group of intellectuals devoted to the study of Schelling and like-minded philosophers, was himself a convinced theosophist and owner of a sizeable library of the proscribed works of Boehme and Saint-Martin. Another member of the circle, Stepan P. Shevyrev (1806–64), who subsequently became a distinguished historian of Russian literature, was profoundly influenced by Boehme because of his studies in Munich under Franz von Baader (1765–1841), one of the last great disciples of Boehme in Germany who was widely known by his work.

The most prominent member of Odoevsky's circle was Ivan Kireyevsky (1806–56), who would later become one of the main representatives of Slavophilism. By the mid-1830s, after he had gained an impressive store of theosophic and romantic knowledge, Kireyevsky accidentally discovered that certain theological concepts used by the Eastern Patristic writers resembled the ideas of Schelling and his other favourite authors. This discovery allowed the Slavophiles to pose as the true and only descendents of a religious tradition which, they claimed, went back to the Greek Church Fathers of late Antiquity. The Fathers' spiritual heritage had been temporarily obscured by the violent reforms carried out by Peter the Great and his successors, but was newly incarnated in the Slavophile movement. Its adherents were consequently ardent readers of the *Philokalia*, a collection of texts written between the fourth and the fifteenth centuries by what were considered spiritual masters of the Orthodox Christian tradition. One of its major pieces is the 'One Hundred Chapters' of the *Praktikos* by Evagrius. First published in Venice in 1782, a Slavonic translation of the *Philokalia* followed just nine years later.

Topitsch's suggestion, referred to earlier, that the popularity of Hegel and Schelling among the *intelligentsia* ought to be seen in the context of an Orthodox-Evagrian spirituality must therefore be slightly revised. For the Slavophiles at least, it was not Evagrius who prepared their reception of Schelling but rather their reading of Schelling and Boehmian theosophy which made them rediscover Maximus the Confessor and Evagrius.

Kireyevsky's philosophy distinguished between two types of social bonds. The first, based on external coercion, characterised Latin and Germanic societies; the second was founded on accord, harmony, a shared faith and love, and belonged to the Russian people. This distinction between a 'mechanical', coercive and 'external' bond and a 'genuine', mutual love is also discussed by Franz von Baader, one of the first to suggest that Divine Providence had protected the Russian Church and the Russian people from the destructive influence from the West. At the end of his life, Baader, who had earlier been given the task of preparing a textbook of religious instruction for the Russian clergy, wrote to Minister Uvarov that Russia remained the last bastion of the true bond of humanity, the only power which could advance a spiritual renaissance in Europe. In contrast to the corruption of the West, to its 'iron barriers of unchangeable social classes' and to the disdain and jealousy between them, the mysterious depth of the Russian people would ensure the survival of the true spirit of *communitas* and conciliation which his contemporary Aleksei Khomyakov (1804–60) had called *sobornost.*[2] Therefore, given the corruption elsewhere, Russia's interests coincided with the highest interests of humanity as a whole.

A theosophic background was not a distinct feature of Slavophilism. For example, Alexander Herzen (1812–70), at one point an outspoken critic of Slavophile beliefs and supporter of the 'Westernisers', had a profound knowledge of Boehme and related mystics. In his reading of Boehme during his forced stay at Viatka (1835–6), Herzen received encouragement from his fellow exile and former member of the 'Dying Sphinx', Alexander L. Vitberg (1787–1855).

Perhaps the most important impact of Boehme and theosophy on Russian thought occurred through Vladimir Sergeevich Solovyov (1853–1900). Through his studies in Moscow, Solovyov had come in contact with theosophic literature, especially Boehme, Swedenborg and Paracelsus. As he realised that prominent writers such as Gichtel, Arnold and even Saint-Martin were all followers of Boehme, his respect for the shoemaker increased. In his treatises of the late 1870s, Solovyov acknowledged that his own religious and philosophical views paralleled the most important insights of the Boehmian school. Solovyov's Boehmian speculations played a leading role in the *intelligentsia*'s turn towards idealism and mysticism in the late nineteenth century, long after the demise of Slavophilism. Nicolai A. Berdiaev (1874–1948), for example, became one of the most important champions of Boehme in Russia and Europe.

Solovyov's theosophy envisioned how humanity could resume its ideal nature and domination over the rest of creation and thereby reincarnate the divine Sophia in the world through mystic-artistic activity. At the conclusion of this process of *apocatastasis*, Sophia would have reabsorbed the World-Soul which had been her antagonist in the fallen world. In a radical transformation, the humans were asked to close the circle of time and become again the creators of themselves and their world. These ideas had a significant influence on leading figures of Russian Marxism such as Alexander Bogdanov and Anatoly Lunacharsky. Lenin was also affiliated with their circle for some years. Bogdanov and Lunacharsky were particularly concerned with resolving the apparent contradiction between Boehmian 'idealism' *à la* Solovyov and Marxist materialism. For this purpose they drew on the work of Richard Avenarius and Ernst Mach, one of the ancestors of the Vienna Circle. Arguing that attributes of the material world such as colour, shape and texture are conferred on objects by the human mind, Mach attempted to eliminate the dualism between the spiritual and physical worlds which, for him, dominated the natural sciences. Lenin, however, was unable to see anything but 'idealism' and 'solipsism' in positions which did not apodictically presuppose the materialism of Feuerbach, Marx and Engels. After reading Bogdanov, he complained that he 'became frenzied with indignation' out of fear that the Bolsheviks might draw their understanding of dialectics from 'the putrid well of some French 'positivists' or other'.[3]

Crucial to Lenin's formation as a thinker was his reading of Nicholas Chernyshevsky (1828–89), the main inspiration behind the Enlighteners of the 1860s in Russia. As the revolutionary mood gained momentum Chernyshevsky grew into the role of the intellectual leader of the radical camp including revolutionary activists such as Shelgunov, Mikhailov and Utin. In 1862 he was arrested and condemned to fourteen years' hard labour and banishment for life to Siberia. While still in prison, he wrote his famous novel *What is to be done? Stories about New People* (1862), which paints an idealised portrait of a generation of 'new men', guided by 'rational egoism' which identifies self-interest with the interests and welfare of society as a whole. The fact that Lenin encountered Chernyshevsky shortly after his brother's execution no doubt intensified the reading experience. According to his wife's memoirs, Lenin was able to recall the work in every detail. The most important of all his works in historical influence, *What is to be done?* (1902), was named after Chernyshevsky's novel.

Like many other members of his generation, Lenin acknowledged that reading Chernyshevsky transformed his 'whole outlook' and provided 'inspiration for a lifetime'. He learned not only that 'every right-thinking and really honest man must be a revolutionary' but also 'what a revolutionary must be like, what his principles must be, how he must approach his aim, and what methods he should use to achieve it'.[4] Chernyshevsky's highest philosophical authority was Feuerbach, from whom he took over the fusion of materialism and anthropocentrism. He was also one of the first thinkers to formulate a general theory of accelerated social change which did not draw on capitalist methods, thereby allowing for the possibility that Russia could bypass the capitalist stage on the route towards socialism. In spite of some important doctrinal differences, the Chernyshevsky tradition was later continued, in the 1870s, by the revolutionary Populists, the *narodniki*, who blended ideas on the special and exceptional development of Russia with the remnants of Slavophilism.

THE THIRD ROME

Solovyov formulated his views on the special mission of the Slavs and the Russian people in terms of the concept of the 'Third Rome'. He knew Auguste Comte's conception of the three stages in the development of knowledge in history but, drawing on Boehme, his understanding of history was far more spiritual and religious. Solovyov believed firmly in the progressive work of the Trinity throughout history. The historical movement whereby one stage was replaced by another was dialectical, and ended in a synthesis which corresponded to the reunion of the Eastern and Western Churches. This reunion would be brought about by a 'third force' which would give human evolution its 'absolute content' through a revelation of a 'divine higher world'. This force was to be a people 'free from limitedness and one-sidedness', which would give life and wholeness to a 'disrupted and benumbed humanity' through its union with the divine principle.[5] While the attempts of Constantine and Charlemagne to establish God's kingdom on earth failed, the task of uniting the first two Romes in a synthesis of social Christianity fell to Russia. At some point, Solovyov urged Alexander III to become the 'new Charlemagne'.

Although such concepts seem to convey Joachimite traditions, the 'Third Rome' is a political concept which existed quite independently of Joachimism. After Rome had fallen to heresy, and after the fall of Constantinople in 1453, Moscow saw itself initially as the liberator of the one true empire. However, after the marriage of Ivan III in 1472 to the heiress of the Greek imperial family, a new, even more potent role emerged. In a charter of 1492, Zozimus, the Metropolitan of Moscow, argued that Ivan III was the new Emperor Constantine of the new Constantinople-Moscow. The classic formulation of the doctrine comes from Philotheus, a monk of Psov, who wrote to Tsar Vassily III at the beginning of the sixteenth century that 'all the empires of Christendom are united in thine, for two Romes have fallen and the third exists and there will not be a fourth; thy Christian empire will not pass to others'.[6] Drawing on the Book of Daniel, the apocryphal Apocalypse of the Fourth Ezra, and the Pseudo-Methodius, Philotheus urged that the Third Rome must be the champion of Christendom in the face of the expected Last Things.

Such visions were institutionalised when Ivan IV (The Terrible) had himself crowned, in 1547, as the Tsar of the Orthodox Church. In 1589, Constantinople was compelled to give the Metropolitan of Moscow the title of Patriarch. The official document explaining the reason for this elevation expressed the belief in Moscow as the Third Rome, and the installation charter repeated Philotheus's epistle almost word by word. Accordingly, it was Russia's destiny to continue the work of the Roman Empire and to unite in one organic whole the diverse nations of the East and the West. Russia was the last stronghold of the orthodox faith and as such distinguished from all Western nations as the imperial representative of Christian truth. When the Emperor Maximilian I tried to integrate Russia into the West by offering a royal crown to Ivan the Great, Ivan refused because his authority, in his understanding, stemmed from his ancestors and the blessing of God. In 1576, Maximilian II offered Ivan IV recognition as the Emperor of the Greek East and again the offer was rejected. Napoleon concluded in

1802 that there were only two nations in the world, Russia and the Occident.

Drawing on Comtean Positivism as well as Boehmian and Hegelian dialectics, trinitarian speculations about Russia's role in the history of humanity preoccupied a number of important Russian thinkers – including theorists of 'Russian Socialism' like Alexander Herzen; 'Westernisers' such as Vissarion Belinsky (1811–48); leading Pan-Slavists such as Nikolai Danilevsky (1822–85); and Populists such as Nikolai Mikhailovsky (1842–1904). To Danilevsky, the Russian people represented the third embodiment of the people chosen by God after Israel and Byzantium. As I explained above, such discussions continued a tradition originally independent of Joachimism. In the nineteenth century, however, Joachim influenced the messianic expectations sweeping through the *intelligentsia* indirectly at least. The medium of influence was George Sand's sequence of novels, *Spiridion*, *Consuelo*, and *La Comtesse de Rudolfstadt*, in which she expressed her vision of historical progress and its imminent apotheosis.[7]

The eponymous hero of the first novel, Spiridion, was born as a Jew, converted to Christianity and then reached, via a Protestant phase, a new spirituality which he believed would transcend Christianity. After his death, his disciples found his hidden 'Book of Revelation' and read the secret of the new religion. In the first version of the novel, the Book contained Spiridion's testament and a recapitulation of his spiritual pilgrimage. Unhappy with this ending, Sand revised it for a second edition. In the new 1842 edition the disciples discover not just one but three texts. The first document is the Gospel according to John written in the hand of Joachim of Fiore; the second is the Introduction to the *Eternal Evangel* of 1254, which Sand believed to be written by John of Parma, and the third is Spiridion's testament. The version read by Herzen and Belinsky was probably the original, and hence did not contain the reference to Joachim. Still, Sand's editing of the text reveals how close, in her own understanding, her viewpoint was to Joachim's.

In this fermentation of ideas and beliefs, the thought that a Socialist revolution in Russia could ignite, like a spark, a truly international revolution in the Western nations would appear plausible, if not laudable, from a number of perspectives and angles. Indeed, given the mystic and apocalyptic underpinnings of these perspectives, it is far from suprising that Russian Marxism tended to emphasise the messianic and spiritual aspects of Marx's system over its 'scientific' part, its political economy. After the Revolution, once it had become obvious that the international aspirations of Communism were illusory at least in the short term, conservative doctrines like Stalin's 'Socialism in one country' could no less draw on Russia's self-understanding as a special, isolated, civilisational entity. In *this* sense, the Third International, which chose Moscow as its seat, and Soviet imperial policies after the Second World War were in striking accordance with the prophecy that Moscow had a message of salvation for both the East and the West, as universally significant as Rome or Constantinople.

THE NEW WORLD

In the fifteenth and sixteenth centuries, the anticipation of the end of all things was very much part of the spirit of the times in Europe, transcending all religious divisions. For all the parties involved, the very struggles of Reformation and Counter-Reformation manifested nothing less than the machinations of Antichrist. The discovery of a New World had to assume providential meaning under these circumstances. Europe became aware of America only a generation before the start of the Protestant Reformation. As late as 1776 Thomas Paine suggested that the discovery of a new continent had preceded the Reformation as a deliberate part of God's plan to 'open a sanctuary to the persecuted in future years, when home should afford neither friendship nor safety'.[8] The European exploration of America was intensified during the Counter-Reformation, followed swiftly by colonisation in the seventeenth century – the first English settlement was established in 1607 – at a time when the divisions of the European Reformation assumed institutional and intellectual permanence. The very timing of these events ensured that European patterns of religious life were exported to the New World.

Puritan eschatology was undoubtedly the most important source of inspiration for the millenarian and apocalyptic excitement which mystified the European settlement of America. In the first half of the seventeenth century, the Puritans incorporated into their world view a strong millenarian character which gave the English nation a cosmic purpose in the evolving history of Christendom.[9] The Puritans in New England did not hesitate to transfer their missionary zeal to their new habitat.[10] Called from home to endure unimaginable rigour and ordeal in a dangerous land, they were to build the 'City upon a Hill', with the eyes of all people upon them as in Revelation 21:10. According to Edward Johnson (1598–1672), who was speaker of the House of Deputies in 1655, New England was 'the place where the Lord will create a new Heaven, and a new Earth'. The Lord Christ intended 'to make his New England Souldiers the very wonder of this Age'.[11] The discovery of America, its settlement and colonisation was divine prophecy fulfilled.

It is no mere accident that the great Puritan migration to the New

World took place when it appeared as if opportunities for reform were closed off in England. In 1625 James I was succeeded by Charles I, who not only had Roman Catholic sympathies but was also determined to rule England on the grounds of what he considered to be his 'divine rights' as King. From 1629 onwards he tried to rule without calling Parliament into session. In 1628, a group of Puritans purchased a controlling interest in a trading company, the New England Company, which was then reorganised to emphasise colonisation instead of commerce. The first migration in 1630 brought more than a thousand settlers to Massachusetts Bay. While for some of them America was an asylum, others simply refocused their millenarian expectations on the New World.

Apocalyptic excitement was not, however, peculiar to Puritanism. There was a substantial Catholic presence in the New World before any British Protestant appeared on the scene. Spanish Catholics were attempting to convert the Native Americans in the southwest, and French Catholics pursued similar missionary activities in what is now Canada and along the Mississippi River long before the Puritan missions. For the Catholics too the discovery of the New World had providential relevance. Although one of the least-studied features of the European 'Age of Discovery', apocalyptic excitement was one of the main driving forces behind geographical exploration, colonisation and missionary work. Revelation 7:9 provides an important link between discovery and apocalypse: there it is said that *all* the races and languages of mankind would be represented among the predestined in the Heavenly Kingdom. The instauration of the Millennium thus required both the discovery of *all* the races of mankind and their conversion to Christianity. The conversion of the heathens was, as explained earlier, also part of Joachim's Third Status. It is consequently no mere coincidence that Joachimism enjoyed a revival in Spain during Ferdinand and Isabella's reign.

The most striking evidence of this revival is Christopher Columbus himself. Columbus saw the possibility of converting all the races of the world as an apocalyptic and messianic vision. In his late self-understanding he was the God-made messenger of 'the new heaven and the new earth of which [God] spoke in the Apocalypse of St John after having spoken of it through the mouth of Isaiah'. God even showed him the 'spot where to find it'.[12] In his *Book of Prophecies*, a commentary on the Psalms, as well as in his letters, Columbus refers to Joachim several times – twice in order to support his argument that the man who is to rebuild the temple of Mount Sion is to come from Spain. He clearly attempted to surround himself with the magical aura which the name of Joachim evoked by proclaiming himself the Joachimite messiah. After the Second Voyage, he revealed his leanings towards the Spiritual Franciscans by walking in the streets of Seville dressed in the sackcloth of a Franciscan penitent. On his deathbed, he took the habit of the Third Order of St Francis, the branch which was open to laymen.[13]

The whole problematic of the final conversion of the heathens just prior to the climax of history inevitably led to the question of the fate of Israel's Ten Lost Tribes.[14] In the Middle Ages and afterwards, it was believed that ten of the twelve tribes of Israel had not returned from their exile in Assyria. According to the Book of Revelation 7:4–9, however, the lost tribes were to reappear on the day of the Last Judgement. In addition, the passage in 1 Chronicles 5:26 to the effect that the ten tribes were there 'unto this day' as well as the prophecy of Ezekiel 37:19–24 kept alive the belief that descendants of the tribes still existed and that the fulfilment of the prophecies depended on their fate. If the Ten Tribes had disappeared, the literal fulfilment of the prophecies would be impossible. If they had not disappeared, they would have to exist somewhere, most probably under a different name.

Accordingly, the Ten Lost Tribes of Israel figured prominently in a number of interpretations of providential history throughout the centuries. Right up to the late nineteenth century, British writers were still trying to prove the 'Israelitish origins' of the Anglo-Saxons. In the fifteenth and sixteenth centuries, however, one of the most celebrated New World myths was that the native Indians were the descendants of Israel's Lost Tribes. At The Hague in 1644, the famous Puritan reformer John Dury, who had worked with Hartlib and Comenius, heard a story about one Antonio de Montezinos who had come upon an Ecuadorian community of Indians who recited the Shema from Deuteronomy 6:4–9 and acknowledged Abraham, Isaac and Jacob as their forefathers. Dury also added a long 'Epistolicall Discourse' to Thomas Thorowgood's *Jews in America, or Probabilities that the Americans are of that Race* (1650). Dury firmly believed that the discovery of the 'American Jews' was a clear sign that knowledge of Christ would soon fill the earth, allowing the Indians to return to Judea.

In the mid-seventeenth century, both England and America were pouring out numerous texts which located the Indians' conversion in biblical prophecy by relating the time of their 'coming in' to the calling of the Jews. The year 1650 also saw the publication of the English translation of Menasseh Ben Israel's *The Hope of Israel*, a work which predicted that the Twelve Tribes would shortly be restored to Jerusalem. The book proved highly influential at a time when Cromwell was negotiating the Jews' admission to England – again a prophetic event in the context of Deuteronomy 28:64, which had prophesied Israel's world-wide dispersal. Admitting the Jews to England, however, could reverse the diaspora by exposing them to an evangelical English gospel.

The theory that the native Americans were of Jewish origin provided the sought-after explanation for their origins. Its popularity, however, stemmed largely from the apocalyptic mood of the time and the corresponding urgency to resolve the fate of the Jews. If the Indians were the Lost Tribes, their discovery would be convincing evidence that the world was soon to end. And by converting them to Christianity, missionaries could actively assist and accelerate providential history. In 1609, the Virginia Company instructed the Governor of the colony, Sir Thomas Gates, that his missionaries must have children taken from their parents if necessary since the Indians 'were so wrapped up in the fogge and miserie of their iniquity' that they would have to be forced, when still young, into the good Christian life. The missionary zeal then turned into a zeal of destruction and a mere fight for survival soon after signs of failure became obvious. In 1622 the Virginia Indians attempted to wipe out the English colonists and thereby assured their own annihilation. The Indian Wars were easily reinterpreted as evidence that Satan was putting up a last fight against his Puritan adversaries.[15]

The close link between millenarian anticipations and missionary work in New England is well illustrated by John Eliot's attempt to plant Christ's monarchy among Christianised natives. Eliot studied the Algonquin tongue and began an Indian ministry in the belief that he was thereby advancing the great historical sequences towards their prophesied climax. His own Indian flock at Natick was destined to take the first step towards the Millennium. Eliot knew of the research done by Dury and Thorowgood, with whom he was in correspondence. In the late 1640s he began to believe that his Indian theocracy should eventually be extended to England where, after the execution of the King, the formation of a new order was required. His appeal to the brethren at home, *The Christian Commonwealth*, which was finished around 1651, became an important document for the Fifth Monarchy movement in England.[16]

This movement demonstrates how easily Puritan millenarians could shift their centre of hope from England to America and back again. The Fifth Monarchists expected the imminent Kingdom of Christ on earth, a theocratic regime in which the Saints would reign over the unregenerate masses and prepare for the Second Coming. They were unique in that they claimed the right and duty of taking arms to overthrow existing regimes and establish the Millennium. The group formulated detailed political, social and economic guidelines for the organisation of the promised kingdom. The name 'Fifth Monarchists' stems from Daniel 7:1–27, which was read as a prophecy of four successive, degenerating world-empires, after which would follow a kingdom that would endure forever. By the late Middle Ages the four were normally taken to be Babylon, Assyria, Greece and Rome. The question of where the 'Fifth' and eternal empire would arise occupied the minds of scholars for many centuries.

The Fifth Monarchists believed that the Civil War was the prelude to the establishment of an everlasting English empire. The movement was well connected with the mainstream of political affairs in the years following the execution of Charles I in 1649. But in the second half of the 1650s its members became disillusioned. Whereas Cromwell had earlier been God's 'chosen instrument', the Protector, as well as his son Richard, later came to be seen as a drag on the unfolding of revealed events. The first partisan organisation for the Fifth Monarchy surfaced in 1649, but serious agitation did not begin before 1653. In the spring of 1657 Fifth Monarchy men were convinced that their time had come, that the 'Saints must do it'. They had to pull down Babylon and bind 'kings in chains'. They plotted in April but were foiled when their scheme was leaked to the government. Many of their leaders were arrested and executed.

The same preoccupation with Last Things which had drawn Puritans to the New World also made many planters return to England. After the Puritan Revolution began to unfold, the planters felt their home country called upon them to be 'helpfull in advancing the Kingdome of Christ, and casting down every strong house of sinne and Satan'.[17] The Fifth Monarchy movement in England provided American Puritans with an articulate, organised forum and channel for millenarian agitation, something which they had failed to establish in the New World. Eliot's *Christian Commonwealth* was printed by Livewell Chapman's Fifth Monarchy Press as a New England version of the Fifth Monarchy, although Eliot himself remained in Massachusetts. Two main figures of the movement, William Aspinwall and Thomas Venner, had a New England background.

The turmoil surrounding radical Puritanism in England also provides the background for the rise of Quakerism. According to George Fox (1624–91), every man and woman could be 'enlightened by the divine light of Christ' through an immediate call. The light of Christ was sufficient for salvation with little outward help from Scripture, books, teaching, or a professional clergy. Quakers believed that their people can be so possessed of the light that they become, in the words of Ephraim Pagitt, 'prophets, Christs or Saviours'. The first-generation Quakers insisted that they were able to participate in the primitive spiritual relationship which existed between God and humanity before the Scriptures. Quakerism was particularly relevant in the development of religious pluralism in the New World because William Penn's 'Holy Experiment' in America, 'Pennsylvania', soon provided one of the most secure homes for religious toleration in the world. Penn

(1644–1718) considered Quakerism ‘primitive Christianity revived’. However, although the inner light guided the Quaker and freed him from authority, it did not deify. It was left to the Ranters to exceed such limits. Ranters considered themselves perfectionists in spiritual things. They were infallible, amoral, libertines and sinned in public in order to prove it.[18]

Puritan eschatology, Old Testament prophecy and Joachimism are not the only continuities and links between American self-perceptions and lines of meaning permeating European spirituality. The struggle of Reformation and Counter-Reformation led members of many unorthodox groups to escape from the Old to the New World. For them, the escape could amount to purification, to a retreat from sin and corruption, and ultimately to the realisation of perfection.[19] The achievement of perfection and purity – sometimes understood as a return to Adam’s innocence before the fall – could evoke a radical antinomianism, expressed in the refusal to obey law and authority. Such attitudes were present, for example, amongst Anabaptist groups immigrating from Europe and among members of the so-called ‘Family of Love’. Arrival in the New World was equated with *communitas*, with a release from hierarchy, even the hierarchy of dogma. The inner light of the believers took precedence over Scripture. As liminal beings, filled with the Spirit, members of such groups required neither instruction nor guidance.

Apart from Anabaptists, whose reputation even in the New World suffered from the disaster of Anabaptist rule in Münster (1534), the New World also attracted Rosicrucian groups from Germany as well as Moravians from Bohemia. The Moravians were groups from the Unity of Brethren, with which Comenius was affiliated, and claimed that their genealogy showed a direct apostolic succession after Jan Hus. The linkages between these Moravian groups and the origins of Methodism are well established.[20] America also provided a haven for groups of French Huguenots, especially after the Catholic Louis XIV revoked the Edict of Nantes in 1685. Many of them considered the Albigenses as their spiritual forebears.

These and many other movements, as well as the Puritans, brought with them the writings of Jacob Boehme. Just as in Europe, Boehme was extremely popular in America. He had great influence on Familists, Quakers and Ranters, Fifth Monarchists and many others. George Whitefield, William Blake and Ralph Waldo Emerson were all admirers of Boehme. The German shoemaker was also a major source of inspiration for Father George Rapp, who led a small German sect, the Harmony Society, to Beaver County, Pennsylvania, in 1805. In 1815, the Rappites moved briefly to Indiana before they returned to Pennsylvania. They sold their property in Indiana to Robert Owen, who then set up his first American Socialist Eden in the colony and named it 'New Harmony'.

Millenarian and illuminist leanings were popular with many more religious groups in America. Certainly the Shakers, the Millerites and even the Mormons deserve some discussion, but space unfortunately prohibits this. The Shakers, for example, called upon the Marcionites, Manichaeans, Bogomilians, Cathari, Beghards, Picards, Waldenses, Albigenses, Anabaptists and Quakers as witnesses to the truth of God during the reign of Antichrist which began shortly after the death of the Apostles.[21] Friedrich Engels referred to the Shakers as examples of profitable and practical Communist communities.[22] However, the sheer number and variety of these movements should not distract from the fact that it was from New England that the most articulate and influential statement of America's millenarian role was to come.

PROPHETIC EVENTS IN AMERICAN HISTORY

The self-understanding of Americans as the 'redeemer nation' surfaced, developed and gained influence in response to key events in the development of the American republic. Among those events are often mentioned the Great Awakening, the Anglo-French War, the Revolution and subsequent independence, the Civil War, the Spanish–American War, the two World Wars, and the Cold War.

Many scholars have argued that the religious enthusiasm of the Awakening during the 1730s and 1740s led directly to the political enthusiasm of the Revolution.[23] The religious revivals are said to have prepared and ultimately provoked the Revolution in at least three ways. First the revivalists, primarily concerned with the conversion of individual sinners into children of God and thus with the restoration of a close relationship between individuals and God, democratised America's religion before the Revolution democratised its government. The ability of the itinerant preacher to persuade his listener to act upon his own individual free will transformed the colonists into citizens who acted out of their own conscience. Moreover, itinerancy itself, as a form of communication, had an impact on authority relationships. It provided an alternative to the official dogma of the parish, tax-supported, Church. The itinerant spoke as one individual to another, outside of any temporal or territorial location.[24]

Second, it is argued that the Awakening transformed the colonists' conservative 'premillenarian' into a 'postmillenarian' outlook. While earlier the Second Coming was thought to be necessary *prior* to the instauration of the Millennium because humans were held to be too wicked, postmillenarian optimism assigned them an active role in the preparation of the new realm. In this latter view, humanity played an active role in bringing about the transfiguration of the world. Christ would return, then, once human effort had effectively set the stage for the reign of Christ. The activism of the later outlook implied an urgent need to fight the corruption of the Old World in open rebellion.

Finally, as America's first truly national event, the Great Awakening evoked a new kind of intercolonial unity, and thereby prepared the country for the Revolution. The movement's scope and success affected even the revolutionary struggle and its outcome. By 1765 the New Light revivalists had come to predominate in most of the Protestant denominations. As a consequence, the anticlericalism of the French and Russian Revolution where the clergy allied themselves with the old order could be avoided in America. Usually, only the parish priests of the Anglican Church, who were appointed directly by the King's authority, sided with the old regime. The Great Awakening was thus the precondition and beginning of the convergence of millenarian and republican thought which nurtured the Revolution.

However, the view that the Great Awakening was the key to America's 'civil millenarianism' must be approached with caution. In an important sense, the piety of the Great Awakening was *opposed* to the millenarian excitement of the Revolution. Indeed, the late 1740s witnessed a significant decline of apocalyptic hope. In 1742, Jonathan Edwards still understood the Awakening as an extraordinary work of God.

> [W]hat is now seen in America, and especially in New England, may prove the dawn of that glorious day; and the very uncommon and wonderful circumstances and events of this work seem to me strongly to argue that God intends it as the beginning or forerunner of something vastly great.[25]

Five years later, Edwards was complaining about the woeful decay of religion in America. He included America – 'at present very sorrowful and dark' – in his pessimism about the spiritual decadence of the whole British Empire.[26]

It is true that Jonathan Edwards had a postmillenarian view of the future. But, for him, the progressive course of history depended on the spread of piety, individual repentance, conversion, and, in general, spiritual introspection. The perceived need for religious regeneration grew out of an intense feeling of guilt. Earlier generations of settlers – who still had to struggle to win a beachhead on the stern frontier along the coast – had enjoyed a particularly close relationship with God and had, therefore, felt close to each other. This proximity to God now seemed lost. Instead, in all the colonies people began to argue and fight over questions of mercantile and land development. The many opportunities to grow rich tempted normally decent people to pursue their private profits in aggressive, competitive ways, often cutting moral corners in their anxiety. For those who became aware of the change of attitude and behaviour, the tyrant on the horizon was sin, and not the English Parliament. When revivalists spoke of the Millennium, they mostly had in mind the advance of Christ's Kingdom through the effusion of God's spirit in widespread and genuine revivals. What was at stake in this movement was not the externalisation of evil but, on the contrary, the acknowledgement of sin, repentance and reform from within.

The event which transformed spiritual introspection into its opposite, the externalisation of evil, was the Anglo-French War. The French Wars provided New Englanders with an opportunity to underscore their collective role in the last decisive struggle with Satan. Their ministers began to glorify a British past which they constructed from their understanding of providential history. History was a continuous battle between liberty and tyranny in which the British constitution, 'the admiration and envy of the world', represented the forces of liberty and French Catholicism the tyranny of Antichrist. For Jonathan Edwards, military victories against the French Catholics were 'temporal mercies', mere incentives to the more important works of repentance and revival,[27] but for the New England clergymen of the 1760s they came to represent the inevitable progress towards a Millennium of both civil and religious liberty. The distinction between the Kingdom of God and the New England political community became blurred.

The millenarianism of the American Revolution resulted from the consolidation of the religious-political framework established during the Anglo-French Wars. While in the French Wars, millenarian hope followed military success, the conflict with Britain was fought in cosmic terms from the outset. Expectations of a new age appeared even when the war was still in its darkest hour. Animated by the expulsion of France from North America, New Englanders expected the total destruction of the forces of Antichrist. It was not too difficult, then, to interpret the struggle with Britain along those lines. However, as the enemy was no longer Catholic, millenarian hopes tended to be expressed in civic rather than religious terms. The primary enemy was the Antichrist of civil oppression rather than that of religious dogma; freedom, not Protestantism, was the cause of God.

Once it was felt that liberty was 'expiring and gasping for life' in Britain, the struggle for American independence was no longer a fight Americans fought for themselves. They fought for the well-being of the whole world because America was to be the permanent sanctuary of liberty, the cause of God. As such, America was to be the permanent source and centre of the unfolding of the divine plan. The country was the divine agent to initiate the Millennium, and its ability to live up to its prophetic role depended on the outcome of the war against Britain. The conflict was fought, then, as a crusade of heaven against hell.[28]

American attitudes towards Britain changed surprisingly late. Right up to the Stamp Act Crisis of 1765, Britain continued to be idealised as the 'favourite nation' of divine providence. For many revolutionaries, the American Revolution was not directed against English political ideas but against a tyrannical and despotic monarch. For a long time Americans believed that in taking up arms they were defending the true rights of Englishmen and that they were acting as legitimate heirs of a proud tradition which went back to the Magna Charta. However, almost overnight the Stamp Act Crisis turned British Israel into Assyria and the servants of God into the offspring of 'their father the Devil'. During the war, it was common for ministers to preach sermons explaining how closely British oppression resembled the beast described in the Book of Revelation, 13:1–18. America was compared to the stone from the Book of Daniel 2:31–45 that strikes 'the image of the beast', becomes a 'great mountain' filling all the earth, and leads to the time when 'discord shall cease, and tyrants be no more'.[29]

The Civil War too was a period of heightened millenarian expectations.[30] The evangelism of both sides, North and South, can in part be traced back to the revivalism of the so-called 'Second Great Awakening' of the early nineteenth century.[31] Unlike the millenarian hope of the revivals of the 1730s and 1740s, the millenarianism of the Second Great Awakening was political from the outset. National union had fostered the conflation of biblical and secular historical worlds because, under conditions of religious pluralism, no single American denomination could maintain exclusive claims to truth. Instead, the nation itself had to develop 'the soul of a church'.[32] Numerous publications with titles such as 'Armageddon, or the overthrow of Romanism and Monarchy; the existence of the United States foretold in the Bible, its future greatness, [...] its expansion into the millenial republic, and its dominion over the whole world [...]' (Samuel Davies Baldwin, 1854) show that, by the mid-nineteenth century, the identification of the United States as 'God's New Israel' had become a commonplace in the country.[33] The famous catchphrase of 'manifest destiny', which reflected the assumption that divine providence had intended the United States to control the entire American continent, was coined in 1845 by a New York editor.

However, the two Awakenings in American history are not only separated by the different natures of their millenarian visions. There are also differences in their theologies. Revivalists of the colonial period stressed the inability of sinners to save themselves. God's sovereignty in all things and thus the need for renewal through repentance was at the centre of the message of itinerists like Edwards and Whitefield. In contrast, leading revivalists of the early nineteenth century in both the North and South came to emphasise the individual's capacity to work out his own salvation. They suggested that God had bestowed on all people the ability to come to Christ. With the nation as the reinforced carrier and focus of divine truth, and with the more activist stance of the Second Great Awakening, the Civil War was in effect fought in defence of the 'sacred aura of the fabric of national civilisation' (Noll, 1992) that, from Northern perspectives, was threatened by the South and, from Southern perspectives, imperilled by the North.

The late nineteenth and early twentieth centuries are commonly regarded as a turning-point in the way in which American élites understood their country's relationship to the outside world.[34] By 1890 there was for the first time a continuous band of states stretching from the Atlantic to the Pacific. A 'new' United States seemed to have miraculously appeared as the true legacy of the Civil War. The word 'nation' referred henceforth to a continent conquered and tamed. Internal consolidation and the external assertion of American values were on the agenda after the completion of the Western settlement. During the last decade of the nineteenth century, the rise of Protestant missions from America was very much part of the actual expansion of the United States. American imperialism understood itself as an 'imperialism of righteousness', as a means for the enterprise of universal evangelisation.[35] President McKinley described his decision to annex the Philippines as resulting from a religious experience. After he had unsuccessfully sought counsel from all sides, he prayed for guidance and received the answer that

> there was nothing left for us to do but to take them all, and to educate the Filipinos, and uplift and civilize and Christianize them, and by God's grace do the very best we could by them as our fellow-men for whom Christ also died.[36]

American expansionism at the turn of the century was nurtured by a widespread feeling that the time was ripe for a great Christian advance. The war with Spain, for some still the representative of that home of Antichrist, the papacy, as well as the impending collapse of the old Chinese order seemed to offer supreme missionary and crusading opportunities. Prophets of expansion such as Josiah Strong easily combined Darwinian biology and Spencer's sociology with the divine will. 'If human progress follows a law of development ..., our civilisation should be the noblest, ' he wrote in 1885. In his *New Era* (1893), Strong advocated that the Hebrews, Greeks and Romans had separately developed humanity's qualities, and that now, for the first time in the history of mankind,

> the three great strands pass through the fingers of one predominant race to be braided into a single supreme civilisation in the new era, the perfection of which will be the Kingdom fully come. ... All unite in the one Anglo-Saxon race, indicating that this race is pre-eminently fitted, and therefore chosen of God, to prepare the way for the full coming of His Kingdom on earth.

Convinced that 'Anglo-Saxondom' would spread itself over the earth, he asked the rhetorical question: 'can anyone doubt that the result of this competition of races will be the "survival of the fittest"?'[37]

The rise of such attitudes, however, was also made possible by the increasing influence of evangelical Protestantism in American government and administration leading right up to the puritanism of the Progressive Movement. Josiah Strong was also one of the leading figures in the crusade for social justice at home which inspired the municipal reformers of the Progressive Era.[38] For a long time, Strong was head of the American Institute of Social Service, the religious agency devoted to collecting sociological data for reform purposes. Indeed, the administrative and political reforms of the early twentieth century, their positivist governmentality, the 'Dry Utopia' of the Prohibition years, [39] as well as Wilson's missionary diplomacy were to a large extent driven and supported by a postmillenarian activism similar to the one advocated by Strong.[40] Wilson wanted the United States to show people 'the way to liberty'. 'We are a sort of pure air blowing in world politics,' he declared, 'destroying illusions and cleaning places of morbid miasmatic gases.' In a sense, he intended to continue the reform begun by the Puritans in England: 'The Anglo-Saxon people have undertaken to reconstruct the affairs of the world, and it would be a shame upon them to withdraw their hand.' He believed that 'we are chosen and prominently chosen to show the way to the nations of the world how they shall walk in the paths of liberty'. Knock writes that Wilson's League of Nations was to be the 'supreme covenant between God and the United States'.[41]

Before and during the wars, American activist mysticism surfaced in Wilson's 'war to end all wars', fought to make the world 'safe for democracy', as well as in Franklin D. Roosevelt's insistence on 'unconditional surrender' as the only acceptable way of ending the Second World War. The very effort of fighting the war could only be justified by promising the ultimate defeat and eradication of the forces of evil. Because such an attitude rejected considerations of costs as well as limitations of violence short of the destruction of the enemy, it implicitly presumed that the American cause was 'holy'.

The Cold War, finally, provided another arena where the crusading impulse of American civil millenarianism could be lived out. The crusade was fought at home as much as abroad. In his play *The Crucible* (1953), Arthur Miller aptly compared the anti-Communist witch-hunting of the early 1950s with the Salem witch trials of 1692.

In the external realm, 1950 saw the drafting of NSC-68, the first document of the Policy Planing Staff prepared under George F. Kennan's successor as director, Paul H. Nitze. NSC-68 offered the first *systemic* approach to the Cold War and as such was capable of being communicated throughout the bureaucracy.[42] According to its authors, the Soviet Union posed an entirely new kind of threat because it was 'animated by a new fanatic faith' which was 'antithetical' to the American faith. The conflict amounted to a 'polarisation' of the world into the forces of 'slavery' and 'liberty' which were represented by the Soviet 'design' and the American 'purpose' respectively.[43] The Soviet 'design' was absolute in the sense that it 'seeks to impose its absolute authority over the rest of the world.' It 'calls for the complete subversion or forcible destruction of the machinery of government and structure of society in the countries of the non-Soviet world and their replacement by an apparatus and structure subservient to and controlled from the Kremlin'.

At the same time, it was clear to the authors of NSC-68 that the idea of liberty was 'the most contagious idea in history'. The existence of the idea of liberty posed a permanent threat to the 'foundation of the slave society'. The Soviet Union's design must be expected, therefore, to include the complete eradication of liberty from the earth. The 'assault on free institutions is world-wide now, and in the context of the present polarization of power a defeat of free institutions anywhere is a defeat everywhere'. In this situation, it was impossible for the United States to remain passive. At stake was – once again – the very survival of the principle of liberty among mankind. Thus, holding out was not enough. '[B]eyond affirming our values our policy and actions must be such as to foster a fundamental change in the nature of the Soviet system.' Because it was not 'an adequate objective merely to seek to check the Kremlin design', the United States had to accept, in its own interest, 'the responsibility of world leadership' in order to 'bring about justice and order by means consistent with the principles of freedom and democracy'. Although the conflict was ultimately a struggle for the minds and personal convictions of human beings, meeting the Soviet challenge necessitated above all 'a build-up of military strength by the United States and its allies to a point at which the combined strength will be superior to the forces that can be brought to bear by the Soviet Union and its allies'.

Other sections of the document are less sweeping. The text acknowledged, for example, that the principle of liberty imposes limitations on the means used to defend the American 'purpose' against the Soviet 'design'. The importance of leadership by example – a principle passionately upheld by Nitze's predecessor, Kennan – is emphasised. In fact, although Kennan played no direct role in the formulation of NSC-68, he had some indirect influence. In preparing the report, Nitze drew on an earlier NSC document – NSC-20/4 – which was based on a draft – PPS-38 – written by Kennan. However, as will be explained in the next chapter, NSC-68's activist stance, its implied universal commitment to the cause of liberty, and in particular the overwhelming weight it assigned to military measures marked a significant departure from Kennan's conception of United States interests.

The extent to which the universalism of the document marks a turning-point in American attitudes towards the Communist challenge is controversial among Cold War historians. Arguably, the Truman Doctrine had pointed already in this direction. But, at least on the part of President Truman, the actual shift in attitude – not to mention its *implementation* – was still to come. Indeed, the American defence budget decreased sharply after the Second World War and remained nearly constant from 1947 to 1950. Even after reading the document in April 1950, Truman did not revise his commitment to a constant if not decreasing budget. However, NSC-68 became a plan of action in response to the Korean War.[44]

NOTES

1. See Ernst Benz, 'Die geistigen Grundlagen des Russischen Bolshewismus', in Deutsche Gesellschaft für Osteuropakunde (ed.), *Russland und Wir: Betrachtungen über Russland und den Bolshewismus* (Stuttgart: Deutsche Verlags-Anstalt, 1951), pp. 49–77; Alain Besançon, *The Intellectual Origins of Leninism* (trans. Sarah Matthews), (Oxford: Basil Blackwell, 1981 (1977)), Chapter 4; Zdenek V. David, 'The Influence of Jacob Boehme on Russian Religious Thought', in *Slavic Review*, 21: 1 (March 1962), pp. 43–64; Boris Groys, 'Elemente des Gnostizismus im Dialektischen Materialismus (sowjetischen Marxismus)', in Peter Koslowski (ed.), *Gnosis und Mystik in der Geschichte der Philosophie* (Zürich: Artemis, 1988), pp. 352–67; Andrzej Walicki, *A History of Russian Thought* (Oxford: Clarendon, 1988).
2. Kireyevsky is quoted in Besançon, p. 71.
3. Quoted in Dmitri Volkogonov, *Lenin: Life and Legacy* (trans. Harold Shukman), (London: HarperCollins, 1995), p. 28.
4. From a conversation reported in Nicolay Valentinov, *Encounters with Lenin* (trans. Paul Rosta and Brian Pearce), (New York: Oxford University Press, 1968), pp. 66–8.
5. Quotations in Marjorie Reeves and Warwick Gould, *Joachim of Fiore and the Myth of the Eternal Evangel in the Nineteenth Century* (Oxford: Clarendon, 1987), pp. 305–6.
6. Quoted in Reeves and Gould, *Joachim of Fiore*, p. 301; see also Voegelin, *The New Science of Politics: an Introduction* (Chicago: University of Chicago Press, 1952), pp. 114–17.
7. Reeves and Gould, pp. 93–8.
8. Quoted in David S. Lovejoy, *Religious Enthusiasm in the New World: Heresy to Revolution* (Cambridge, MA: Harvard University Press, 1985), p. 8.
9. See, for example, Joy Gilsdorf, *The Puritan Apocalypse: New England Eschatology in the Seventeenth Century* (New York: Garland, 1989); Peter Toon (ed.), *Puritans, the Millenium and the Future of Israel: Puritan Eschatology 1600–1660* (London: Clarke, 1970).

10. See Ernest Lee Tuveson, *Redeemer Nation: The Idea of America's Millennial Role* (Chicago: University of Chicago Press, 1968), pp. 17–25. Also Mark A. Noll, *A History of Christianity in the United States and Canada* (Grand Rapids: Eerdmans, 1992), pp. 32–53.
11. Edward Johnson in Perry Miller and Thomas H. Johnson (eds), *The Puritans*, Vol. I (New York: Harper, 1963), pp. 145, 152.
12. Columbus quoted in Pauline Moffitt Watts, 'Prophecy and Discovery: On the Spiritual Origins of Christopher Columbus's "Enterprise of the Indies"', *American Historical Review*, 90: 1 (February 1985), pp. 73–102 (73).
13. See John Leddy Phelan, *The Millennial Kingdom of the Franciscans in the New World* (Berkeley: University of California Press, second edn, 1970), pp. 19–22.
14. See Joseph Jacobs, 'The Lost Ten Tribes', *The Jewish Encyclopedia*, Vol. XII (New York: Funk and Wagnalls, 1906), pp. 249–53; Louis Isaac Rabinowitz, 'The Lost Tribes', *Encyclopaedia Judaica*, Vol. 15 (Jerusalem: Keter, 1971), pp. 1003–6.
15. Cf. Roy H. Pearce, *Savagism and Civilization: A Study of the Indian and the American Mind* (Baltimore: Johns Hopkins Press, 1971), Chapter I.
16. See J. F. Maclear, 'New England and the Fifth Monarchy: The Quest for the Millennium in Early American Puritanism', *The William and Mary Quarterly*, Third Series, 32: 2 (April 1975), pp. 223–60. Also B. S. Capp, *The Fifth Monarchy Men: A Study in Seventeenth-century English Millenarianism* (London: Faber & Faber, 1972).
17. From Edward Johnson's *Wonder-Working Providence of Sions Savior*, quoted in Maclear, 'New England and the Fifth Monarchy', p. 248.
18. Lovejoy, *Religious Enthusiasm*, pp. 111–16. Pagitt's quote is on p. 112.
19. Cf. Lyman Tower Sargent, 'Utopianism in Colonial America', *History of Political Thought*, 4: 3 (Winter 1983), pp. 483–522.
20. Lovejoy, *Religious Enthusiasm*, pp. 162–4.
21. Stephen A. Marini, *Radical Sects of Revolutionary New England* (Cambridge, MA: Harvard University Press, 1982), p. 151.
22. Michael J. St Clair, *Millenarian Movements in Historical Context* (New York: Garland, 1992), pp. 291, 298.
23. See, for example, Alan Heimert, *Religion and the American Mind: From the Great Awakening to the Revolution* (Cambridge, MA: Harvard University Press, 1966). Also William G. McLoughlin, 'Enthusiasm for Liberty: The Great Awakening as the Key to the Revolution', in Jack P. Greene and W. G. McLoughlin, *Preachers and Politicians: Two Essays on the Origins of the American Revolution* (Worcester: American Antiquarian Society, 1977), pp. 47–73.
24. Cf. Harry S. Stout, 'Religion, Communications, and the Ideological Origins of the American Revolution', *The William and Mary Quarterly*, Third Series, Vol. 34 (1977), pp. 519–41.
25. From Edwards, 'Some Thoughts Concerning the Present Revival of Religion', Darrett B. Rutman (ed.), *The Great Awakening: Event and Exegesis* (New York: John Wiley, 1970), pp. 79–86 (86).
26. Nathan O. Hatch, *The Sacred Cause of Liberty: Republican Thought and the Millennium in Revolutionary New England* (New Haven: Yale University Press, 1977), p. 33.
27. Hatch, *The Sacred Cause*, pp. 30, 49.
28. Hatch, *The Sacred Cause*, p. 88.
29. Typical quotations in Noll, *History of Christianity*, p. 118.
30. See in particular James H. Moorhead, *American Apocalypse: Yankee Protestants and the Civil War 1860–1869* (New Haven: Yale University Press, 1978).
31. For this argument see Richard J. Carwardine, *Evangelicals and Politics in Antebellum America* (New Haven: Yale University Press, 1993).
32. Hatch, *The Sacred Cause*, pp. 141–2.
33. Noll, *History of Christianity*, p. 317.
34. See, for example, Robert H. Wiebe, *The Search for Order 1877–1920* (New York: Hill and Wang, 1967), especially Chapter 9, and Robert L. Beisner, *From the Old Diplomacy to the New, 1865–1900* (Arlington Heights, IL: Harlan Davidson, second

edn, 1986). See also Maldwyn A. Jones, *Limits of Liberty: American History 1607–1980* (New York: Oxford University Press, 1983), pp. 396–9.

35. The term 'imperialism of righteousness' was coined by Alexander Blackburn in an article for the *Standard* published in August 1898. See Julius W. Pratt, *Expansionists of 1898: The Acquisition of Hawaii and the Spanish Islands* (Gloucester, MA: Peter Smith, 1959), pp. 279–316 (293).
36. Quoted in Pratt, *Expansionists*, p. 316.
37. See Julius W. Pratt, *America's Colonial Experiment* (New York: Prentice-Hall, 1950), pp. 21–8 (24); the quotes are in Arthur M. Schlesinger Jr, 'The Theory of America: Experiment or Destiny?', in Schlesinger, *The Cycles of American History* (London: Penguin, 1989), pp. 3–22 (14–15), and Richard Hofstadter, *Social Darwinism in American Thought* (Boston: Beacon Press, second edn, 1959), pp. 178–9.
38. Arthur A. Ekirch Jr, *Progressivism in America: A Study of the Era from Theodore Roosevelt to Woodrow Wilson* (New York: Franklin Watts, 1974), pp. 92–3; on Strong see also Tuveson, *Redeemer Nation*, pp. 137–8, 165–9.
39. See, for example, James H. Timberlake, *Prohibition and the Progressive Movement, 1900–1920* (New York: Atheneum, 1970), especially pp. 34–8; and Norman H. Clark, *Deliver us from Evil: An Interpretation of American Prohibition* (New York: Norton, 1976).
40. See Arthur S. Link, *Woodrow Wilson and the Progressive Era 1910–1917* (New York: Harper & Row, 1954), especially Chapter 4 on 'Missionary Diplomacy'.
41. Quotes from John M. Mulder, *Woodrow Wilson: The Years of Preparation* (Princeton, NJ: Princeton University Press, 1978), p. 231, and Thomas J. Knock, *To End all Wars: Woodrow Wilson and the Quest for a New World Order* (New York: Oxford University Press, 1992), pp. 11, 14. Tuveson, *Redeemer Nation*, discusses Wilson on pp. 209–13.
42. See John Lewis Gaddis, *Strategies of Containment: A Critical Appraisal of Postwar American National Security Policy* (New York: Oxford University Press, 1982), Chapter Four, on the rationale of NSC-68, and Melvyn P. Leffler, *A Preponderance of Power: National Security, the Truman Administration, and the Cold War* (Stanford, CA: Stanford University Press, 1992), Chapter 8, on the historical background.
43. 'A Report to the National Security Council by the Executive Secretary on United States Objectives and Programs for National Security' (NSC-68), 14 April 1950, in US Department of State, *Foreign Relations of the United States 1950, Volume I (National Security Affairs, Foreign Economic Policy)*, (Washington, DC: Government Printing Office, 1977), pp. 235–92.
44. See John Lewis Gaddis, 'Was the Truman Doctrine a Real Turning Point?', *Foreign Affairs*, Vol. 52, January 1974, pp. 386–402; and also John Newhouse, *War and Peace in the Nuclear Age* (New York: Alfred Knopf, 1989), pp. 81–5.

8
Parrhesia against *Gnosis*: George F. Kennan on the spiritual dimension of the Cold War

The introductory chapter distinguished between *following* and *contemplating* lines of meaning. Once such a line has been followed and thereby laid open, the analyst can proceed to reflect on its underlying experience or problem. It is to this task, to the contemplation of the 'history' outlined in the previous chapters, that I will turn now.

In the first chapter I also pointed out that such contemplation, when communicated to others, can re-enter the temporal flow and become a constituent of history. Indeed, for the three major periods considered – late Antiquity, the Renaissance and the twentieth century – one can find contemporary witnesses who reflected on the spiritual conditions of their own times in terms which, in some sense, anticipate my own inquiry into the spiritual dimension of the Cold War. There is even a sense in which the thoughts and acts of the three thinkers I have in mind have become 'constituents' of history, although perhaps not always the way they were intended to.

It is clear that for late Antiquity St Augustine represents just such a witness. Raised in a predominantly Christian household, Augustine became a Manichaean auditor at the age of nineteen. After a short Neo-Platonic phase, he converted to Christianity in AD 386, when aged thirty-one. After his conversion and baptism, he confronted the Manichaeans in his writings as a man who had once been one of them. For him, therefore, the 'Gnostic problem' was a *personal* problem. This fact, together with the enormous influence which he later had on the development of Christian doctrine, turns his work into more than a mere historical reference.

However, the Renaissance, too, had an important and influential witness in Niccolò Machiavelli. To suggest the Florentine diplomat in this context will surprise those who associate him only with Leo Strauss's classic interpretation. Machiavelli's crucial contribution to political philosophy, according to Strauss, was the insight that 'one must lower the standards in order to make probable, if not certain, the actualisation of the right or desirable social order or in order to conquer chance'. This lowering of standards, Strauss argued, represented a radical departure from the classical teaching with its emphasis on human excellence.[1] Indeed, the view that it is in Machiavelli's writings where one can see most clearly the break-up of the medieval spiritual order and the beginning of the modern concern with order and science has become widely accepted. While most would agree that *Il Principe* is somehow about the 'lowering of standards', its author's position becomes far more interesting once one begins to ask exactly *whose* 'standards' are implicated in his writings. If those standards are defined by the anthropological optimism of the Renaissance preachers of the 'Golden Age', *i tempi aurei*, then Machiavelli's position appears far more balanced than is usually acknowledged.

Finally, for the twentieth century, I propose to look at the life and work of the American diplomat George F. Kennan as a starting point for a *noetic* reflection on the Cold War experience – a reflection, that is, which pertains to the question of how this experience both exposed and shaped the order of individual souls and society. Kennan was fully aware of the conflict's spiritual aspects; in fact, there is a sense in which, to him, the spiritual dimension actually *defined* it. Warning from the outset that the greatest danger for the Americans was to become like their adversaries, he saw his worst fears confirmed in the nuclear arms race between the superpowers. The spiritual disease which, according to Kennan, not only afflicted the two main protagonists of the conflict but Western society in general was the tendency to the 'total externalisation of evil', amounting to a 'failure of self-knowledge' which he considered 'profoundly un-Christian'. Kennan developed his analysis of the Cold War into a general diagnosis and criticism of the spiritual condition of Western society.

As the Cold War is now our focus, most of this chapter centres on Kennan. However, in two brief excursions I will also state my own assessment of Augustine and Machiavelli and their positions within the overall context of my inquiry. For this purpose I draw especially on Peter Brown's and Johannes van Oort's work on Augustine and Sebastian de Grazia's analysis of Machiavelli. The literature on Kennan's contribution is far less developed. Biographical work typically focuses on Kennan's influence as a diplomat and foreign policy adviser,[2] but to date there has been little interest in him as a philosopher.

EXCURSION I: MANI, AUGUSTINE AND THE TWO CITIES

Augustine submitted to the Manichaean sect in a 'spirit of total surrender'.[3] For nine years, he was affiliated with the group and engaged in their practices and rituals as a 'hearer' or 'auditor'. A man of great intellectual force, Augustine was first attracted to the Manichaeans because of the sharpness and wit with which they deconstructed the beliefs of simple, uneducated Christians. He was repelled by the obscurity of the Latin Bible, which he read in a primitive version written by inexperienced missionaries in the second century. Its barbarous style could not match the eloquence and subtlety of the works of Cicero, Virgil and Varro with which Augustine was familiar. The Manichaeans were famous for their attempts to subject faith to the critique of logic and consistency. Their system, after all, was a 'scientific' system in the sense that their mythology claimed to provide an account of what was 'objectively' visible in the night sky. The Milky Way *was* the Column of Glory. Mani's light could actually be seen. Hence, where others could only 'believe', the Manichaeans offered the open and undiluted truth, even if full access to such truth was reserved for their spiritual élite.

Augustine became suspicious of his own Manichaean beliefs and the claims of his sect's leaders as his knowledge of astrology grew. Mani's revelations of the workings of the universe appeared to be insufficient, if not simply inadequate, to explain what was clearly visible. There were, for example, no explanations for solstices or eclipses. In the *Confessions*, Augustine observed that what he was commanded to believe 'was entirely at variance and out of keeping with the principles of mathematics and the evidence of my own eyes'.[4] To him, this insight implied much more than that one theory was wrong and had to be replaced by another. He came to question not only the scientific truth of his beliefs but, more substantially, the misguided sense of certainty and the complete lack of guilt which, in his own assessment, had been the most conspicuous features of his Manichaean phase. The first of these issues – certainty – refers to the problem of knowledge, the second – guilt – to the problem of evil.

As he moved towards an ideal of wisdom which resulted from a prolonged quest without endings, Augustine had to leave the Manichaean certainty. The Manichaean system was a total system; it claimed to provide the *final* answer to *all* questions. As he understood very well, the system's attraction was precisely that it deluded the mind into a state of rest which, in truth, turned out to be a dead end. He rebelled against Mani's vision not because it contained errors but, more fundamentally, because his soul resisted the attempt to compress, once and for all, its experience of reality into a system.

There simply was no end to the soul's development in this life.

> Whoever thinks that in this mortal life a man may so disperse the mists of bodily and carnal imaginings as to possess the unclouded light of changeless truth, and to cleave to it with the unswerving constancy of a spirit wholly estranged from the common ways of life – he understands neither what he seeks, nor who he is who seeks it.[5]

Ultimate fulfilment can only come after death; in this life, the quest never ends, not even with baptism. If taken literally, this position seems to question the purpose of cosmic existence; but its symbolic significance lies precisely in the fact that it protects the meaningfulness of life in its entirety. To proclaim that fulfilment or perfection is a goal to be reached in this life entails a denigration of all those real aspects of life which cannot live up to the standards of perfection. To embrace the *whole* of human experience, in contrast, means to postpone the question of fulfilment.

The Bishop's position on the problem of evil confirms these insights. During his Manichaean phase, he was able to abnegate responsibility for evil and sin.

> I still thought that it is not we who sin but some other nature that sins within us. It flattered my pride to think that I incurred no guilt and, when I did wrong, not to confess it ... I preferred to excuse myself and blame this unknown thing which was in me but was not part of me.[6]

Augustine condemns the externalisation of evil as a substance, as an active power of its own because the problem of evil cannot be contained unless we begin to think of ourselves as sinners. It is absolutely crucial, therefore, that evil is not understood as an independent force which actively opposes the good, but as a mere privation of the good which is inherent in all forms of existence.

Evil cannot be externalised; it has existence only in those who turn away from the good. The view that fulfilment is impossible during mortal existence corresponds here to the position that the human being can never be declared free from sin in this world. Augustine dramatises this position in the symbol of the Original Sin, which, first incurred by Adam, affected all mankind by hereditary transmission. To one of his most eloquent critics, the Pelagian Bishop Julian of Eclanum, speaking of sin by transmission meant making sin a *necessary* component of human existence. This assumption, Julian continued, merely repeated the traditional error of the Manichaeans, for whom the very existence of the cosmos required a precosmic departure from divine perfection. The Original Sin, however, does not denote a 'necessity of sin', but a 'solidarity of sin', a common humility.

Humanity was firmly placed on the 'other side' of perfection; no human being was able to raise himself above this humility by his own merits. For Augustine, 'solidarity in sin' defined a community, and not boundaries such as the ones the Donatists and Pelagians drew around themselves. The symbol of the Original Sin was thus opposed to the latter's self-evoked, ascetic perfection. In accordance with these views, Augustine saw salvation as utterly dependent on God. 'Men place the initiative in their salvation on a wrong footing by placing it in themselves'.[7] If they do think they can find salvation on their own, they are bound to insert divisions among themselves.

Similar themes are present also in Augustine's greatest and most influential work, *The City of God*. This *magnum opus* has traditionally been at the centre of accusations that, in spite of his conversion, Manichaeism somehow survived in Augustine's thinking. Julian of Eclanum was not the only, and certainly not the last, critic to advance such charges.[8] The *City of God* presents the universe as divided into the *civitas Dei* and the *terrena civitas*. The two cities are distinguished by two kinds of loves: 'the earthly by the love of self, even to the contempt of God; the heavenly by the love of God, even to the contempt of self'. The division originated in the prideful revolt of the (now fallen) angels in heaven, which preceded and paralleled humanity's fate on earth. Humans had lived in peace and comity until the fall, which brought evil into the world. On earth, the fall signifies the beginning of the historical course of the two cities, which continues until the Day of Judgement.[9] This is the age called the time of the world.

As has frequently been pointed out, Augustine's presentation of the historical development of the opposition between the two cities resembles the structure of Manichaean mythology in a number of aspects. There is first of all the implied dualism of the two *civitates* which are separated, according to Augustine, by an unbridgeable gap. Secondly, just like Manichaean cosmogony, *City of God* divides the history of the world into three epochs: an epoch of separation and division which brings the two cities into existence, an era of co-existence and mixing, and finally a destined end in which the *civitas Dei* will have returned to what it was in the beginning. Finally, the work accentuates the sense of alienation among the citizens of the *civitas Dei* in this life. The faithful are soujourning on earth as aliens. The citizen of the *civitas Dei* is a 'resident stranger', a *peregrinus*, a pilgrim whose true home is elsewhere.

These similarities have traditionally been understood as evidence that the doctrine of the two cities, which after Augustine assumed world-wide significance, was directly taken over from Manichaeism. But the argument does not stand up to scrutiny. For, in spite of obvious correspondences, Augustine's *City of God* is fundamentally opposed to Manichaean dualism. Nowhere in the book does he propose a doctrine of evil as an eternal power separate from God. The devil has forsaken the truth, but he has not had an evil nature from the beginning.[10] And even after evil has entered the stage, Satan remains under God's jurisdiction. Moreover, although it is true that the *terrena civitas* represents a merging of identity into the things of this world, the latter are not deprived of goodness. The things of this world are God's gifts and as such are to be used by the members of the *civitas Dei*. Gold in itself, for example, is not evil; instead, what is evil is to love gold in the wrong manner. The dualism of Augustine's two cities is thus not an ontological, but a moral dualism.

It is also important to realise that, although the Manichaeans were familiar with a doctrine of two cities, the doctrine did not originate with them. As van Oort has argued, the similarities between Mani's system and Augustine's *civitates* need not derive from a direct influence of the former on the latter but can be explained by their common background. The actual source of the doctrine of the two cities 'is most likely the pre-Augustinian Christian, the Jewish and particularly the archaic Jewish-Christian tradition', which survived in Africa right up to the times of Augustine.[11]

Whatever the sources of its symbolism, the argument and concern of the *City of God* suggest that its author used a 'dualistically coloured phraseology' (van Oort, 1991) as a *means* in the same way in which Plato used myths to convey central elements of his philosophy. To present human sin as darkness, and the battle against evil as a conflict against the powers of the *terrena civitas*, allowed Christian thinkers to speak of the power of sin in the emphatic language of moral dualism without assigning Being to evil alongside the Being of God. This is not to say that the doctrine of the two cities was an allegory. In many places, Augustine says clearly that the *civitates* are real. At the same time, however, he asserts that the boundary between them is invisible. Who belonged to the devil's party and who did not was a secret. 'For in this world this is a secret, for we cannot tell whether even a man who seems to stand shall fall, or whether he who seems to lie shall rise again.' Even in the Christian Church both, 'he who breaks what he teaches and he who does it, the one being least, the other great', existed together.

> Consequently, where both classes exist, it is the Church as it is now, but where only the one shall exist, it is the Church as it is destined to be when no wicked person shall be in her. Therefore the Church even now is the Kingdom of Christ, and the Kingdom of Heaven. Accordingly, even now His Saints reign with Him, though otherwise than as they shall reign thereafter; and yet, though the tares grow in the Church along with the wheat, they do not reign with Him.[12]

Hence, the relevance of the division between the two cities is primarily eschatological. The boundary between the two will be revealed at the end of time, and only then. The whole construction has the function of an exhortation, an eschatological summons, even if the separation could not be an object of human action. In this sense, it is plainly wrong to say that Manichaeism entered Christian doctrine through the imprints it had left on its former auditor. When he argued against Mani's religion, Augustine knew exactly what he was doing.

In the long run, however, the Bishop of Hippo may have overestimated his readers. It is a frequent phenomenon in the history of political philosophy that the sophistication and sharpness of a great thinker is abused, probably unintentionally, by disciples of lesser talent. Augustine fought the sectarian consciousness of the Donatists, and yet the moral dualism of his *civitates* became easy prey for sectarian distortions. Anselm of Lucca and the other ideologists of the Investiture Contest ransacked his writings in order to patch together, from selective quotations, a Catholic theory of a 'holy' war. In the realm of theory, these developments heralded the Crusades.

EXCURSION II: THE MYTH OF THE PRINCE

In the tradition of the *speculum principis*, the question of good government was primarily a question of the ruler's moral qualities. The good ruler cultivated virtues such as compassion, trustworthiness, honesty and integrity as permanent parts of his character. The most important counsel given in these texts was therefore: Be good until you die. Sebastian de Grazia refers to this attitude as an 'ethics of being', in which the moral quality of government depends on the governor's personality, his 'being'. Machiavelli, de Grazia continues, replaced this ethics with an 'ethics of doing', in which the morality of an action depends entirely on its consequences.[13] In the face of changing circumstances, the blind adherence to principles, regardless of the respect they command, may prove disastrous not only for the ruler but also for his subjects. For the Florentine, therefore, there was no act which was intrinsically 'good'. After all, 'one sees a ruler flourishing today and ruined tomorrow, without having changed at all in character or qualities'.[14]

A prince who follows Machiavelli's 'ethics of doing' can never rest. He can never be sure of himself or of his position because his qualities can never be proven to be 'good' or 'bad' in themselves; at all times, they are merely 'held to be good' or 'thought to be bad'.[15] Both his fate and moral worth depend on the use made of such reputed qualities and on the consequences of princely action. Machiavelli's advice to the prince is therefore inevitably paradoxical. The only guideline which can claim some generality is that the ruler must be wary of generalisations. When discussing various courses of princely actions, the author of *The Prince* insists that 'one cannot give definite rules' (as to how to win over the people), and that 'definite judgements cannot be passed' (on whether the building of fortresses is useful), that the usefulness of certain actions 'depends on the circumstances', and that 'it is very difficult to generalise about this, since men and circumstances vary'.[16]

The prince must be sufficiently flexible and open to deal with contingencies, and he must not allow himself to be lulled into the false confidence of routines and principles. 'All courses of actions involve risks, for it is in the nature of things that when one tries to avoid one danger another is always encountered.'[17] A republic too, 'if she wants to be kept free, requires new acts of foresight every day'.[18]

Machiavelli's ethical framework has two important implications. If the moral quality of an act rests on its actual, intended and unintended, consequences, full moral assessments remain provisional. For at what point does an action or event no longer have consequences? And if the act continues indefinitely to have consequences, how can we ever draw a conclusion about its goodness? Certainty about the moral attributes of courses of events could only be achieved from a comprehensive perspective on the whole of human history. This perspective, however, is reserved to God. The true measure of justice, therefore, is God's unseen measure. The ultimate standards of justice – that is, knowledge of the distinction between good and evil – belong therefore to a realm 'beyond the things of the world', 'beyond the things of men'; a realm which 'human intelligence cannot grasp'.[19]

Because the monopoly of judgement rests with God, and because everyone is subject to his judgement, it is difficult for Machiavelli to write about politics and military affairs without mentioning God. He has more than one hundred references to God, none of which are trivial; they reveal a pious man who speaks of God in the conventional reverential manner. God's existence is taken for granted. Some people may have lost their fear of God but this does not in any sense question his reality. The fact that Machiavelli does not embellish God with racy metaphors and does not systematically address the nature of his existence does not reflect casualness but, on the contrary, reverence. Machiavelli's God is the creator, providential, real, universal, personal, and above all, 'a judge, just and forgiving, rewarding and punishing, awesome, a force transcendent, separate from but operative in the world'.[20] God is of 'infinite goodness' and never indifferent towards humans. In turn, human actions are liable to God's judgement because humans have free will. 'God does not want to have to do the whole thing, for he likes to leave us our free will so we can lay claim to part of the glory by earning it.'[21] The choice to act towards good or evil is an individual's choice; the ultimate judgement is God's.

The second implication of Machiavelli's approach to the problem of good and evil is that assessments of the moral appropriateness of actions cannot but draw on some notion of 'success'. Modern readers often tend to misconstrue this aspect of his thinking as an expression of moral relativism. But to say that a human being's moral judgement remains, in a sense, provisional does not imply that all judgements are the same. The 'success' the Italian has in mind is *inclusive* rather than a personal 'success'. In order to appreciate such 'success' properly, one must adopt a comprehensive view which looks, as much as possible, at *all* the consequences as they unfold from an action into the future. From this perspective, the ruler's 'success' transcends his personal fate. For the 'health' (*salute*) of the republic or kingdom it is not sufficient that it has a ruler who governs well for as long as he lives; instead, a leader is required who orders it in such a way that it can be maintained when he dies.[22]

The most comprehensive 'success' the ruler – and the ruled – can aim at is the common good – *il bene commune*, *il utile publico* or *il bene publico*. In his *Discourse of Florentine Public Affairs* (1520), Machiavelli seems to imply that the common good is best realised in an order in which 'no citizen of whatever rank either out of fear for himself or out of ambition would have to desire innovation'.[23] Thus, the *bene commune* correlates to a state of balance, an equilibrium, in which all citizens are both secure and content with their respective social positions and the opportunities they entail. The equilibrium does not exclude innovation altogether, but bans a desire for change based on the wrong motives.

In the early sixteenth century, however, the good end – *il fine buono* – could hardly have been more remote from the Italians. As he was writing *The Prince*, Machiavelli found Italy more slave than the Hebrews before Moses, more servant than the Persians before Cyrus, and more scattered than the Athenians before Theseus. Indeed, Italy was 'without head, without order, beaten, despoiled, lacerated, devastated, subject to every sort of ruination'.[24] It must be remembered that, prior to the French invasion in 1494, Italy had been a prosperous and wealthy country, perhaps the most civilised area in Europe. The destruction of the cultural and social order through the successive invasion of French, Spanish and German armies could therefore not be rationalised in terms of 'progression' as if economically progressive countries had invaded an economically-backward region. Further, the upheaval was neither the result of social revolution, nor apparently due to moral or political principles. It was a clear case of stronger powers with a better military organisation degrading a weaker, less-equipped power.[25] The apparent meaninglessness of the events made it all the more difficult to discern the force of organised human existence behind them.

The trauma of a dissolution of order can provoke various kinds of responses. Fatalism is one of them. The view that the affairs of this world are completely governed by fortune and fate, and that humans cannot control them was 'more popular' in his own times, Machiavelli wrote in the twenty-fifth chapter of *The Prince*, 'because of the great changes that have taken place'. It was this view which drove his contemporaries into despair or indifference; or into Hermetic magic, alchemy or science as a means of elevating humanity above the forces of law-like fate. The Italian even admits that he was sometimes tempted to adopt this opinion. In the end, however, he resisted. Man still controlled half of his actions. In order to illustrate both human limitations and possibilities in facing the unforeseen, he likened fortune to a river. Rivers, he observed in the same chapter,

> when they get angry, break their banks, knock down trees and buildings, strip the soil from one place and deposit it somewhere else. ... Nobody can resist them at any point. But although they are so powerful, this does not mean men, when the waters recede, cannot make repairs and build banks and barriers so that, if the waters rise again, either they will be safely kept within the sluices or at least their onrush will not be so unregulated and destructive.

Machiavelli's response to the crisis does not appeal to magic remedies which, once found, put humans forever in charge of their affairs. To him, the ultimate roots of the crisis do not lie in external forces to which humans are unavoidably exposed but in people's lack of preparation, their inability to look beyond their most immediate surroundings and their personal ambitions. Florence and Italy are helpless not because the cosmos works against them but because the centrifugal forces of self-interest and unlimited ambition undermine any attempt at a co-ordinated, united and effective response to the challenges. The crisis turns Machiavelli into a social critic who appeals to his fellow Italians for a reform from within.

The Florentine formulates his criticism in such a way that the crisis he perceives implies its own solution. Just as the Hebrews had their Moses, the Persians their Cyrus, and the Athenians their Theseus, the Italians must and will find their redeemer among themselves. The redeemer's task is to install or restore the common good by assigning everyone to his place. The ordering force by which he will achieve this Machiavelli calls *virtù ordinata*. Yet, because the measure of justice is transcendent, the individuals who possess such force and succeed in founding or restoring a just social order must somehow be 'favoured by God'; indeed they were 'friends of God'.[26] All four 'most excellent' men mentioned again and again in his writings – Moses, Cyrus, Theseus and Romulus – were thought to have enjoyed special relationships with the Divine.

The redeemer would therefore be a man of *charisma*. His actions and behaviour are performed in the power of a special, divine enabling. A *charisma* is a spiritual gift or talent granted by God not for the sake of the recipient but for the benefit of others. Numbers 11:14–17 implies that such *charisma* is a prerequisite for the right governing of a people.

For Paul, *charismata* were spiritual gifts from God which were meant to lead to the edification of the community.[27]

Machiavelli knew that the true candidates for the task would hesitate as they knew that they risked their souls when they entered evil.

> To reconstitute political life in a city presupposes a good man, whereas to have recourse to arms in order to make oneself prince in a republic supposes a bad man. Hence very rarely will there be found a good man ready to use bad methods in order to make himself prince, though with a good end in view, nor yet a bad man who, having become prince, is ready to do the right thing and to whose mind it will occur to use well that authority which he has acquired by bad means.[28]

For Plato, too, the coincidence of power and philosophy was a paradox and hence required chance or providence to become a reality.[29] Machiavelli, however, is impatient; he does not want to wait for chance. After all, the opportunity for restoration is there for 'so many factors come together at the moment to help out a new ruler'; indeed, one could not be sure if 'there has ever been a more propitious time for such a man'. Italy was awaiting its saviour.

The purpose of writing *The Prince*, or at least its last version which included the twenty-sixth chapter, was to recruit the man who would prove his *virtù ordinata* by reordering Italy. The text offered both the technical advice necessary to survive in a corrupt society as well as the encouragement for an unknown reader to seize the opportunity and recognise his calling. After all, God is offering his friendship. In the last chapter, the author addresses his prince directly. Machiavelli believed him to be a member of the Medici family, a family which was 'favoured by God' and, after Giovanni de Medici had become Pope, 'by the Church'. However, the Florentine thinker never hesitated to adjust the dedication to the necessities. Giuliano, the first candidate, died young; so did Lorenzo, to whom *The Prince* was actually dedicated. After Lorenzo's death, his hopes seem to have centred on Giovanni delle Bande Nere, son of Giovanni de Medici and Catherina Sforza. But he too died at an early age. Still, Machiavelli never gave up his hope that the redeemer would hear his calling. In a sense, *The Prince* is not addressed to any specific individual. Having been the victim of *fortuna* too often, its author considered himself a man of little *virtù*. Thus, not being a prophet himself, he could not tell who the true prophet would be. *The Prince* was meant to be encouraging and useful 'for whoever may understand it'.[30]

GEORGE F. KENNAN

Having joined the Foreign Service in 1926, aged twenty-two, Kennan soon established himself as a specialist in Russian and Soviet affairs. In 1933 he had his first assignment at the Embassy in Moscow, where he worked as an aide and interpreter to Ambassador Bullit. After a year as consul and second secretary in Vienna, he returned to Moscow in November 1935 (until August 1937) as second secretary, then again later in July 1944 (until April 1946) as minister-counsellor and chargé d'affaires, and in 1952 as ambassador. The ill-fated ambassadorship ended within only a few months when the Soviet government declared him a *persona non grata* after Kennan publicly compared the treatment he received in Moscow with the treatment he received from the Germans during his war internment in Bad Nauheim.[31] In between he served at the Soviet desk in the State Department (October 1937–August 1938), as second secretary and consul in Prague (from September 1938 for a year), as counsellor and chargé d'affaires in Lisbon, and briefly as a counsellor to the European Advisory Commission in London.

Kennan's career took a dramatic turn in response to his famous 'Long Telegram' which he sent from Moscow at the State Department's request in February 1946. The situation has been commented upon so many times that it is by now a commonplace to note the Telegram's extraordinary impact.[32] Kennan was at odds with American policy towards the Soviet Union at least since he had come to Moscow to serve under Harriman in 1944. For reasons to which I return later, he felt that the American administration and public were unprepared for the 'problem of dealing with Russia'. Before the United States could face this problem, an entirely different approach to the 'wider problems and techniques of [American] foreign policy in general' was required, for the Soviet Union was not just any partner or opponent in world politics; it was a force animated by a metastatic faith in an imminent transfiguration of the world through revolution. In a letter of 21 January 1946, to Elbridge Durbrow, Chief of the Eastern European Division in the State Department, he announced his resignation for the needed change in approach could not be initiated 'within the walls of a diplomatic chancery or in subordinate positions in the Department of State'. Kennan felt that he could have a greater effect on public opinion 'at home' if he left the Foreign Service.[33]

Less than two weeks later, on 9 February, Stalin explained in one of his rare public appearances that the Second World War could have been avoided if there had existed a method for the periodic redistribution of resources and markets between nations according to need. Because capitalism, as he added, had no such method most observers concluded that Stalin believed capitalism and peace were incompatible. Pondering upon the purpose and meaning of Stalin's address, the Treasury Department decided to ask Kennan for his views on why Moscow did not show more enthusiasm about the World Bank and International Monetary Fund.

Previously, Washington had not responded to Kennan's numerous cables analysing Soviet developments, leading him to believe that he was entirely ignored. When the request eventually reached him, two weeks after despair had driven him into resignation, he felt that he had nothing to lose: 'They had asked for it. Now, by God, they would have it.'[34] Driven by 'impatience and disgust' at Washington's *naïveté*, Kennan composed a brilliantly-written eight thousand-word telegram in which he analysed the nature of the Soviet challenge. The fact that the Soviet Union was 'inaccessible to considerations of reality in its basic reactions', that Soviet party line was 'not based on any objective analysis of [the] situation beyond Russia's borders' meant that the Soviet leaders could not be persuaded by rational argument in negotiations. In fact, 'the very disrespect of Russians for objective truth – indeed, their disbelief in its existence – leads them to view all stated facts as instruments for furtherance of one ulterior purpose or another'.[35]

Washington's reaction to the telegram 'was nothing less than sensational'.[36] The State Department sent its author a message of commendation and sent copies of the telegram to diplomatic missions around the world. Secretary of the Navy James Forrestal had it reproduced and made required reading for hundreds, if not thousands, of higher officers in the armed services. Kennan believes that it was due to Forrestal's influence that he was assigned as a deputy commandant for foreign affairs to the National War College in Washington, and later chosen by General Marshall to head the newly-established Policy Planning Staff.[37] As Director of the Planning Staff, Kennan was largely responsible for the design and implementation of the Marshall Plan.

That there was a serious danger that his position could be misunderstood in a fundamental way must have become clear to Kennan at the latest after the publication of the famous 'X' article and the subsequent public uproar over its contents.[38] Since attempts to conceal his authorship soon failed, the article was given an unwanted, and in many ways mistaken, quasi-official character. 'Mr X' was bombarded with press comments and felt 'like one who has inadvertently loosened a large boulder from the top of a cliff and now helplessly witnesses its path of destruction in the valley bellow, shuddering and wincing at each successive glimpse of disaster'.[39]

The irony, if not tragedy, of the situation was that Kennan failed to express his views clearly and became affiliated with the 'sweeping language' and 'sweeping commitments' (Kennan, 1967) of the Truman Doctrine. The press picked up the concept of 'containment' and elevated it to the status of a 'doctrine' of which Kennan was considered the author. He later self-critically identifies a number of deficiencies in his article. Most serious of all was his failure 'to make clear that what

[he] was talking about when [he] mentioned the containment of Soviet power was not the containment by military means of a military threat, but the political containment of a political threat'.[40] By pointing out the specific nature of Soviet power, he had demanded a different approach to American foreign policy, but at the same time, his presentation of Soviet Communism unwillingly aroused the proponents of the United States' missionary role in the exorcism of the world from evil.

As the 'oversimplified and highly militarized view of the Russian problem'[41] reflected in NSC-68 came to dominate American policies towards the Soviet Union, Kennan's recommendations no longer carried the weight they once had. After leaving the Policy Planning Staff, he took a long leave of absence and spent two years at the Institute for Advanced Study in Princeton before he accepted, with some hesitation, the ambassadorship in Moscow. He hesitated for the simple reason that he 'had misgivings about undertaking to represent, in a capital as important and sensitive as Moscow, a policy' which by then he 'neither fully understood nor believed in'.[42]

In the summer of 1953, Kennan retired from the Foreign Service and became a member of the Institute for Advanced Study. With the exception of a brief ambassadorship in Yugoslavia under the Kennedy administration (1961–63), he avoided further direct involvement in politics and found a new home in the academic world of which he became a much respected member. Through his writings, lectures and public appearances, Kennan seems by now, in the words of Alex Danchev, the 'putative philosopher-king of the American republic'.[43]

KENNAN AS A PHILOSOPHER

For Kennan the soul is the centre of the human being. With the soul 'there developed in man ... a capacity for self-awareness, for self-scrutiny, and for consciousness of the moral qualities of his own behaviour, and indeed a certain ability to perceive and hold in mind the distinctions between right and wrong'.[44] He sees the soul

> not only as a sort of self-awareness that was not present in the animal, but also as the emergence in individual man of a certain moral autonomy – an ability to make choices and to design, within the limits of his mortality and his semi-animalistic nature, his own path.[45]

The soul has to operate in between two deities, the Primary Cause and the Spirit. The Primary Cause is the creator of the natural order of things and, in this role, is not entirely responsive to human desires. 'The Primary Cause must, after all, have had a great many other things to think about'. Hence, humans are in no position to transgress the natural order of things – neither through actions of their own nor through prayers.

However, the soul is not alone in the order of things.

> Simultaneously with the emergence of the soul there seems to me to have become evident the existence, and the involvement with human life, of a Deity of another sort ... filled with understanding and compassion for the agonies inflicted on man by the conflict between his two natures,

physical and spiritual. This Deity, 'if not indeed the creator of the innovation in man's nature called the soul, was and is the companion to it'. It is a 'loving and caring companion', and perhaps even more: 'a part of the human person itself, sharing in its trials and dilemmas, and lending the strength necessary for their endurance'. Referring to John 4:24, Kennan envisions this merciful Deity as a 'Substance, a Spirit, as Jesus himself is said once to have described it'. He distinguishes the Spirit from the 'all-powerful Deity of established Christian doctrine' because the Spirit 'bears no responsibility for the natural order of things in which the human individual is compelled to live'. The Spirit regards this order as a 'given' factor in the defining of the human predicament – 'as one of the inalterable terms of the human problem; and it starts from there in the search for a response to that problem'. The problem is thus reduced 'to the question of how, within the framework of a natural order already established, the individual is to conduct himself in a manner consistent with the divine purpose'.[46]

In the context of this problem, of living in harmony with the 'divine purpose' in an order given to man, the Spirit's intercession is required and will be forthcoming 'if suitably asked for'. Kennan suggests that the Spirit can speak to human beings in moments of despair. 'I, the Spirit says, am a part of you. I am partly outside you, but also partly within you.' The Spirit can help only to the extent that the believer welcomes the help and puts 'forward [his] best effort to help [himself]'. It is the believer who, 'by the dimensions of [his] own effort, define[s] the limits of [the Spirit's] usefulness'. The 'usefulness' of the Spirit lies in the fact that It is a 'fellow sufferer', that it gives 'understanding' and, 'to the extent that [the believer] deserve[s] it, compassion'. Because the Spirit is 'stronger' than the believer, It can give strength so that human efforts can 'extend' beyond mortality. The actions of the Spirit are not 'entirely intelligible' to humans. Some of them 'will have to be taken on faith'; in fact, they are offered only 'on the assumption that faith is forthcoming'.

Kennan is at pains to point out that the tension between the given order of things and the merciful Deity is to be endured rather than artificially removed. There is hope, but no happy ending. He 'decisively' rejects 'any and all suggestions' that mankind might be perfectible. The human being was a 'cracked vessel'. There was 'a real flaw in human nature – a flaw which places definite limitations on man's happiness, whether personal or social, the correction of which lies in part beyond the limits of his own powers'. Man was not 'perfectible' for the 'fissures in the human psyche are profound and elemental', a fact which should 'warn us against any and every sort of utopian purpose or expectation'. 'Marxists and the other materialists' failed to recognise that 'a measure of tragedy is built into the very existence of the human individual; and it is not to be overcome by even the most drastic human interventions into the economic or social relationships among individuals'. Hope can come only from the 'preeminent involvement and responsibility of the single human soul, in all its loneliness and frailty'.[47]

By establishing a strong link between the soul and the merciful Deity, Kennan presents the soul as an individual's sensorium of transcendence. The duality between the Primary Cause and the Spirit is not resolved in some cosmic drama but remains the fundamental condition of human existence. Humans must bear the tension of standing in-between, of the Platonic *metaxy*. He is adamant that the human condition is no reason for despair. The struggle 'can have, and does have, its glorious moments'. Moreover, 'true glory' will not be found in the 'visible prospects of success' but in the 'inherent worthiness of the struggle'.[48]

In Kennan's view, the 'problem of religious faith' concerns the 'effort of a single man to establish his relationship to forces beyond the reach of his own rational perception – forces upon the interaction with which he knew the ultimate value of his own life to depend'.[49] Thus, it is not left to the individual to determine the ultimate value of his own life. Accordingly, in his writings, Kennan tries 'to avoid judgements on [himself], [his] doings, [his] attempts to understand the life of [his] time' for 'all that would have to be left, [he] thought, to a deity held – if only by faith – to be benevolent'.[50] Still, it is important to him that, at the moment of judgement, he will be able to say that he 'had, after all, simply done [his] best'.[51] As a *parrhesiast*, Kennan acts on his own with 'nothing to look to but his own consciousness', but he still acts in front of God. The ultimate responsibility of the individual for his actions, for the way in which he relates to other individuals 'in his daily duties and doings', is 'a responsibility before his conscience and his God; it is not polluted by association with that of other men for worldly purposes'. The extent to which the individual lived up to this responsibility was the key, at least in theory, to 'the possibility of saintliness'.[52]

The Christian faith 'has its part' in life where humans acknowledge that God's measure is 'unseen'. Awaiting judgement through a bigger power, the individual can do only what he can, 'with as much fidelity as [he] can muster to [his] own nature and [his] own values'. For humans see 'only dimly, their justice is imperfect, and they do not really know what is right and what is wrong. They know only whether they have done their best'.[53] We all carry individual responsibility for our deeds precisely because we can never be mere agents of divine will. God's purposes are not visible; and his ways are 'truly unfathomable'.[54] The soul gives the individual a sense of 'right' and 'wrong', a sense of his being subject to God's measure, the full contents of which remains, however, elusive.

PHILOSOPHY, POLITICS AND THE LIMITS OF POWER

In the political realm, the elusiveness of God's measure imposes *philosophical* limits on the projection of American or Western power to the rest of the world. It was not just pragmatic but also *moral* reasons that demanded that Americans appreciate the limitations of their country's power. In this context, it is worthy noting that Kennan was one of the earliest critics of the Vietnam War. He insisted that

> there are problems in this world that we will not be able to solve, depths into which it will not be useful or effective for us to plunge, dilemmas in other regions of the globe that will have to find their solution without our involvement.[55]

'We must bear in mind that there are things we do not know and cannot know.' Therefore, 'we cannot conclude that everything we want automatically reflects the purpose of God'.[56] In particular, it was beyond the 'political and moral possibilities' of the United States to 'govern, even temporarily, great numbers of people in other parts of the world'.

If it is an essential aspect of the human condition that God's measure is 'unseen', then no people is justified in applying its own measure to other peoples of the world. 'No people can be the judge of another's domestic institutions and requirements', and Americans 'have no need to be apologetic to anyone, unless it be ourselves, for the things we do and the arrangements we enforce within our own country'. If Americans were able to act accordingly, to 'lay upon [themselves] this sort of restraint', and if in addition they were able 'to refrain from constant attempts at moral appraisal', then, Kennan suggested, 'posterity might look back upon our efforts with fewer and less troubled questions'.[57]

Moral crusades, which demand great changes in the lives of other people, were 'simply not in character' for the United States.[58] Against the 'legalism' and 'moralism' of the immediate post-war period, Kennan proposed to 'get back more closely to some of the concepts of the Founding Fathers of this country if we are to cope with the problems of modern times'.[59] His study of American diplomatic history showed him that the 'lucid and realistic thinking of early American statesmen of the Federalist period' got lost in the 'cloudy bombast of their successors of later decades'. He traced the utopian expectations, legalistic methodology and moralistic demands of the post-Kennan American diplomacy back to the statesmen of the period from the Civil War to the Second World War.

For Kennan, the annexation of the Philippines, Puerto Rico, Guam and the Hawaiian Islands marks a turning-point 'in the whole concept of the American political system. They represented the first instance of sizeable populations being taken under our flag with no wide anticipation that they would ever be accepted into statehood'.[60] He sees here the first manifestations of 'a sort of Rotarian idealism, a dogoodiness' in American foreign policy, which he relates to the late nineteenth-century outburst of missionary activities overseas. According to Kennan, it was the very same idealism which determined the American attitude towards the First World War as the opportunity to make the world 'safe for democracy', that determined American policies behind the Kellogg Pact, the World Trade Organisation, the United Nations and UNESCO.[61] He regards such 'ostensibly idealistic and pretentious undertakings' as concealments for 'our failure to have a genuine foreign policy addressed to the real problems of international relations in a changing world'.[62] Instead, statesmen devoted themselves to what Kennan calls 'the American dream' – the dream to appear (rather than to be) before 'the mirror of our own adolescent self-esteem' something 'lofty, something noble, something of universal significance'.[63]

Yet, in reality, the only way of exerting external influence which was 'in character' for the United States was leadership by example. In a speech given at Scranton in January 1953, Kennan quoted the passage from John Quincy Adams about 'America being the well-wisher to the freedom and independence of all, but the champion and vindicator only of her own'. He called upon his fellow-countrymen to 'take pride in our institutions and our political ideas', to 'commend them *by their successful application* in our own country'.[64] Again and again, he repeated that the power of example was far greater than the power of precept.

> The greatest service this country could render to the rest of the world is to put its own house in order and then make American civilisation an example of decency, humanity, and societal success from which others could derive whatever they might find useful to their own purposes.[65]

Kennan never departed from the principle of 'leadership by example'. It reappears in the early 1990s as 'the greatest help' Americans could give to the Russians after the end of the Cold War though the example would, of course, 'depend upon the quality of our own civilisation'.[66]

An important implication of the elusiveness of the measure is that, for Kennan, 'our belief in our own institutions is still something in the nature of faith, a habit and a predilection.' It was not a belief 'which can be justified to others on incontestable empirical grounds'. Whether American public institutions are able 'to bear society through the vicissitudes of social and economic change and to continue to provide a successful framework for progress in a society where the development of technology is placing ever greater strains on the structure of public authority' was, as he wrote in 1950, the undecided issue of the present. In a 'changing and imperfect world', the issue will never be entirely decided so that 'our adherence to our own institutions must remain, legitimately and understandably, an act of faith, not a pragmatic experience'. Therefore, again, 'any attempt on our part to recommend our institutions to others must come perilously close to the messianic tendencies of those militant political ideologies which say, in effect, "You should believe because we believe"'.[67]

PHILOSOPHICAL LEADERSHIP AND THE NEED FOR INTROSPECTION

In one of the papers of the Policy Planning Staff, Kennan argued that 'a truly stable world order can proceed, within our lifetime, only from the older, mellower and more advanced nations of the world'. For these were the nations for which 'the concept of order, as opposed to power, has value and meaning'. Unless these nations, 'through that combination of political greatness and wise restraint which goes only with a ripe and settled civilisation', find the strength to hold 'real leadership in world affairs today', Plato's vision that 'cities will never have rest from their evils, – nor the human race, as I believe' will come true.[68] It is remarkable that Plato's *Republic* could find its way into the papers of the main advisory body of the State Department. The quote is very revealing for it was meant to place the (ongoing) ERP, the European Recovery Program (Marshall Plan), into a context. The context becomes clear once it is understood that Plato's warning in the *Republic* 474d–e refers to a situation in which the city fails to combine philosophy and political power. In Kennan's analysis, then, the task of the Marshall Plan was to prepare the grounds for the re-emergence of philosophical leadership among the nations of the world. As such it also expressed an acknowledgement that the 'fountainheads of most of [America's] own culture and traditions' lay in Europe. By abandoning Europe, 'we would be placing ourselves in the position of a lonely country, culturally and politically. To maintain confidence in our own traditions and institutions, we would henceforth have to whistle loudly in the dark'.[69]

In Kennan's outlook, then, the European Recovery Program was based on philosophical and, therefore, *civilisational concerns*.

> Involved in the continuation of the present conditions in Europe [was] nothing less than the possibility of a renunciation by Europeans of the values of individual responsibility and political restraint which have become traditional to their continent. This would undo the work of centuries and would cause such damage as could only be overcome by the effort of further centuries.

In addition, the United States, 'in common with most of the rest of the world, would suffer a cultural and spiritual loss incalculable in its long-term effects'.[70]

The need to provide spiritual leadership by example imposes on American (and Western) society the need for introspection.

> It is because no country can hope to be, over the long run, much more to others than it is to itself that we have the moral duty to put our own house in order, if we are to take our proper part in the affairs of the rest of the world.[71]

In 1951, in a paper which he considered to be a 'second "X"-Article', Kennan was still sufficiently optimistic to assert that Americans, if in accord with themselves, could 'compel the respect and confidence of a world which, despite all its material difficulties, is still more ready to recognise and respect spiritual distinction than material opulence'.[72] Much less optimistic assessments of the attraction of 'spiritual distinction' followed later. In 1972, he observed that Americans had 'simply not faced up successfully to [their] own internal problems' and had lost, 'just since World War II, a great deal of [their] value, and [their] potential influence, as an example to other people'.[73]

National strength was above all 'a question of our internal strength; of the health and sanity of our own society'. For this reason, Americans could not afford 'to be indifferent to internal disharmony, dissension, intolerance, and the things that break up the moral and political structure of our society at home'.[74] The picture of a 'harmonious' society he takes from a book by Lewis Mumford, *The Culture of Cities* (1938). The book contains an illustration of a 'holy procession' in medieval Florence which had no spectators. 'Everyone in town was in the procession, because everyone in town had some relation to the public life of the place.' 'Everybody fitted in somewhere.' According to Kennan, this is 'how life should be'. 'And this is what we have lost.'[75]

The need for introspection and *internal* reform followed from more than the obvious lack of *philosophical* leadership in world politics. Kennan's prophecies gained an additional sense of urgency from his belief in the inevitability of decline. Unless precautions are taken, nature will always claim her own 'in her usual implacable way, attacking the products of all human intrusions upon her favoured uniformities, cracking foundations, rotting walls, spreading spiderwebs, overgrowing lawns, meadows, and all other products of the human effort at "improvement"'.[76] He read Spengler's *The Decline of the West* at the age of twenty-two and was a great admirer of Edward Gibbon (1737–94), the chronicler of the fall and decline of the Roman Empire.[77] 'For years,' Kennan admitted in the late 1960s, 'Gibbon's dictum that "under a democratical government the citizens exercise the powers of sovereignty; and those powers will be first abused, and afterwards lost, if they are committed to an unwieldy multitude" has lain at the heart of [his] political philosophy.'[78] On another occasion he quotes from Gibbon that 'from enthusiasm to imposture the step is perilous and slippery'.[79]

The implication of such views is that decline is inevitable unless American society takes care of itself. Kennan is adamant that the celebration of 'democracy' alone was not enough. 'Democracy in all its modern forms, and particularly as it now exists in the US, is not the final answer to political problems.' For 'the value of a democratic society in the Christian sense depends not just on the fact of its enjoying certain rights and liberties but on the nature of the use made of them'.[80] Democratic liberties are *means*, not ends. And the question of ends, of improvement, naturally involves spiritual aspects of human existence. The response to the 'great social bewilderments of this age' must lie predominantly in the 'spiritual, moral, and intellectual shaping of the individual with a view to the development of his qualities of leadership, rather than on the prospects for unaided self-improvement on the part of the leaderless masses'.[81] He openly commits himself to a form of 'élitism'. The required élite must be an élite 'of service to others, of conscience, of responsibility, of restraint of all that is unworthy in the self, and of resolve to be to others more than one could ever hope to be to one's self'.[82]

TOTALITARIANISM AS THE CORRUPTION OF THE SOUL

According to Kennan, one of the most important and most disturbing hallmarks of Soviet totalitarianism, and indeed of any kind of totalitarianism, is its opposition to the quest for truth. 'Persons really committed to Soviet ideology … could not simultaneously be committed to that rigid dogma and total intellectual discipline, on the one hand, and to the freedom of the mind in the quest for objective truth … on the other.'[83] In their 'feverish political imaginations', Soviet leaders cultivated falsehood as a deliberate weapon of policy. 'They began by adopting an attitude of complete cynicism about objective truth, denying its value if not its existence, declaring the lie to be no less useful and respectable than the truth if only it served the purposes of the party'. Once the possibility of truth is denied, falsehood becomes a means for the Soviet leaders of 'deceiving others and exploiting their credulity' as well as of 'comforting and reassuring themselves'.[84] To them, truth was created rather than a constant. Truth was nothing but 'the most recent manifestation of the wisdom of those in whom the ultimate wisdom is supposed to reside, because they represent the logic of history'.[85]

The resistance to the quest for truth is always followed by the creation of a 'second reality'.

> In tens of thousands of instances, over the course of the years, real events had to be denied, false ones invented, or true facts distorted beyond recognition, in order to produce a version that was compatible with the party's neurotic vision of the environment in which it lived and of its own reaction to that environment.[86]

Kennan gives an example of this procedure in his memoirs. In the negotiations at Potsdam, Stalin complained that all ports of the Baltic freeze. Demanding at least one ice-free port at the expense of Germany, Stalin asked for the cession of the city of Königsberg to the Soviet Union. His request went unchallenged. In his personal report on the Potsdam Conference, Truman later informed the American public that he had agreed to satisfy the 'age-old Russian yearning' for an ice-free port. But, as Kennan points out, Königsberg is *not* ice-free. It lies forty-nine kilometres from the open sea, at the end of an artificial canal which is frozen several months of the year. However, the second, post-war edition of the *Soviet Encyclopaedia*, published in 1953, specifically describes Königsberg as 'ice-free'. The earlier edition made no such allegation. Kennan believes that 'the grounds for this assertion can be no other than Stalin's statement'. Geographic conditions were apparently created by the 'political convenience of the Soviet government. If anyone thought, after 1945, that he saw ice in the canal at Königsberg, he didn't. It was an illusion fed by anti-Soviet prejudice'.[87]

Kennan reflected on the philosophical implications of the Soviet denial of truth and its implications for American-Soviet relations in a long memorandum 'Russia – Seven Years Later' written in September 1944 in Moscow. Later he explained that the memo was 'actually basic to the understanding of the later ones' written from the embassy in Moscow between 1944 and 1946. Hence, it must have been 'basic' also to the analysis of the Long Telegram.[88]

As a reflection on the changes that had occurred in the Soviet Union since his last visit in 1937, 'Russia – Seven Years Later' contains a remarkable discussion of the problem of the philosopher to distinguish shadows from reality.[89] '[R]ight and wrong, reality and unreality, are determined in Russia not by any God, not by any innate nature of things, but simply by men themselves. Here men determine what is true and what is false.' This 'serious fact' was 'the gateway to the comprehension of much that is mysterious in Russia'. According to Kennan, 'Bolshevism has proved some strange and disturbing things about human nature. It has proved that what is important for people is not what is there but what they conceive to be there.' Given unlimited control over people's minds, it was possible to make them feel and believe 'practically anything'. And it made 'no difference whether that "anything" is true, in our conception of the word. For the people who believe it, it becomes true. It attains validity, and all the powers of truth.' The shadow which is taken for reality can arouse 'unspeakable violence' on the part of both those who fight for it and those who fight against it. He concludes that the 'power of autosuggestion' played a 'tremendous part in Soviet life'.

This is Kennan's depressing analysis of life in the cave of Soviet Russia of 1944. What did he think, at that time, about the possibility of the philosophical ascent out of the cave? First, he warns Americans that they do not stand above 'these disturbing phenomena of the Russian world. Unless he is a man of great mental obtuseness or of great mental strength', the American too,

> upon the first contact with Russian life, will begin to react strongly to these man-made currents, the reality of which he would have contemptuously rejected from a distance. He will soon take them as real forces, as real threats or as real promises.

He will be right 'but he will not know what he is doing. He will remain the tool, rather than the master, of the material he is seeking to understand'. Kennan concludes that there was 'little possibility that enough Americans will ever accomplish these philosophical evolutions to permit of any general understanding of Russia on the part of our government or our people'.

The understanding of such 'disturbing phenomena', however, was not impossible even if 'it would imply a measure of intellectual humility and a readiness to reserve judgement about ourselves and our institutions, of which few of us would be capable'. Hence, loneliness is the immediate implication of the 'apprehension of what is valid in the Russian world', an altogether 'unsettling and displeasing' experience. And whoever succeeds in this enterprise is unlikely to

> find his satisfaction in the achievement of anything practical for his people, still less in any official or public appreciation for his efforts. The best he can look forward to is the lonely pleasure of one who stands at long last on a chilly and inhospitable mountain top where few have been before, where few can follow, and where few will consent to believe that he has been.[90]

Kennan describes in these passages the loneliness of the philosopher-diplomat whose peculiar existence between (at least) two societies has given him insights which are unwanted in both of them.

The dismissal of the quest for truth corresponds to the systematic destruction of *parrhesia* in Soviet society. Once the Party committee has made its decision, 'it is incumbent upon the individual member to support that decision with every evidence of conviction and enthusiasm, no matter what may have been his feelings before that decision was taken'. As a result, the individual link in the chain of command enjoys the 'happy privilege of feeling no worry about that which has been done, and of being free to direct attention solely to the problems of the future'. If the collective decision turns out to be unfortunate, the individual conscience is absolved through the collective principle.[91] Hence, Soviet society is geared towards the eradication of *parrhesiasts*, of people whose actions flow from their own individual conscience.

Other features of Soviet totalitarianism include its 'exaggerated fear of the outside world', the 'universal pretensions' of its ideology, the 'jealous and intolerant eye of the Kremlin' which can distinguish, 'in the end, only vassals and enemies', its excessive secrecy, and the fact that its leaders recognised 'no restrictions, either of God or man, on the character of their methods'.[92] And because of the distorted relation Soviet ideologists had with truth, their 'suspicions' could not be 'altered or assuaged by personal contacts, rational arguments or official assurances'.[93] Moreover, the Soviet perspective was self-confirming:

> It is an undeniable privilege of every man to prove himself right in the thesis that the world is his enemy; for if he reiterates it frequently enough and makes it the background of his conduct he is bound eventually to be right.[94]

And if the Soviets are animated 'by implacable hostility to all that they do not control, they can only assume those whom they do not control are animated by a similar hostility toward them'. Thus, the Kremlin must conclude 'that their power must be absolute if it is to be effective'.[95] Moreover, Kennan observed the intrinsic need for Soviet ideology to present itself in the form of an all-encompassing system for 'a regime which forbids individuals to formulate their own political thought must itself always have an answer for everything ...'.[96]

With its denial of the quest for truth, the Soviet system was 'an attempt at the destruction of Western civilisation', as Kennan remarked in a Policy Planning Staff paper.[97] Nevertheless, he was confident that Communism had no future. It had no future because, as his friend Charles Bohlen once observed, 'it had no answer to the phenomenon of death. ... The Marxist outlooks included no recognition that the individual human condition embraced within itself elements of tragedy (man's mortality was only one) that could not be overcome by even the most drastic manipulations of social environment'.[98] The Kremlin leaders, although armed with a formidable ideology, had no 'answers to any of the great riddles of humanity, the riddles of birth and love and ambition and death which have accompanied man from the beginning of civilisation'.[99] And yet it was necessary to be on guard against the further spread of messiaism for those who are 'determined to achieve the elimination of evil and the realisation of the Millennium within their own time' do more harm than the efforts of those who 'have tried to create a little order and civility and affection within their own intimate entourage, even at the cost of tolerating a great deal of evil in the public domain'.[100]

Kennan refused to discuss Soviet ideology as if it were to be taken at face value. Soviet Communism, with its 'messianic quality' was not, in his view, a new philosophy about to revolutionise the world but the latest manifestation of a historical tradition which in earlier times had celebrated Russia as 'Holy Russia' and Moscow as the 'Third Rome'. Behind

> those grim old walls surrounding the palaces and churches of the Kremlin was not a new revelation of human or divine genius, not a new idea destined to change the ethics of man and to open a brighter page in the history of humanity, but only ... a streamlined version of a despotism as old as human society itself.[101]

Soviet ideology purported to be a 'rival religion' but as such it was 'no less Byzantine in conception and no less Russian in method' than the Orthodox Church.[102]

'Russia', Kennan explains, has never been a territorial notion. Russia

> stopped where the infidel began ... There were no geographical barriers, no mountains, no seas, no fastflowing rivers to mark it. It was as limitless as the horizon of the Russian plain itself. And it is no wonder then that the Russians saw no final limit to the possible extension of their power.

In his lectures at the National War College, he quotes from an American envoy who reported from St Petersburg in the nineteenth century that 'these people are obsessed with a strange superstition that they are destined to conquer the world'. The historical continuity of Russian messiaism implied that, at a deeper level, the problem of Soviet totalitarianism was *not* a problem of Marxist ideology. 'In summary, then, the role of ideology in Soviet political psychology, while of tremendous importance, is not primarily that of a basic determinant of political action'.[103]

My analysis must shift, therefore, from Kennan's evaluation of Soviet ideology to the problem of totalitarianism in general. After having spent more than ten years of his life in totalitarian countries, there was no doubt in Kennan's mind that totalitarianism was 'the most shocking and cynical disservice one can do to the credulity and to the spiritual equilibrium of one's fellow men'.[104] Totalitarianism was the 'social equivalent of mental illness'; both often began with 'the sense of being the innocent victim of unseen conspirational forces'.[105] Thus, significantly, totalitarianism was not a national phenomenon;

> it is a disease to which all humanity is in some degree vulnerable. To live under such a regime is a misfortune that can befall a nation by virtue of reasons purely historic. ... Where circumstances weaken the powers of resistance, to a certain crucial degree, the virus triumphs.

The Russians, in other words, had become victims of a 'virus' which exploited 'the evil and weakness in man's nature'. It attempted 'to live by man's degradation, feeding like a vulture on his anxieties, his capacity for hatred, his susceptibility to error, and his vulnerability to psychological manipulation'.[106]

It was simply not true that 'the human impulses which give rise to the nightmares of totalitarianism were ones which Providence had allocated only to other peoples and to which the American people had been graciously left immune'. Moreover, there were 'openly totalitarian forces already working in [American] society'. In fact,

> there is a little bit of the totalitarian buried somewhere, way down deep, in each and every one of us. It is only the cheerful light of confidence and security which keeps this evil genius down at the usual helpless and invisible depth.

Those who think that the work of building freedom in the United States was accomplished completely and for all time by our forefathers 'lull themselves to sleep'. Quoting from Goethe, Kennan concluded that 'freedom has to be reconquered every day'.[107]

The vulnerability of the human soul to the dangers of totalitarianism created a bond between Russians and Americans. Kennan asked his compatriots to

> rise above these easy and childish reactions and consent to view the tragedy of Russia as partly our own tragedy, and the people of Russia as our comrades in the long hard battle for a happier system of man's coexistence with himself and with nature on this troubled planet.[108]

And because confidence – or faith – was decisive in fighting off the virus of totalitarianism, the threat

> which has lain behind Soviet armies, ... and behind the aberrations of confused American left-wingers, will not be overcome until we have learned to view ourselves realistically and to purge ourselves of some of our prejudices, our hypocrisies, and our lack of civil discipline.[109]

In the end, the 'most important factor in determining the ultimate outcome of the Cold War was the spiritual distinction of our own civilisation'. For 'whether we win against the Russians is primarily a question of whether we win against ourselves'. In 1957, in his BBC Reith Lectures, Kennan insisted that 'the fortunes of the Cold War will begin to turn in our direction as and when we learn to apply ourselves resolutely to many things that have, superficially viewed, nothing whatsoever to do with the Cold War at all'.[110]

The ossification of the Cold War, however, was strong evidence for Kennan that the Americans were failing in their efforts to avoid contagion with the virus of totalitarianism. The Marshall Plan was the appropriate beginning of the 'containment' policy, but this is precisely what it was supposed to be: a *beginning*. 'It would lay the foundation for a new sense of purpose in Western society' – a sense of purpose needed 'not just for our protection against an outward threat but to enable us to meet a debt to our own civilisation …, to accomplish what we would have owed it to ourselves to accomplish, *even had such a thing as international communism never existed*'.[111] All those things that needed to be done to combat Communism needed to be done 'anyway – even in the absence of a Communist threat – to assure the preservation and advance of civilisation'.[112]

This broader meaning of 'containment' brings the term close to the classical notion of *arete*, to a balanced existence, a taking care of oneself, the ability to preserve the openness of reality by resisting the slavery of addictions, and to virtue. Thus, beneath the problem of the relative importance of political and military means of containing the Soviet Union, there is a philosophical concern at the centre of Kennan's containment. He makes this concern explicit by acknowledging that 'we can no longer apply that term [containment] to the Soviet Union alone'. For 'there is much in our own life, here in this country, that needs early containment. It could in fact be said that the first thing we Americans need to learn to contain is, in some ways, ourselves'. There were many aspects of modern Western life which needed 'containment' – 'environmental destructiveness' and the 'tendency to live beyond our means' were just two examples. Kennan proposes to 'develop a wider concept of what containment means, a concept more closely linked to the totality of the problems of Western civilisation at this juncture in world history'.[113]

In this broader sense, 'containment' is directed against a form of existence which does not recognise limits. Limitless existence, Kennan clarifies, was partly the immediate consequence of the unconditional acceptance of the logic of the marketplace.

> A foreigner easily gains the impression that we … have resigned ourselves helplessly to the workings of our economic system; and that we are content to move wherever that system carries us, regardless of the effect on the esthetic taste, the intellectual health, and the emotional freshness of our people.

Once one loses a sense of limits, one loses a sense of what should not be done, and hence becomes unable to understand how and, in fact, why one should direct one's life in a purposeful and cautious manner.

And once orientation has gone lost, one cannot give an example to others: 'only he is capable of exercising leadership over others who is capable of some real degree of mastery over himself'.[114]

In the context of American–Soviet relations, containment was never meant to 'perpetuate the status quo' but 'to tide us over a difficult period'. At one point in the mid-1940s, Kennan thought that this 'difficult period' would last about ten to fifteen years.[115] The path of containment he had envisioned was left when 'containment' was transformed into a doctrine, into an 'indestructible myth'. This, he reflects, was one of the unfortunate effects of the 'X-Article'. In a sense, then, containment itself did not fail but the intended follow-up never occurred.[116] Instead, there followed the militarisation of the conflict.

Henceforth Kennan was again at odds with American foreign policy. While the United States had failed to recognise that the 'Soviet Union [was] a new, different type of power' until 1946, the country shifted to the opposite extreme after 1949.

> [T]here emerged one of those great and forbidding apparitions to the credence in which mass opinion is so easily swayed: a monster devoid of all humanity and of all rationality of motive, at once the embodiment and the caricature of evil, devoid of internal conflicts and problems of its own, intent only on bringing senseless destruction to the lives and hopes of others.[117]

Soviet power became so 'demonic, monstrous, incalculable, inscrutable' in American eyes that it was unthinkable that 'we admit to a share in the responsibility for [Soviet] behaviour'.[118] To his dismay, Americans came 'unconsciously' to accept the Soviet thesis that 'every Soviet gain is automatically our loss and to see our salvation as dependent on our ability to outpace Russia in every single phase of her economic progress'.[119] The Cold War, in other words, had become a zero-sum game for *both* players. Kennan felt it necessary to respond to these developments with a plea for 'a new act of faith in the ultimate humanity and sobriety of the people on the other side', a plea which, addressed to both sides, implied that the common bond of mankind had been broken between the two adversaries.[120]

Kennan complains about the subsequent intolerance, secretiveness, suspicion and cruelty Americans demonstrate in their relations to the outside world. The 'witch-hunting' of the McCarthy era brought out the worst in Americans: cheap provincial chauvinism, anti-intellectualism, mistrust of thought, a demand for uniformity and the tendency 'to draw about us the same sort of iron curtain that we resented when we saw it surrounding our communist adversaries'. Again he recognises the attempt to suppress *parrhesia*, but this time on the American side. In the hunt for Communist conspiracies, the accusers, 'like the victims of some totalitarian brainwashing', arrogated to their individual selves the powers of the spiritual and temporal law-giver, to make the definition of social conduct a matter of fear in the face of vague and irregular forces, rather than a matter of confidence in the protecting discipline of conscience and the law.[121]

Moreover, as the United States assumed more and more responsibilities, the American 'administrative responses to world problems' were increasingly marked by 'the flight from the individual, the striving for the creation of machinery to replace individual insight and judgement, the labored diffusion of power'. In place of the *parrhesia* of the philosopher-diplomat, whose personality is 'revealed, tried and tested' in confrontation with the '"differentness" of a foreign environment',[122] the Foreign Service offered nothing but 'an uncomfortable sense of being at the mercy of forces unknown and unseen, a condition that grips subordinate and superior together in a sort of Kafka-esque nightmare to which there is no end and from which there is no escape'.[123]

The 'tendency to the total externalisation of evil (in bodies of people just as in individuals)' had finally infected American society. 'Psychically and practically' there was nothing more dangerous than this 'failure of self-knowledge'. The struggle against evil was always in part 'an overcoming of self. We cannot for this reason identify ourselves self-righteously with all that is good and clothe whatever opposes us in the colors of unmitigated evil'.[124]

This externalisation of evil was what gave the 'problem of Soviet–American relations' its 'religious connotations'. The conflict seemed to lead

to an effort on the part of a great many people to externalize evil, to attribute to the Soviet leadership and the Soviet people every sort of iniquity and indeed a sort of monopoly on iniquity; and what is worse, to see in their supposed total iniquity the proof of our own total virtue.

Such 'monstrous oversimplifications' Kennan finds 'profoundly un-Christian'.[125] Once humans become unable to detect themselves in the behaviour of others, 'human forces easily take on dark, sinister and repellent aspects'.[126] With some despair, Kennan concluded that, while fighting the Soviets, the Americans increasingly became like them, a danger he had warned against already in the Long Telegram.[127]

If one fought against an enemy ostensibly because of his methods, and permitted oneself to be impelled by the heat of the struggle to adopt those same methods, who, then, could be said to have won? … Whose outlook could be said to have triumphed?[128]

THE DECLINE OF THE WEST

The ironic success of Soviet totalitarianism turned Kennan into a prophet of the 'decline of the West'. The Cold War as a war between two similarly closed self-understandings of human existence showed the extent to which the contamination of civilisation with the virus of totalitarianism had advanced. In the late 1960s Kennan warned that the very survival of Western civilisation – in both the 'spiritual and physical sense' – was endangered, and that the dangers lay within rather than outside Western civilisation.[129] In the mid-1990s he concluded that the twentieth century was a 'tragic one in the history of European (including American) civilisation', a 'sad' and 'disturbing' century.[130]

On several occasions Kennan identified as the major cause and symptom of the present crisis what was also, in a sense, the essence of totalitarianism: the inability to distinguish reality from unreality. In the contemporary political world, Kennan wrote in 1988, 'artificially created images are considered more significant than realities'. In our age,

> there is a real danger that we may lose altogether our ability to distinguish the real and the unreal, and, in doing so, lose both the credibility of true moral behaviour and the great force such behaviour is, admittedly, capable of exerting.[131]

The Western world is about to lose its 'sense of the fitness of things', and this *is* the meaning of decadence.[132]

However, the symptoms of the crisis went far beyond the realm of politics. Kennan refers to the 'appalling shallowness of the religious, philosophic and political concepts' which pervaded a society inflicted by 'sickly secularism'; he mentions 'overpopulation, precipitate urbanization, the feverish hyperintensity of communication, the destruction of the natural environment'. Again and again he laments the destruction of urban life through the automobile, through the 'quiet nocturnal stream of temporary moving prisons'. Americans had succeeded in creating a 'fine end-of-the-world' in their cities. The 'sad climax of individualism' as well as widespread 'attitudes of hopelessness, skepticism, cynicism, and bewilderment' qualify this society 'as a "sick" one'. While Kennan considers the 'noise' of the present age 'a nightmare', Americans justify themselves 'by the fact that the sun shines and that life is easy'. They often do not really seem to live 'but to await death' in a 'sort of trancelike unreal state of existence, drugged by the sedatives of advertising, TV, and the wheel of the automobile'.[133] The 'decadence and demoralisation' of American society was partly due to the fact that 'the whole process of communication' was dominated by the 'advertising industry'. The excesses of advertising posed a threat to civilisation because they 'de-train people for any sustained attention to the truth'.[134]

Decadence is in turn what makes societies susceptible to the evil of totalitarianism. There was a direct correlation between the 'apocalyptic disasters of society' listed above and the degree of vulnerability to totalitarian tendencies. The establishment or maintenance of indigenous totalitarian systems is much easier, for example, for societies of a scale

> so vast and complicated that the individual can no longer sense or survey his relation to the whole and is obliged to feel himself ... as a helpless and superfluous entity in the hands of demoniac forces beyond his power to understand or influence.

Similarly, if the pace of social change violates the 'continuity of the generations' or destroys 'the individual's confidence in his environment', the 'totalitarian virus' would encounter much less resistance.[135]

The clearest indication of spiritual decline for Kennan was the nuclear arms race. Nuclear deterrence manifested a spiritual and philosophical derangement of the first order; it was, literally, 'madness', 'a form of illness', 'morbid in the extreme'. It could be understood only as some form of 'subconscious despair on the part of its devotees – some sort of death wish, a readiness to commit suicide for fear of death', 'a lack of faith, or better a lack of the very strength that it takes to have faith, as countless of our generations have had it before us'.[136] To threaten, by holding nuclear weapons, 'the very intactness of the natural environment in which, and in which alone, civilisation would have a future' seemed 'to be "simply wrong", wrong in the good old-fashioned meaning of the term. It involves an egocentricity on our part that has no foundation either in religious faith or in political philosophy'.[137] Humans were too weak to manage or even deserve the power placed in their hands by weapons of mass destruction.[138] The preposterous gesture of accumulating such power made people lose their humanness. Already in the late 1950s, when the nuclearisation of Europe was at its very beginning, Kennan felt tempted to join those 'who say, "Let us divest ourselves of this weapon altogether; let us at least walk like men, with our heads up, so long as we are permitted to walk at all"'.[139]

The philosopher-diplomat insists that

> warfare should be a means to an end other than warfare, an end connected with the beliefs and the feelings and the attitudes of people, an end marked by submission to a new political will and perhaps a new regime of life, but an end which at least did not negate the principle of life itself.

What characterises nuclear weapons is that they 'cannot really be reconciled with a political purpose directed to shaping, rather than destroying, the lives of the adversary'. Thus, 'they fail to take account of the ultimate responsibility of men for one another, and even for each other's errors and mistakes'. Therefore, 'they reach backwards beyond the frontiers of Western civilisation, to the concepts of warfare which were once familiar to the Asiatic hordes'.[140]

To place the natural environment, the only environment which makes human existence possible, at stake 'just for the sake of the comforts, the fears, and the national rivalries of a single generation' involved an 'element of sacrilege'. Kennan anticipates that, in this modern age, his attitudes may be dismissed as 'religious'. He adds, therefore, that 'the renunciation of self-interest, which is what all morality implies, can never be rationalised by purely secular and materialistic means'. All morality rests, 'consciously or otherwise, on some foundation of religious faith'.[141] And if the highest form of freedom was the successful containment of totalitarianism and decadence – two faces of one coin – then freedom had to entail 'a system of restraints', a sense of limits. These restraints had to be sought, Kennan explained, in 'the wisdom of the ages, and in the ethical codes that the great religions of civilization have developed'.[142]

Paradoxically, the urgency of his exhortations reveals that Kennan never lost the hope of the reformer. The decline of the West was not 'a fully accomplished fact'. And one could not 'regard American society as *hopelessly* diseased'.[143] After all, there was his 'defiant faith – a desperate, unreasoning faith, if you will – but faith nevertheless in the endurance of this threatened world, faith in the total essentiality of historical continuity'.[144] But at the same time, he never felt at home in the century in which he was born. He was, in his own words, 'an expatriate in time rather than in place', and felt like a 'disembodied spirit'. He could not 'help but regret that [he] did not live fifty or a hundred years sooner' for life was 'too full in these times to be comprehensible' and began to seem 'like a movie, with hundreds of kaleidoscopic scenes flashing on and off our field of perception – gone before we have time to consider them'.[145] Although never without hope, Kennan acknowledged that the 'America of today' was not and never could be again the 'wonderful old America'. The memory and inspiration of the past had to be preserved but it would be an escape from reality to belief in its restoration.[146]

In response to the 'discomfort' he experiences as a contemporary of the twentieth century, Kennan tends to 'seek in the interpretation of history a usefulness [he] could not find in the interpretation of [his] own time'.[147] But the writing of history is not an escape from the present. As the 'spectacular mechanical and scientific creations of modern man tend to conceal from him the nature of his own humanity and to encourage him in all sorts of Promethean ambitions and ions', it is precisely history which can 'expose the nature of man as revealed in simpler and more natural conditions, where that which was elemental was less concealed by artificialities'. The modern individual needs to be reminded 'of the nature of the species he belongs to, of the limitations that rest on him, of the essential elements, both tragic and helpful, of his own condition'.[148]

NOTES

1. Cf. Leo Strauss, *What is Political Philosophy?* (Westport, CT: Greenwood, 1977), pp. 40–9, and Strauss, *Thoughts on Machiavelli* (New York: Free Press, 1958).
2. C. Ben Wright was the first to embark on a biography of Kennan. But his views, summarised in 'Mr. X and Containment', *Slavic Review*, 35: 1 (March 1976), pp. 1–31, provoked a hostile response from Kennan (pp. 32–6). Wright's project was never completed but has been an important source of information for subsequent 'Kennan-scholarship'. Works on Kennan include Barton Gellman, *Contending with Kennan: Toward a Philosophy of American Power* (New York: Praeger, 1984); Walter L. Hixson, *George F. Kennan: Cold War Iconoclast* (New York: Columbia University Press, 1989); David Mayers, *George Kennan and the Dilemmas of US Foreign Policy* (New York: Oxford University Press, 1988); Wilson D. Miscamble, *George F. Kennan and the Making of American Foreign Policy 1947–1950* (Princeton, NJ: Princeton University Press, 1992); Michael Polley, *A Biography of George F. Kennan: The Education of a Realist* (New York: Mellen Press, 1990); Anders Stephanson, *Kennan and the Art of Foreign Policy* (Cambridge, MA: Harvard University Press, 1989). Very useful is Laurel F. Franklin's *George F. Kennan: An Annotated Bibliography* (Bibliographies of American Notables 3) (Westport: Greenwood Press, 1997).
3. Johannes van Oort, *Jerusalem and Babylon: A Study into Augustine's City of God and the Sources of his Doctrine of the Two Cities* (Leiden: Brill, 1991), p. 360. See also Samuel N. C. Lieu, *Manichaeism* (Tübingen: Mohr, second edn, 1992), Chapter 5.
4. Augustine, *Confessions* (trans. Henry Chadwick), (New York: Oxford University Press, 1991), Book 5, Section 3.
5. *The Harmony of the Gospels*, quoted in Peter Brown, *Augustine of Hippo: A Biography* (Berkeley: University of California Press, 1967), p. 147.
6. Augustine, *Confessions*, Book 5, Section 10.
7. Augustine quoted in Brown, *Augustine*, p. 403.
8. For a recent example see Bjørn Qviller, 'The Machiavellian Cosmos', *History of Political Thought*, 17: 3 (Autumn 1996), pp. 326–53 (331–40), who finds a 'Gnostic' anthropology in Augustine and Machiavelli.
9. Augustine, *The City of God* (trans. Henri Bettenson), (Harmondsworth: Penguin, 1984), Book 15, Section 1; Book 14, Section 28.
10. van Oort, *Jerusalem and Babylon*, p. 225.
11. van Oort, *Jerusalem and Babylon*, p. 364.
12. Augustine, *City of God*, Book 20, Sections 7 and 9.
13. Sebastian de Grazia, *Machiavelli in Hell* (Princeton, NJ: Princeton University Press, 1989), p. 315.
14. Niccolò Machiavelli, *The Prince* (ed. Quentin Skinner and Russell Price), (Cambridge: Cambridge University Press, 1988), Chapter 25.
15. Machiavelli, *The Prince*, Chapter 18.
16. Machiavelli, *The Prince*, Chapters 9, 20.
17. Machiavelli, *The Prince*, Chapter 21.
18. Machiavelli, *Discorsi*, Book 3, Chapter 49.
19. The three quotes in this sentence are from Machiavelli, *Discorsi*, Book 2, Chapter 29; Book 1, Chapter 6; *The Prince*, Chapter 11.
20. de Grazia, *Machiavelli*, p. 58.

21. Machiavelli, *The Prince*, Chapter 26.
22. Machiavelli, *Discorsi*, Book 1, Chapter 11.
23. Quoted in de Grazia, *Machiavelli*, p. 380.
24. See Machiavelli, *The Prince*, Chapters 12, 25, 26; and *Discorsi*, Book 1, Chapter 12; etc.
25. Cf. Eric Voegelin, 'Machiavelli's Prince: Formation and Background', *The Review of Politics*, Vol. 13 (1951), pp. 142–68 (147).
26. Machiavelli, *The Prince*, Chapter 26.
27. 1 Corinthians 12–14.
28. Machiavelli, *Discorsi*, Book 1, Chapter 18.
29. Plato, *Republic* (trans. D. Lee), (Harmondsworth: Penguin, 1987), 473e, 499b.
30. Machiavelli, *The Prince*, Chapter 15.
31. George F. Kennan, *Memoirs (Volume II) 1950–1963* (Boston: Little, Brown, 1972), p. 159.
32. See, for example, John Lewis Gaddis, *The United States and the Origins of the Cold War 1941–1947* (New York: Columbia University Press, 1972), pp. 302–4.
33. The letter is now in the George F. Kennan Papers, Box 28, Folder '1946', Seeley G. Mudd Collections, Princeton, New Jersey.
34. George F. Kennan, *Memoirs 1925–1950* (Boston: Little, Brown, 1967), p. 293.
35. The full text of the telegram is in US Department of State, *Foreign Relations of the United States 1946, Volume VI (Eastern Europe, the Soviet Union)*, (Washington, DC: Government Printing Office, 1970), pp. 696–709 (699, 701, 706).
36. Kennan, *Memoirs 1925–1950*, p. 294.
37. Kennan, *Memoirs 1925–1950*, p. 355.
38. George F. Kennan (Mr. 'X'), 'The Sources of Soviet Conduct', *Foreign Affairs*, Vol. 25, July 1947, pp. 566–82.
39. Kennan, *Memoirs 1925–1950*, pp. 354–67 (356).
40. Kennan, *Memoirs 1925–1950*, p. 358.
41. Kennan, *Memoirs 1925–1950*, p. 134.
42. Kennan, *Memoirs 1950–1963*, p. 105.
43. Alex Danchev, 'To and from Russia with love', *The Times Higher Educational Supplement*, 5 July 1996, p. 22.
44. George F. Kennan, *Around the Cragged Hill: A Personal and Political Philosophy* (New York: Norton, 1993), p. 38.
45. Kennan, *Around the Cragged Hill*, p. 44.
46. Kennan, *Around the Cragged Hill*, pp. 45–6.
47. Kennan, *Around the Cragged Hill*, pp. 27–8, 36, 258; see also Kennan, *Democracy and the Student Left* (Boston: Little, Brown, 1968), pp. 9–10.
48. Kennan, *Around the Cragged Hill*, p. 27.
49. Kennan, *Around the Cragged Hill*, p. 51.
50. George F. Kennan, *Sketches from a Life* (New York: Pantheon, 1989), p. vii.
51. Kennan, *Memoirs 1925–1950*, p. 156.
52. George F. Kennan, 'The Relation of Religion to Government', *The Princeton Seminary Bulletin*, Winter 1969, pp. 42–7 (44)
53. Kennan, *Democracy and the Student Left*, pp. 238–9.
54. Kennan, *Memoirs 1950–1963*, pp. 166–7, 324; and *Sketches from a Life*, p. x.
55. George F. Kennan, *American Diplomacy* (Chicago: University of Chicago Press, 1984), p. 178.
56. George F. Kennan, 'Foreign Policy and Christian Conscience', *Atlantic Monthly*, May 1959, pp. 44–9 (45); George F. Kennan, 'World Problems in Christian Perspective', in Abraham S. Eisenstadt (ed.), *American History: Recent Interpretations* (New York: Crowell, 1962), pp. 460–76 (468).
57. Kennan, *American Diplomacy*, pp. 53–4.
58. Kennan, *Sketches from a Life*, p. 213.
59. George F. Kennan, *Measures Short of War: the George F. Kennan Lectures at the National War College 1946–47* (ed. Giles D. Harlow and George C. Maerz), (Washington, DC: National Defence University Press, 1991), p. 214.
60. Kennan, *American Diplomacy*, p. 14.

61. Kennan, *Measures Short of War*, p. 297.
62. Kennan, *Memoirs 1950–1963*, pp. 70–1.
63. George F. Kennan, *Realities of American Foreign Policy* (London: Oxford University Press, 1954), pp. 15–16.
64. Kennan quotes from his own speech in *Memoirs 1950–1963*, pp. 171–3. My emphasis.
65. Kennan, *American Diplomacy*, pp. 153, 178; *Around the Cragged Hill*, pp. 209–10.
66. See, for example, George F. Kennan, 'Communism in Russian History', in George F. Kennan, *At a Century's Ending: Reflections 1982–1995* (New York: Norton, 1996), pp. 43–61 (60).
67. 'Memorandum by the Counselor of the Department (Kennan) to the Secretary of State', Washington, 29 March 1950, in US Department of State, *Foreign Relations of the United States 1950, Volume II (The United Nations, the Western Hemisphere)*, (Washington, DC: Government Printing Office, 1976), pp. 616–17.
68. US Department of State, *State Department Policy Planning Staff Papers*, Vol. II (1948), (New York: Garland, 1983), p. 126.
69. Kennan, *Measures Short of War*, pp. 167–8.
70. US Department of State, *State Department Policy Planning Staff Papers*, Vol. I (1947), (New York: Garland, 1983), pp. 31–2.
71. Kennan, *Around the Cragged Hill*, p. 182.
72. George F. Kennan, 'America and the Russian Future', *Foreign Affairs*, 29: 3 (April 1951), pp. 351–70; here quoted from Kennan, *American Diplomacy*, pp. 129–54 (154).
73. George F. Kennan, '"X" plus 25', *Foreign Policy*, No. 7 (Summer 1972), pp. 5–21 (18).
74. Kennan, *Measures Short of War*, pp. 14–15.
75. George F. Kennan and George Urban, 'A Conversation', in Kennan et al., *Encounters with Kennan* (London: Cass, 1979), pp. 1–83 (34); George F. Kennan and Melvin J. Lasky, 'A Conversation', in *Encounters with Kennan*, pp. 189–215 (204). Kennan acknowledged that Lewis Mumford had a 'formative influence' on his thought (ibid.). The illustration of the Holy procession in Florence is in Lewis Mumford, *The Culture of Cities* (London: Secker & Warburg, 1938), p. 36.
76. Kennan, *Sketches from a Life*, p. 360.
77. On Kennan and Spengler see John Lamberton Harper, *American Visions of Europe* (Cambridge: Cambridge University Press, 1996), pp. 142, 160–1.
78. Kennan, *Democracy and the Student Left*, p. 206. For Kennan's admiration of Gibbon see also Kennan, 'History as Literature', *Encounter*, 12: 4 (April 1959), pp. 10–16 (12).
79. Kennan, *American Diplomacy*, p. 109.
80. Kennan, 'Foreign Policy and Christian Conscience', p. 45; and 'World Problems in Christian Perspective', p. 468.
81. Kennan, *Around the Cragged Hill*, pp. 68, 258.
82. Kennan, *Around the Cragged Hill*, pp. 130–3.
83. Kennan, *Memoirs 1950–1963*, p. 199.
84. George F. Kennan, *Russia, the Atom and the West* (Westport, CT: Greenwood, 1974), pp. 20–1.
85. Kennan, *American Diplomacy*, p. 117.
86. Kennan, *Memoirs 1925–1950*, p. 245.
87. Kennan, *Memoirs 1925–1950*, pp. 263–4.
88. See 'George Kennan to John Lukacs, January 18, 1995', in George F. Kennan and John Lukacs, *George F. Kennan and the Origins of Containment 1944–1946. The Kennan–Lukacs Correspondence* (Columbia: University of Missouri Press, 1997), p. 27.
89. Kennan, 'Russia – Seven Years Later', *Memoirs 1925–1950*, pp. 503–31.
90. Kennan, 'Russia – Seven Years Later', pp. 529–31.
91. Kennan, *Measures Short of War*, pp. 124–5, 231.
92. Kennan, *Memoirs 1925–1950*, pp. 129, 227; and *American Diplomacy*, pp. 111, 115.
93. 'The Chargé in the Soviet Union (Kennan) to the Secretary of State', 20 March 1946, in US Department of State, *Foreign Relations of the United States 1946,*

Volume VI (Eastern Europe, the Soviet Union), 1942–1950 (Washington, DC: Government Printing Office, 1961–1976), p. 721.

94. Kennan, *American Diplomacy*, p. 112.
95. Kennan, *Measures Short of War*, p. 59.
96. 'The Chargé in the Soviet Union (Kennan) to the Secretary of State', Moscow, 4 October 1945, in US Department of State, *Foreign Relations of the United States 1945, Volume V (Europe)*, (Washington, DC: Government Printing Office, 1967), p. 888.
97. *State Department Policy Planning Staff Papers*, Vol. II (1948), p. 393.
98. Kennan, *Around the Cragged Hill*, p. 98.
99. Kennan, *Measures Short of War*, p. 85.
100. Kennan, *Democracy and the Student Left*, p. 9.
101. Kennan, *Measures Short of War*, pp. 84–5. Also Kennan, 'Communism in Russian History'.
102. 'The Chargé in the Soviet Union (Kennan) to the Secretary of State', Moscow, 3 February 1945, in *Foreign Relations of the United States 1945, Volume V (Europe)*, p. 1117.
103. Kennan, *Measures Short of War*, pp. 114, 116.
104. Kennan, *Memoirs 1950–1963*, p. 225.
105. George F. Kennan, 'The Ethics of Anti-Communism', in *University: A Princeton Quarterly*, No. 24 (Spring 1965), pp. 3–5 (5).
106. Kennan, *American Diplomacy*, pp. 147–8.
107. Kennan, *Measures Short of War*, p. 168.
108. Kennan, *American Diplomacy*, p. 147.
109. Kennan, *Measures Short of War*, pp. 86–7.
110. Kennan writes of 'spiritual distinction' in a letter of January 1952, referred to in *Memoirs 1950–1963*, p. 84; the remaining quotations are from *Russia, the Atom and the West*, pp. 14, 96.
111. Kennan, *Russia, the Atom and the West*, p. 90. My emphasis.
112. 'Draft Memorandum by the Counselor (Kennan) to the Secretary of State', Washington, 17 February 1950, in US Department of State, *Foreign Relations of the United States 1950, Volume I (National Security Affairs, Foreign Economic Policy)*, (Washington, DC: Government Printing Office, 1977), pp. 163–4.
113. George F. Kennan, 'Containment: Then and Now', in Kennan, *At a Century's Ending*, pp. 110–15 (114–15).
114. George F. Kennan, *Realities of American Foreign Policy* (London: Oxford University Press, 1954), p. 114.
115. 'Memorandum of Canadian–United States Defense Conversations held in Ottawa in Suite "E", Chateau Laurier Hotel, December 16 and 17, 1946', in US Department of State, *Foreign Relations of the United States 1946, Volume V (The British Commonwealth, Western and Central Europe)*, (Washington, DC: Government Printing Office, 1969), p. 70.
116. Kennan, *Memoirs 1925–1950*, pp. 356, 365.
117. George F. Kennan, 'The United States and the Soviet Union 1917-1976', *Foreign Affairs*, 54: 4 (July 1976), pp. 670–90 (680, 682).
118. Kennan, *Memoirs 1925–1950*, p. 499.
119. Kennan, *Russia, the Atom and the West*, p. 9.
120. George F. Kennan, 'A European Settlement', in Edward Reed (ed.), *Peace on Earth – Pacem in Terris* (New York: Pocket, 1965), pp. 77–83 (82).
121. Quotations from Kennan, *Realities of American Foreign Policy*, p. 118; *Memoirs 1950–1963*, pp. 223–5.
122. George F. Kennan, 'The Future of Our Professional Diplomacy', *Foreign Affairs*, Vol. 33 (1955), pp. 566–86 (572).
123. George F. Kennan, 'America's Administrative Response to Its World Problems', *Daedalus*, 87: 2 (Spring 1958), pp. 5–24 (14, 17).
124. Kennan, 'The Ethics of Anti-Communism', p. 5.
125. George F. Kennan, 'Nuclear Weapons and Christian Faith', in *At a Century's Ending*, pp. 69–71 (69). On the externalisation of evil see also Kennan, 'Western

Decadence and Soviet Moderation', in Martin F. Herz (ed.), *Decline of the West? George Kennan and His Critics* (Washington, DC: Ethics and Public Policy Center, 1978), pp. 3–9 (8–9).

126. Kennan, *Memoirs 1950–1963*, p. 222; and *Democracy and the Student Left*, p. 143.
127. *Foreign Relations of the United States 1946, Volume VI*, p. 709.
128. Kennan, *Memoirs 1925–1950*, p. 198; *Memoirs 1950–1963*, p. 87; also 'Foreign Policy and Christian Conscience', p. 45.
129. Kennan, *Democracy and the Student Left*, pp. 224–5, 228.
130. George F. Kennan, 'Foreword', in Kennan, *At a Century's Ending*, pp. 7–13 (7, 11, 13).
131. George F. Kennan, 'The Gorbachev Prospect', pp. 219–29 (229), and 'Morality and Foreign Policy', pp. 269–82 (282), both in Kennan, *At a Century's Ending*.
132. Kennan and Urban, 'A Conversation', p. 20.
133. Kennan, *Democracy and the Student Left*, pp. 216–17; and *Sketches From a Life*, pp. 43, 225, 288–9; also *Memoirs 1950–1963*, pp. 81–2; and *Around the Cragged Hill*, p. 158. See also George F. Kennan, 'To Prevent A World Wasteland', *Foreign Affairs*, 48: 3 (April 1970), pp. 401–13.
134. Kennan and Urban, 'A Conversation', p. 16.
135. All quotations in this paragraph from George F. Kennan, 'Totalitarianism in the Modern World', in Carl J. Friedrich (ed.), *Totalitarianism: Proceedings of a Conference held at the American Academy of Arts and Sciences* (Cambridge, MA: Harvard University Press, 1954), pp. 17–31 (26, 28).
136. George F. Kennan, 'On Nuclear War', in Phil Braithwaite (ed.), *George Kennan on NATO, Nuclear War and the Soviet Threat* (Evesham: West Midlands CND Sales, 1985), pp. 33–9 (39).
137. Kennan, *Memoirs 1950–1963*, p. 247.
138. See, for example, George F. Kennan and Martin Agronsky, 'A Different Approach to the World: An Interview', in *The New York Review of Books*, 23: 21 & 22 (20 January 1977), pp. 12–17 (14–15).
139. Kennan, *Sketches From a Life*, p. 294; and *Memoirs 1950–1963*, p. 247; also *Russia, the Atom and the West*, p. 54.
140. 'Memorandum by the Counselor (Kennan), Washington, January 20, 1950', in US Department of State, *Foreign Relations of the United States 1950, Volume I*, p. 39. On the same set of problems see also Kennan, 'Foreign Policy and Christian Conscience', pp. 47–9; and 'World Problems in Christian Perspective', pp. 471–4.
141. Kennan, 'Morality and Foreign Policy', in *At a Century's Ending*, pp. 269–82 (281).
142. Kennan, 'Totalitarianism in the Modern World', pp. 30–1.
143. Kennan and Urban, 'A Conversation', p. 63; Kennan and Lasky, 'A Conversation', p. 197. My emphasis.
144. George F. Kennan, 'Acceptance Speech. Gold Medal for History' (1984), in *At a Century's Ending*, pp. 307–8 (308).
145. Kennan, *Sketches From a Life*, pp. 7, 183, 363; and *Memoirs 1925–1950*, p. 77; also *Memoirs 1950–1963*, pp. 117, 311; George F. Kennan, 'Flashbacks', in *At a Century's Ending*, pp. 30–42 (40).
146. Kennan, *Realities of American Foreign Policy*, p. 109.
147. Kennan, *Memoirs 1950–1963*, pp. 88–9.
148. George F. Kennan, 'The Experience of Writing History', in Abraham S. Eisenstadt (ed.), *The Craft of American History* (New York: Harper, 1966), Vol. 2, pp. 270–8 (277–8).

9
Epilogue

'In watching the flow of events over the past decade or so, it is hard to avoid the feeling that something very fundamental has happened in world history.' Thus wrote Francis Fukuyama in his infamous 'The End of History?' in 1989. The article could hardly have provoked the ensuing debate if Fukuyama had not so successfully captured the fairly widespread 'sense of epoch' that followed the end of the Cold War and the demise of Soviet Communism. He observed in his contemporaries, and probably shared, a dim awareness 'that there is some larger process at work, a process that gives coherence and order to the daily headlines'. A few years later, in spite of all controversy and criticism, the State Department analyst still gave an affirmative answer to the question of 'whether, at the end of the twentieth century, it makes sense for us once again to speak of a coherent and directional History of mankind that will eventually lead the greater part of humanity to liberal democracy'.[1]

Fukuyama sensed a further advance of Hegel's Absolute Spirit – just as Hegel himself had in the early nineteenth century after momentous political changes. Indeed, the years preceding the publication of the *Phenomenology* saw Napoleon proclaimed Emperor of the French (May 1804) and Francis II assume the title of Emperor of Austria. The year 1805 witnessed the War of the Third Coalition, with Trafalgar and Austerlitz, ending with the Treaty of Pressburg. The Napoleonic reorganisation of Europe through the Federative System and the Confederation of the Rhine followed in 1806. In August of that year, Francis II surrendered to French pressure. He resigned the dignity of a Roman Emperor and declared the Roman–German Empire extinct. One month later, on 18 September 1806, Hegel concluded his lecture series on speculative philosophy by explaining to his students that

> [w]e find ourselves in an important epoch of time, in a ferment; the *Geist*, with a sudden jerk, has moved to advance beyond its previous *Gestalt* and to assume a new one. The whole mass of hitherto accepted conceptions and concepts, the bonds of the world, have been dissolved and collapse like a dream image.[2]

Fukuyama acknowledged, much to his credit, that 'the notion of the end of history [was] not an original one'. He recognised in Hegel the great predecessor of his own enterprise. Although he tried to broaden the empirical and philosophical basis of his work in his later book, Fukuyama's account of the changes in the late twentieth century remains fundamentally a Hegelian speculation on the progressive manifestation of the *logos* in history through Western liberalism. The end of the Cold War is thereby inevitably turned into another step towards the imminent 'universalisation of Western liberal democracy as the final form of human government'; a development which marks the 'end point of mankind's ideological evolution'.[3]

We should realise that much of the controversy surrounding his article concerned the use of Hegelian dialectics to label the end of the Cold War the end of 'history'. However, fewer have questioned his pronouncement of a 'Western triumph' consisting in the 'total exhaustion of viable systematic alternatives to Western liberalism' and the world-wide spreading of the 'consumerist Western culture'.[4] Whatever it was that passed away with Soviet Communism, it did not implicate Western practices; on the contrary, the latter were finally validated by history through the demise of their opponents. Liberal democratic principles were henceforth celebrated as the undoubted remedies for societies in crisis.

With or without Hegelian foundation, such assessments – although assessments of historical change – reflect a profound continuity in the self-understanding of Western societies. As Eric Voegelin has pointed out, the strength of constitutional democracy, especially in the Anglo-Saxon countries, rests on 'the eschatological tension left over from the Puritan Revolution which endows the constitutional form with a character of "finality" as the successful experiment in organising a society with a classical and Christian tradition'.[5] The end of the Cold War seemed to offer the opportunity, in theory and practice, to extend this vision to the whole world. Notions of a 'new world order' and 'globalisation' became paramount to the contemporary search for the *renovatio mundi* – a global transfiguration which would turn present wars fought in the name of principles into transitory police actions necessary to remove the last obstacles on the route towards a 'culture of peace'.

There has always been an awareness in United Nations circles that the changes required to implement such visions do not just concern institutions but must ultimately affect human consciousness. The Preamble of UNESCO's constitution declares that 'it is in the minds of men that defences of peace must be constructed'. With UNESCO, Comenius's *pansophic* vision of total education – discussed in Chapter 5 – has found a powerful institutional expression. It is hence no mere coincidence that the General Conference of UNESCO decided at its ninth session, held in New Delhi in November and December 1956, to publish a volume of excerpts from Comenius's work on education. In the Preface, the editors declare that '[i]t was the desire of the General Conference that UNESCO should be associated in the homage which educators throughout the world are paying to one of the first men to propagate the ideas which UNESCO took for its guidance at the time of its establishment'.[6]

In response to the UN Secretary-General's 'Agenda for Peace', UNESCO launched its 'Culture of Peace' programme. This is perhaps the most ambitious attempt so far to implement its mission. Starting from the presumption that 'one is not born this way or that way; one is made', presented as a scientific truth, the 'Culture of Peace' programme sees the universal elimination of violence within the reach of human action. Systematic education will adapt human consciousness to the project's requirements. Just like their Puritan predecessors, the First International Forum on the Culture of Peace recognised that the task could only be accomplished through the 'participation of people at all levels – in their relations with each other and with the environment and at community, national, regional and international level', and through the 'thorough mobilization of all means of education and communication, both formal and non-formal'. All people were to be educated, in a 'joint-effort, including every single person in the society'.[7] Both Boutros-Ghali's 'Agenda for Peace' and UNESCO's 'Culture of Peace' implied that the end of the Cold War provided at last a window of opportunity to resolve the problems haunting mankind.

Hence, if there was any reflection on the meaning of the Cold War experience it tended to confirm and revive visions much older than the Cold War itself. In terms of both institutional practices and intellectual reflection the post-Cold War world offers plenty of evidence that the line of meaning followed in previous chapters extends beyond the Cold War into the present. The outcome of the conflict was primarily understood as corroborating positions which had earlier sustained the conflict.

There are, however, alternative ways of looking at the developments of the last decade which appreciate that Western thought and practices were implicated in the fate of Soviet Communism. Eric Voegelin, for example, understood the confrontation with Communism in the twentieth century as a sign that the corruption of Western culture of the nineteenth century had finally come 'home to us with a vengeance'. For, if liberalism was understood as 'the immanent salvation of man and society', Communism was its 'most radical expression'.[8] There is indeed a sense in which the Communist Revolution *continued* earlier attempts to emulate modern Western governmental rationality in Russia. The ultimate conclusion of the eighteenth-century 'science of the state' was to apply the science of Marx to society.

Similar questions have shaped the intellectual development of Hannah Arendt. Work on the *Origins of Totalitarianism* convinced her that Marxist totalitarianism – unlike racism – had grown out of the central Western philosophical tradition. This led her to re-examine the latter's fundamental assumptions in *The Human Condition*.[9] According to Shmuel Eisenstadt, the Great Occidental Revolutions, including the French and Russian, are the most dramatic, and possibly most successful, attempts in the history of mankind to implement on a macro-societal scale a utopian vision 'with strong Gnostic components'.[10] For Eisenstadt, the Great Revolutions represent the culmination of the sectarian, heterodox potentialities which developed in Axial civilisations and were brought to the forefront through the cultural and political programme of modernity. As a result, the whole of modernity is implicated in the tragedy which is manifested in both the rise and fall of Soviet Communism. In contrast to Fukuyama's 'end of history', the interpretations of Voegelin, Arendt and Eisenstadt are careful not to celebrate a 'triumph' of the Western world. They perceive the Cold War as a *shared* tragedy involving both 'East' and 'West'.

It seems, therefore, that in considering the Cold War crisis a choice has to be made. To what extent should the 'victors' reflect on their opponent's failure as a *common* failure? Prior to all questions of historical evidence, this is primarily a question of *where* one is prepared to look for the causes of, and responsibility for, a crisis of meaning. I have argued throughout this book that the choices made in this context originate, to a large extent, from the realm of experience referred to as 'spirituality'. It is this very question – the question of the responsibility for evil – which forms the centre in the cluster of problems which are explicated in the line of meaning presented in previous chapters.

Augustine, Machiavelli and Kennan seem to agree with Plato that the most important response to a profound historical transition and the concurrent uncertainty was a change *from within*. Experiencing life as a *participation* in a cosmic order which is both harmonious and given, they concluded that evil cannot have a separate existence but stems exclusively from the actions of human beings who turn away from the divine order of being. In their frameworks, ignorance and malice tend to coincide as the reason for this turning away. Malicious acts are therefore misguided acts, and those who commit them are in need of guidance. Because nobody is immune from error, the misguided acts of others always mirror the potential spectrum of our own failures. Like Plato, the three thinkers from the previous chapter refused to locate the source of the disorder and confusion of their times in just one group, race or ideological system remote from themselves.

Because they are parts of the order of being, human beings share in the respect which the latter commands. Thus, although Augustine, Machiavelli and Kennan clearly testify that there are situations in which the use of violence can be justified, they emphasise that there are limits to what human beings could do to each other. It is true that Augustine advocated religious coercion in his struggle with the Donatists. But even in these attempts to put an end to the eighty-five-year-old pattern of mutual hostility between Catholics and Donatists in Hippo he continued to consider 'coercion' as a positive process of corrective treatment rather than as a punitive measure.[11] He opposed the death penalty as a matter of principle because it excluded the possibility of repentance. Augustine did not depart from the classical teaching that God had made the human being free to choose between good or evil but argued that the individual act of free 'self-determination' was always embedded in an order which lay outside the range of such self-determination. Although the final act of choice must be spontaneous, not forced, it could be preceded by a long process which humans did not necessarily choose for themselves.

At numerous places in his writings, Augustine opposed torture, capital punishment or any discipline that went beyond what a truly loving father might administer to an erring son. Even in conflict, the adversary remained a 'brother': 'The man you cannot put right is still yours: he is part of you; either as a fellow human being, or very often as a member of your church, he is inside with you.' Accordingly, 'there is only one remedy: do not think ill of your brother. Strive humbly to be what you would have him be; and you will not think that he is what you are not'.[12]

Although he was not sure whether 'one can speak well of evil', Machiavelli considered Romulus's foundation of Rome as evidence that evil acts may at times bring good results. In Chapter 8 of *The Prince*, Machiavelli distinguishes between 'badly-used' and 'well-used' cruelties. 'Cruel deeds may be called well committed when they are all committed at once, because they are necessary for establishing one's power, and are not afterwards persisted in, but changed for measures as beneficial as possible to one's subjects.' Cruelty that goes beyond the 'founding act' of a new order is a clear sign of failure on the part of the (new) ruler. The Florentine never hesitates to condemn those who committed inexcusable crimes. Regardless of the circumstances, cruelty cannot be 'well-used' if the acts in question exterminate, mutilate, or exile a great part of the community. Because of his 'bold achievements' (*le azione e virtù*), Agathocles, tyrant of Syracuse from 317 BC to 289 BC, might have been a candidate for admission to the circle of great leaders and founders, but 'one ought not, of course, to call it *virtù* to massacre one's fellow citizens, to betray one's friends, to break one's word, to be without mercy and without religion'. Because of 'his inhuman cruelty and brutality, and his innumerable wicked actions ... it would be wrong to praise him as the finest of men'.[13]

Philip Macedon, father of Alexander the Great, was reported to have moved 'men from province to province as shepherds move their sheep'. Machiavelli insists that

> these methods are the cruellest and the enemies of every way of life, not only Christian but the human; and any man ought to flee them, and to wish rather to live as a private person than as king with so great a destruction of men.[14]

Of all his verdicts, Machiavelli's description of Ferdinand of Aragon's 'pious cruelty' is perhaps the most famous. Ferdinand 'exploited religion', 'expropriating and expelling from his kingdom the Marranos: an act without parallel and truly despicable'.[15] The whole practice of the Inquisition is implied in Machiavelli's criticism. Even Leo Strauss pointed out that Machiavelli was the only non-Jew of his time to have expressed this view.[16]

Like Augustine and Machiavelli, Kennan detested violence but was not a pacifist. His outspoken criticism of the nuclear arms race reveals an Augustinian attitude towards the use of coercion. And as I demonstrated in some detail in the preceding chapter, Kennan saw in the tendency to 'externalise evil' the singlemost important *spiritual* problem of the Cold War conflict.

Their assessment of the possibilities and limitations of human existence compelled Augustine, Machiavelli and Kennan to criticise unified and comprehensive world views which emanate from the firm possession of a central vision. Those who claim to possess this absolute vision place themselves directly within the divine understanding.

Of course, the classical tradition in Western philosophy, too, assumes that the order of being has a centre. The classical and scholastic thinkers considered human action 'rational' only if it was oriented beyond all intermediate ends and means to a last end; that is, to the Platonic *agathon*, the Aristotelian *nous*, the Thomistic *ratio aeterna*, or the *summum bonum*. However, the exponents of such tradition also insisted that full knowledge of this centre – the end beyond all ends – was reserved to the Divine. Human existence is therein understood as the continuing striving for attunement to God's unseen measure. Although it is to them possible to learn and advance in this endeavour, the quest itself does not come to an end in this life.

The 'knowledge' we can have of the form of the Good is different from the knowledge we have of objects or the working principles of man-made machines. This is underlined by the fact that, in many classical accounts, the highest end is sometimes related to *eudaimonia*, which is commonly translated into English as 'happiness'. The meaning of 'happiness' is here not understood as referring to an object or a proposition, to a 'this' or a 'that', but entails a balanced state of mind capable of distinguishing the immediacy of 'pleasure' from the comprehensive and lasting satisfaction that comes with the proper 'care of the soul' (*epimelesthai sautou*).[17] And yet, although it cannot be intended in the same sense in which a table is the desired end-product of a carpenter's work, 'happiness' is a recognisable state of mind; we are able to recognise a state of mind as 'happiness' when we encounter it. It is consequently possible to build up a wisdom – a discriminating power – concerning the meaning of 'happiness'. However, the very nature of this wisdom is provisional and practical rather than final and theoretical. The philosopher's 'knowledge' of the form of the Good is of this kind.

By stressing the transcendence of the divine measure, the classical tradition reaffirms human limitations. The human being participates in, and is not above or outside, the order of things.[18] In contrast to this outlook, Mani's *gnosis* presents itself in terms of an objective account of the visible world and beyond. The Manichaean religion gives access to the central vision which overlooks the whole and thus answers all questions about its parts. At the same time as this vision puts an end to the dynamics of the human quest for knowledge, it accelerates the dynamics of cosmic history. Knowing the full history of the cosmos brings that very history closer to its conclusion. The human being thereby becomes a liquidator of a decrepit state rather than a participator in a given order. Accepting this role of liquidator does not constitute a change of identity. On the contrary, through *gnosis* the Manichaean becomes aware of who he is and always has been.

A similar gesture is present in both Hegel's understanding of 'absolute knowledge' and in Marx's attempt to call forth the revolution by 'informing' the workers of its inevitability. Nothing could be further removed from Augustine's understanding of religious conversion as the *beginning* of an *endurance* of tensions rather than their final relaxation. For Augustine, baptism might save the life of a wounded man found close to death, but he still needed to endure, for the rest of his life, a prolonged and precarious convalescence in the community of the Christian Church. Therefore, for Augustine human nature always bordered on uncertainty.

The absolutist position *gnosis* provides results from a generalisation: that of the experience of forlornness and alienation. Once alienation and suffering are no longer felt to be the consequence of a deviation from normality, and have themselves become the new norm by which the world is examined, the sufferer has effectively elevated himself above the vicissitudes of cosmic existence. He can no longer be surprised or disappointed. At that point, the soul has of course shut itself off from the order of being. But the dilemma finds an obvious solution in the Hegelian dialectics of the Spirit: if the soul cannot find its way through the cosmos back to God, God must be alienated from himself and drawn into the human state of alienation.

Gnosis promotes the soul, in its self-understanding, to an absolute position high above the un-reality of cosmic ignorance and suffering. From this outpost, the world must indeed appear as a totality, a 'system'. Through *gnosis* the actual experience of alienation is transformed into the 'distance' required to be able to observe the cosmos from outside. The *moral* significance of this transformation, however, lies in the absoluteness of the boundaries which it creates between human beings. For if *gnosis* elevates the soul above the cosmos, beyond Plato's *chorismos*, the unbridgeable gap which the classical thinkers perceived between the human and divine realms mutates into a gap between those with *gnosis* and those without. The common bond of mankind is effectively broken between these two groups as soon as both consider themselves in possession of absolute vision. They will then fight a war driven by *gnosis*, a 'Gnostic war'.

This book proposed to study the Cold War as an instance of just such a 'Gnostic war'. In order to give historical substance to this interpretation, it was necessary to lay open a line of meaning which extends through Manichaeism to the ideologies that have sustained the conflict. How can a 'Gnostic war' possibly end? The antagonists live in different worlds, logic and reason have little to do with the termination of the conflict. There is no *logical* need for a 'Gnostic war' to end. In practice, of course, nothing lasts forever. Differences in actual power and the physical exhaustion of resources will eventually break up the stalemate. The outcome establishes the opponents as either 'winner' and 'loser' and thereby gives the impression of a genuine conclusion. Yet, the nature of the situation is such that the underlying dynamics of the tragedy remains hidden. The games of power can dissolve one of the two absolute positions but they fail to identify the absoluteness as the foundation of the conflict. On the contrary, their victory will compel the 'victors' to see their absolute position confirmed and to shape the world in its image.

A victory gained in practice does not remove, therefore, the need for theoretical reflection and introspection. Kennan's exhortations are as urgent today as they have been for the last half century. My earlier question – To what extent should the 'victors' reflect on their opponent's failure as a *common* failure? – is therefore of more than just theoretical interest. It is central not only to an understanding of the spiritual dimension of the Cold War, but also for an appreciation of the continuity between the conflict and the crusading impulse that today informs Western conceptions of 'globalisation'. UNESCO's Culture of

Peace Programme is just one of numerous global projects which, supported by today's powerful communication technologies, make the Puritan utopias of Hartlib and Comenius look like antiques. As the world moves towards the beginning of a new millennium, and as the practice of international politics embraces the entire globe, eschatological tensions are bound to increase.

NOTES

1. See Francis Fukuyama, 'The End of History?', *The National Interest*, Vol. 16 (Summer 1989), pp. 3–18 (3), and his subsequent book *The End of History and the Last Man* (Harmondsworth: Penguin, 1992), p. xii.
2. Hegel quoted in Eric Voegelin, 'On Hegel: A Study in Sorcery', in J. T. Fraser, F. C. Haber and G. H. Müller (eds), *The Study of Time* (Berlin: Springer, 1972), pp. 418–51 (435).
3. Fukuyama, 'The End of History?', p. 4.
4. Fukuyama, 'The End of History?', p. 3.
5. Eric Voegelin, 'Industrial Society in Search of Reason', in Raymond Aron (ed.), *World Technology and Human Destiny* (Ann Arbor: University of Michigan Press, 1963), p. 37.
6. UNESCO (eds), *John Amos Comenius: Selections* (Paris: UNESCO, 1957). The volume features an introductory essay by Jean Piaget on the 'significance of Comenius at the present time'.
7. 'First Consultative Meeting of the Culture of Peace Programme', Final Report (CPP-94/CONF.601/3), (Paris: UNESCO, October 1994), p. 2, quoted in Ramin Kaweh, 'A Study in the Political Philosophy of Globalisation: The Case of UNESCO's Culture of Peace Programme' (unpublished MA Dissertation, University of Kent at Canterbury, 1996), p. 22.
8. Voegelin, 'Industrial Society in Search of Reason', p. 45; Voegelin, *The New Science of Politics: An Introduction* (Chicago: University of Chicago Press, 1952), p. 175.
9. Cf. Margaret Canovan, 'Hannah Arendt and the Human Condition', in Leonard Tivey and Anthony Wright (eds), *Political Thought since 1945* (Hants: Edward Elgar, 1992), pp. 72–90 (76–7).
10. Shmuel N. Eisenstadt, 'O Sectarianismo da Idade Axial e as Antinomias da Liberdade', *Gepolis*, No. 5 (1998), pp. 117–36 (123).
11. Cf. Peter Brown, 'St Augustine's Attitude to Religious Coercion', *Journal of Roman Studies*, Vol. 54 (1964), pp. 107–16.
12. Quoted in Brown, *Augustine*, pp. 208–9.
13. Niccolò Machiavelli, *The Prince*, Chapter 8.
14. Niccolò Machiavelli, *Discorsi*, Book 1, Chapter 26.
15. Machiavelli, *The Prince*, Chapter 21.
16. Leo Strauss, *What is Political Philosophy?* (Westport, CT: Greenwood, 1977), p. 44.
17. Cf. Chapter 2, pp. 30–1, above.
18. George F. Kennan is linked to this tradition *via* the Founding Fathers. See John Zvesper, 'The American Founders and Classical Political Thought', *History of Political Thought*, 10: 4 (Winter 1989), pp. 701–18; J. G. A. Pocock, *The Machiavellian Moment: Florentine Political Thought and the Atlantic Republican Tradition* (Princeton: Princeton University Press, 1975).

Bibliography

Allan, Pierre and Kjell Goldmann (eds), *The End of the Cold War: Evaluating Theories of International Relations* (Dordrecht: Nijhoff, 1992)

Angelov, Dimiter, *The Bogomil Movement* (Sofia: Sofia Press, 1987)

Arendt, Hannah, *The Human Condition* (New York: Doubleday, 1959)

– *Between Past and Future* (London: Faber & Faber, 1961)

– *The Origins of Totalitarianism* (New York: Harcourt, 1973)

Armstrong, A. H., *Plotinian and Christian Gnosis* (London: Variorum, 1979)

Augustine, *The City of God* (trans. Henri Bettenson), (Harmondsworth: Penguin, 1984)

– *Confessions* (trans. Henry Chadwick), (New York: Oxford University Press, 1991)

Bainton, Roland, *Here I stand* (Icknield Way: Lion Publishing, 1983)

Barnes, Robin Bruce, *Prophecy and Gnosis: Apocalypticism in the Wake of the Lutheran Reformation* (Stanford: Stanford University Press, 1988)

Barns, J. W. B., 'Greek and Coptic Papyri from the Covers of the Nag Hammadi Codices', in Martin Krause (ed.), *Essays on the Nag Hammadi Texts in Honour of Pahor Labib* (Leiden: Brill, 1975), pp. 9–17

Barrett, C. K., 'Gnosis and the Apocalypse of John', in A. H. B. Logan and A. J. M. Wedderburn (eds), *The New Testament and Gnosis* (Edinburgh: Clark, 1983), pp. 125–37

Bauer, Walter, *Orthodoxy and Heresy in Earliest Christianity* (London: SCM Press, 1972 (1935))

Baur, Ferdinand Christian, *Die Christliche Gnosis oder Die Christliche Religionsphilosophie in ihrer geschichtlichen Entwicklung* (Tübingen: Osiander, 1835)

Becker, Marvin B., 'Florentine Politics and the Diffusion of Heresy in the Trecento: A Socioeconomic Inquiry', *Speculum*, Vol. 34 (1959), pp. 60–75

Behm, J. and E. Würthwein, 'Metanoia' in Gerhard Kittel (ed.), *The Theological Dictionary of the New Testament*, Vol. 4 (Grand Rapids: Eerdmans, 1967), pp. 975–1008

Beisner, Robert L., *From the Old Diplomacy to the New, 1865–1900* (Arlington Heights, IL: Harlan Davidson, second edn, 1986)

Benz, Ernst, *Ecclesia Spiritualis: Kirchenidee und Geschichtstheologie der Franziskanischen Reformation* (Stuttgart: Kohlhammer, 1934)

– 'Die geistigen Grundlagen des Russischen Bolshewismus', in Deutsche Gesellschaft für Osteuropakunde (ed.), *Russland und Wir: Betrachtungen über Russland und den Bolshewismus* (Stuttgart: Deutsche Verlags-Anstalt, 1951), pp. 49–77

– 'Creator Spiritus: Die Geistlehre des Joachim von Fiore', in Olga Fröbe-Kapteyn (ed.), *Der Mensch und das Schöpferische* (Zürich: Rhein-Verlag, 1957), pp. 285–355
– *Die Christliche Kabbala: Ein Stiefkind der Theologie* (Zürich: Rhein-Verlag, 1958)
Berlin, Isaiah, 'A Remarkable Decade', in Berlin, *Russian Thinkers* (eds Henry Hardy and Aileen Kelly), (London: Hogarth Press, 1978), pp. 114–209
Besançon, Alain, *The Intellectual Origins of Leninism* (trans. Sarah Matthews), (Oxford: Basil Blackwell, 1981 (1977))
Blackman, E. C., *Marcion and his Influence* (London: SPCK, 1948)
Bloch, Ernst, *Das Prinzip Hoffnung*, 'Freiheit und Ordnung: Abriss der Sozialutopien', in Bloch, *Gesamtausgabe* (Frankfurt a.M.: Suhrkamp, 1977), Vol. 5, pp. 590–8
Bloomfield, M., 'Joachim of Flora: A Critical Survey of His Canon, Teachings, Sources, Biography, and Influence', in Delno C. West (ed.), *Joachim of Fiore in Christian Thought: Essays on the Influence of the Calabrian Prophet*, Vol. I (New York: Burt Franklin, 1975), pp. 29–91
Boehme, Jacob, *The Aurora* (trans. John Sparrow), (London: Watkins, 1914)
– *The Signature of All Things and other Writings* (London: Clarke, 1969)
– *Concerning the Three Principles of the Divine Essence: Of the Eternal, Dark, Light, and Temporary World* (trans. John Sparrow), (London: Watkins, 1910)
Broek, Roelof van den and Wouter J. Hanegraaff (eds), *Gnosis and Hermeticism: From Antiquity to Modern Times* (New York: SUNY Press, 1998)
Brown, Peter, 'St. Augustine's Attitude to Religious Coercion', *Journal of Roman Studies*, Vol. 54 (1964), pp. 107–16
– *Augustine of Hippo: A Biography* (Berkeley: University of California Press, 1967)
Bühler, Karl, *Sprachtheorie: Die Darstellungsfunktion der Sprache* (Stuttgart: Fischer, second edn, 1965)
Burkitt, F. C., *Church and Gnosis: A Study of Christian Thought and Speculation in the Second Century* (Cambridge: Cambridge University Press, 1932)
Canovan, Margaret, 'Hannah Arendt and the Human Condition', in Leonard Tivey and Anthony Wright (eds), *Political Thought since 1945* (Hants: Edward Elgar, 1992), pp. 72–90
Capp, B. S., *The Fifth Monarchy Men: A Study in Seventeenth-century English Millenarianism* (London: Faber & Faber, 1972)
Carwardine, Richard J., *Evangelicals and Politics in Antebellum America* (New Haven: Yale University Press, 1993)
Charlton, D. G., *Positivist Thought in France During the Second Empire 1852–70* (Oxford: Clarendon, 1959)
Clark, Norman H., *Deliver us from Evil: An Interpretation of American Prohibition* (New York: Norton, 1976)
Cohen, I. Bernard (ed.), *Puritanism and the Rise of Modern Science: The Merton Thesis* (New Brunswick: Rutgers University Press, 1990)
Cohn, Norman, *The Pursuit of the Millennium: Revolutionary Millenarians and Mystical Anarchists of the Middle Ages* (London: Paladin, 1970)

– *Cosmos, Chaos and the World to Come: The Ancient Roots of Apocalyptic Faith* (New Haven: Yale University Press, 1993)
Comenius, see UNESCO
Comte, Auguste, *System of Positive Polity or Treatise on Sociology: Instituting the Religion of Humanity* (New York: Franklin, 1966), four volumes
Copenhaver, Brian P. (ed.), *Hermetica: The Greek* Corpus Hermeticum *and the Latin* Asclepius *in a new English translation* (Cambridge: Cambridge University Press, 1992)
Couliano, Ioan P., *The Tree of Gnosis: Gnostic Mythology from Early Christianity to Modern Nihilism* (trans. H. S. Wiesner and Ioan P. Couliano), (San Francisco: Harper, 1990)
Danchev, Alex, 'To and from Russia with love', *The Times Higher Educational Supplement*, 5 July 1996, p. 22
David, Zdenek V., 'The Influence of Jacob Boehme on Russian Religious Thought', in *Slavic Review*, 21: 1 (March 1962), pp. 43–64
Deghaye, Pierre: 'Jakob Böhmes Theosophie: die Theophanie in der ewigen Natur', in Peter Koslowski (ed.), *Gnosis und Mystik in der Geschichte der Philosophie* (Zürich: Artemis, 1988), pp. 151–67
– 'Jacob Boehme and His Followers' in Antoine Faivre and Jacob Needleman (eds), *Modern Esoteric Spirituality* (London: SCM Press, 1993), pp. 210–47
Dobbs, Betty J. T., *The Foundations of Newton's Alchemy or, 'The Hunting of the Greene Lyon'* (Cambridge: Cambridge University Press, 1975)
– 'Newton's *Commentary* on the *Emerald Tablet* of Hermes Trismegistus: Its Scientific and Theological Signifance', in Ingrid Merkel and Allen G. Debus (eds), *Hemeticism and the Renaissance: Intellectual History and the Occult in Early Modern Europe* (Cranbury, NJ: Associated University Presses, 1988), pp. 182–91
– *The Janus faces of genius: The role of alchemy in Newton's thought* (Cambridge: Cambridge University Press, 1991)
Drijvers, Han J. W., *Bardaisan of Edessa* (trans. G. E. van Baaren-Pape), (Assen: VanGorcum, 1966)
– *East of Antioch: Studies in Early Syriac Christianity* (London: Variorum Reprints, 1984)
Dunn, John, 'The Identity of the History of Ideas', *Philosophy*, 43: 164 (April 1968), pp. 85–104
Eisenstadt, Shmuel N., 'Cultural Traditions and Political Dynamics: the Origins and Modes of Ideological Politics', *British Journal of Sociology*, 32: 2 (June 1981), pp. 155–81
– 'Dissent, Heterodoxy and Civilizational Dynamics: Some Analytical and Comparative Indications', in Eisenstadt (ed.), *Orthodoxy, Heterodoxy, and Dissent in India* (New York: Mouton, 1984), pp. 1–9
– 'Comparative Liminality: Liminality and Dynamics of Civilization', *Religion*, 15: 3 (July 1985), pp. 315–38
– 'The Axial Age Breakthroughs – Their Characteristics and Origins', in Eisenstadt (ed.), *The Origins and Diversity of Axial Age Civilisations* (Albany, NY: SUNY Press, 1986), pp. 1–25
– 'Frameworks of the Great Revolutions: Culture, Social Structure, History

and Human Agency', *International Social Science Journal*, 44: 133 (August 1992), pp. 385–401

– 'O Sectarianismo da Idade Axial e as Antinomias da Liberdade', *Gepolis*, No. 5 (1998), pp. 117–36

Ekirch Jr, Arthur A., *Progressivism in America: A Study of the Era from Theodore Roosevelt to Woodrow Wilson* (New York: Franklin Watts, 1974)

Erdmann, Carl, *The Origin of the Idea of Crusade* (trans. M. W. Baldwin and W. Goffart), (Princeton: Princeton University Press, 1977)

Evans, R. J. W., *Rudolf II and his World: A Study in Intellectual History 1576–1612* (Oxford: Clarendon Press, 1984)

Faivre, Antoine and Jacob Needleman (eds), *Modern Esoteric Spirituality* (London: SCM Press, 1993)

Feuerbach, Ludwig, *The Essence of Christianity* (trans. George Eliot), (New York: Harper Torchbooks, 1957)

– *Principles of the Philosophy of the Future* (trans. M. H. Vogel), (New York: Bobbs-Merrill, 1966)

Foucault, Michel, *Discourse and Truth: The Problematization of Parrhesia*, Notes to the Seminar given by Foucault at Berkeley in autumn 1983, manuscript edited by Joseph Pearson

– 'Hermeneutik des Subjekts', in Helmut Becker and Lothar Wolfstetter (eds), *Freiheit und Selbstsorge* (Frankfurt a.M.: Materialis, 1985), pp. 32–60

– *The Care of the Self* (New York: Pantheon, 1986)

– 'Technologies of the Self', in Luther H. Martin, Huck Gutman and Patrick H. Hutton (eds), *Technologies of the Self: A Seminar with Michel Foucault* (London: Tavistock, 1988), pp. 16–49

– 'The Ethics of Care for the Self as a Practice of Freedom', in James Bernauer and David Rasmussen (eds), *The Final Foucault* (Cambridge, MA: MIT Press, 1988), pp. 1–20

Fowden, Garth, *The Egyptian Hermes: A Historical Approach to the Late Pagan Mind* (Cambridge: Cambridge University Press, 1986)

Frank, Erich, *Philosophical Understanding and Religious Truth* (New York: Oxford University Press, seventh printing, 1963)

Franklin, Laurel F., *George F. Kennan: An Annotated Bibliography* (Bibliographies of American Notables 3), (Westport: Greenwood Press, 1997)

Fukuyama, Francis, 'The End of History?', *The National Interest*, Vol. 16 (Summer 1989), pp. 3–18

– *The End of History and the Last Man* (Harmondsworth: Penguin, 1992)

Gadamer, Hans-Georg, *The Idea of the Good in Platonic-Aristotelian Philosophy* (trans. P. Christopher Smith), (New Haven: Yale University Press, 1986)

Gaddis, John Lewis, *The United States and the Origins of the Cold War 1941–1947* (New York: Columbia University Press, 1972)

– 'Was the Truman Doctrine a Real Turning Point?', *Foreign Affairs*, Vol. 52, January 1974, pp. 386–402

– *Strategies of Containment: A Critical Appraisal of Postwar American National Security Policy* (New York: Oxford University Press, 1982)

– *The Long Peace: Inquiries into the History of the Cold War* (New York: Oxford University Press, 1987)

— *Russia, the Soviet Union, and the United States: An Interpretive History* (New York: McGraw-Hill, second edn, 1990)

— *The United States and the End of the Cold War: Implications, Reconsiderations, Provocations* (New York: Oxford University Press, 1992)

— *We Now Know: Rethinking Cold War History* (Oxford: Clarendon Press, 1998)

Garsoïan, Nina G., *The Paulician Heresy: A Study of the Origin and Development of Paulicianism in Armenia and the Eastern Provinces of the Byzantine Empire* (The Hague: Mouton, 1967)

Gellman, Barton, *Contending with Kennan: Toward a Philosophy of American Power* (New York: Praeger, 1984)

Gennep, Arnold van, *The Rites of Passage* (London: Routledge & Kegan Paul, 1960)

Gibbon, Edward, *The Decline and Fall of the Roman Empire* (London: Encyclopaedia Britannica, twenty-second printing 1978 (1952))

Gilsdorf, Joy, *The Puritan Apocalypse: New England Eschatology in the Seventeenth Century* (New York: Garland, 1989)

Grant, R. M., *Gnosticism and Early Christianity* (New York: Harper and Row, 1966)

Grazia, Sebastian de, *Machiavelli in Hell* (Princeton, NJ: Princeton University Press, 1989)

Groys, Boris, 'Elemente des Gnostizismus im Dialektischen Materialismus (sowjetischen Marxismus)', in Peter Koslowski (ed.), *Gnosis und Mystik in der Geschichte der Philosophie* (Zürich, Artemis, 1988), pp. 352–67

Haardt, Robert (ed.), *Gnosis: Character and Testimony* (trans. J. F. Hendry), (Leiden: Brill, 1971)

Hamilton, Bernard, *Monastic Reform, Catharism and the Crusades* (London: Variorum, 1979)

Harnack, Adolf, *Monasticism: Its Ideals and History, and: The Confessions of St Augustine. Two Lectures* (trans. E. E. Kellett and F. H. Marseille), (London: Williams and Norgate, 1913)

Harper, John Lamberton, *American Visions of Europe* (Cambridge: Cambridge University Press, 1996)

Hartman, Chester and Pedro Vilanova (eds), *Paradigms Lost: The Post Cold War Era* (London: Pluto Press, 1992)

Hatch, Nathan O., *The Sacred Cause of Liberty: Republican Thought and the Millennium in Revolutionary New England* (New Haven: Yale University Press, 1977)

Hegel, G. W. F., *The Philosophy of History* (trans. J. Sibree), (New York: Dover, 1956)

— *Lectures on the History of Philosophy* (trans. E. S. Haldane and F. H. Simson), (London: Routledge & Kegan Paul, 1963), three volumes

— *Logic (Part One of the Encyclopaedia of the Philosophical Sciences)*, (trans. William Wallace), (Oxford: Oxford University Press, 1968 (rep. from the second edn, 1892))

— *Philosophy of Nature (Part Two of the Encyclopaedia of the Philosophical Sciences)*, (trans. A. V. Miller), (Oxford: Clarendon, 1970)

— *Lectures on the Philosophy of Religion*, three volumes (ed. Peter C. Hodgson,

trans. R. F. Brown), (Berkeley: University of California Press, 1984–7)
– *The Letters* (trans. Clark Butler and Christine Seiler), (Bloomington: Indiana University Press, 1984)
– *Elements of the Philosophy of Right* (ed. Allen W. Wood, trans. H. B. Nisbet), (Cambridge: Cambridge University Press, 1991)
Heimert, Alan, *Religion and the American Mind: From the Great Awakening to the Revolution* (Cambridge, MA: Harvard University Press, 1966)
Hill, Christopher, *The World Turned Upside Down: Radical Ideas During the English Revolution* (London: Temple Smith, 1973)
Hingley, Ronald, *Nihilists: Russian Radicals and Revolutionaries in the Reign of Alexander II* (New York: Delacorte Press, 1967)
Hixson, Walter L., *George F. Kennan: Cold War Iconoclast* (New York: Columbia University Press, 1989)
Hofstadter, Richard, *Social Darwinism in American Thought* (Boston: Beacon Press, second edn, 1959)
Hogan, Michael J., *The End of the Cold War: Its Meaning and Implications* (Cambridge: Cambridge University Press, 1992)
Hook, Sidney, *From Hegel to Marx* (Ann Arbor: The University of Michigan Press, 1966)
Inglis, Fred, *The Cruel Peace: Everyday Life and the Cold War* (New York: Basic Books, 1991)
Jacob, Margaret C., *The Radical Enlightenment: Pantheists, Freemasons and Republicans* (London: Allen & Unwin, 1981)
Jacobs, Joseph, 'The Lost Ten Tribes', *The Jewish Encyclopedia*, Vol. XII (New York: Funk and Wagnalls, 1906), pp. 249–53
Jaspers, Karl, *The Origin and Goal of History* (New Haven: Yale University Press, 1953)
Johannisson, Karin, 'Magic, Science, and Institutionalization in the Seventeenth and Eighteenth Centuries', in Ingrid Merkel and Allen G. Debus (eds), *Hermeticism and the Renaissance: Intellectual History and the Occult in Early Modern Europe* (Cranbury, NJ: Associated University Presses, 1988).
Jonas, Hans, *Gnosis und Spätantiker Geist – Erster Teil: Die mythologische Gnosis* (Göttingen: Vandenhoeck & Ruprecht, third edn, 1964)
– *Gnosis und Spätantiker Geist – Zweiter Teil: Von der Mythologie zur mystischen Philosophie* (Göttingen: Vandenhoeck & Ruprecht, second edn, 1966)
Jones, Maldwyn A., *The Limits of Liberty: American History 1607–1980* (New York: Oxford University Press, 1983)
Kaweh, Ramin, 'A Study in the Political Philosophy of Globalisation: The Case of UNESCO's Culture of Peace Programme' (unpublished MA Dissertation, University of Kent at Canterbury, August 1996)
Keller, Carl-A., 'Das Problem des Bösen in der Apokalyptik und Gnostik', in Martin Krause (ed.), *Gnosis and Gnosticism* (Papers read at the seventh International Conference on Patristic Studies, Oxford 1975), (Leiden: Brill, 1977), pp. 70–90
Kennan, George F. (Mr. 'X'), 'The Sources of Soviet Conduct', *Foreign Affairs*, Vol. 25, July 1947, pp. 566–82

– 'America and the Russian Future', *Foreign Affairs*, 29: 3 (April 1951), pp. 351–70

– 'Totalitarianism in the Modern World', in Carl J. Friedrich (ed.), *Totalitarianism: Proceedings of a Conference held at the American Academy of Arts and Sciences* (Cambridge, MA: Harvard University Press, 1954), pp. 17–31

– *Realities of American Foreign Policy* (London: Oxford University Press, 1954)

– 'The Future of Our Professional Diplomacy', *Foreign Affairs*, Vol. 33 (1955), pp. 566–86

– 'The Challenge of Freedom', in *The New Leader*, 20 June 1955, pp. 11–12

– 'America's Administrative Response to Its World Problems', *Daedalus*, 87: 2 (Spring 1958), pp. 5–24

– 'History as Literature', *Encounter*, 12: 4 (April 1959), pp. 10–16

– 'Foreign Policy and Christian Conscience', *Atlantic Monthly*, May 1959, pp. 44–9

– 'World Problems in Christian Perspective', in Abraham S. Eisenstadt (ed.), *American History: Recent Interpretations* (New York: Crowell, 1962), pp. 460–76

– 'A European Settlement', in Edward Reed (ed.), *Peace on Earth – Pacem in Terris* (New York: Pocket, 1965), pp. 77–83

– 'The Ethics of Anti-Communism', in *University: A Princeton Quarterly*, No. 24 (Spring 1965), pp. 3–5

– 'The Experience of Writing History', in Abraham S. Eisenstadt (ed.), *The Craft of American History* (New York: Harper, 1966), Vol. 2, pp. 270–8

– *Memoirs 1925–1950* (Boston: Little, Brown, 1967)

– *Democracy and the Student Left* (Boston: Little, Brown, 1968)

– 'The Relation of Religion to Government', in *The Princeton Seminary Bulletin*, Winter 1969, pp. 42–7

– 'To Prevent A World Wasteland', *Foreign Affairs*, 48: 3 (April 1970), pp. 401–13

– *Memoirs (Volume II): 1950–1963* (Boston: Little, Brown, 1972)

– '"X" plus 25', *Foreign Policy*, No. 7 (Summer 1972), pp. 5–21

– *Russia, the Atom and the West* (Westport, CT: Greenwood, 1974)

– 'The United States and the Soviet Union 1917–1976', *Foreign Affairs*, 54: 4 (July 1976), pp. 670–90

– 'Western Decadence and Soviet Moderation', in Martin F. Herz (ed.), *Decline of the West? George Kennan and His Critics* (Washington, DC: Ethics and Public Policy Center, 1978), pp. 3–9

– *American Diplomacy* (Chicago: University of Chicago Press, 1984)

– 'On Nuclear War', in Phil Braithwaite (ed.), *George Kennan on NATO, Nuclear War and the Soviet Threat* (Evesham: West Midlands CND Sales, 1985), pp. 33–9

– 'The View from Russia', in Thomas T. Hammond (ed.), *Witnesses to the Origins of the Cold War* (Seattle: University of Washington Press, 1986), pp. 27–33

– *Sketches from a Life* (New York: Pantheon, 1989)

– *Measures Short of War: the George F. Kennan Lectures at the National War*

College, 1946–47 (ed. Giles D. Harlow and George C. Maerz), (Washington, DC: National Defense University Press, 1991)

— *Around the Cragged Hill: A Personal and Political Philosophy* (New York: Norton, 1993)

— *At a Century's Ending: Reflections 1982–1995* (New York: Norton, 1996)

Kennan, George F. and Martin Agronsky, 'A Different Approach to the World: An Interview', in *The New York Review of Books*, 23: 21, 22 (20 January 1977), pp. 12–17

Kennan, George F. and John Lukacs, *George F. Kennan and the Origins of Containment 1944–1946. The Kennan–Lukacs Correspondence* (Columbia: University of Missouri Press, 1997)

Kennan, George F. et al., *Encounters with Kennan* (London: Cass, 1979)

Kirwin, G. F., 'Metanoia' in *The New Catholic Encyclopedia*, Vol. 9 (New York: McGraw-Hill, 1967), p. 724

Klíma, Otakar, *Manis Zeit und Leben* (Prag: Tschechoslowakische Akademie der Wissenschaften, 1962)

Knock, Thomas J., *To End all Wars: Woodrow Wilson and the Quest for a New World Order* (New York: Oxford University Press, 1992)

Koslowski, Peter (ed.), *Gnosis und Mystik in der Geschichte der Philosophie* (Zürich: Artemis, 1988)

Kristeller, Paul Oskar, *Renaissance Thought and its Sources* (ed. Michael Mooney), (New York: Columbia University Press, 1979)

Lambert, Malcolm, *Medieval Heresy: Popular Movements from the Gregorian Reform to the Reformation* (Oxford: Blackwell, second edn, 1992)

Lasch, Cristopher, 'Gnosticism, Ancient and Modern: The Religion of the Future?', in *Salmagundi*, No. 96 (Fall 1992), pp. 27–42

Lawrence, C. H., *Medieval Monasticism: Forms of Religious Life in Western Europe in the Middle Ages* (London: Longman, second edn, 1989)

— *The Friars: The Impact of the Early Mendicant Movement on Western Society* (London: Longman, 1994)

Lebow, Richard Ned and Janice Gross Stein, *We All Lost the Cold War* (Princeton: Princeton University Press, 1994)

Lebreton, Jules and Jacques Zeiller, *Heresy and Orthodoxy* (trans. Ernest C. Messenger), (New York: Collier, 1962)

Lee, Philip J., *Against the Protestant Gnostics* (New York: Oxford University Press, 1987)

Leff, Gordon, *Heresy in the Later Middle Ages* (Manchester: Manchester University Press, 1967)

Leffler, Melvyn P., *A Preponderance of Power: National Security, the Truman Administration, and the Cold War* (Stanford, CA: Stanford University Press, 1992)

Lerner, Robert E., 'Refreshment of the Saints: The Time After Antichrist as a Station for Earthly Progress in Medieval Thought', *Traditio*, Vol. 32 (1976), pp. 97–144

Lieu, Samuel N. C., *Manichaeism* (Tübingen: Mohr, second edn, 1992)

Link, Arthur S., *Woodrow Wilson and the Progressive Era 1910–1917* (New York: Harper & Row, 1954)

Lovejoy, David S., *Religious Enthusiasm in the New World: Heresy to Revol-*

ution (Cambridge, MA: Harvard University Press, 1985)

Luhmann, Niklas, 'The Autopoiesis of Social Systems', in Felix Geyer and Johannes van der Zouwen (eds), *Sociocybernetic Paradoxes: Observation, Control and Evolution of Self-steering Systems* (London: Sage, 1986), pp. 172–92

– 'Was ist Kommunikation?', *Information Philosophie*, Vol. 1 (1987), pp. 4–16

– *Soziale Systeme* (Frankfurt a.M.: Suhrkamp, fourth edn, 1991)

Lundestad, Geir and Odd Arne Westad (eds), *Beyond the Cold War: New Dimensions in International Relations* (Oslo: Scandinavian University Press, 1993)

Machiavelli, Niccolò, *The Prince* (ed. Quentin Skinner and Russell Price), (Cambridge: Cambridge University Press, 1988)

– *The Chief Works and Others* (trans. Alan Gilbert), (Durham, NC: Duke University Press, 1989), three volumes

– *Il Principe e altre opere politiche* (Milan: Garzanti, 1993)

– *Selected Political Writings* (ed. and trans. David Wootton), (Indianapolis: Hackett, 1994)

Maclear, J. F., 'New England and the Fifth Monarchy: The Quest for the Millennium in Early American Puritanism', *The William and Mary Quarterly*, Third Series, 32: 2 (April 1975), pp. 223–60

Macrae, George, 'Apocalyptic Eschatology in Gnosticism', in David Hellholm (ed.), *Apocalypticism in the Mediterranean World and the Near East* (Tübingen: Mohr, 1983), pp. 317–25

Mahé, Jean-Pierre, 'Gnostic and Hermetic Ethics' in Roelof van den Broek and Wouter J. Hanegraaff (eds), *Gnosis and Hermeticism: From Antiquity to Modern Times* (New York: SUNY Press, 1998), pp. 21–36

Manuel, Frank E., *The New World of Henri Saint-Simon* (Cambridge, MA: Cambridge University Press, 1956)

– *The Prophets of Paris* (Cambridge, MA: Harvard University Press, 1962)

– *The Religion of Isaac* Newton (Oxford: Clarendon, 1974)

Manuel, Frank E. and Fritzie P. Manuel, *Utopian Thought in the Western World* (Oxford: Basil Blackwell, 1979)

Marini, Stephen A., *Radical Sects of Revolutionary New England* (Cambridge, MA: Harvard University Press, 1982)

Martin, Edward James, *A History of the Iconoclastic Controversy* (New York: AMS Press, 1978)

Marx, Karl, see McLellan

Masters, G. Mallary, 'Renaissance Kabbalah', in Antoine Faivre and Jacob Needleman (eds), *Modern Esoteric Spirituality* (London: SCM Press, 1993), pp. 132–53

Mayers, David, *George Kennan and the Dilemmas of US Foreign Policy* (New York: Oxford University Press, 1988)

McGinn, Bernard, *The Calabrian Abbot: Joachim of Fiore in the History of Western Thought* (London: Collier Macmillan, 1985)

McKnight, Stephen A., *The Modern Age and the Recovery of Ancient Wisdom: A Reconsideration of Historical Consciousness 1450–1650* (Columbia: University of Missouri Press, 1991)

McLellan, David, *The Young Hegelians and Karl Marx* (London: Macmillan, 1969)

— (ed.), *Karl Marx: Selected Writings* (Oxford: Oxford University Press, 1977)

— *The Thought of Karl Marx* (London: Macmillan, third edn, 1995)

— *Karl Marx: A Biography* (London: Papermac, 1995)

McLoughlin, William G., 'Enthusiasm for Liberty: The Great Awakening as the Key to the Revolution', in Jack P. Greene and W. G. McLoughlin, *Preachers and Politicians: Two Essays on the Origins of the American Revolution* (Worcester: American Antiquarian Society, 1977), pp. 47–73

Meier, Christian, *Die Entstehung des Politischen bei den Griechen* (Frankfurt a.M.: Suhrkamp, 1980)

Merkel, Ingrid and Allen G. Debus (eds), *Hermeticism and the Renaissance: Intellectual History and the Occult in Early Modern Europe* (Cranbury, NJ: Associated University Presses, 1988)

Merton, Robert K., *Science, Technology and Society in Seventeenth Century England* (New York: Howard Fertig, 1970)

Miller, Perry and Thomas H. Johnson (eds), *The Puritans* (New York: Harper, 1963), two volumes

Miscamble, Wilson D., *George F. Kennan and the Making of American Foreign Policy 1947–1950* (Princeton, NJ: Princeton University Press, 1992)

Moore, R. I., *The Origins of European Dissent* (Oxford: Basil Blackwell, 1985)

Moorhead, James H., *American Apocalypse: Yankee Protestants and the Civil War 1860–1869* (New Haven: Yale University Press, 1978)

Mulder, John M., *Woodrow Wilson: The Years of Preparation* (Princeton, NJ: Princeton University Press, 1978)

Mumford, Lewis, *The Culture of Cities* (London: Secker & Warburg, 1938)

— *The Transformation of Man* (New York: Collier Books, 1956)

Nadel, Alan, *Containment Culture: American Narratives, Postmodernism, and the Atomic Age* (Durham: Duke University Press, 1995)

Newhouse, John, *War and Peace in the Nuclear Age* (New York: Alfred Knopf, 1989)

Noll, Mark A., *A History of Christianity in the United States and Canada* (Grand Rapids, Michigan: Eerdmans, 1992)

Obolensky, Dimitri, *The Bogomils: A Study in Balkan Neo-Manichaeism* (Cambridge: Cambridge University Press, 1948)

Oort, Johannes van, *Jerusalem and Babylon: A Study into Augustine's City of God and the Sources of his Doctrine of the Two Cities* (Leiden: Brill, 1991)

— 'Manichaeism' in Roelof van den Broek and Wouter J. Hanegraaff (eds), *Gnosis and Hermeticism: From Antiquity to Modern Times* (New York: SUNY Press, 1998), pp. 37–51

O'Regan, Cyril, *The Heterodox Hegel* (New York: SUNY Press, 1994)

Orlandi, Tito, 'A Catechesis against Apocryphal Texts by Shenute and the Gnostic Texts of Nag Hammadi', in *Harvard Theological Review*, 75: 1 (January 1982), pp. 85–95

Pagel, Walter, *Paracelsus: An Introduction to Philosophical Medicine in the Era of the Renaissance* (Basel: Karger, 1985)

Pagels, Elaine, *The Gnostic Gospels* (London: Weidenfeld and Nicolson, 1979)

Pearce, Roy H., *Savagism and Civilisation: A Study of the Indian and the American Mind* (Baltimore: Johns Hopkins Press, 1971)

Phelan, John Leddy, *The Millennial Kingdom of the Franciscans in the New World* (Berkeley, CA: University of California Press, second edn, 1970)

Piórczynski, Józef, 'Jakob Böhme als Vorläufer der Hegelschen Absoluteslehre', in *Reports on Philosophy*, Vol. 9 (1985), pp. 33–9

Pizzorno, Alessandro, 'Politics Unbound', in Charles S. Maier (ed.), *Changing Boundaries of the Political: Essays on the Evolving Balance between the State and Society, Public and Private in Europe* (Cambridge: Cambridge University Press, 1987), pp. 27–62

Plato, *Apology*, in Plato, *The Last Days of Socrates (Euthyphro, Apology, Crito, Phaedo)*, (trans. H. Tredennick and H. Tarrant), (Harmondsworth: Penguin, 1993), pp. 29–67

– *Laws* (trans. T. J. Saunders), (Harmondsworth: Penguin, 1975)

– *Phaedrus and The Seventh and Eighth Letters* (trans. W. Hamilton), (Harmondsworth: Penguin, 1973)

– *Philebus* (trans. J. C. B. Gosling), (Oxford: Clarendon, 1975)

– *Republic* (trans. D. Lee), (Harmondsworth: Penguin, 1987)

– *Timaeus* (trans. D. Lee), (Harmondsworth: Penguin, 1971)

Pocock, J. G. A., 'The History of Political Thought: A Methodological Inquiry', in Peter Laslett and W. G. Runciman (eds), *Philosophy, Politics and Society* (second series), (Oxford: Basil Blackwell, 1964), pp. 183–202

– *The Machiavellian Moment: Florentine Political Thought and the Atlantic Republican Tradition* (Princeton, NJ: Princeton University Press, 1975)

Polley, Michael, *A Biography of George F. Kennan: The Education of a Realist* (New York: Mellen Press, 1990)

Pratt, Julius W., *America's Colonial Experiment* (New York: Prentice-Hall, 1950)

– *Expansionists of 1898: The Acquisition of Hawaii and the Spanish Islands* (Gloucester, MA: Peter Smith, 1959)

Prior, Moody E., 'Bacon's Man of Science', in Brian Vickers (ed.), *Essential Articles for the Study of Francis Bacon* (Hamden, CT: Archon Books, 1968), pp. 140–63

Qviller, Bjørn, 'The Machiavellian Cosmos', *History of Political Thought*, 17: 3 (Autumn 1996), pp. 326–53

Rabinowitz, Louis Isaac, 'The Lost Tribes', *Encyclopedia Judaica*, Vol. 15 (Jerusalem: Keter, 1971), pp. 1003–6.

Raven, J. E., *Plato's Thought in the Making* (Cambridge: Cambridge University Press, 1965)

Reeves, Marjorie, *The Influence of Prophecy in the Later Middle Ages: A Study in Joachimism* (Oxford: Clarendon, 1969)

– *Joachim of Fiore and the Prophetic Future* (London: SPCK, 1976)

– 'The Originality and Influence of Joachim of Fiore', *Traditio*, Vol. 36 (1980), pp. 269–316

Reeves, Marjorie and Warwick Gould, *Joachim of Fiore and the Myth of the Eternal Evangel in the Nineteenth Century* (Oxford: Clarendon, 1987)

Reitzenstein, Richard, *Poimandres: Studien zur griechisch-ägyptischen und frühchristlichen Literatur* (Leipzig: Teubner, 1904)

Reuter, Ulrike, Lothar Wolfstetter, Hermann Kocyba and Bernd Heiter (eds), *Michel Foucault: Das Wahrsprechen des Anderen* (Frankfurt a.M.: Materialis Verlag, 1988)

Riley-Smith, Jonathan, *The Crusades: A Short History* (London: Athlone Press, 1987)

– *The First Crusade and the Idea of Crusading* (London: Athlone, 1995)

Robb, Nesca A., *Neoplatonism of the Italian Renaissance* (New York: Octagon, 1968)

Roberts, C. H., 'Review of The Facsimile Edition of the Nag Hammadi Codices (Leiden: Brill, 1979)', in *The Journal of Theological Studies*, New Series, Vol. 32 (1981), pp. 265–6

Robinson, James M. (ed.), *The Nag Hammadi Library in English* (Leiden: Brill, third edn, 1988)

Rossi, Paolo, *Francis Bacon: From Magic to Science* (Chicago: The University of Chicago Press, 1978)

Rousseau, Philip, *Pachomius: The Making of a Community in Fourth-century Egypt* (Berkeley: University of California Press, 1985)

Rowland, Christopher, *The Open Heaven: A Study of Apocalyptic in Judaism and Early Christianity* (London: SPCK, 1982)

Rudolph, Kurt, *Die Gnosis: Wesen und Geschichte einer spätantiken Religion* (Göttingen: Vandenhoeck & Ruprecht, third edn, 1994)

Runciman, Steven, *The Medieval Manichee: A Study of the Christian Dualist Heresy* (Cambridge: Cambridge University Press, 1960)

Rutman, Darrett B. (ed.), *The Great Awakening: Event and Exegesis* (New York: John Wiley, 1970)

St Clair, Michael J., *Millenarian Movements in Historical Context* (New York: Garland, 1992)

Sargent, Lyman Tower, 'Utopianism in Colonial America', *History of Political Thought*, 4: 3 (Winter 1983), pp. 483–522

Schlesinger Jr, Arthur M., 'The Theory of America: Experiment or Destiny?', in Schlesinger, *The Cycles of American History* (Harmondsworth: Penguin, 1989), pp. 3–22

Schlier, Heinrich, 'Parrhesia' in Gerhard Kittel (ed.), *The Theological Dictionary of the New Testament*, Vol. 5 (Grand Rapids: Eerdmans, 1967), pp. 871–86

Scholem, Gershom G., *Major Trends in Jewish Mysticism* (New York: Schocken, 1961)

– *Jewish Gnosticism, Merkabah Mysticism, and Talmudic Tradition* (New York: The Jewish Theological Seminary of America, 1965)

– 'Kabbalah', in *Encyclopaedia Judaica* (Jerusalem: Keter Publishing, 1973), Vol. 10, pp. 490–654

– *Origins of the Kabbalah* (Princeton: Princeton University Press, 1990 (1962))

Schwartz, Benjamin J., 'The Age of Transcendence', *Daedalus*, 104: 2 (Spring 1975), pp. 1–8

Shea, William R., *The Magic of Numbers and Motion: The Scientific Career of René Descartes* (Canton, MA: Science History Publications, 1991)

Skinner, Quentin, 'History and Ideology in the English Revolution', *The*

Historical Journal, 8: 2 (1965), pp. 151–78
– 'Meaning and Understanding in the History of Ideas', in *History and Theory*, Vol. 8 (1969), pp. 3–53
– 'Conventions and the Understanding of Speech Acts', *Philosophical Quarterly*, 20: 79 (April 1970), pp. 118–38
– 'Some Problems in the Analysis of Political Thought and Action', *Political Theory*, 2: 3 (August 1974), pp. 277–303
Solon, 'Elegiac Poems' in J. M. Edmonds (trans. and ed.), *Elegy and Iambus with the Anacreontea. Part I: Elegiac Poets from Callinus to Critias* (London: Heinemann (Loeb Classical Library), 1931), pp. 114–44.
Spitz, Lewis W., *The Religious Renaissance of the German Humanists* (Cambridge, MA: Harvard University Press, 1963)
Stephanson, Anders, *Kennan and the Art of Foreign Policy* (Cambridge, MA: Harvard University Press, 1989)
Stern, Peter, 'Marx's Critique of Philosophy', in *Interpretation*, 5: 3 (Spring 1976), pp. 266–87
Stout, Harry S., 'Religion, Communications, and the Ideological Origins of the American Revolution', *The William and Mary Quarterly*, Third Series, Vol. 34 (1977), pp. 519–41
Strauss, Leo, 'On Classical Political Philosophy', in *Social Research*, 12: 1 (February 1945), pp. 98–117
– *Thoughts on Machiavelli* (New York: Free Press, 1958)
– *What is Political Philosophy?* (Westport, CT: Greenwood, 1977)
Taubes, Jakob, *Abendländische Eschatologie* (Bern: Francke, 1947)
Tigerstedt, E. N., *The Decline and Fall of the Neoplatonic Interpretation of Plato: An Outline and some Observations* (Helsinki: Societas Scientiarum Fennica, 1974)
Timberlake, James H., *Prohibition and the Progressive Movement, 1900–1920* (New York: Atheneum, 1970)
Toon, Peter (ed.), *Puritans, the Millenium and the Future of Israel: Puritan Eschatology 1600–1660* (London: Clarke, 1970)
Topitsch, Ernst, 'Marxismus und Gnosis', in Topitsch, *Sozialphilosophie zwischen Ideologie und Wissenschaft* (Berlin: Luchterhand, third edn, 1971), pp. 261–96
Tucker, Robert, *Philosophy and Myth in Karl Marx* (Cambridge: Cambridge University Press, second edn, 1972)
Turner, Victor W., *The Forest of Symbols: Aspects of Ndembu Ritual* (Ithaca: Cornell University Press, 1967)
– *The Ritual Process: Structure and Anti-Structure* (Chicago: Aldine, 1969)
Tuveson, Ernest Lee, *Redeemer Nation: The Idea of America's Millennial Role* (Chicago: University of Chicago Press, 1968)
UNESCO (eds), *John Amos Comenius: Selections* (Paris: UNESCO, 1957)
US Department of State, *Foreign Relations of the United States*, 1942–1950 (Washington, DC: Government Printing Office, 1961–76)
– *The State Department Policy Planning Staff Papers* (New York: Garland, 1983), three volumes (1947, 1948, 1949)
Valentinov, Nikolay, *Encounters with Lenin* (trans. Paul Rosta and Brian Pearce), (New York: Oxford University Press, 1968)

Versluis, Arthur, 'Christian Theosophy and Ancient Gnosticism', in *Studies in Spirituality*, Vol. 7 (1997), pp. 228–41

Vielhauer, P., 'Apocalypses and Related Subjects: Introduction', in E. Hennecke and W. Schneemelcher (eds), *New Testament Apocrypha. Volume Two* (London: SCM Press, 1975), pp. 581–607

Voegelin, Eric, *Über die Form des Amerikanischen Geistes* (Tübingen: J. C. B. Mohr, 1928)

– 'The Formation of the Marxian Revolutionary Idea', *The Review of Politics*, 12: 3 (July 1950), pp. 275–302

– 'Machiavelli's Prince: Formation and Background', *The Review of Politics*, Vol. 13 (1951), pp. 142–68

– *The New Science of Politics: An Introduction* (Chicago: University of Chicago Press, 1952)

– *Israel and Revelation* (Volume 1 of *Order and History*), (Baton Rouge: Louisiana State University Press, 1956)

– *The World of the Polis* (Volume 2 of *Order and History*), (Baton Rouge: Lousiania State University Press, 1957)

– *Plato and Aristotle* (Volume 3 of *Order and History*), (Baton Rouge: Louisiana State University Press, 1957)

– 'Religionsersatz: Die Gnostischen Massenbewegungen unserer Zeit', *Wort und Wahrheit*, 15: 1 (1960), pp. 5–18

– 'Industrial Society in Search of Reason', in Raymond Aron (ed.), *World Technology and Human Destiny* (Ann Arbor: University of Michigan Press, 1963), pp. 31–46

– 'On Hegel: A Study in Sorcery', in J. T. Fraser, F. C. Haber and G. H. Müller (eds), *The Study of Time* (Berlin: Springer, 1972), pp. 418–51

– *Science, Politics and Gnosticism* (Chicago: Regnery Gateway, 1968)

– *The Ecumenic Age* (Volume 4 of *Order and History*), (Baton Rouge: Louisiana State University Press, 1974)

– *From Enlightenment to Revolution* (ed. John H. Hallowell), (Durham, NC: Duke University Press, 1975)

– *Anamnesis* (trans. and ed. Gerhart Niemeyer), (Notre Dame: University of Notre Dame Press, 1978)

– *In Search of Order* (Volume 5 of *Order and History*), (Baton Rouge: Louisiana State University Press, 1987)

– *Ordnung, Bewußtsein, Geschichte* (ed. Peter J. Opitz), (Stuttgart: Klett, 1988)

– *Autobiographical Reflections* (Baton Rouge: Louisiana State University Press, 1989)

– *History of Political Ideas Volume I: Hellenism, Rome, and Early Christianity* (The Collected Works of Eric Voegelin Vol. 19), (ed. Athanasios Moulakis), (Columbia: University of Missouri Press, 1997)

Volkogonov, Dmitri, *Lenin: Life and Legacy* (trans. Harold Shukman), (London: HarperCollins, 1995)

Walicki, Andrzej, *A History of Russian Thought* (Oxford: Clarendon, 1988)

Walker, Daniel P., *Spiritual and Demonic Magic from Ficino to Campanella* (Notre Dame: University of Notre Dame Press, 1975)

Walsh, David, *The Mysticism of Innerworldly Fulfillment: A Study of Jacob*

Boehme (Gainesville: University Presses of Florida, 1983)
Watts, Pauline Moffitt, 'Prophecy and Discovery: On the Spiritual Origins of Christopher Columbus's "Enterprise of the Indies"', *American Historical Review*, 90: 1 (February 1985), pp. 73–102
Webster, Charles, *The Great Instauration: Science, Medicine and Reform 1626–1660* (London: Duckworth, 1975)
Weeks, Andrew, *Boehme: An Intellectual Biography of the Seventeenth Century Philosopher and Mystic* (New York: SUNY Press, 1991)
– *Paracelsus: Speculative Theory and the Crisis of the Early Reformation* (New York: SUNY Press, 1997)
Wehr, Gerhard, *Jakob Böhme* (Reinbek: Rowohlt, 1971)
Weinstein, Donald, *Savonarola and Florence: Prophecy and Patriotism in the Renaissance* (Princeton, NJ: Princeton University Press, 1970)
Whitfield, Stephen J., *The Culture of the Cold War* (Baltimore: The Johns Hopkins University Press, 1991)
Widengren, Geo, *Mani and Manichaeism* (trans. Charles Kessler), (London: Weidenfeld and Nicolson, 1965)
Wiebe, Robert H., *The Search for Order 1877–1920* (New York: Hill and Wang, 1967)
Williams, Michael Allen, *Rethinking 'Gnosticism': An Argument for Dismantling A Dubious Category* (Princeton: Princeton University Press, 1996)
Wilson, R. McLachlan, *Gnosis and the New Testament* (Oxford: Basil Blackwell, 1968)
Wirszubski, Ch., 'Giovanni Pico's Companion to Kabbalistic Symbolism', in E. E. Urbach, R. J. Zwi Werblowsky and Ch. Wirszubski (eds), *Studies in Mysticism and Religion presented to Gershom Scholem* (Jerusalem: Magnes Press, 1967), pp. 353–62
Wisse, Frederik, 'Gnosticism and Early Monasticism in Egypt', in Barbara Aland (ed.), *Gnosis: Festschrift für Hans Jonas* (Göttingen: Vandenhoeck & Ruprecht, 1978), pp. 431–40
Wood, Gordon S., *The Creation of the American Republic 1776–1787* (Chapel Hill: University of North Carolina Press, 1969)
Wright, C. Ben, 'Mr. X and Containment', *Slavic Review*, 35: 1 (March 1976), pp. 1–31
Yates, Frances A., *The Occult Philosophy in the Elizabethan Age* (London: Routledge & Kegan Paul, 1979)
– *Ideas and Ideals in the North European Renaissance. Collected Essays Vol. 2* (London: Routledge & Kegan Paul, 1984)
– *The Rosicrucian Enlightenment* (London: ARK Paperbacks, 1986)
– *Giordano Bruno and the Hermetic Tradition* (Chicago: The University of Chicago Press, 1991 (1964))
Zvesper, John, 'The American Founders and Classical Political Thought', *History of Political Thought*, 10: 4 (Winter 1989), pp. 701–18

GENERAL TEXTS AND ENCYCLOPAEDIAS

The New Jerusalem Bible (Study Edition), (London: Darton, Longman & Todd, 1994)
The New Catholic Encyclopedia (New York: McGraw-Hill, 1967)
Gerhard Kittel (ed.), *The Theological Dictionary of the New Testament* (Grand Rapids, Michigan: Eerdmans, 1964–72)
The Holy Quran (trans. A. Y. Ali), (Beirut: Dar Al Arabia, 1968)
The Jewish Encyclopedia (New York: Funk and Wagnalls, 1901–06)
Encyclopaedia Judaica (Jerusalem: Keter, 1971–4)

Index

Abraham, 106, 172
Académie des Sciences, 130
Adam, 41, 51–2, 66, 106, 124, 127, 131, 144, 150, 175, 189
  in Boehme's theosophy, 144
  in Manichaeism, 66
  in the Old Testament, 41
  in the 'Script without Title', 51–2
Adams, John Quincy, 203
Addas, 64, 87
Adoptionism, 74–5
aeons, 50, 62, 132, 148
Agapius, 68
Agathocles, 227
agathon see form of the Good
'Agenda for Peace', 225
Aglaophemus, 124
agnoia, 53
Albigenses, 81, 105, 175, 176
Albigensian Crusade, 82, 113
Albinus, 117
alchemy, 104, 126, 128, 146, 195
Alexander I, 164
Alexander VI, 137
Alexander the Great, 38, 60, 228
Alexius, 96
alienation, 53, 55, 156, 190, 229–30
'Allegory of the Cave', 25–36, 43, 208
'American dream', 203
American Revolution, 176, 178–9
Ammonius Saccas, 90
Anabaptist movement, 72, 116, 175–6
anamnesis, 33
anchorites, 87, 104
Angelic Pope, 107, 113, 116
Anglo-French War, 176, 178
Anselm of Lucca, 192
Antichrist, 97, 103, 107, 109, 113, 170, 176, 178, 180
antinomian tendencies, 57, 78
antinomianism, 76, 175
apocatastasis, 92, 96, 128, 166
Apelles, 62
apocalypse, 94–9, 123, 171
Apocalypse of John see Revelation
apocalyptic beliefs, 73, 94–9, 151
  and the Crusades, 96–7
apocalypticism, 94–9
  and asceticism, 94
'Apostle of the Light', 64, 66, 69
archons, 51–3, 58, 65–6
Arendt, Hannah, 226
aretai, 57
Arians, 63
Aristippus, Henricus, 118
Aristotle, 27, 40, 145, 149, 152
Arnold, Gottfried, 164, 166
asceticism, 48, 57, 74, 84–6, 88, 90, 94–7, 99, 130
  antinomian, 130
  Christian, 84
  and dualism, 74
  and eschatological excitement, 94–7, 99
  Manichaean, 76, 84
  as preliminary stage of 'Gnosticism', 90
Asclepius, 120–4, 127, 136
Ashmole, Elias, 129
astrology, 120, 126
Athanasius, 85–6
'athletes of God', 82
auditores, 67
Avenarius, Richard, 166
Axial Age, 11–14, 37

Baader, Franz von, 164, 165
Bacon, Francis, 127–8, 147
Bahir, 132
baptism, 68, 75, 189
bar nasa, 42
Bardaisan, 63, 126, 127
Barns, John, 85
Baronius, Cesare, 125
Basil the Great, 86
Basilides, 47, 59, 148
Bauer, Walter, 59
Baur, Ferdinand Christian, 142, 148

beatific vision, 43
Beguins, 112–14
Behem, Abraham, 146
'being-in-the-world', 52, 54–5, 57, 69
Belinsky, Vissarion, 169
Bengel, Johann Albrecht, 138, 151
Berdiaev, Nicolai A., 166
Besançon, Alain, 142
Blake, William, 175
Boehme, Jacob, 17, 138, 142–7, 148–9, 150, 151, 152, 163–7, 175
Bogdanov, Alexander, 166
Bogomil, 78
Bogomilism, 79–81
Bogomils, 64, 72, 73, 78–81, 84, 176
  ascetic élite, 79, 84
  auditors, 79
  Byzantine, 79, 80
Bohlen, Charles, 209
Bolsheviks, 67, 166
Bolshevism, 208
Book of Revelation *see* Revelation
Bousset, Wilhelm, 60
Boutros-Ghali, Boutros, 225
Brahe, Tycho, 146
brahmins, 13
'breaking the vessels', 134
Broek, Roelof van den, 49
Brown, Peter, 67, 187
Buddha, 66, 126
Buddhism, 13, 63
Bühler, Karl, 15
Burkitt, F. C., 98

Cabala, 130–8, 144–5, 146
  and Catharism, 131–2
Cabalist mysticism, 104, 125, 128
Cabalistic texts, 99
Calcidius, 117–18
Callinice, 76
Candidus, 63
Campanella, Tommaso, 3
Carbeas, 76
'care of the soul', 31, 229
Carolingians, 77, 81, 88
Casaubon, Isaac, 125, 127, 128
Cathar Council at Saint-Félix-de-Caraman, 80, 82
Catharism, 80–4, 99, 103, 113, 131–2
Cathars, 64, 72, 73, 74, 80–4, 88, 99, 131–2, 176
  and apostolic liminality, 82
  ascetic élite, 80–2, 84
Catherine the Great, 164
Celestine V, 113
Celsus, 60
Cerdo, 60
Chaldaean Oracles, 118, 120
charisma, 195–6
Charlemagne, 168
Charles I, 171, 174
Chernyshevsky, Nicholas, 167
chiliasm *see* millenarianism
chorismos, 12, 27, 32, 37, 41, 230
Christ, 43, 58, 69, 77, 79, 103, 104, 106, 123, 125, 126, 129, 174, 177, 178, 180
  as healer, 123
  in Marcionism, 61
  in Origen's system, 92
  in Ptolemy's system, 62–3
  as 'saved saviour', 58
'Christian Cabala', 17, 137–8
Christianity, 9, 11, 14, 22, 25, 39–45, 48, 59–60, 63, 66, 68, 74, 123–4, 125, 127, 136, 137, 149, 151, 171, 173, 175, 186
  and the *chorismos*, 41
  and 'Gnosticism', 59–60
  Lutheran, 151
  and mutuality in the divine-human encounter, 40
  and Paulicianism in Bulgaria, 77–8
  prophesied in the *Asclepius*, 123–4
  Syriac, 74
Chrysochir, 76
Chrysoloras, Manuel, 118
Cicero, 2, 188
Cistercianism, 84, 104, 105
'civil millenarianism', 177, 181
Civil War, 176, 179, 203
civitas Dei, 190
Clarenists, 112–14
Clareno, Angelo, 112–14
Clement of Alexandria, 62
Cluniacs, 88–9
Cluny, 88–9, 96, 105
Cold War, 1, 163, 176, 181–3, 186–7, 203, 211–13, 215, 224–6, 228, 230
Columbus, Christopher, 171–2
Column of Glory, 66–7, 188
Comenius, John Amos, 128–130, 147, 172, 175, 224–5, 231
Communist Manifesto, 154, 159
Communist Revolution, 160, 225
Communist society, 155, 157, 159
Communism, 67, 157, 160, 169, 209, 212, 225
  two phases of, 160
  see also Soviet Communism
Communists, 160
communitas, 5–11, 26, 34–5, 38, 44, 69, 89–90, 94, 95, 99, 103, 104, 108, 175
  abstract vision of, 10, 69
  actualisation of, 9–11
  and community, 6–11

during the Millennium, 95
and Manichaeism, 69
as a model of human interrelatedness, 5
and monasticism, 89–90
as a realm of reflection, 7
and space, 9–10, 69
struggle for, 9
and time, 9–10, 69
Comte, Auguste, 116, 153–4, 167, 169
Condorcet, Marie-Jean-Antoine-Nicolas de Caritat, Marquis de, 154
consolamentum, 81, 83
Constantine, 87, 168
Constantine Copronymus, 77
Constantine-Silvanus, 76
containment, 198–9, 212–13
Copernicus, Nicolaus, 127
Corpus Hermeticum, 118–30
alleged antiquity of, 124
and *gnosis*, 126
cosmos, 29, 49–58, 63, 65, 68, 84, 91, 92, 104, 116, 131
in Greek philosophy, 29, 68
in the *Interrogatio Johannis*, 81
in Origen's system, 91
in Ptolemy's system, 63
as the result of an accident, 50
and the World-Soul, 91
Couliano, Ioan P., 59, 60, 93
Counter-Reformation, 125, 145, 170, 175
credentes, 80, 81
Cromwell, Oliver, 172, 174
crucifixion, 58, 68
Crusade, First, 96–7
Crusaders, 82
Crusades, 105, 192
'Culture of Peace', 225, 230–1
Cyrus, 194, 195

Danchev, Alex, 199
Danilevsky, Nikolai, 169
Darwinian biology, 180–1
Decembrio, Uberto, 118
Decius, 87
decline of the West, 215–18
demiurge, 49–51, 53, 61–2, 63
as a lower deity in Marcionism, 61–2
in Ptolemy's system, 63
democracy, 4–5, 206
in Athens, 4
and *parrhesia*, 4–5
spiritual preconditions for, 4–5
Descartes, René, 127–8
diadochai, 60
'dialectical materialism', 157
dialectics, 33–4, 143, 156–7, 224, 230
dangers of, 34
Marx's understanding of, 156–7
modern understanding of, 143
Dietzgen, Joseph, 157
Diocletian, 87
Dion, 32
Dionysius (Corinth), 47
Dionysius (Syracuse), 32
Dionysius the Areopagite, 125
Docetism, 58, 75, 76, 79, 148
Dominic, 83, 108
Dominican Order, 84
Dominicans, 73, 83, 108–9
Donatists, 189, 192, 227
'double negation', 55, 157
Drijvers, Han J. W., 127
Drittes Reich, 116
Drugunthia, Church of, 80, 83
'Dry Utopia', 181
dualism, 49–50, 52–4, 58, 60, 63, 65, 67, 75, 79, 81, 83, 97–8, 122, 190–2
absolute, 50, 79, 83
anticosmic, 49–50, 58, 79, 122
and apocalypticism, 97–8
Bogomil belief in, 79
in the *City of God*, 190–1
of darkness and light, 52–3, 65
'Gnostic', 67
Manichaean, 63, 65, 190
Massalian belief in, 79
moderate, 50, 79, 81
monistic, 50
moral, 191–2
and Paulician doctrine, 75
Persian, 60
radical, 50
Zoroastrian, 60, 63
Zurvanite, 60
Dury, John, 128–30, 172, 173
'Dying Sphinx', 164, 166

Edwards, Jonathan, 177, 178, 180
Eisenstadt, Shmuel N., 12, 14, 226
ekklesia, 44, 55
ekstasis, 91
electi, 67
Elijah, 106
Eliot, John, 173, 174
emanation, 90–1, 132, 134
Emerson, Ralph Waldo, 175
Encyclopaedists, 154
Ender, Karl, 145
Engels, Friedrich, 154, 166, 176
Enlightenment, 142
ennoia, 62
Ên Sôph, 133–4
Enoch, 127
enthusiasm, 73, 94–9, 104, 176
apocalyptic, 94–9

Ephraim the Syrian, 126
Epicur, 152
epimelesthai sautou see 'care of the soul'
Epiphanius of Constantia, 49, 62
epistrophe, 39, 55, 63
eschatological, 50, 73, 94, 97, 98, 103, 109, 110, 113, 151, 191, 224, 231
eschatology, 96, 110, 130, 160, 170, 175
Eternal Evangel, 111–12, 154, 169
'ethics of being', 192
'ethics of doing', 192
European Recovery Program, 204–5
Evagrius Ponticus, 86, 92–3, 96, 165
Eve, 51–2, 66
  in Manichaeism, 66
  in the 'Script without Title', 51–2
experience, 14, 19–21, 29
  equivalence of, 19–21
  self-interpretations of, 14
  sharing of, 19
  and symbolisation, 14
  of the 'turning around', 29
externalisation of evil, 178, 187, 189, 214

fate *see heimarmene*
Faustus of Milevis, 67, 126
Ferdinand of Aragon, 228
Feuerbach, Ludwig, 152–8, 166, 167
Fichte, Johann Gottlieb, 93
Ficino, Marsilio, 73, 116–125, 135, 136, 137, 145
  and his 'Academy', 73
Fifth Monarchy movement, 173–4, 175
First World War, 176, 181, 203
Forrestal, James, 198
'forms' *see* Plato
form of the Good, 28–34, 39, 43, 52, 69, 228–9
  elusiveness of, 32, 36
  knowledge of, 28, 228–9
  as 'measuredness', 36
  as a 'mixture', 36
  and political order, 31, 34–7
  transcendence of, 28–9, 33, 37
  as the ultimate ground of being, 29
Founding Fathers, 202
Fourier, François-Marie-Charles, 154
Fowden, Garth, 122, 125, 126
Fox, George, 174
Francis II, 223
Franciscans, 73, 83, 103, 108–16
  and the issue of poverty, 109–10
Francke, August, 163
Francke, Gotthilf, 163
Franckenberg, Abraham, 146
Frank, Erich, 116
fraticelli, 113–16
  and the *Ciompi* rebellion, 115
  and the Clarenists, 113–14
  in Florence, 114–16
  il populo di Dio, 115
Frederick II, 82
freedom, as the cause of God, 178
Freemasonry, 127, 164
French Revolution 11, 116, 154, 177, 226
  and the Eternal Evangel, 116
Freud, Sigmund, 48
Fukuyama, Francis, 223–4, 226
'fullness of God' see *pleroma*
Futtuq, 64, 86

Gans, Eduard, 154
Garsoïan, Nina, 74–5
Genesis, 62, 68, 124
Gennep, Arnold van, 5
Gerard of Borgo San Donnino, 111–12
German Idealism, 116, 142, 152, 163, 164
Ghibellines, 82
Gibbon, Edward, 59, 72, 74, 206
Gichtel, Johann Georg, 145, 166
Giovanni delle Bande Nere, 196
'globalisation', 224
gnosis, 47–9, 51, 63, 68, 98, 122, 131, 132, 152, 186, 229–30
'Gnostic' Christology, 58
'Gnostic War', 22, 230
'Gnosticism', 22, 47–60, 62, 63, 68–70, 85–6, 98, 122, 126, 131, 142, 146, 148
  antipathy towards philosophy, 55
  and apocalypticism, 98
  cannot be defined as 'ideal type', 22, 48
  and classical culture, 68–70
  Jewish and rabbinic, 131
  origins of, 59
  'parasitic' nature of, 59
'Gnostics', 58, 75, 86, 120, 126, 148
  and anchoritic and cenobitic movements, 86
  and secrecy, 58
  self-descriptions of, 58
'Golden Age', 104, 138, 187
Grant, R. M., 98
Grazia, Sebastian de, 187, 192
Great Awakening, 176–8
Gregorian revolution, 89
Gregory VII, 89
Gregory the Theologian, 86
Guelfs, 82

Haak, Theodore, 130
Haardt, Robert, 67
hades, 53
Hadrian, 59
happiness, 228–9
Harnack, Adolf von, 60
Harranians, 126–7

Hartlib, John, 128–30, 172, 231
Hasidim, 132
Heavenly Jerusalem, 95, 97–8
Hecht, Koppel, 144–5
Hegel, Georg Wilhelm Friedrich, 17, 48, 99, 142, 143, 147–55, 157, 158, 159, 164, 165, 223–4, 229
  on Boehme, 148–9, 150
  on Christianity, 149
  and Joachim, 151
  on philosophy, 151
heimarmene, 53–4
Helmont, Franciscus Mercurius van, 138, 145
Henry IV, 89
Heracleon, 63
Heraclitus, 12, 29
heresiologists, 47, 59, 62
Hering, Samuel, 147
Hermaioi, 126
Hermes Trismegistus, 119–30, 135
Hermetic texts, 99, 119–30
  technical, 125–6
  theoretical, 126
Hermeticism, 104, 119–30, 136, 137, 146, 148
Hermeticists, 120–30, 146
Herzen, Alexander, 166, 169
Hesiod, 12
Hinduism, 63
Hippolytus, 47, 49, 62, 63
Historia Manichaeorum, 76
history, 19–21
Homer, 11, 37
Hugh de Digne, 112
Huguenots, 175
humanity
  in 'Gnostic' mythology, 50–2
  pneumatisation of, 104
Hus, Jan, 128, 175
Hussite movement, 72
Hussite Wars, 145

Iamblichus, 117, 126
Ibn al-Nadim, Mohammed, 64
iconoclasm, 75
Iconoclastic Controversy, 77
Iconoclasts, 75
  Byzantine, 75
Idris, 127
ignorance, 31, 36, 55
Illiad, 11
Imitatio Christi, 83
'immortalising', practice of, 43
'imperialism of righteousness', 180
incarnation, 42, 68, 84
Innocent III, 82, 83
Innocent VIII, 136–7
Inquisition, 80, 82, 84, 113–15, 137, 228
intelligentsia, 93, 165, 166, 169
Interrogatio Johannis, 80–1
Investiture Contest, 73, 89, 192
Irenaeus, 47, 49, 58, 62
Isaiah, 124
Islam, 14, 63, 97, 126–7
Israel, Menasseh Ben, 172
Israel's Ten Lost Tribes, 172–3
Ivan III, 168
Ivan IV, 168

Jacob, Margaret, 127
Jacobi, Friedrich Heinrich, 149
James I, 125, 171
Jean d'Olivi, 112–14
Jesus, 39, 40, 41–5, 58, 60, 61, 62, 66, 69, 74, 75, 83, 106, 126, 148
  in Adoptionism, 74
  as 'Apostle of Light', 66
  and the beatific vision, 43
  in 'Gnostic' myth, 58
  and the Jews, 44
  in Paulicianism, 75
  in Ptolemy's system, 62
  his role in Marcionism, 61
  and salvation, 41–2
  as the suffering messiah, 42
  and Thomas, 44
Jewish mysticism, 17, 130–8
  and Catharism, 131–2
Joachim of Fiore, 18, 103–16, 152, 169, 171
  and ecumenism, 108
  his method, 105–6
  life, 104–5
  and monastic reform, 105
  reputation during his lifetime, 109
Joachimism, 83–4, 103–16, 151, 168, 169, 171, 175
  influence of, 116
Joachimite speculation, 73, 103–16, 151, 154
Johannine spirituality, 95
John XIX, 89
John of Parma, 111–12, 169
John the Apostle, 94
John the Divine, 95
Jonas, Hans, 47–58, 60, 90, 93, 122, 126
Johnson, Edward, 170
Judaism, 14, 41, 66, 131, 145
Julian of Eclanum, 189, 190
Jung, Carl G., 48

Kennan, George F., 22, 182–3, 186–7, 196–218, 226, 227, 228, 230
  on decadence, 215–16
  on democracy, 206

on human nature, 199–202
on 'leadership by example', 203
life, 196–9
on the nuclear arms race, 216–17
'totalitarianism', 206–14
Kepler, Johannes, 146
Khomyakov, Aleksei, 165
'Kind Stranger', 61, 69, 70
Kireyevski, Ivan, 164–5
Knock, Thomas J., 181
Knorr von Rosenroth, Christian, 137–8, 145
Korean War, 183
Kristeller, Paul Oskar, 118

Labzin, Alexander, 164
Lactantius, 120, 123
League of Nations, 181
Lenin, Vladimir Ilich, 157, 166–7
Leo IX, 89
Leonardo da Pistoia, 119
Lessing, Gotthold Ephraim, 116
Liberato, 113
liberty, 178, 182
libertinism, 57–8
liminality, 5–11, 14, 25, 34, 69–70, 82, 83, 84, 89–90, 94, 95, 103, 108
as contact with sacred powers, 6
and contingency, 8
dangers of, 8, 34
van Gennep's definition of, 5
as a moment of truth, 6, 9–10
and monasticism, 89–90
in rites of passage, 5
'status' of, 9, 11
see also communitas
lines of meaning, 15–21, 22, 25, 48–9, 70, 73, 93, 97, 99, 104, 130, 163, 175, 186, 225, 226, 230
as communication, 15–16
contemplation of, 20
definition of, 15
exploration of, 17–18
and the study of 'Gnosticism', 48–9
literati, 13, 65
logos, 29, 39, 53, 116, 224
Lollard movement, 72
'Long Telegram', 197–9, 207, 214
Louis VIII, 82
Louis IX, 82
Louis XIV, 175
Löw, Jehudah, 146
Lucifer, 143–4, 150
Luhmann, Niklas, 15–16
Luke, Archbishop of Cosenza, 105
Lunacharsky, Anatoly, 166
Luria, Isaac, 133–5, 137, 138
Lurianic Cabala, 131, 133–5
Luther, Martin, 3, 99

McCarthy era, 213
Mach, Ernst, 166
Machiavelli, Niccolò, 22, 186–7, 192–6, 226–8
McLellan, David, 157
Macrobius, 118
magic, 104, 120, 123–4, 126, 127, 136, 195
Cabalist, 136
demonic, 123
natural, 123, 136
pneumatic, 123
Magna Charta, 179
Mani, 47, 63–70, 72, 73, 74, 75, 76, 87, 126, 145, 188, 191, 229
as 'Apostle of Light', 66
and Hermes, 126
Manichaean Church, 64
Manichaeans, 57–8, 67–8, 73–6, 79, 80, 84, 85, 87, 98, 120, 126, 176, 186, 187–192, 229
auditores, 67
electi, 67
élite and ordinary members, 57–8
Manichaeism, 21, 60, 62, 63–70, 72, 79, 85, 87, 93, 97, 99, 145, 163, 187–192, 230
and asceticism, 67
and permanent liminality, 69
Marcion, 60–2, 63, 64, 69–70, 77, 147
Marcionism, 22, 59, 60–2, 69–70, 75, 77, 176
Marcus, 63
Marshall, George C., 198
Marshall Plan, 198, 204–5, 212
Marx, Karl, 142, 152–60, 166, 225, 229
departing from Feuerbach, 155
on dialectics, 157–8
on human nature, 155
on revolution, 156–7
and the 'total individual', 158
Marxism, 130, 166
Massalians, 79, 84
'materialism', 153
Maximilian I, 168
Maximilian II, 168
Maximus the Confessor, 165
Medici, Cosimo de, 117, 119
Medici, Lorenzo de (Il Magnifico), 137
Meister Eckhart, 147, 151
mendicant orders, 83, 103, 109, 111
Merezhkovsky, D. S., 116
Merton, Robert K., 140n–141n
messiah, 42, 44, 61, 136, 171
Messina Conference on the Origins of Gnosticism, 47, 60

metabolism, 157–8
metanoia, 25, 39–41, 55
metaxy, 20, 201
Methodism, 175
Mikhailovsky, Nikolai, 169
millenarian movements, 94–9
millenarianism, 73, 94–9, 130, 170–1, 173, 176, 177, 178, 179
  and monasticism, 96–7
  and republican thought, 177
Millennium, 95–9, 103, 138, 171, 173, 176, 178, 210
Miller, Arthur, 181
Millerites, 176
Mithridates, Flavious, 136
Moeller van den Bruck, Arthur, 116
monastic reform movement, 73, 88, 99
monasticism, 73, 84–90, 96–7, 99, 130
  and the Crusades, 96–7
  and heresy, 84–90
Monophysites, 75
Montanist movement, 73, 104
Montanus, 94
Moravians, 175
More, Henry, 138
Mormons, 176
Moses, 41, 108, 119, 123, 124, 125, 130, 131, 135, 194, 195
Moses de Leon, 132–3
Mughtasilah, 64, 87
Mumford, Lewis, 205
Müntzer, Thomas, 116
mysticism, 86, 90–3, 130–8, 147, 152, 163, 166, 181
  activist, 152, 181
  Christian, 147
  and heresy, 90–1
  Merkabah, 131
  Neo-Platonist, 99
myth, 8, 35, 191
  gennaion pseudos, 35
  and rites of passage, 8

Nag Hammadi, 48, 49, 51, 58, 85–6, 98, 120, 126
Napoleon, 168–9, 223
Nazarius, 80
Neander, August, 148
Neo-Manichaeans, 72
Neo-Manichaeism, 72
neophytes, 5–10
Neo-Platonism, 25, 73, 90–3, 117–20, 124, 125, 132, 135, 136, 137, 138, 146, 147–8, 186
  as the foundation of Eastern spirituality, 93
  and 'Gnosticism', 93
  as a line of meaning, 93
  and mysticism, 90–3
New Testament, 40, 43, 64, 76, 94, 106, 107, 108, 111, 132
New World, 163, 170–83
'new world order', 224
Newton, Isaac, 128, 147, 154
Nicetas, 80, 82–3
Nitze, Paul H., 182
NSC-68, 182–3, 199
'nuclear apocalypse', 163
nuclear weapons, 216

Odoevsky, Vladimir, 164
Odyssey, 11–12
Oetinger, Friedrich Christoph, 138, 144–5, 147, 151
Old Testament, 39, 41–2, 60, 64, 75, 79, 106, 107, 108, 111, 124, 130, 132, 175
Oort, Johannes van, 187, 191
O'Regan, Cyril, 147, 150
Origen, 62, 63, 90, 91–3
  and Catharism, 93
  as 'Christianised Gnosis', 93
  his Christology, 92
  and the doctrine of freedom of will, 91
Original Sin, 150, 189
Orlandi, Tito, 86
Orpheus, 119, 124, 135
orthodoxy, 13, 59–60, 99
  in early Christianity, 59–60, 99
  and heterodoxy in Axial Age civilisations, 13
Owen, Robert, 154, 175

Paine, Thomas, 170
pansophia, 128–30
Paracelsus, 142, 146, 147, 166
Parmenides, 12
parrhesia, 2–5, 14, 43, 186, 201, 209, 213–14
  apostolic, 43
  and Jesus, 43
  and liminality, 14
  and rhetoric, 2
patarenes, 80
pataria, 80
Paul of Samosata, 75
Paulicianism, 74–8, 79, 84
  Armenian, 74–5
  Byzantine, 75
  and Christianity, 76
Paulicians, 64, 72–8, 84
'Peace of God', 88, 96
Peasant Wars, 72
Pelagians, 189
Penn, William, 174
Pentecost, 44
periagoge, 29–34, 36, 39

cannot be taught, 33, 36
and the classical virtues, 33
as a moment of truth, 30
and the order of the soul, 29, 31–2
and transcendence, 29
Peter of Fossombrone *see* Clareno
Peter of Macerata *see* Liberato
Peter of Sicily, 74–7
Peter the Great, 164, 165
Petracius, 83
Petrarch, 118
philia politike, 40
Philip II of Macedon, 38, 228
Philip of Gortyna, 47
Philo, 148
Philokalia, 165
Philolaus, 124
Philotheus, 168
philosopher-diplomat, 208, 214, 216
philosophy, 13, 34–5, 153
and the Axial Age, 13
and democracy, 13
Feuerbach's understanding of, 153
and liminality, 34–5
'Phoenician Tale', 35
Photius, 68
phronesis, 36
Picatrix, 127
Pico della Mirandola, 17, 122, 125, 130, 135–7, 145
Pietism, 99, 138, 152, 163–4
Pimander, 120–2, 124, 126
'pious cruelty', 228
Pizzorno, Alessandro, 89
Plato, 4, 18, 20, 22, 25–38, 40, 43, 52, 68–9, 73, 116–19, 124, 126, 135, 191, 196, 204, 226, 230
at Dionysius's court, 32
on 'forms', 27, 52
on the size of the *polis*, 38
and Solon, 37–8
translations of, 117–18
Platonic Academy, 73, 116, 119
Plekhanov, Georgy Valentinovich, 157
pleroma, 50–1, 54–6, 58, 62, 63, 131
Plethon, Georgios Gemistus, 118–19
Plotinus, 73, 90–1, 117, 119, 120, 126, 135
departing from Plato, 90
and his 'Gnostic' students, 90–1
pneuma, 51–8, 63, 104, 120
Poimandres see Pimander
Policy Planning Staff, 198, 199, 204, 209
polis, 4, 35, 55, 69
and liminality, 14
and Solon's reforms, 37–8
Populists, 167
Porphyry, 90, 117, 118, 120
Positivism, 130, 153, 167, 169
postmillenarian outlook, 176, 177
premillenarian outlook, 176
prisci theologi, 135, 137
Proclus, 90, 117, 119, 147, 148
Progressive Era, 181
Progressive Movement, 181
Prometheus, 68–9, 71n
Psellos, Michael, 118–19, 120, 127
Pseudo-Dionysius, 90, 117, 125
Pseudo-Methodius, 168
psyche see soul
Puritan eschatology, 170-6
Puritan movement, 128–30
Puritan Revolution, 128–30, 147, 174, 224
Puritanism, 170–6
Puritans, 116
Ptolemy, 62
Pythagoras, 119, 124, 128, 135

Quakerism, 174–5, 176
Quran, 127

Ranters, 175
Rapp, George, 175
ratio aeterna, 228
reason, 36
Reeves, Marjorie, 111
Reformation, 99, 116, 151, 170, 175
Reitzenstein, Richard, 125
Renaissance syncretism, 103
renovatio mundi, 224
resurrection, 43, 44–5, 68
Reuchlin, Johannes, 137, 145
Revelation, Book of, 94–9, 105, 111, 151, 170–2, 179
Rhodon, 47
Riley-Smith, Jonathan, 96
rite of passage, 5–11, 26
Romulus, 195, 227
Roosevelt, Franklin D., 181
Rosicrucian movement, 116, 127, 128, 175
Royal Society, 129–30
Rudolph, Kurt, 60
Runciman, Steven, 67
Russia, 78, 163–9, 197, 198, 207–208, 210, 211, 213, 225
Russian Marxism, 166, 169
Russian Revolution, 93, 169, 177, 226
Russian Socialism, 169

sabi'a, 127
St Antony, 84–5
St Augustine, 22, 64, 95, 120, 123–4, 186–92, 226–7, 228, 229
on the Millennium, 95, 103–4

St Benedict, 106
St Francis, 83, 109–14, 172
eschatological significance of, 109, 112
testament of, 110
St Odilo, 89
St Pachomius, 84–6
St Paul, 40, 43, 61, 66, 77, 108, 125, 196
Saint-Martin, Claude de, 164, 166
Saint-Simon, Claude-Henri de Rouvroy, Comte de, 154
Salutati, Coluccio, 118
salvation, 41, 55–6, 58, 61, 81, 104, 106, 120, 126, 149, 170, 174, 225
according to Marcion, 61
in Catharism, 81
Christian understanding of, 41
and *gnosis*, 56
in 'Gnostic' mythology, 55–6
in Hermeticism, 120, 126
Samuel of Ani, 73
Sand, George, 169
sangha, 13
Sarug, Israel, 135
Sassanians, 74
Satan, 50, 79, 81, 95, 98, 132, 133, 150, 173, 190
Savonarola, Girolamo, 116
Schelling, Friedrich von, 93, 116, 142, 147, 149, 164, 165
Schleiermacher, Friedrich Ernst Daniel, 142, 147, 149
Scholem, Gershom, 131, 132, 134
science, 104, 127–30, 187, 188, 195
'Script without Title', 51
and the inversion of Genesis, 52
Scultetus, Bartolomäus, 146
Second Coming, 94, 95, 97, 103, 138, 151, 176
Second Great Awakening, 179
'second reality', 56, 207
Second World War, 176, 181, 183, 197, 203, 205
Secret Supper, 80
sefiroth, 132–3
self-alienation, 152–3
Septuagint, 39, 43
Serapion of Thmuis, 85
Sergius, 76
Sforza, Catherina, 196
Shakers, 176
Shenute, 86
Shevyrev, Stepan P., 164
Silvanus, 76
Simon Magus, 50
Skinner, Quentin, 16, 18
Slavophilism, 165–6, 167
sobornost, 165
Societas Regia Scientiarum, 130
sociology, 156
Socrates, 26, 28, 31–6, 43
Solon, 37–8
Solovyov, Vladimir Sergeevich, 166, 167–8
Son of God, 74
Son of Man, 42
Sophists, 4, 33
soul, 28, 29–30, 33, 52, 54–5, 63, 69, 188, 199–201, 211, 229–30
and *gnosis*, 229–30
immortality of, 33
negation of, 52, 54–5
as sensorium of transcendence, 29–30, 52, 201
Soviet Communism, 142, 199, 210, 223, 224, 225, 226
Soviet Union, 182, 197, 198, 199, 207, 212, 213
Spaeth, Johann Jakob, 145
Spanish-American War, 176, 180–1
spark *see pneuma*
Sparrow, John, 147
speculum principis, 192
Spencer, Herbert, 181
Spengler, Oswald, 206
Spirit, 44–5, 58, 62–3, 79, 81, 83–4, 103, 104, 106–9, 148–9, 151, 152–3, 158, 175, 200–1, 230
as *aeon* in Ptolemy's system, 62–3
in Catharism, 81
Hegel's understanding of, 148–9, 151, 230
Jesus as, 58
in Joachimism, 106–9
Kennan's understanding of, 200–1
Massalian understanding of, 79
of Pentecost day, 44–5
progressive unfolding of, 104
of the Resurrected, 45
third dispensation of, 103, 106
spiritual dimension of political order, 4–5
and history, 11–14
and liminality, 11
Spiritual Franciscans, 72, 110–16, 172
and Catharism, 113
spiritual intelligence, 107, 138
spirituality, 2–5, 14, 226
empirical study of, 14
and religion, 2
Spirituals *see* Spiritual Franciscans
Sprat, Thomas, 129
Stamp Act Crisis, 179
Stalin, Joseph, 169, 197, 207
Stobaeus, 126
Strauss, Leo, 20, 186–7, 228
Strong, Josiah, 180–1
summum bonum, 228

Swedenborg, Emanuel, 138, 164, 166
Symeon, 78
syncretism, 17, 86, 124, 146
Synesius, 117
system 47, 49, 50, 53, 55–7, 62–3, 64, 67, 68, 132, 142, 154, 159–60, 188, 230
  Cabalist, 132
  Hegelian, 142
  as a literary form, 55–7
  Marx's, 159–60
  Ptolemy's system, 62–3
  Valentinian, 62
Taborites, 116
terrena civitas, 190
Tertullian, 47, 61–2
  on Marcionism, 61–2
theodicy, 52
Theodore, 86
Theodoret of Cyrus, 77
Theodotus, 63
Theophilus, 47
Theseus, 194, 195
Third Rome, 163, 167–70, 210
'third status', 73, 103, 107–8, 110, 111–12, 171
  transition to, 111–12
Thorowgood, Thomas, 172, 173
tikkun, 135
Timothy of Alexandria, 85
Topitsch, Ernst, 93, 142, 165
totalitarianism, 206–14, 215, 216, 226
transcendence
  experience of, 29
  and the *periagoge*, 29
  and the temporal order, 11–14, 37
'transvaluation of all values', 69
Tree of Knowledge, 51, 124, 150
Trinity, 68, 105, 106–8, 149, 167
Truman, Harry S., 183, 207
Truman Doctrine, 183, 198
truth-telling *see parrhesia*
tsimtsum, 134
Turner, Victor, 5–7, 34
'turning around' *see periagoge; metanoia*

UNESCO, 203, 224–5, 230
Ungrund, 143, 149
United Nations, 203, 224–5
United States, 163, 179, 180–3, 197, 199, 202, 203, 205, 211, 213, 214
Unity of Brethren, 128, 175
'unseen measure', 37, 68, 69, 193, 201, 202, 228
Urban II, 96–7

Valentinian, 64
Valentinians, 63, 98, 126, 148
  'Italian school', 63
  'oriental school', 63
  see also Valentinus
Valentinus, 47, 62–3, 68–9, 126
  and Hermes, 126
Varro, 188
Vassily III, 168
Vienna Circle, 153, 166
Vietnam War, 202
Virgil, 188
virtù, 227
virtù ordinata, 195–6
virtues, 33, 57
Vitberg, Alexander L., 166
Voegelin, Eric, 20, 44, 60, 68, 142, 224, 225, 226

Waldenses, 72, 176
Wallis, John, 129
Walter, Balthasar, 146
Weber, Max, 1
Weigel, Valentin, 142, 146, 151
Westphalen, Ludwig von, 154
Whitefield, George, 175, 180
Williams, Michael Allen, 48
Wilson, Woodrow, 181
Wisse, Frederick, 85–6
World-Soul, 91, 93, 166

'X'-article, 198–9, 205, 213
Xenophanes, 12

Yates, Frances A., 123
Yohai, Simeon ben, 132, 138, 145
Young Hegelians, 152, 154

Zohar, 132–3, 135, 138, 144
Zoroaster, 66, 118, 119, 126
Zoroastrian priests, 64
Zoroastrian tradition, 63
Zozimus, 168